WEED CONTROL HANDBOOK

Issued by

THE BRITISH WEED CONTROL COUNCIL

Edited by

E. K. WOODFORD

O.B.E. Ph.D.

Director, A.R.C. Weed Research Organisation;
Chairman, Recommendations Committee of the
British Weed Control Council

and

S. A. EVANS

B.Sc. Dip.Agric.

National Agricultural Advisory Service Liaison Officer,
Weed Research Organisation;
Secretary, Recommendations Committee of the
British Weed Control Council

THIRD EDITION

BLACKWELL
SCIENTIFIC PUBLICATIONS
OXFORD

PREFACE

Progress in chemical weed control is very rapid and demands frequent new editions of the handbook. In 1958 a permanent form was adopted for the handbood; this was repeated in 1960 and is continued in this 1962 edition.

The handbook is unique in the agricultural world in that the principal interested commercial and official bodies have been brought together to produce an agreed statement. As in previous years, the material for this edition has been prepared by the Recommendations Committee of the British Weed Control Council. Many other people have helped and the Committee is very grateful for their assistance.

The handbook is intended for all who are interested in the practical or the technical aspects of the subject and the aim has been to make the volume complete; to cover all questions that can arise in the chemical control of weeds. Thus it deals with those weed killers which are established in use and also gives the available information about those which are not yet fully proven, their chemistry, their effects and recommended dosages. It lists the weeds and their susceptibilities, the crops and their resistances. Methods of application of herbicides are described and sections are devoted to such matters as spray drift and the legal aspects of herbicide use. If anything has been omitted the Committee would like to know about it and any suggestions for improvement in future editions should be sent to the Secretary of the Recommendations Committee, A.R.C. Weed Research Organization, Begbroke Hill, Kidlington, Oxford.

Every effort has been made to ensure that the recommendations and statements made are correct but the British Weed Control Council cannot accept responsibility for any loss, damage or other accident arising from carrying out the methods advocated in the handbook.

H. G. SANDERS M.A. PH.D
Chief Scientific Adviser to the Minister of Agriculture,
President, British Weed Control Council

SPECIAL NOTES
CONCERNING THE USE OF CHAPTERS II TO VI

(i) This book is concerned primarily with herbicides. The chemical names, structural formulae and common unabbreviated name of all the herbicides mentioned are given in Appendix III and considered in Chapter I (page 1). The recommendations concerning herbicides are given for each crop and habitat. The paragraphs are numbered consecutively throughout Chapters II–VI.

(ii) The choice of the correct herbicide to apply in any given situation depends upon many considerations, but will be determined primarily by the tolerance of the crop and the susceptibility of the weeds that are present or expected. These two aspects are considered together, but wherever there is sufficient information available, separate tables for crop tolerance and/or weed susceptibility are given under each crop (e.g. cereals) or habitat (e.g. water). But usually the recommendations refer mainly to the acceptable doses of herbicides, and the response of weeds to those herbicides are grouped together with Tables of Weed Susceptibility in Chapter V.

(iii) The recommendations made are for the United Kingdom. Statements in Chapters II to VI may be taken as firm recommendations except where warnings are inserted at the beginning of a paragraph. If more experience of a treatment is desirable before a firm recommendation can be made then the paragraph is preceded by [**Tentative**]. Treatments in paragraphs marked [**For Information**] are in no way recommended. They are included mainly in order to indicate treatments which show some promise but for which there is insufficient evidence regarding reliability under varying conditions to allow any recommendations to be made.

(iv) The manner in which a herbicidal chemical is formulated influences its selective toxicity to crop and weed. This book is concerned primarily with recommendations for basic formulations of herbicides (see page 11) without added surface-active agents (except where such an agent has to be included in the formulation of emulsifiable concentrates). Surface-active agents ('wetters' and 'spreaders') should not be added to the spray unless recommended. It is essential that if there is doubt on the dose to apply, the condition for use or the method of application the manufacturers advice should be sought.

(v) Doses of MCPA, 2,4-D, 2,4,5-T, MCPB, 2,4-DB, MCPA plus/2,3,6-TBA, MCPA plus 2-methoxy 3,6-dichlorobenzoic acid, mecoprop, dichlorprop, dalapon and sodium or ammonium trichloracetate are given in terms of the quantity of acid equivalent (a.e.) per acre. Mecoprop and dichlorprop are produced commercially as a mixture of dextro- and laevo-rotatory isomers, in equal amounts, one of which is active as a herbicide the other inactive. Doses are given as the total of both isomers. Doses of dinoseb and DNOC refer to the quantity of parent nitrated phenol and doses of pentachlorphenol refer to the parent chlorinated phenol. Doses of maleic hydrazide, amino triazole, simazine, atrazine, monuron, fenuron, diuron, propham, chlorprophan, sodium monochloracetate and 2,4-DES refer to amounts of active ingredient (a.i.). Doses of sulphuric acid are in terms of 100 per cent acid (see pages 217–218 for an explanation of the methods of expressing the active content of herbicide formulations). Where 'salt' is used to explain the type of herbicide it denotes the following derivatives of an acid: sodium potassium, ammonium or amine. See pages 1 and 286 regarding chemical nomenclature.

(vi) Crops are referred to by their common names only. Weeds are given their botanical name and a common name, the authority for the former being the *Flora of the British Isles*, 2nd ed., 1962, by Clapham, Tutin and Warburg (Cambridge University Press) (see Chapter I, page 1). Where a stage of growth of a crop or weed is referred to in terms of leaf numbers, this always refers to the number of true leaves and never includes the cotyledons.

(vii) All recommendations for the use of herbicides in crops apply only to healthy, well-grown crops. Plants lacking in vigour are more liable to damage

TABLE OF CONTENTS

LIST OF TABLES

(xi)

PAGE

LIST OF FIGURES

PAGE

CHAPTER I

INTRODUCTION TO HERBICIDES

The control of weeds in crops by chemical methods has been one of the outstanding developments of the twentieth century. Starting in 1896 with the chance discovery in France that a solution of copper sulphate killed *Sinapis arvensis* (charlock) without affecting oats, this revolutionary method of weed control has expanded and developed until at the present time several million acres are being sprayed annually in Great Britain alone and a large range of herbicides is available for a multitude of different purposes. During the past two decades the widespread acceptance of herbicides in agriculture, horticulture, and forestry, and the rapid introduction of new chemicals and application techniques have resulted in a situation where even those intimately connected with the subject cannot readily keep in touch with the new developments. The *Weed Control Handbook* is an up-to-date reference book in which can be found information and recommendations on the many different aspects of this new and complex subject.

If full use is to be made of this handbook it is essential to be familiar with the technical terms and abbreviations adopted in the text and to know something of the chemicals that are in use as herbicides. This introductory chapter refers briefly to the terminology that has grown up with the development of chemical weed control and classifies and gives notes on the more important herbicides commonly used in Great Britain and for which recommendations are made in this book. Methods of formulation are briefly described. Herbicides which have only recently become available or are still in the experimental stage are considered in Chapter XIII.

TERMINOLOGY

Throughout the book, crops are referred to by their common names only, but weeds are usually given both a common name and a botanical name; for the latter, the authority used has been the *Flora of the British Isles*, 1962, 2nd ed., by Clapham, Tutin and Warburg (Cambridge University Press). Many weeds have more than one common name and although one common name has been used in the text, additional names, up to three for each weed, have been listed in the main index at the back of the book.

The chemical names and structural formulae of all the herbicides mentioned

1

in this book are given in Appendix III. The majority of these names are too long and cumbersome for frequent use and many chemicals have in consequence been given either a coined name or an abbreviation. An alphabetical list of all common names and chemical abbreviations used in this book is given in Appendix II.

In every case, the name or abbreviation refers to the basic chemical which is active as a herbicide. If the chemical is an acid, it may be used in the form of various derivatives or salts: for example, MCPA is available as a sodium, potassium or amine derivative of MCPA acid, 2,4-D as an amine or an ester derivative of 2,4-D acid. The nomenclature for derivatives such as these conforms with that approved by the British Standards Institution (B.S. 1831: 1961); thus the potassium salt of MCPA is referred to as MCPA-potassium, an ester of 2,4-D as 2,4-D-ester. Where the derivative type '-salt' is used, it denotes the following derivates: sodium, potassium, ammonium or amine. Doses or concentrations of acid derivatives are expressed in terms of the parent acid (acid equivalent), not in terms of the actual derivative (see page 217).

For an explanation of other technical terms used in this book, reference should be made to the Glossary, Appendix I.

CLASSIFICATION OF HERBICIDES

Broadly speaking herbicides are applied to the foliage of weeds or to the soil where they kill weed seeds as they germinate or affect established weeds by being taken up through the roots. Some herbicides are effective whether applied to the foliage or soil, which makes it unsatisfactory to use a classification system for herbicides on such categories as 'foliage-acting' or 'soil-acting'.

Herbicides can, however, be considered with little risk of confusion as 'contact' herbicides or 'translocated' herbicides. Contact herbicides are those which do not move far from the point of application and kill only the tissues with which they come into contact. In contrast, translocated (systemic) herbicides move from the site of application to other parts of the plant, so that localized application may in fact result in the death of the entire plant.

These two properties of herbicides provide the basis for a useful and flexible system of classification which does not so much attempt to label each herbicide as of a particular type but rather to list herbicides according to the way they are used to control weeds, i.e. the type of *treatment* for which they are used.

The basic divisions, for clarification, are as follows:

(1) foliage treatment of the weed $\Big\langle \begin{array}{l} \text{contact} \\ \text{translocated} \end{array}$

(2) soil treatment ⟨ contact (causing localized death of roots in vicinity of herbicide)
translocated

This can be made more useful by incorporating information of the timing of the application of each herbicide treatment in relation to the crops in which the weeds are to be controlled. The full framework of this classification then becomes:

TABLE 1. CLASSIFICATION OF HERBICIDE TREATMENTS

A. Weed	B. Herbicide	C. Crop
Foliage	{ contact translocated	{ pre-planting pre-emergence post-emergence
Soil	{ contact translocated	

It will be seen that this system incorporates (1) foliage application and (2) soil applications with respect to weeds and also to crops. It should be noted that pre-planting and pre-emergence applications are made either on to the weed foliage or the soil, no crop being yet visible; post-emergence applications are made onto crop foliage and either onto the weed foliage or the soil. There are thus six typical situations:

Weed ⟨ foliage / soil ⟩ × Crop ⟨ pre-planting / pre-emergence / post-emergence ⟩

in which herbicides can be used with reference to the control of weeds in crops. These situations are depicted diagrammatically in Fig. 1, page 4.

If the division of herbicides into 'contact' and 'translocated' is accepted, then herbicide treatments can be considered to fall into the following categories:

(1) contact foliage treatment (weed) pre-sowing (crop)
(2) ,,   ,,   ,,   ,,   pre-emergence (crop)
(3) ,,   ,,   ,,   ,,   post-emergence (crop)
(4) translocated foliage treatment (weed) pre-sowing (crop)
(5) ,,   ,,   ,,   ,,   pre-emergence (crop)
(6) ,,   ,,   ,,   ,,   post-emergence (crop)
(7) contact soil treatment (weed) pre-sowing (crop)
(8) ,,   ,,   ,,   ,,   pre-emergence (crop)
(9) ,,   ,,   ,,   ,,   post-emergence (crop)
(10) translocated soil treatment (weed) pre-sowing (crop)
(11) ,,   ,,   ,,   ,,   pre-emergence (crop)
(12) ,,   ,,   ,,   ,,   post-emergence (crop)

Where the herbicide is being used for non-selective (total) weed control (i.e. where no crop is concerned), there are the basic four treatments: (i) contact foliage (ii) translocated foliage (iii) contact soil (iv) translocated soil.

For convenience, and because relatively little is known about the mode of action of many herbicides when applied to the soil, the two soil treatments (iii) and (iv) can be joined under the general term *residual soil treatment*, both

RESIDUAL TREATMENTS   CONTACT OR TRANSLOCATED
(soil acting)   FOLIAGE TREATMENTS

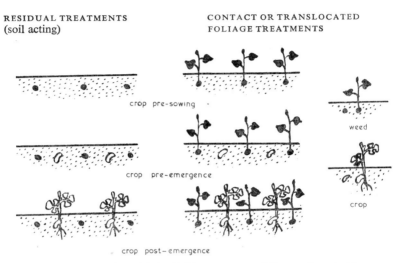

crop   pre-sowing

weed

crop   pre-emergence

crop

crop   post-emergence

FIG. 1.—Situations in which herbicides may be used for weed control in crops.

in connection with selective as well as non-selective weed control. This term is fully explained below.

The addition of a further application category 'water' can be made to accommodate in this classification those herbicides that are directly applied to water for the control of aquatic weeds.

This basic framework of herbicide treatments applies to all herbicides known at present and allows the herbicides themselves to be placed in categories appropriate to the treatments for which they are, or can be, employed (Table 2). This system breaks away from that hitherto employed in previous editions of the *Weed Control Handbook* which attempted to label the herbicides, themselves, for example, 'pre-emergence herbicides' or 'foliage-acting

TABLE 2. CLASSIFICATION OF HERBICIDES ACCORDING TO THE METHOD OF APPLICATION TO WEEDS AND THEIR MODE OF ACTION

Application to weed foliage		Application to soil ('residual')		Application to water
Contact	Translocated	Contact	Translocated	
Cresylic acids	Amino triazole*	Dinoseb	Amino triazole	Acrolein
Calcium cyanamide	Atrazine	DNOC	Atrazine*	Copper sulphate
Dinoseb*	Barban	Formalin	Borates	Dichlone
DNOC*	4-CPA*	Pentachlorophenol	Chlorpropham	
Ferrous sulphate	2,4-D*		4-CPA	
Gas liquor	2,4-DB*		2,4-D	
Mineral oils	Dalapon*		2,4-DB	
Pentachlorphenol*	Dichlorprop*		2,4-DES($\to$2,4-D)	
Potassium cyanate	Diquat		Dalapon	
Sodium mono- chloroacetate	Endothal		Di-allate	
Sodium nitrate	Fenoprop*		Dichlorprop	
Sulphuric acid	MCPA*		Diuron	
Tar oil winter wash	MCPB*		Endothal*	
	Maleic hydrazide*		Fenoprop	
	Mecoprop*		Fenuron	
	3,6-dichloro-2-methoxy benzoic acid*		Maleic hydrazide	
	Paraquat		MCPA	
	Sodium chlorate		MCPB	
	2,4,5-T*		Mecoprop	
	2,4,5-TB*		3,6-dichloro-2-methoxy benzoic acid	
	2,3,6-TBA*		Monuron	
	Trichloracetic acid		Neburon	
			Propham	
			Simazine	
			Sodium chlorate*	
			2,4,5-T	
			2,4,5-TB	
			2,3,6-TBA	
			Trichloroacetic acid*	

* The more important application of a herbicide when it occurs in more than one column.

herbicides' with the inevitable difficulty that a herbicide that acted both through root or shoot or one that was effective when applied both pre- and post-emergence could not be accommodated.

In Table 2 all the more important herbicides for which a recommendation is given in this book are listed according to the appropriate type of treatment for which they can be used. The following points should be observed:

(a) The chemicals are arranged in alphabetical order in each column.

(b) When a chemical occurs in both 'foliage' and 'soil' columns, this indicates that it can be appreciably active as a herbicide when applied to the leaves of weeds as well as to the soil. An asterisk marks the more important application.

(c) The absence of a herbicide from a particular column does not necessarily mean that it cannot have the type of activity indicated at the top of the column but that it is either unimportant or not sufficiently well known to justify inclusion.

(d) The position of chemicals in the table must be liable to revision as further information becomes available concerning their mode of action.

NOTES ON THE MORE IMPORTANT TYPES OF HERBICIDE TREATMENTS

PRE-SOWING OR PRE-PLANTING TREATMENTS

CONTACT FOLIAGE

A contact pre-sowing or pre-planting foliage treatment is one which is used to kill annual weeds that have already emerged in order to clear the ground for sowing or planting the crop. The herbicides used for this purpose have little or no residual action and therefore do not control weeds which germinate after spraying. This type of application is useful where the ground has been prepared for a crop some time in advance and no further cultivation is to be carried out before sowing. An example of a contact pre-sowing foliage treatment is the use of vaporizing oil sprays on forest tree seed-beds. This type of treatment is not widely used in this country although it can be valuable in certain circumstances, for example, when a seed-bed has been prepared and sowing is delayed by dry weather. If annual weeds germinate during this period it may be preferable to kill them by the use of a non-persistent contact herbicide rather than by cultivations which might cause further loss of soil moisture.

TRANSLOCATED FOLIAGE

Translocated pre-sowing or pre-planting foliage treatments may be used for the control of perennial weeds, such as couch, creeping thistle and field bindweed. For spring-sown crops, applications during the previous autumn are often convenient and effective, for example, dalapon for couch and 2,4-D for bindweed, both applied to the weeds growing in cereal stubble. Another instance is the treatment of grassland with MCPA shortly before ploughing to reduce perennial weeds such as creeping thistle or rushes in the following crop. The exact timing of the treatment is determined partly by the need to apply the herbicide at a time when the weed can be controlled and partly by the cropping programme. The persistence of the herbicide used must be such that no injury is caused to the following crop.

RESIDUAL

Residual pre-sowing and pre-planting soil treatments consist of applications to the soil of relatively persistent, root-absorbed herbicides prior to sowing or planting a crop. Such treatments are now being carried out on a limited scale both to eradicate specific perennial weeds which are difficult to control selectively in the growing crop and to control annual weeds which germinate during the early stages of crop growth. TCA, for example, has been used for several years as a pre-sowing treatment for killing couch grass prior to arable cropping. The control of wild oats in peas and sugar beet has been achieved by pre-sowing applications of TCA and also of propham, the latter controlling some broad-leaved weeds as well. More recently di-allate has been suggested as a specific herbicide against wild oats in field beans and sugar beet. All these herbicides are most effective if thoroughly mixed into the soil by means of cultivations. For annual weed control this can usually be done when the seed bed is prepared.

The timing of a pre-sowing or pre-planting application depends upon the persistence of the chemical, the dose required for weed control, and the tolerance of the crop towards the chemical. For the control of perennial weeds a high dose may be needed and a long interval, possibly several months, may then be necessary between spraying and sowing. In the case of annual weeds treatment is made less than a month, and in some cases immediately before sowing or planting a tolerant crop. If the crop is not completely resistant to the dose which is needed for good weed control, the period between spraying and sowing should be long enough to allow some of the chemical to disperse before the crop germinates. If the chemical is lost too rapidly, weed control may be poor, but if it remains for too long in the upper layer of soil a sensitive crop may be affected. For these reasons the effectiveness of this type of application tends to be less reliable than that of post-emergence sprays, but it does provide a method of attacking weeds which are very difficult to control by other means.

PRE-EMERGENCE TREATMENT

CONTACT FOLIAGE

The term 'contact foliage pre-emergence' denotes the application, made after the weeds have emerged, of contact herbicides which have negligible residual activity, in order to kill seedling weeds which have emerged before the crop. Chemicals which can be used in this way include diquat, paraquat, sulphuric acid, mineral oils, emulsifiable formulations of pentachlorophenol and formulations of cresylic acids. The two essential requirements are: first, that the majority of weed seedlings should have emerged before the crop, and secondly, that the chemical used should be an efficient contact herbicide that does not persist in toxic form in the soil. It must be stressed that the contact foliage pre-emergence method does not necessarily remove the need for later cultural weed control, since the effect is usually temporary, but a successful application ensures that the seed-bed is clean when the crop emerges; weed competition in the early stages is thereby greatly reduced and subsequent cultural operations are faciliated. A disadvantage of the method is that it allows very little latitude in timing the spray, and bad weather at the critical time may mean that spraying has to be abandoned. A second drawback is that the weeds may not all appear in one flush but may continue to germinate over an extended period of time, a large proportion not appearing until after the crop has emerged. This often happens with autumn-sown crops, and under such conditions little benefit is derived from the use of a contact foliage pre-emergence spray.

The method was originally developed for use in crops which germinate slowly, such as onions and leeks, but certain other crops such as parsnip and sugar beet germinate sufficiently slowly for it to be used. The success of the technique depends on the correct timing of the spray application; ideally it should be two or three days before the crop begins to appear. In practice this stage is not always easy to determine and the procedure is sometimes adopted of sowing with the crop seed a small proportion of the seed of a marker crop such as radish. The spraying is then carried out when the marker crop emerges. The only disadvantage is that if bad weather prevents spraying, the marker crop itself may present an awkward problem.

This method can be modified, on crops which germinate rapidly, by the use of the 'stale seed-bed technique'. This, in pre-emergence work, involves preparing the seed-bed, waiting until the weeds have emerged, sowing the crop with as little soil disturbance as possible and then applying the spray immediately or within a day or two. The advantage over simply harrowing the flush of weeds before sowing lies in the absence of soil disturbance, so that further weed seeds are not stimulated to germinate. This method has given good results with a variety of crops, but the delay necessary in order for the weeds to emerge may lead to deterioration of the seed-bed on some soils.

RESIDUAL

The term 'residual pre-emergence' indicates an application, made at any time between the sowing and emergence of a crop, of a herbicide which will persist in the soil and kill weed seedlings for a considerable period afterwards. The chemicals employed usually have a low solubility in water and tend to remain in the surface layer of the soil, being absorbed by the weed seedlings germinating there. For this type of application to be successful, it is necessary either that the crop seeds shall be protected from the chemical by being sown deeply, or that the young crop plants shall be inherently tolerant to the particular chemical used. The first condition can be met with large-seeded crops such as beans. There is, however, some risk that heavy rain may cause the chemical to be washed down to the root zone of the crop, with resultant damage. An added complication occurs with many chemicals in that they tend to be adsorbed on organic matter and soil colloids so that the effect of a given dose varies according to the soil type. These two factors, rainfall and soil type, constitute a serious obstacle to the development of safe residual pre-emergence herbicides for direct-sown crops unless the second condition of physiological tolerance on the part of the crop is satisfied, as in the case of simazine or atrazine on maize. Formulations of chlorpropham containing diuron or fenuron are being used successfully on broad beans, peas, onions and certain other crops. Lack of damage is the combined result of partial crop tolerance and of protection of the crop by means of the relative placement of the crop roots and the herbicide.

With crops which have underground storage organs, such as bulbs, corms, rhizomes or storage roots, the soil above them may afford considerable protection from herbicides applied to the soil surface. In some of these crops residual pre-emergence weed control has proved feasible, as for example, in the use of monuron for annual weed control in established asparagus and the use of several different herbicides in bulb crops.

POST-EMERGENCE TREATMENT

Most of the vast area sprayed each year with herbicides is treated by means of post-emergence foliage applications, the aerial parts of both crops and weeds receiving the chemical. Treatments of this type, which are so well known as to require only brief mention here, are dealt with in detail in the later chapters of this book, and cover a wide range of situations including the selective control of weeds in cereal crops, the eradication of scrub from grassland and the control of perennial weeds in bush fruit.

CONTACT FOLIAGE

This technique consists of an overall spray of a contact herbicide applied when both crop and weeds are above ground. The main object is to kill annual weeds. Examples are: the use of DNOC on cereal crops, dinoseb on peas, sulphuric acid on onions and kale, and oils on forest tree seedlings. The action of contact sprays is usually rapid and their selectivity is largely governed by differential retention by crop and weed. Such factors as volume rate, droplet size, uniformity of application and weather conditions have an important effect on the success or otherwise of the application.

TRANSLOCATED FOLIAGE

In contrast to contact herbicide treatments, the main basis of selectivity in translocated foliage treatments is the different reaction of crop and weed to the chemical once it has penetrated into the plant. The effects are usually slow to develop, as the chemical interferes increasingly with the normal development of susceptible plants and several weeks may elapse between application of the herbicide and death. A useful property of many translocated herbicides is that, at sub-lethal doses, they may suppress the growth of treated weeds for a long period and prevent them from competing with the crop in which they are growing. This, in conjunction with the inhibition of seed production, may often be as useful as a rapid kill. Translocated herbicides are less influenced than contact herbicides by factors such as volume rate, droplet size and uniformity of application.

Examples of translocated post-emergence treatments for which recommendations are made in this book include the use of MCPA and 2,4-D for the control of annual and perennial weeds in cereal crops and grassland, and MCPB for weed control in leguminous crops.

RESIDUAL

Residual post-emergence treatment is a relatively recent innovation which up to the present time has been largely restricted to certain horticultural crops but its importance is rapidly increasing. Although the application is sometimes made overall, the object is to get the chemical on to the soil where it can kill weed seedlings as they germinate. The herbicides used generally have little effect once the weeds have passed the very early seedling stage, so that in this type of application it is important that the ground should be clean at the time of spraying. It may be necessary first to carry out a cleaning cultivation in order to ensure this. An example of the use of a residual post-emergence treatment during the growing season is that of 2,4-DES on strawberries (page 109). This particular chemical is inactive until partial breakdown in the soil has occurred. Other herbicides may be more suitable for use during the dormant season, for example, chlorpropham when used for weed control in blackcurrants (page 104).

NON-SELECTIVE HERBICIDE TREATMENTS

Non-selective applications of herbicides are generally made with the object of killing all the vegetation present. The herbicides may be applied to the foliage of the plants to be killed, or to the soil, according to the requirements of the treatment and the mode of action of the chemical used. If the treatment is required only to kill the existing vegetation, the minimum dose to accomplish this is used, but often it is desirable that the treatment should, in addition, keep the treated area free from plant growth for a considerable period. In this case a higher dose than is necessary merely to kill the vegetation may have to be applied to provide residual toxicity in the soil, or alternatively, a combination of herbicides can be used, each with its own task. Thus sodium chlorate at a comparatively low dose or diquat, paraquat, mineral oils etc., can be used to destroy existing vegetation followed up by a subsequent application of a persistent herbicide such a monuron or simazine applied to the bare soil to keep the area free of weeds for a long period. Non-selective (total) weed control is discussed in Chapter VI.

Another non-selective use of herbicides is the pre-harvest desiccation of potato haulm and forage legumes grown for seed. In this case quick-acting herbicides with a short-term residual toxicity are used to kill the foliage of the crop in order to facilitate harvesting (see Chapter II section (iv)).

FORMULATION OF HERBICIDES

With a few exceptions, chemicals which are employed as herbicides are applied at such low doses that they have to be mixed with a suitable carrier so that they can be evenly distributed over the treated area. The carrier may be liquid or solid according to the properties of the active ingredient and the type of application required.

LIQUID FORMULATIONS

For application in liquid form, water is the cheapest carrier and most chemicals can be suitably formulated so that dilution with water may be easily carried out. Water-soluble active ingredients are sold either as solids or aqueous concentrates, for example, sodium monochloroacetate and MCPA-salt respectively. Chemicals which are insoluble in water require special treatment. They may be dissolved in an oil or other organic solvent together with suitable emulsifying agents to form a miscible oil or emulsifiable concentrate, which, when added to water, forms an emulsion either of the oil-in-water or water-in-oil (invert emulsion) type according to whether the water or oil respectively is the continuous phase. Water-insoluble active ingredients may, alternatively, be formulated as pastes or wettable powders or dispersible liquids which form suspensions when diluted with water.

For special purposes, it may be necessary to use a mineral oil or other organic solvent as a carrier for the active ingredient; in this case the latter may be dissolved directly in the carrier when required for use or formulated in an organic solvent as a concentrated solution that can be diluted as required with the oil carrier.

An important aspect of the formulation of herbicides for liquid application concerns the addition of surface active agents, activators, etc., to the basic formulation of a product, in order to modify the herbicidal properties of the active ingredient. Recommendations and information in this book relate to herbicides without such additives unless specifically stated.

Solid Formulations

Herbicides may be applied in solid form (a) to suit a particular method of application, (b) to gain increased selectivity or effectiveness, (c) because the dose is sufficiently large to make liquid application impracticable or (d) for convenience. If the active chemical has to be diluted with an inert carrier, it may either be mixed directly with the carrier or dissolved in a suitable solvent and sprayed on to the carrier. Solid formulations are generally in the form of dusts for general application, or as granules (pellets) for special purposes such as aquatic weed control or where selectivity requires to be enhanced in the case of residual post-emergence treatments. A wide range of herbicides in granular form is available for experimental work. These are of special interest for band treatment (see page 208) of crops grown in wide rows using special application equipment. Herbicides may be formulated as granules also in an attempt to control the release of the active chemical in the soil. Herbicides applied as dusts may, as with liquids, be specially formulated in order to modify their biological properties. For instance, the adherence of dusts to different leaf surfaces may be modified by additives such as lubricating oil.

NOTES ON HERBICIDES USED IN GREAT BRITAIN

The chemical formulae for the herbicides discussed below are given in Appendix III; for details of new or experimental herbicides, see Chapter XIII.

See page 28 for note on the safe use of these herbicides.

INORGANIC CHEMICALS

Ammonium Sulphamate

This is a colourless crystalline solid, very soluble in water; it absorbs moisture when exposed to damp air. It is of low toxicity to animals. In solution it is corrosive to some metals, particularly brass. Ammonium sulphamate is used mainly to kill woody plants and is applied to stems or cut stumps, as an aqueous overall spray to the foliage, or as a solid or concentrated aqueous solution in frill-girdles, auger holes or bark notches.

BORATES

Borax and crude sodium borates are the most common borate-containing materials used in Great Britain for non-selective weed control. They are normally applied dry at doses of 15 to 40 cwt per acre. Borates are not broken down in the soil but they are readily leached. The duration of effect may be for one or more years and depends upon the dose used, the weed species, the rainfall and the soil type. They do not give rise to any particular hazards, being low in mammalian toxicity, non-corrosive and non-inflammable.

Borates are slow acting and the full effects may not be visible for several weeks following application. Other herbicides such as sodium chlorate or monuron are sometimes added to borate herbicides to give more rapid or more persistent results respectively.

COPPER SULPHATE

Copper sulphate, a freely soluble salt, has been used for many years to control algae and submerged water weeds. It is used at concentrations of 0·5 to 2 parts per million of water. It has the disadvantage of often being toxic to fish at the concentrations required for killing weeds.

FERROUS SULPHATE

This is a constituent of 'lawn sand' used for the control of moss, pearlwort, and other weeds of lawns.

MERCURY COMPOUNDS

Mercurous chloride ('calomel') is a salt of comparatively low mammalian toxicity which may be used in lawns for the control of moss. Mercuric chloride ('corrosive sublimate') is also effective against moss and fungi in turf but this salt, on the other hand, is highly poisonous and is included in Part II of the Poisons List Order (see page 236).

SODIUM ARSENITE

As a result of an agreement by the manufacturers of agricultural chemicals, sodium arsenite is no longer available in Great Britain for use as a herbicide or desiccant in agriculture. Recommendations for its use have therefore been excluded from the handbook.

The toxic nature of sodium arsenite inevitably gives rise to very considerable hazards to man, to domestic animals and to wild life when it is used as an agricultural spray. Because of its efficiency and low cost however, it had in recent years become extensively used for the destruction of potato haulm, for clover desiccation and various weed control purposes.

SODIUM CHLORATE

Sodium chlorate is probably the most widely used non-selective herbicide at the present time. It is applied at doses of 50 to 400 lb per acre according to the species to be killed and the duration of effect required. It is available as a colourless crystalline solid or in concentrated aqueous solution. It is very soluble in water and the solid takes up water when exposed to damp air. Applied as a spray or in solid form, it can give rise to a serious fire hazard in dry weather by rendering dry organic material such as plant remains, timber, clothing, etc. highly inflammable. Commercial products based on sodium chlorate may contain a fire-depressant such as calcium chloride to reduce this hazard. Sodium chlorate is of low mammalian toxicity; its aqueous solutions are somewhat corrosive to certain metals, e.g. zinc, mild steel.

SODIUM NITRATE

Sodium nitrate, applied as an aqueous spray at doses of 2·5 to 3 cwt per acre is of limited use as a selective herbicide for certain young annual weeds in beet crops. The product used must be completely soluble in water and free from foreign matter that might cause blocking of nozzles. Sodium nitrate is of low mammalian toxicity, and its aqueous solutions are not particularly corrosive to metals.

SULPHURIC ACID

Sulphuric acid has been used for many years as a selective herbicide for the control of annual weeds in cereals and onions. More recently, it has been recommended for selective weed control in leeks and kale and also for pre-emergence weed control in horticultural crops. It kills a wide range of weeds and is not greatly affected by weather conditions. In this country it is still used for potato haulm destruction and can be used as a pre-harvest desiccant spray for leguminous seed crops. (See Chapter II.)

In cereals, sulphuric acid is seldom used, having been replaced by more effective, cheaper and more easily applied herbicides. It is still applied occasionally, however, in order to reduce the 'flag' of winter cereal crops. Sulphuric acid treatment has been claimed to be of assistance in controlling Eyespot disease of wheat and barley (*Cercosporella herpotrichoides* Fron.).

The usefulness of sulphuric acid as a herbicide is greatly reduced by its corrosive action on machinery and clothing. Special acid-resisting spraying equipment is available but expensive, and this, together with the unpleasantness of handling the chemical, tends to restrict its use to specalist spraying contractors.

Sulphuric acid is generally available in the form known as BOV (brown oil of vitriol), a commercial grade containing 77 per cent by volume of sulphuric acid. Purer grades of sulphuric acid are now available and care should be taken to ascertain the concentration before using as a herbicide, particularly as recommendations are often in terms of BOV. (In this handbook, all recommendations are in terms of 100 per cent sulphuric acid.)

Sulphuric acid is generally used at concentrations varying between 5 and 12 per cent applied at about 100 gallons per acre, but BOV is sometimes used undiluted with water at 10 to 20 gallons per acre, in which form it is less corrosive than the diluted acid.

ORGANIC CHEMICALS
I. AUXIN TYPE GROWTH REGULATORS

These are frequently described as 'hormones' or 'hormone weed killers', terms that are misleading, hormones being growth regulating substances produced in plant or animal tissues.

MCPA AND 2,4-D

The synthetic growth regulators MCPA and 2,4-D, which were discovered in 1942, revolutionized weed control by their ability to kill many annual and perennial weeds without harming cereal and other graminaceous crops and by their low cost and ease of application in small volumes of water or as dusts. They are absorbed by both roots and shoots and are readily translocated within herbaceous plants. They are of low mammalian toxicity, non-staining and non-inflammable.

Doses in agricultural crops vary from 4 oz to about 32 oz per acre. In contrast with the contact type of selective herbicide, a useful measure of growth suppression, as opposed to kill, may often be obtained with these and other growth regulator herbicides on weeds that are not easily killed outright or on susceptible weeds at very low doses.

Several forms of MCPA and 2,4-D are available commercially as selective herbicides, the following being the most important: MCPA-sodium or potassium, MCPA-amine, 2,4-D-amine and 2,4-D-ester. The specific amine or ester used may vary from product to product, as may the formulation of the active ingredient. Commercial formulations may or may not contain added surface-active agents. The metallic salt or amine derivatives are generally formulated as aqueous solutions, the ester derivatives as emulsifiable oils.

Whereas commercial 2,4-D products usually contain only the 2,4-dichloro isomer, MCPA products may contain as impurities small amounts of isomers other than the 4-chloro-2-methyl isomer, the most important being the 6-chloro-2-methyl isomer. These other isomers are not appreciably active as herbicides and it is usual to quote the concentration of a particular product in terms of the active 4-chloro-2-methyl isomer.

The early MCPA products also contained sufficient chlorocresols as impurities to give the characteristic odour associated with MCPA. The chlorocresols were responsible for imparting taint to certain crops, particularly tomatoes, growing near sprayed areas or near stored MCPA products. This taint problem has now been largely overcome by reducing the chlorocresol content of the MCPA products, which are now almost odourless.

The drift hazard with MCPA and 2,4-D is a serious one because of the high activity of the sprays and dusts against many crop plants and the relatively high concentration of herbicide at low volume spray dilutions. Neither the metallic salt nor amine derivatives have an appreciable vapour drift hazard, but drifting of vapour may occur on very warm days with the more volatile lower alkyl ester derivatives. The higher esters are much less volatile and do not give rise to an appreciable vapour drift hazard.

In general terms, MCPA and 2,4-D are very similar in effect both on crops and weeds. Differences that are well established by experiment and commercial practice are indicated in the appropriate sections of this handbook. Examples are the greater selectivity of MCPA compared with 2,4-D when applied to spring oats, and the lower dosage of 2,4-D required to obtain an equivalent effect on certain annual weeds.

Both herbicides are broken down in the soil, normally within a few weeks of application, the rate of breakdown being influenced by soil type, moisture and temperature. For conditions in Great Britain, the length of time that MCPA exists in the soil in toxic amounts after an application of 32 oz per acre is generally agreed to be about 2 to 3 months; 2,-4D is less persistent and under similar conditions is likely to be broken down within a month of application.

MCPB AND 2,4-DB

Closely related to MCPA and 2,4-D are the phenoxybutyric acid derivatives MCPB and 2,4-DB. These chemicals are active as herbicides because some plants are able to convert them to MCPA and 2,4-D respectively; other plants may not be able to do this or may be inefficient at bringing about the change. This is the basis for the enhanced selectivity of MCPB and 2,4-DB for various situations where the weeds convert these chemicals to MCPA or 2,4-D more effectively than the crop: MCPB is well known for the control of certain weeds in undersown cereals, established grassland and peas; 2,4-DB has recently become available for use in lucerne, undersown cereals and grassland. Both herbicides are potentially important for the treatment of cereals before the crop has reached a stage when MCPA or 2,4-D can be applied without injury. MCPB and 2,4-DB at the generally used dose range of 24 to 48 oz per acre are effective only on a limited range of weeds and mixtures of these herbicides with MCPA or 2,4-D have been developed.

MECOPROP (CMPP)

Mecoprop was introduced in 1956 as a complementary herbicide to MCPA and 2,4-D because of its ability to control in particular *Galium aparine* (cleavers) and *Stellaria media* (chickweed), two important cereal weeds that could previously only be selectively killed by DNOC or sulphuric acid. It controls most weeds that are also susceptible to MCPA. It has proved just as safe as MCPA and 2,4-D to cereals and, moreover, can be applied to oats, barley and to Koga II and Jufy wheat before the 5-leaf stage with much less risk of injury to the crop. This makes it potentially very valuable for controlling a wide range of weeds before most other herbicides can be used. Mecoprop cannot be used on undersown crops.

Mecoprop is produced commercially as a mixture of the two different optically active isomers in equal amounts one of which is active as a herbicide, the other inactive. Doses are normally expressed in terms of the mixture of isomers. The dose range in current use is 24 to 40 oz per acre.

Mecoprop is safe to use, being of no greater toxicity to mammals than MCPA. It is generally applied in about 20 gallons of water per acre.

DICHLORPROP (2,4-DP)

Dichlorprop was introduced in 1961 as a further addition to the range of auxin type growth regulator herbicides because of its property of being able to control in particular Polygonaceous weeds in addition to a range of weeds generally similar to those controlled by MCPA. It may be used on cereals after the 5-leaf stage but should not be used on undersown crops. Dichlorprop is, like mecoprop, produced as a mixture of two isomers in equal amounts, one active and the other inactive, and doses are normally expressed in terms of the mixture of isomers. The dose normally used is about 56 oz per acre.

Dichlorprop is safe to use, being of no greater toxicity to mammals than MCPA. It is generally applied in about 20 gallons of water per acre.

2,3,6-TBA PLUS MCPA

British work has shown that a water-soluble formulation of 2,3,6-TBA is very effective, at low doses, as a post-emergence spray for the control of many broad-leaved weeds that are resistant to MCPA and 2,4-D. In addition, at these low doses it is relatively non-toxic to cereals in the tillering stage. Hence proprietary mixtures of 2,3,6-TBA and MCPA have been developed for use in cereals.

Mixtures of 2,3,6-TBA and MCPA control, in addition to weeds controlled by MCPA alone: *Anthemis* spp. (mayweed), *Galium aparine* (cleavers), *Matricaria recutita* (wild chamomile), *Polygonum persicaria* (redshank), *Stellaria media* (chickweed) and *Tripleurospermum maritimum* ssp. *inodora* (scentless mayweed). In addition they give better control than does MCPA of *Polygonum aviculare* (knotgrass), *P. convolvulus* (black bindweed), *Solanum nigrum* (black nightshade), *Sonchus arvensis* (perennial sowthistle), *S. oleraceus* (annual sowthistle) and *Spergula arvensis* (corn spurrey).

2,3,6-TBA is slower in action than MCPA. It does not cause epinasty of weeds resistant to MCPA, but stops their growth soon after the spray is applied and the growing points slowly become deformed. As little growth takes place after treatment, early spraying prevents the weeds from competing with the crop and from interfering with harvesting. In addition the weeds set little or no seed. They are thus effectively controlled, although, they may not always be killed. A proprietary mixture of 2,3,6-TBA and MCPA in the ratio of 1 to 3 has been shown to be safe on all cereal crops when applied between the four- and six-leaf stages. At later stages of growth it becomes more toxic, especially to spring wheat, and crops should not be sprayed after 'jointing' or 'shooting' has begun.

The mixture gives best results if applied at volumes between 8 and 20 gallons per acre. It must not be used on cereals which have been, or are to be, undersown.

3,6-Dichloro-2-Methoxybenzoic Acid plus MCPA

As 2,3,6-TBA has been added to MCPA to control a wider range of weeds than MCPA alone, so a mixture of 3,6-dichloro-2-methoxybenzoic acid and MCPA has been developed. The mixture will control, in addition to the weeds controlled by MCPA alone: *Galeopsis tetrahit* (hempnettle), *Lapsana communis* (nipplewort), *Polygonum aviculare* (knotgrass), *Polygonum convolvulus* (black bindweed), *Polygonum lapathifolium* (pale persicaria), *Polygonum persicaria* (redshank), *Silene album* (white campion), *Stellaria media* (chickweed).

A proprietary mixture of 3,6-dichloro-2-methoxybenzoic acid and MCPA in an approximate ratio of 1 to 14 may be used on cereal crops which have reached the five-leaf stage but not after 'jointing' or 'shooting'. It should be applied at volumes between 8 and 20 gallons per acre. It cannot be used on crops where grass and clover is to be or has been undersown. It is safe to use, being of low toxicity to animals.

2,4-DES

2,4-DES itself is not active as a herbicide when applied to the foliage of plants but is converted in the soil to 2,4-D, and this can then prevent the establishment of weeds, which otherwise would grow from seed. It is used particularly in perennial crops such as strawberries, and other soft fruit, bush fruits and nursery stock at a dose of 2 to 5 lb per acre, which is generally sufficient to keep the ground free of annual weeds for 3 to 4 weeks under moderate rainfall conditions. Moist and warm soil is needed for conversion to 2,4-D but subsequent dry weather prolongs activity. It is important that the ground should be free from established weeds before 2,4-DES is applied. 2,4-DES may be used in conjunction with other residual herbicides such as chlorpropham and fenuron.

2,4,5-T

The most important application of 2,4,5-T is for killing woody plants, several species of which have been shown to be more susceptible to 2,4,5-T, than to MCPA and 2,4-D. Both amine and ester derivatives are available commercially, the latter being the most important; the esters are applied either in emulsions for overall foliage sprays or in solution in a mineral oil such as vaporizing oil or diesel oil for local application to frill girdles, or to stumps, or by the 'basal bark' technique. Commercial products often contain a mixture of 2,4-D and 2,4,5-T esters for reasons of economy and the greater range of effectiveness on different plant species gained by including the two chemicals.

Like the other auxin type herbicides, 2,4,5-T is of low mammalian toxicity, non-staining and non-inflammable. It is generally less effective on herbaceous species than MCPA and 2,4-D; it is much more persistent in the soil.

2,4,5-TB

This compound is much less toxic to most weeds than is MCPB or 2,4-DB. However, it does possess a high degree of selectivity for the control of *Convolvulus arvensis* (field bindweed) and *Calystegia sepium* (bellbine) in blackcurrants, which may be sprayed safely before or after fruiting (see page 105).

4-CPA

4-CPA-ester, formulated as a miscible oil, has recently become commercially available as a specific herbicide for the control of *Pteridium aquilinum* (bracken). See page 76. 4-CPA is toxic to a wide range of plants but little attention has been given to its evaluation as a herbicide apart from its role as a treatment for bracken.

II. OTHER GROWTH REGULATORS

AMINO TRIAZOLE

This herbicide is active on many plants at low doses. It can enter the plant through roots and foliage and is readily translocated. Its most striking effect is the production of chlorotic or albino shoots due to interference with chlorophyll production. The intensity of effect and the extent of recovery from it depends largely on the dose applied.

A recent development has been the use of ammonium thiocyanate as an activator for this herbicide. The addition of this compound applied at a similar dose to the amino triazole greatly improves the effect of the latter on *Agropyron repens*. It is claimed that the activator may also enhance its activity on stoloniferous species of *Agrostis* and certain other plants.

No large degree of selectivity has been reported for amino triazole and its main use appears to be for the control of grasses and broad-leaved weeds in fallow or uncultivated land. It has also shown promise for the control of certain woody plants and some emergent aquatic weeds. For all purposes it is normally applied as a foliage spray. The dose generally recommended is 4 to 8 lb per acre.

Amino triazole is available commercially as an aqueous concentrate containing ammonium thiocyanate.

Amino triazole has a lower persistence in the soil than dalapon at an equivalent dose and susceptible crops can normally be sown within a few weeks of application.

BARBAN

This herbicide, discovered in the U.S.A. has been developed for use in the U.K. for the control of *Avena fatua, Avena ludoviciana* (wild oats) and *Alopecurus myosuroides* (blackgrass) in cereals, field beans and peas. It is a foliage-applied post-emergence herbicide that is applied at low volume to the seedling weeds. The stage of growth of the weed is critical. It causes cessation of growth of *Avena* spp. at the normal dose used in cereals, 5 oz per acre, with much delayed or little recovery. To enhance this effect competition from the crop is important. At higher doses *Avena* spp. may be killed and in peas and beans, which do not normally offer as much competition as cereals in the early stages, the dose normally used is 10 oz per acre. It may be used on wheat and most varieties of barley in autumn or spring. Winter cereals may not be sprayed in the period mid-January to the end of February. Most broad-leaved weeds are resistant to this herbicide.

Barban is of low mammalian toxicity but it may cause irritation of the skin and care should be taken when mixing and applying it.

DALAPON

Dalapon is a translocated herbicide, toxic to grasses and many other monocotyledons. It is most active when applied to the foliage, but is also effective when taken up from the soil. For good results the treated plants must be in active growth at the time of treatment; thus spring, summer or autumn applications are generally favoured, although in milder districts treatments in winter have also given satisfactory results.

Dalapon is commercially available as the sodium salt, a powder which dissolves readily in cold water for application at medium-high volume rates according to the type of vegetation to be sprayed. Proprietary formulations may include a wetting agent to enhance activity. Dalapon is an exceptionally safe herbicide with a very low toxicity to mammals and fish. Its solutions are not highly corrosive.

The principal use for dalapon is for the control of *Agropyron repens* and other perennial weed grasses of arable land as an alternative to cultural measures or to other herbicides such as TCA or sodium chlorate. The subject is discussed in some detail on page 167. It is also recommended for the control of weed grasses in lucerne. In horticulture, dalapon is recommended for the control of couch grass in a variety of crops such as asparagus, blackcurrants and apples and reference should be made to specific crops of interest to the reader in Chapter III.

Other uses being developed for dalapon include the destruction of grass swards with the object of surface reseeding without ploughing, the control of aquatic vegetation to facilitate the maintenance of drainage ditches, river banks, etc., and the control of grasses in paths, industrial sites and similar situations. The dose of dalapon used varies from 4 to 40 lb acid equivalent per acre according to the species to be treated, the degree of control required, whether mechanical cultivations are employed to aid the herbicide treatment and whether repeated applications are envisaged. Individual recommendations are made in appropriate sections of this book.

The persistence of dalapon in the soil varies according to temperature, soil type, rainfall and the dose applied. It is generally considered safe to plant susceptible crops after an interval of 6 to 8 weeks following an application of 15 lb dalapon per acre, but this period may have to be extended if the weather is exceptionally dry or cold.

ENDOTHAL

This herbicide was developed as a defoliant principally for cotton in the United States of America but investigation of its herbicidal properties has led to its use in Britain as a soil-applied pre-emergence herbicide. It has only limited selectivity in most crops. However, sugar beet shows a useful tolerance to pre-emergence applications which control a number of annual weeds. The control of some weeds such as *Stellaria media* (chickweed) and *Avena fatua* (wild oats) is improved by using a mixture of endothal and propham in the ratio of 1 part propham to 1·3 parts of endothal. It is used mainly in sugar beet but has also shown promise in certain Brassica crops. The dose varies

3

widely from about 2·5 to 7 lb total active ingredients per acre according to soil type and mechanical analyses of the soil are required to be able to determine the correct dose. The efficiency of the mixture is influenced by soil moisture, rainfall and temperature. Treatment is costly and band application over the crop rows is generally employed to reduce the quantity of herbicide required per acre. Endothal has a high mammalian toxicity and is included in the Agriculture (Poisonous Substances) Regulations (see Chapter VIII).

DI-ALLATE

This is a soil-applied herbicide which controls *Avena fatua* and *A. ludoviciana* (wild oats). It has to be incorporated into the soil immediately after spraying and before sowing field beans or sugar beet. It kills germinating *Avena* spp. (wild oats) and has little effect on them if they have emerged. The normal dose is 1 to 1·5 lb per acre. It has been extensively used in barley but recommendations are not made in the Handbook because of risk of crop injury. Persistence in the soil may be sufficient to control wild oats germinating up to 8 weeks after treatment.

It is formulated as an emulsifiable concentrate which has to be carefully mixed with the water before spraying. The volume rate used is normally 20 to 40 gallons per acre. Di-allate is of low mammalian toxicity but may cause skin irritation.

MALEIC HYDRAZIDE

This compound possesses certain growth inhibitory as well as herbicidal properties. Applied in the early spring at a dose of 4 to 6 lb per acre it will inhibit the growth of perennial grasses for periods up to 16 weeks, thereby reducing the need for mowing on sites such as road verges. Further details are given in Chapter VI, Section (ii). Maleic hydrazide should not be used on fine turf.

In all uses of maleic hydrazide the addition of a wetting agent is likely to improve the effect.

Maleic hydrazide is of low toxicity to animals and is supplied as an aqueous concentrate. Its use on all non-edible crops has been accepted.

PROPHAM AND CHLORPROPHAM (CIPC)

For many years propham has been known to possess selective herbicidal properties when applied to soil in which crops and weeds are germinating. Except for sugar beet it has been largely superseded by chlorpropham which is now used on a field scale as a selective residual herbicide treatment for the control of annual weeds in a wide variety of established perennial crops—principally fruit and nursery stock. With a few exceptions such as *Stellaria media* (chick-weed), chlorpropham is relatively ineffective on established weeds, the che-mical being absorbed by the roots and not by the foliage. It is normally applied to the soil in order to prevent the establishment of weeds growing from seed. Some weeds, notably *Senecio vulgaris* (groundsel), *Sonchus* spp. (sowthistle) and *Sinapis arvensis* (charlock), are not controlled by chlorpropham, hence the development of mixtures of chlorpropham and other residual herbicides such as diuron and endothal.

For the control of wild oats in sugar beet and peas, propham has given results comparable with those obtained with trichloroacetic acid when applied in the same way—before the final seed-bed cultivations; many broad-leaved weeds are also controlled.

Propham and chlorpropham are relatively insoluble in water and are form-ulated for use either as wettable powders or emulsifiable concentrates. Doses are in the range of 1 to 6 lb per acre.

QUATERNARY AMMONIUM COMPOUNDS: DIQUAT AND PARAQUAT

These are new British herbicides which have been under development since their discovery in 1955. They are cationic and may be produced with various anions such as chlorine, bromine and methylsulphate. The normal method of stating the dose is in terms of the diquat or paraquat cation. They are rapidly absorbed by the foliage of plants, and act quickly, killing the aerial parts normally within a few hours. They are translocated to some extent within the plant and they differ in this respect from conventional contact herbicides. They are therefore less dependent on application factors such as volume rate. A particularly useful property is that they are inactivated immediately on contact with the soil, thus allowing susceptible crops to be sown as soon as desired after an application.

They will kill a wide range of annual plants and will desiccate the tops of perennials; as their action does not normally extend below soil level, regrowth may occur with plants equipped for regeneration from the root or underground stem systems.

Diquat is commercially available as an aqueous concentrate, with or with-out an added wetting agent. At a dose of 8 to 11 oz per acre diquat without added wetter has proved an effective potato haulm killer. A volume rate of 20 gallons per acre has been satisfactory. Leaf kill is rapid (3 to 4 days) while kill of stem takes place more slowly (10 to 14 days). At these doses, diquat will deal effectively with most weeds present at the time of harvesting the potatoes. Diquat may also be used for the pre-harvest desiccation of legumes grown for seed. Diquat with added wetting agent is used as a foliage-applied contact pre-emergence treatment.

Paraquat is also available as an aqueous concentrate and is generally more toxic to grasses than is diquat. It is being developed for killing swards so that new swards can be established without ploughing. It is also useful in many other ways including the control of vegetation at the base of fruit trees etc. Both diquat and paraquat are used as a means of destroying vegetation prior to applying a non-selective residual herbicide.

Diquat is of low toxicity to animals and although paraquat is rather more toxic neither are included in the Agriculture (Poisonous Substances) Regulations.

SUBSTITUTED UREA HERBICIDES: FENURON, MONURON AND DIURON

Fenuron, monuron and diuron are three closely related compounds which have the common properties of long-term persistence in the soil and high activity against a wide range of plants. At high doses, 30 lb per acre or more, they will kill most plants and keep the soil free from vegetation for at least a year. Monuron is generally used in this way as a non-selective persistent herbicide. At doses in the range 0·25 to 2 lb per acre, they may be used selectively in certain perennial crops for the control of annual weeds, which are killed soon after emergence following a soil application of the herbicide; for this purpose fenuron and diuron have received the greatest attention and are recommended alone or in combination with chlorpropham for certain horticultural crops.

The successful use of these herbicides at low doses in crops is largely determined by their low solubility in water and hence their restricted movement downwards into the rooting zone of the crop. After application to the soil surface, they can be absorbed only by the roots of plants. Fenuron is the most soluble and diuron the least. For details of the solubility of these compounds refer to Appendix III. All four compounds are slowly broken down in the soil by micro-organisms. They are generally formulated as wettable powders and agitation of the spray liquid is required during application. They are low in mammalian toxicity and are non-corrosive.

The substituted urea herbicides should be used on cultivated land with special care in order to avoid damage to the treated crops and to subsequent crops which can occur as a result of over-dosing. Great care is also required when applying monuron as a non-selective herbicide to keep it away from valuable trees, shrubs and herbaceous plants, and from flowing water.

TRIAZINE HERBICIDES: SIMAZINE AND ATRAZINE

Simazine is the best known of the large group of herbicidal compounds, the substituted triazines. It is characterized by its high toxicity to a large range of plants when applied to the soil and by its persistence in the soil, properties which make it valuable for long-term non-selective weed control. For this purpose it is applied at a dose of 10 lb or more per acre. At doses in the range 0·5 to 2 lb per acre it can be used selectively for the control of annual weeds in certain annual crops, notably maize which is markedly tolerant to this herbicide. Simazine is almost insoluble in water (5 p.p.m.) and it moves downwards in the soil very slowly after application to the soil surface; it is absorbed only by the roots of plants and it is therefore being developed as a selective pre-emergence herbicide in certain deeply sown annual crops such as field beans which, unlike maize, are not completely resistant to simazine. It can also be used for the control of annual weeds in certain perennial crops, particularly those that either have a deep root system or are large in relation to the dose required for controlling the weeds, e.g. annual weeds in black-currants, asparagus, certain tree crops and shrubs.

Simazine is commercially available as a wettable powder. It is safe to use, and has low mammalian toxicity, but great care must be exercised when applying it on cropped land to prevent over-dosing and consequent damage to the treated and to the subsequent crops.

Atrazine is very similar to simazine except that it is rather more soluble and more independent of soil moisture for effective weed control. It is preferable to simazine for use in maize. The doses used are 1 to 1·5 lb per acre.

Trichloroacetic Acid (TCA)

Trichloroacetic acid is available commercially as the sodium salt, a crystalline solid containing about 92 per cent a.e. The salt is readily soluble in water. Applied as a spray to the soil it will kill seedling grasses at 10 lb per acre or less and perennial grasses such as *Agropyron repens* (couch grass) at a higher dose, the chemical treatment generally being combined with cultivations.

Unlike dalapon, trichloroacetic acid is absorbed mainly by the roots, and the mixing of the chemical with the soil by means of cultivation plays an important part in obtaining successful results. Information on its persistence in the soil and how soon crops can be planted following an application for couch grass control is given on page 168. Recently trichloroacetic acid at about 7 lb per acre has given useful results for the control of wild oats in peas and sugar beet, application being made to the soil prior to the final seed-bed cultivations.

Trichloroacetic acid is of low mammalian toxicity but, as the sodium salt, it is moderately corrosive to most metals.

III. Contact Herbicides

Dinitropheols: DNOC and Dinoseb

DNOC and dinoseb are closely related members of this group of compounds. They are intensely yellow-staining and poisonous to humans and animals by ingestion, inhalation or absorption through the skin. Special precautions to be taken when using them are outlined in the Agriculture (Poisonous Substances) Regulations. (See Chapter VIII, Section (i).)

Both chemicals applied in spray form are very efficient herbicides, killing a wide range of annual weeds. Neither is corrosive to metals.

DNOC

Commercial products for selective weed control in cereals are usually based on one of two forms: DNOC or 'activated DNOC' (DNOC + activator, e.g. ammonium sulphate). Rates of application vary between 4 and 10 lb per acre, those for the activated DNOC being about 25 per cent less than those for the unactivated DNOC. Another form, DNOC-sodium, is sometimes also used for cereals and is specifically recommended for linseed and flax. It is less effective than the parent DNOC at equivalent dosages. DNOC is not very soluble in water and remains as a suspension even when diluted for application in the field. The normal volume rate for DNOC products is 80–100 gallons per acre. The mixing with water must be very thorough and the sprayer should have effective agitation in the liquid tank.

The importance of DNOC herbicides lies in their ability to kill several important annual weeds which are little affected by MCPA or 2,4-D, including *Galium aparine* (cleavers), *Chrysanthemum segetum* (corn marigold), *Matricaria recutita* (wild chamomile), *Tripleurospermu maritimum* ssp. *inodora* (scentless mayweed), *Veronica* spp. (speedwells) and *Spergula arvensis* (spurrey). Some of these can now be more conveniently and more cheaply controlled by mecoprop or mixtures of 2,3,6-TBA and MCPA.

The effectiveness of DNOC is increased by high temperatures at or immediately following spraying. Its efficiency is reduced at temperatures below 55°F. Rolling or harrowing of cereals immediately before or after spraying with DNOC may give rise to crop damage; there should be an interval of ten days before or seven days after spraying.

While being of particular importance as a selective herbicide for cereals, DNOC formulated as an oil-water emulsion or as a solution in oil is an effective non-selective contact herbicide and may be used for potato haulm destruction or for the pre-harvest desiccation of leguminous seed crops.

DINOSEB

Dinoseb products in Great Britain are based either on the ammonium salt or an amine derivative and are used mainly for selectively killing annual weeds in peas, seedling lucerne and undersown cereals. They are generally applied as high volume sprays at doses of 1 to 3 lb dinoseb per acre. At such concentrations these dinoseb salts are completely soluble and agitation is not required. With the increasing number of products containing the more soluble dinoseb-amine there is a trend towards the use of medium volume rates for its application. Since the effect of a given dose of dinoseb may vary markedly according to the physical characteristics of the spray, due consideration should be given before employing spraying pressures, volume rates and jet sizes other than those recommended by the manufacturers of the product.

As with DNOC, dinoseb may also be formulated in oil or oil-water emulsions for non-selective uses such as potato haulm destruction and pre-harvest desiccation.

MINERAL OILS

Certain types of mineral oil can be used for the selective control of young annual weeds in umbelliferous crops, especially carrots. Those recommended in this country are the white spirits (boiling range 140 to 210°C) with aromatic content between 15 and 25 per cent. The white spirits are safer than the vaporizing oils as far as these crops are concerned. Proprietary brands of white spirits are available which are standardized for use as selective herbicides. Vaporizing oils are not standard in respect of their phytotoxic properties. Different brands and different batches of the same brand may vary in their effect on the crop and on the weeds and it is desirable to test each batch on a small area before large scale application.

'Fortified' oils are persistent or non-persistent mineral oils containing DNOC, dinoseb, cresylic acids or pentachlorophenol to increase their phytotoxicity. They are not selective. They may be applied direct or emulsified with water. Their chief uses are in crop desiccation, potato haulm destruction and as contact or residual pre-emergence herbicides.

Crude and waste oils may be used without fortifying agents for non-selective weed control.

PENTACHLOROPHENOL

This compound has been known for many years to have herbicidal properties similar in numerous respects to those of the dinitrophenols, but it has lower mammalian toxicity. However, only comparatively recently have its potentialities been seriously investigated.

Pentachlorophenol is not translocated and can be used, when suitably formulated, as a contact herbicide and as a pre-emergence treatment for the control of germinating weed seeds. Pentachlorophenol may be added as a fortifying agent to oils formulated for general contact weed control. Both pentachlorophenol and its sodium salt may be used as contact and residual pre-emergence treatments on a variety of crops. The phenol, dissolved in oil or in oil-water emulsion, at 1 to 4 lb per acre, has been used as a pre-emergence treatment for beans, sugar beet and other crops. Pentachlorophenol can also be used as a pre-harvest desiccant for leguminous seed crops.

SODIUM MONOCHLOROACETATE

Known for many years as a desiccant in N. America, this compound has more recently been developed in Great Britain as a contact herbicide for annual weeds of various brassica crops including kale and for onions and leeks. It is also recommended for the desiccation of red clover. The commercial grade of this chemical, a white crystalline powder, is very soluble in water and is generally applied at 16 to 30 lb in 10 to 30 gallons water per acre. It is of low toxicity to animals.

Sodium monochloroacetate is not absorbed quickly by weeds and should not be used when rain is imminent. It acts slowly and the maximum effect on the weeds may not appear for up to three weeks after spraying. Satisfactory results are obtained from application in 20 gallons of water per acre and increasing the volume above this rate gives progressively less weed control. However, uniform spray coverage is essential. The addition of a wetting agent may increase weed control but considerably increases the damage to brassica crops. There is some evidence that sodium monochloroacetate persists in the soil for a time after application and this limits its usefulness as a pre-emergence treatment.

TOXIC HAZARDS

For advice concerning the safe use of herbicides mentioned in this chapter readers are referred to the official recommendations published as a loose-leaf dossier entitled 'Chemical Compounds used in Agriculture and Food Storage in Great Britain—User and Consumer Safety—Advice of Government Departments'. These and other aspects of the safe use of herbicides are dealt with in Chapter VIII.

CHAPTER II

RECOMMENDATIONS FOR THE USE OF HERBICIDES IN AGRICULTURE

SECTION (i) CEREAL CROPS

INTRODUCTION

1. The wide range of herbicides available for cereals makes it possible to control nearly all the important annual weeds and nowadays the most troublesome weeds of cereals tend to be perennials such as thistles, docks, and field bindweed which, whilst checked, are not always satisfactorily controlled by herbicides.

The first choice of a herbicide for cereals should be either MCPA or 2,4-D, both of which are effective against many weeds and are relatively cheap. Other more expensive herbicides such as mecoprop, dichlorprop, mixtures of MCPA plus 2,3,6-TBA and MCPA plus 3,6-dichloro-2-methoxybenzoic acid and barban should only be chosen where weeds resistant to MCPA or 2,4-D are present.

The undersowing of cereals with grass and clover, restricts the herbicides that may be used safely to MCPB, 2,4-DB, mixtures of either of these herbicides with small amounts of MCPA, or dinoseb. Commercial preparations of MCPB or 2,4-DB plus MCPA should normally be used on undersown cereals rather than MCPB or 2,4-DB alone, and these mixtures are generally to be preferred to dinoseb, the use of which requires certain precautions, as laid down by the Agriculture (Poisonous Substances) Act (see Chapter VIII). Dinoseb, however, controls several important weeds that are resistant to MCPB plus MCPA and 2,4-DB plus MCPA.

2. Cereals alter in their tolerance of herbicides as they grow older. It is therefore very necessary to be able to define accurately their stage of growth in order to be precise with regard to the recommendations concerning the time of application. This is discussed in paragraph 4.

The volume of liquid in which the herbicide is applied also influences the efficiency of the treatment. This aspect is considered in paragraph 5.

The correct herbicide to use, the amount to apply and the time to apply it in any particular situation will depend upon many considerations, but primarily upon the crop that is being grown and the weeds that are present or

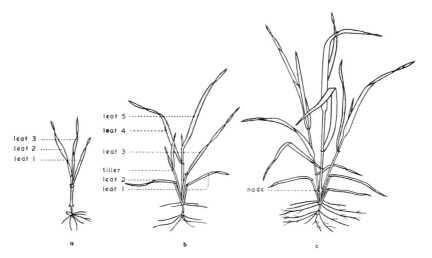

FIG. 2. Stages of growth of cereals: (a) three-leaf stage; (b) five-leaf stage; (c) start of 'shooting' or 'jointing'. All drawings ×¼. (Drawn by R. J. Chancellor from paintings of wheat plants by E. C. Large.)

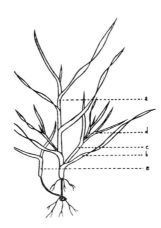

FIG. 3. Diagrammatic representation of the way tillers arise in young cereal plants. a = main shoot; b = first leaf on main shoot; c = primary tiller arising in axil of first leaf of main shoot; d = secondary tiller arising in axil of first leaf of primary tiller; e = tiller arising from seed.

expected. The limits of tolerance of cereal crops to herbicides are indicated in paragraph 6 (Table 4). The correct dose to apply below the maximum permissible on a crop will depend upon the susceptibility of the weed or weeds that infest the crop. This aspect is dealt with in paragraph 7 (Table 5).

The specific crop situations are dealt with in paragraphs 9 to 38 at the end of the section and an index to these is given in Table 3 on page 32.

3. Before studying this and subsequent sections of this Handbook that deal with recommendations, the Special Notes (page v) should be considered.

DETERMINATION OF STAGE OF GROWTH OF CEREALS

4. The development of spring cereals during the early stages of their growth is most conveniently characterized by the number of leaves they have formed, and this criterion is adopted. It is important to define clearly the terms 'one-leaf stage', and 'two-leaf stage', etc, used in this book. The leaf number refers only to those leaves which are fully expanded and are on the main shoot. It does not refer to leaves on secondary shoots or tillers (side shoots). A leaf is considered fully expanded if the tip of the next leaf is just visible. For example, the 1-leaf stage is when the first leaf has expanded and the top of the second leaf is just visible. Extreme care is necessary when counting the leaves as it is easy to miss shrivelled lower leaves. Where lower leaves have shrivelled, tillers will help to identify them; tillers arise from the axils of leaves, generally from the lower ones first. Tillers arising within tillers (secondary tillers) and those arising direct from the seed should be ignored (see Figs 2 and 3 opposite).

The tolerance of winter cereals to herbicides during autumn and winter cannot be correlated reliably with the number of leaves formed. Normally spraying of winter cereals is not carried out until the spring when the crop is 'fully tillered'. This is the stage when it is difficult to distinguish between the main shoot and tillers. Spraying earlier than this is possible with certain herbicides (see paragraphs 9, 11, 13, 16 and 18).

When sampling a crop to determine the stage of growth it is essential to be certain of removing the whole plant from the ground and random samples should be dug rather than pulled, as the latter method may leave tillers behind.

VOLUME RATES

5. All growth regulator herbicides (MCPA, 2,4-amine, 2,4-D-ester, MCPB, 2,4-DB, mecoprop, dichlorprop, MCPA plus 3,6-dichloro-2-methoxybenzoic acid mixtures and MCPA plus 2,3,6-TBA mixtures) are readily diluted with water and application is generally made in the range of 5 to 100 gallons of

TABLE 3. A GUIDE TO THE USE OF HERBICIDES ON CEREALS

		Dicotyledonous weeds				Graminaceous weeds	Para.
		Annual	Para.	Perennial	Para.		
1. Cereals alone	(a) Post-emergence, translocated	MCPA	9–11	MCPA	9–11	Barban (wheat and certain varieties of barley only)	23–24
		2,4-D (not on oats)	12	2,4-D (not on oats)	12		
		MCPB (±MCPA)*	13	MCPB (±MCPA)*	13		
		2,4-DB (±MCPA)*	14	2,4-DB (±MCPA)*	14		
		Mecoprop	15–16	Mecoprop	15–16		
		Dichlorprop	17	Dichlorprop	17		
		MCPA plus 2,3,6-TBA	18	MCPA plus 2,3,6-TBA	18		
		MCPA plus 3,6-dichloro-2-methoxybenzoic acid	19	MCPA plus 3,6-dichloro-2-methoxybenzoic acid	19		
				See footnote†			
	(b) Post-emergence, contact	DNOC	20–21	Nil	—	Nil	—
		Dinoseb	20–21				
		Sulphuric acid	22				
2. Cereals undersown with grass and clover or lucerne	(a) Post-emergence, translocated	MCPB (±MCPA)	31	MCPB (±MCPA)	31	Barban (wheat and certain varieties of barley only)	38
		2,4-DB (±MCPA)	32–33	2,4-DB (±MCPA)	32–33		
		MCPA	37	MCPA	37		
		2,4-D	37	2,4-D	37		
				See footnote†			
	(b) Post-emergence contact	DNOC	34–35	Nil	—	Nil	—
		Dinoseb	34–35				
		Sulphuric acid	36				
3. Cereal legume mixture	(a) Post-emergence, translocated	MCPB (±MCPA)	26	MCPB (±MCPA)	26	Nil	—
		MCPA	27	MCPA	27		
				See footnote†			
	(b) Post-emergence, contact	Dinoseb	28–29	Nil	—	Nil	—

* These herbicides are normally used only on undersown cereals.
† Normally the optimum time for spraying perennial weeds is later than that for spraying annual weeds. Where translocated herbicides are used post-emergence for the control of annual weeds they can be effective on the shoots of the perennial weeds that are present.

water per acre. Applications below 10 gallons per acre normally are not recommended, particularly with MCPB, 2,4-DB, dichlorprop, and mecoprop because of the less reliable weed control which may result. With mecoprop the minimum volume should be 20 gallons per acre where the vegetation is dense — as is often the case, for example, where *Galium aparine* (cleavers) are present — to ensure that the herbicide penetrates sufficiently to give the weed a lethal dose. All growth regulator herbicides give satisfactory results at medium and high volumes (see page 209), except MCPA plus 2,3,6-TBA for which the maximum volume for best results is 30 gallons per acre. Barban should be applied in 10 to 20 gallons of water per acre as this gives the greatest retention of the herbicide on wild oat plants.

The contact herbicides (DNOC, DNOC-amine, dinoseb-ammonium, dinoseb-amine and sulphuric acid) are applied in medium to high volume (20 to 100 gallons per acre). There are two reasons for the higher volume rates. First, as contact herbicides kill only the part of the weed which they touch it is important that the weed is well wetted with the spray. Second, some of the contact herbicides at the normally recommended doses are insoluble or immiscible at low volume rates and DNOC is insoluble even at 100 gallons per acre. The volume rate used should not be less than 60 gallons per acre: the mixture in the spray tank should be continually agitated to keep the chemical mixed with the water. Dinoseb-ammonium and DNOC-amine are soluble when applied in 60–100 gallons and agitation is not necessary. Dinoseb-amine is more soluble than dinoseb-ammonium and DNOC-amine and satisfactory results may be obtained with volume rates down to 40 gallons per acre. Sulphuric acid is normally diluted and applied at 100 gallons per acre of dilute solution. The acid, in the form of 'Brown Oil of Vitriol' is sometimes applied undiluted but weed control by this method is less reliable and crop damage is generally greater.

MAXIMUM SAFE DOSES AND STAGES OF GROWTH AT WHICH HERBICIDES MAY BE APPLIED TO CEREALS

6. The different types of herbicide recommended for selective weed control in cereals are listed in Table 4 which sets out the *maximum* safe dose of each herbicide at stages of growth of the crop from the development of the first leaf until the beginning of 'shooting' or 'jointing'. None of the herbicides are recommended for use after the latter stage of growth.

TABLE 4. MAXIMUM SAFE DOSES AND STAGES OF GROWTH AT WHICH HERBICIDES MAY BE APPLIED TO CEREALS

Amounts of synthetic plant growth regulator herbicides are given as ounces per acre of acid equivalent of active isomer, except mecoprop and dichlorprop where doses are given as the total of dextro- and laevo-rotory isomers. Amounts refer to products not containing an added surface-active agent (except 2.4-D-ester in which such an agent has to be included in the formulation of the normal type of emulsifiable concentrate). The suffix '-salt' indicates sodium, potassium, ammonium and amine formulations.

Amounts of DNOC and dinoseb are given as lb/ac of the parent nitrated phenol.

Note: For recommendations regarding the spraying of dredge corn see paragraphs 25 to 29 and for undersown cereals see paragraphs 30 to 38.

A. WINTER CEREALS

The maximum safe amounts recommended in this section of the table refer to applications to fully tillered crops in the spring as described in the text. For applications earlier than this see paragraphs 9, 11, 13, 16 and 18.

Chemical	Unit of dose	Crop			
		Wheat	Barley	Oats	Rye
MCPA-salt†	oz/acre	32	32	32	32
2,4-D-amine†	oz/acre	24	16	16	24
2,4-D-ester	oz/acre	16	8	4	16
MCPB-salt	oz/acre	48	48	48	(evidence lacking)
2,4-DB-salt	oz/acre	48	48	32	(evidence lacking)
Mecoprop-salt‡	oz/acre	56	56	56	NR
Dichlorprop-salt‡	oz/acre	56	56	56	NR
MCPA plus 3,6-dichloro-2-methoxybenzoic acid-salts	oz/acre	18 + 1·3	18 + 1·3	18 + 1·3	(evidence lacking)
MCPA plus 2,3,6-TBA-salts	oz/acre	12 + 4	12 + 4	12 + 4	12 + 4
DNOC‖	lb/acre	8*	8*	8	8
Dinoseb-ammonium‖	lb/acre	1·5	1·5	1	1·5
Dinoseb-amine‖	lb/acre	2	2	1·5	2
Sulphuric acid**	gal/acre	11·5	10	10	10
Barban	oz/acre	5	5¶	NR	NR

TABLE 4—*continued*

B. SPRING CEREALS

The maximum safe amounts recommended in this section of the table refer to applications as described in the text.

Chemical	Unit of dose	Crop	Stage of growth (see paragraph 3)		
			1 leaf to 3 leaves	3 to 5 leaves	5 leaves to start of 'shooting'
MCPA-salt†	oz/acre	wheat	NR	12‡‡	32
		barley	NR	12‡‡	32
		oats	24	24	32
2,4-D-amine†	oz/acre	wheat	NR	NR	16
		barley	NR	NR	16
		oats	NR	NR	NR
2,4-D-ester	oz/acre	wheat	NR	NR	8
		barley	NR	NR	8
		oats	NR	NR	NR
MCPB-salt	oz/acre	wheat	48	48	48
		barley	48	48	48
		oats	48	48	48
2,4-DB-salt	oz/acre	wheat	NR	NR	48
		barley	48	48	48
		oats	24	24	24
Mecoprop-salt‡	oz/acre	wheat	56§	56§	56
		barley	56	56	56
		oats	56	56	56
Dichlorprop-salt‡	oz/acre	wheat	NR	NR	56
		barley	56	56	56
		oats	56	56	56
MCPA plus 3,6-cidhloro-2-methoxybenzoic acid-salts	oz/acre	wheat	NR	NR	18 + 1·3
		barley	NR	NR	18 + 1·3
		oats	NR	NR	18 + 1·3

TABLE 4—*continued*

Chemical	Unit of dose	Crop	Stage of growth (see paragraph 3)		
			1 leaf to 3 leaves	3 to 5 leaves	5 leaves to start of 'shooting'
MCPA plus 2,3,6-TBA-salts	oz/acre	wheat	NR	NR	12 + 4
		barley	NR	NR	12 + 4
		oats	NR	NR	12 + 4
DNOC‖	lb/acre	wheat	NR	8*	8*
		barley	NR	8*	8*
		oats	NR	8	8
Dinoseb-ammonium‖	lb/acre	wheat	NR	1·5	1·5
		barley	NR	1·5	1·5
		oats	NR	1	1
Dinoseb-amine‖	lb/acre	wheat	NR	2	2
		barley	NR	2	2
		oats	NR	1·5	1·5
Sulphuric acid**	gal/acre	wheat	NR	NR	10
		barley	NR	NR	10
		oats	NR	NR	8
Barban	oz/acre	wheat	5	5	—
		barley	5¶	5¶	—
		oats	NR	NR	—

* Maximum doses may be increased by 25 per cent in very cold weather in spring and for the control of weeds which have reached an advanced stage of growth, but increased scorch of cereal may occur.

‖ Maximum doses should be decreased by 20 per cent in warm, moist weather and may be increased by 20 per cent in cold, dry weather in the spring.

** Volumes of 100 per cent pure acid. Conversion is required for acid content of product used, e.g. multiply by 1·3 for B.O.V. containing 77 per cent v/v of acid.

¶ **Certain** varieties only (see para 23).

‡‡ See para 10 regarding possible occurrence of deformed ears.

† When MCPA or 2,4-D are applied in a dust carrier twice the quantities can be used.

‡ Doses are given as total of dextro- and laevo-rotatory isomers.

§ Koga II and Jufy I only.

NR Not recommended

‖ Unactivated. Where an activated product is used the maximum amount must be reduced by 25 per cent.

THE SUSCEPTIBILITY OF ANNUAL WEEDS TO HERBICIDES USED ON CEREALS

7. Table 5 indicates the response of the annual weeds commonly found in cereal crops to herbicides. The aim is to assist the reader to choose the most appropriate herbicide. The information is based on results obtained with typical products containing the various active chemicals. Some products may have rather different properties as a result, for example, of the addition of wetting agents, and it is recommended that once a particular product has been selected the manufacturer's instructions should be followed carefully. Four categories have been selected to indicate the degree of weed control obtained at either of two stages of growth of the weed by a stated dose of herbicide applied. The categories of **susceptibility** are defined as follows:

S   Susceptible – Complete or almost complete kill.

MS Moderately susceptible – Effective suppression with or without mortality.

MR Moderately resistant – Temporary suppression, the duration depending on the vigour of the crop and the weather.

R   Resistant – No useful effect.

The stages of growth are defined as follows:

Sd   Seedling stage – Cotyledons up to 2–3 leaves.

Yp   Young plant – 3–4 leaves to early flower-bud.

The **doses** chosen for each herbicide at the top of the columns are the upper and lower levels that are most generally used in cereals.

If there is insufficient information to give such detail a single tentative category is given, indicating the general response to a dose within the given range.

Commercial mixtures of some of the herbicides shown in this table are available. The addition of two herbicides is intended to extend the range of weeds controlled. As the proportion of the constituents in commercial products may cover a fairly wide range it is impossible to make any positive recommendations concerning them. It is not possible to deduce from this table the susceptibility of weeds to commercial mixtures. As a practical guide, however, the potential value of a mixture may be estimated by combining the list of species classified as generally susceptible to one constituent with those similarly classified with regard to the other constituent, except where the dose of a constituent is appreciably lower than the lower dose shown in the table.

8. Perennial weeds are dealt with individually in Chapter V.

4

TABLE 5. THE SUSCEPTIBILITY OF ANNUAL WEEDS TO HERBICIDES USED IN CEREALS

Weed (Chemical and dose; oz. acid equivalent per acre)		MCPA-salt 12	24	2,4-D amine 10	20	2,4-D ester 5	10	MCPB-salt 24	32	2,4-DB-salt 24	32	Mecoprop-salt 32†	40†	Dichlorprop-salt 32†	40†	MCPA plus 2,3,6-TBA-salts 12 + 4	MCPA plus 3,6-dichloro-2-methoxybenzoic acid-salt 18 + 1·3	DNOC (i)	Dinoseb-amine and ammonium (ii)	Cross reference (page no.)
1. *Alopecurus myosuroides* (blackgrass)	Sd	R		R		R		R		R		R		R		R	R	R	R	172
	Yp																			
2. *Anagalis arvensis* (scarlet pimpernel)	Sd	MR	MS	MR	MS	MR	MS	MR	MS	MR	MS	MR		MR		MS	S	S	S	
	Yp	R	MR	R	MR	R	MR	R	MR	R	MR	—				MR	MS	S	S	
3. *Anchusa arvensis* (bugloss)	Sd	MR		MR		MR		—		—		—		—		MS		—	MS	
	Yp																			
4. *Anthemis arvensis* (corn chamomile)	Sd	R	MR	R	MR	R	MR	R		R		MR	MR	MR	MR	MS	MR	S	S	
	Yp	R	R	R	R	R	R					R	MR	R	MR	MR	R	R	MR	
5. *Aphanes arvensis* (parsley piert)	Sd	R		R		R		R		R		R		R		R	R	R	S	
	Yp																			
6. *Atriplex patula* (common orache)	Sd	MS	MS	MS	S	MS	S	MR	MS	MS	MS	MS	S	MS	S	S	MS	S	S	
	Yp	MR	MS	MR	MS	MR	MS	R	MR	R	MR	MR	MS	MR	MS	MS	MS	MR	MR	
7. *Avena fatua* (common wild oat)	Sd	R		R		R		R		R		R		R		R	R	R	R	173–4
	Yp																			
8. *Avena ludoviciana* (winter wild oat)	Sd	R		R		R		R		R		R		R		R	R	R	R	173–4
	Yp																			
9. *Brassica nigra* (black mustard)	Sd	S‡	S*	S‡	S	S‡	S	S	MS	MS	S	S	S	S	S	S	S	S	S	
	Yp	S‡	S*	S‡	S*	S	S	S	MS	MS	MS	S	S	S	S		S	S	S	
10. *Brassica rapa* ssp. *campestris* (wild turnip)	Sd	MS	MS	S	S	S	S	MS	MS			MS	S	MS	S	S	S		—	
	Yp	MR	MS	MS	MS	MS	MS	MR	MR			MR	MS	MR	MS		MS		—	
11. *Capsella bursa-pastoris* (shepherd's purse)	Sd	S	S	S	S	S	S	S	S	S	S	S	S	S	MS	S	S	S	S	
	Yp	MS	MS	MS	MS	MS	MS	MR	MS	MR	MS	MS	MS	MS	S	S	S	S	S	
12. *Cerastium holosteoides* (mouse-ear chickweed)	Sd	MR	MS	MR	MS	MR	R	—		—		MS		MS		MS	—	R	R	
	Yp	R	MR	R	R	MR	MS					S		S		MR				
13. *Chenopodium album* (fat hen)	Sd	S	S	S	S	MS	MR	S	S	S	S	S	S	S	S	S	S	S	S	
	Yp	S	S	S	S	S	S	S	MS	MS	S	S	S	S	S	S	S	MR	MR	

TABLE 5—*continued*

Chemical and dose; oz. acid equivalent per acre / Weed		MCPA-salt		2,4-D amine		2,4-D ester		MCPB-salt		2,4-DB-salt		Mecoprop-salt		Dichlorprop salt		MCPA plus 2,3,6-TBA-salts	MCPA plus 3,6-dichloro-2-methoxybenzoic acid-salt	DNOC	Dinoseb-amine and ammonium	Cross reference (page no.)
		12	24	10	20	5	10	24	32	24	32	32†	40†	32†	40†	12 + 4	18 + 1·3	(i)	(ii)	
14. *Chrysanthemum segetum* (corn marigold)	Sd	R		R		R	MR	R		R		R		R		MR	MR	S(w)	S	
	Yp					R	R									R	R	MR(w)	MR	
15. *Echium vulgare* (viper's bugloss)	Sd	MR		MR		MR		—		—		MR		MR		MS	—	—	—	
	Yp															MR				
16. *Erysimum cheiranthoides* (treacle mustard)	Sd	S	S	S	S	S	S	MS	S	MS	S	S	S	S	S	S	S	S	S	
	Yp	S	S	S	S	S	S	MR	MS	MR	MS	MS	S	MS	S	S	S	S	S	
17. *Euphorbia helioscopia* (sun spurge)		MS		MR		MR		—		—		—		—		—	—	MR	MR	
18. *Fumaria officinalis* (fumitory)	Sd	MS	MS	MR	MS	MR	MS	S	S	MS	S	MR	MS	MR	MS	S	S	S(w)	S	
	Yp	MR	MR	R	MR	R	MR	MR	MR	R	MR	R	R	R	R	MR	MS	S(w)	MS	
19. *Galeopsis tetrahit* (common hempnettle)	Sd	MS	S	R	MR	R	MR	MS	MS	R	MR	MR	MS	MR	MS	S	S	S	S	
	Yp	MR	MS	R	R	R	R	MR	MR	R	R	R	MR	R	MS	MS	MS	S	S	
20. *Galium aparine* (cleavers)	Sd	R		R		R		R		R		MS	S	MS	S	S	MR	MS	S	
	Yp											MS	S	MS	S	MS	R	MS	MS	
21. *Geranium molle* (dove's foot cranesbill)		MR		MR		MR		—		—		MS		—		MR	—	MR	MS	
22. *Lapsana communis* (nipplewort)		R		R		R		R		R		—		—		R	S	—	—	
23. *Lithospermum arvense* (corn gromwell)	Sd	MR	MS	MR	MS	MR	MS	—		—		R	MR	R	MR	MS	—	S	S	
	Yp	R	MR	R	MR	R	MR					R	R	R	R	MR	—	S	S	
24. *Matricarta recutita* (wild chamomile)	Sd	R		R		R		R		R		R		R		MS	R	S	S	
	Yp															MR		MR	MR	
25. *Myosotis arvensis* (common forget-me-not)		MS		MS		MS		MR		R		R		R		MS	—	—	S	

TABLE 5—continued

Chemical and dose; oz acid equivalent per acre / Weed		MCPA-salt 12	MCPA-salt 24	2,4-D amine 10	2,4-D amine 20	2,4-D ester 5	2,4-D ester 10	MCPB-salt 24	MCPB-salt 32	2,4-DB-salt 24	2,4-DB-salt 32	Mecoprop-salt 32†	Mecoprop-salt 40†	Dichlorprop salt 32†	Dichlorprop salt 40†	MCPA plus 2,3,6-TBA-salts 12+4	MCPA plus 3,6-dichloro-2-methoxybenzoic acid-salt 18+1·3	DNOC (i)	Dinoseb-amine and ammonium (ii)	Cross reference (page no.)
26. *Papaver rhoeas* (corn poppy)	Sd	MS	S	MS	S	MS	S	MS	S	MS	S	MR	MS	R	MS	MS	S	S	S	
	Yp	MR	MS	MR	MR	MS	S	R	MR	R	MR	R	MS	R	MS	MR	MS	S	MR	
27. *Polygonum aviculare* (knotgrass)	Sd	R	MR	MR	S	MR	MS	MR	MR	MR	R	R	MR	RMS-MR	R	MS	S-MS	S	S	
	Yp	R	R	R	MR	R	MS	R	MS	R	MR	R	R	R	S	MR	MR	MR	MR	
28. *Polygonum convolvulus* (black bindweed)	Sd	R	R	MR	MS	MR	MS	R	R	MR	MS	R	MR	MS	S	MS	MS	S	S	
	Yp	R	R	R	MR	R	MR	R	MS	R	MR	R	R	MR	S	MR	MR	MS	R	
29. *Polygonum lapathifolium* (pale persicaria)	Sd	R	R	MR	MS	MR	MR	R	R	MS	S	MR	MR	S	S	MS	S	S	S	
	Yp	R	R	R	MR	R	MR	R	R	MR	MS	R	R	MS	S	MR	MS	R	R	
30. *Polygonum persicaria* (redshank)	Sd	R	R	MR	S	MR	S	R	MR	MS	S	MR	MR	S	S	S-MS	S	S	S	
	Yp	R	R	R	S	R	S	R	R	MR	MS	R	R	MS	S	MR	MS	R	R	
31. *Ranunculus arvensis* (corn buttercup)	Sd	S	MS	S	S	S	S	S	MS	S	S	S	S	S	S	S	S	S	S	
	Yp	MS	S	MS	S	MS	S	MS	S	S	S	MS	MS	S	S	S	S	S	R	
32. *Raphanus raphanistrum* (wild radish)	Sd	S	S	S	S	S	MR	R	MR	R		S	S	S	S	S	S	S	S	
	Yp	S	MS	S	MS	MS	R	R	R			S	S	S	S	S	S	S	MR	
33. *Scandix pecten-veneris* (shepherd's needle)	Sd	MR	MS	MR	MS	R	R	R		R		—		—		MS	MS	S	S	
	Yp	R	R	R	R	R	MR									MR	R	MR	MR	
34. *Senecio vulgaris* (groundsel)	Sd	MR	MS	MR	MS	MR	MS	MS	S	MR	MS	MR	MS	MR	MS	MS	S	S	S	
	Yp	R	MS	R	R	R	R	MR	MS	R	R	MR	MR	MR	MR	R	MS	S	MR	
35. *Sinapis alba* (white mustard)	Sd	S	S	S	S	S	S	MS	S	MS	S	S	S	S	S	S	S	S	S	
	Yp	S	S	S	S	S	S	MR	MS	MR	MS	S	S	MS	S	S	S	S	S	
36. *Sinapis arvensis* (charlock)	Sd	S‡	S	S‡	S	S‡	S	MS	MS	MS	S	S	S	S	S	S	S	S	S	
	Yp	S*	S	S*	S	S	S	MR	MS	MS	MS	MS	S	MS	S	S	S	S	S	
37. *Silanum nigrum* (black nightshade)	Sd	MR	MS	MR	MS	MR	MS	MS	MS	MS	S	S	S	S	S	MS	—	S	S	
	Yp	R	R	R	R	R	MR	MS	MS	MS	MS	S	S	S	S	MR		R	R	
38. *Sonchus asper* (spiny sowthistle)	Sd	MS	S	MS	S	MS	MS	MS	S	MS	S		MS	MR		S	—	S	S	
	Yp	MR	MS	MR	MS	MR	MS	MR	MS	MR	MS					MS		R	MR	
39. *Sonchus oleraceus* (annual sowthistle)	Sd	MS	S	MS	S	MS	S	MS	S	MS	S	MR	MS	MR	R	S	S	S	S	
	Yp	MR	MS	MR	MS	MR	MS	MR	MS	MR	MS	MR	MR	R	R	MS	MS	R	MR	

TABLE 5—*continued*

Weed (Chemical and dose; oz. acid equivalent per acre)	Sd/Yp	MCPA-salt 12	MCPA-salt 24	2,4-D amine 10	2,4-D amine 20	2,4-D ester 5	2,4-D ester 10	MCPB-salt 24	MCPB-salt 32	2,4-DB-salt 24	2,4-DB-salt 32	Mecoprop-salt 32†	Mecoprop-salt 40†	Dichlorprop-salt 32†	Dichlorprop-salt 40†	MCPA plus 2,3,6-TBA-salts 12+4	MCPA plus 3,6-dichloro-2-methoxybenzoic acid-salt 18+1·3	DNOC (i)	Dinoseb-amine and ammonium (ii)	Cross reference (page no.)
40. *Spergula arvensis* (corn spurrey)	Sd	MR	MS	MR	MS	R	MR	R	R	R	R	R	MR	MS	S	MS	MS	S	MS	182
	Yp	R	R	R	R	R	R	R	R	R	R	R	R	MR	MS	MR	MR	MR	MR	
41. *Stellaria media* (chickweed)	Sd	MR	MR	MR	MR	S	S	R	R	R	R	S	S	MS	S	S-MS	S-MS	S	S	
	Yp	R	R	R	R	MS	S	R	R	R	R	S	S	MS	S	MR	MR	S	S	
42. *Thlaspi arvense* (field pennycress)	Sd	S	S	S	S	S	S	S	MS	—	—	S	S	MS	S	S-MS	S	S	S	
	Yp	S	S	S	S	S	S	MS	R	—	—	S	MS	MS	S	MR	S	S	S	
43. *Tripleurospermum maritimum* ssp. *inodorum* (scentless mayweed)	Sd	R	R	R	R	R	MR	R	R	R	R	MR	MS	R	R	MR	MR	S	S	
	Yp	R	R	R	R	R	R	R	R	R	R	R	MR	R	R	R	R	S	MR	
44. *Urtica urens* (annual nettle)	Sd	MS	S	S	S	MS	S	S	MS	S	S	S	S	S	MS	S	S	S	S	
	Yp	MR	MS	MS	S	MR	MS	S	MS	MS	S	MS	S	MS	S	MR	MR	MR	MR	
45. *Veronica agrestis* (procumbent speedwell)	Sd	MR	MS	MR	MS	R	R	R	R	R	R	R	R	—	—	MS	—	S	S	
	Yp	R	R	R	R	MR	R	R	R	R	R	R	R	—	—	R	—	S	MR	
46. *Veronica arvensis*	Sd	MR	MR	MR	MR	MR	MR	—	—	—	—	MR	MR	—	—	MR	—	S	S	
	Yp	MR	MR	MR	MR	MR	MR	—	—	—	—	MR	MR	—	—	MR	—	S	MS	
47. *Verontca hederifolia*	Sd	MR	MS	MR	MS	R	R	R	R	R	R	MR	MR	—	—	MS	MS	S	S	
	Yp	R	R	R	R	MR	R	R	R	R	R	MR	MR	—	—	R	R	S	MS	
48. *Veronica persica* (buxbaum's speedwell)	Sd	MR	MR	MR	MS	R	R	MR	MS	R	R	MR	MR	MR	MR	MS	MR	S	S	
	Yp	R	R	R	R	MR	R	R	R	MR	R	MR	MR	MR	MR	R	R	S	MR	
49. *Vicia hirsuta* (hairy vetch)	Sd	S	S	S	S	S	S	—	—	—	—	—	—	—	—	S	—	—	MS	
	Yp	S	S	S	S	S	S	—	—	—	—	—	—	—	—	S	—	—	MS	

(i) DNOC at 4 to 6 lb per acre activated, 6 to 8 lb. per acre unactivated. (ii) Dinoseb-ammonium 1·5 lb.;—amine 2 lb per acre.
* S to 5 oz per acre.
† Total acid equivalent in terms of active and inactive isomers in ratio 1 : 1.
‡ S to 2·5 oz per acre.
(w) wetting agent should be used.

A. CEREALS ALONE

MCPA-SALT ON WINTER-SOWN BARLEY, WHEAT AND RYE

9. MCPA-salt may be sprayed on autumn- or winter-sown wheat, barley and rye for the control of annual weeds when the crop is fully tillered until the start of 'shooting' or 'jointing'. If crops are sprayed earlier than recommended, malformation of the head, stem and leaf may occur. The amount of malformation, which increases with the dose applied, is not necessarily correlated with yield reduction. Malformation may affect grain quality and care should be taken that malting barley in particular is fully tillered before spraying. Except where grain quality is unimportant, spraying MCPA-salt earlier than recommended may be desirable to obtain the best weed control. Where MCPA is applied in a dust carrier twice the dose recommended as a spray will be required.

MCPA-SALT ON SPRING-SOWN BARLEY, WHEAT AND RYE

10. MCPA-salt may be sprayed on to spring-sown wheat, barley and rye between the five-leaf stage and the start of 'shooting' or 'jointing'. Spraying earlier than this may induce malformation of the head, stem and leaf. The amount of malformation, which increases with the dose applied, is not necessarily correlated with yield reduction. Malformation may effect grain quality and care should be taken that malting barley in particular is at the 5 leaf stage before spraying. Spraying wheat and barley at the 3 to 5 leaf stages may be desirable providing the maximum dose is no more than 12 oz per acre and the risk of occurrence of ear malformation is acceptable. The advantages of early spraying are that annual weeds are more readily controlled and crop yields are generally better than following spraying at the 5 to 6 leaf stage; in addition a lower dose of herbicide is used and this means a saving in cost. Ear malformation may be absent or slight, but very occasionally fairly severe malformation with a weakening of the rachis of the ear may occur. The conditions leading to this are not fully known, but it is concerned with such matters as the stage of development of the ear primordia (which in different crops may be at variable stages of development between the 3 and 5 leaf stages) and differences in translocation. Early spraying may not be desirable when weather conditions are poor or where few weeds have emerged.

When MCPA or 2,4-D are applied in a dust carrier, twice the quantities recommended as a spray should be used.

MCPA-salt on Oats

11. MCPA-salt may be sprayed on spring oats at any time between the 1 leaf stage and the start of 'shooting' or 'jointing', and the time of spraying may thus be chosen according to the stage of growth of the weed population. The spraying of spring oats with products formulated with a surface-active agent (see Glossary) should be restricted to the time between the 5 leaf stage and the start of 'shooting' or 'jointing'. Oat varieties Ayr Line, Ayr Commando and Yielder are more susceptible than other varieties to MCPA, and amine formulations are more toxic to them than metal salts. If it is necessary to spray these varieties they should be treated as soon as possible after the first-leaf stage and before the 4 leaf stage in the case of Yielder and the 3 leaf stage in the case of Ayr Commando and Ayr Line. Flamande Desprez also appears to be susceptible to MCPA. After being treated with MCPA, all varieties of oat may show some malformity of the panicle, which is not readily observed, but except with the varieties already mentioned the amount of malformity is usually small and it does not result in yield reduction. Winter oats may be sprayed at any time in the spring until the start of 'shooting' or 'jointing'. Spraying should not be carried out when frost is expected.

When MCPA is applied in a dust carrier, twice the quantities recommended as a spray should be used.

2,4-D-amine and -ester on Barley, Wheat and Rye

12. 2,4-D-amine and -ester may be sprayed on spring-sown wheat, barley and rye for the control of annual weeds when the cereal is between the 5 leaf stage and the start of 'shooting' or 'jointing'. Winter-sown wheat, barley and rye may be sprayed in the spring when fully tillered until the start of 'shooting' or 'jointing'.

MCPB-salt and Mixtures of MCPB-salt and MCPA-salt

13. MCPB-salt may be sprayed on spring wheat, barley and oats at any time from the 1 leaf stage to the start of 'shooting' or 'jointing'; winter-sown wheat, barley and oats may be sprayed at any time in the spring, up to the start of 'shooting' or 'jointing': MCPB is much less likely to cause malformities in any cereal than are MCPA and 2,4-D. The long period during which MCPB may be applied safely to cereals allows the stage of development of the weed population to govern the time of application. To improve the control of certain weeds, notably *Sinapis arvensis* (charlock) and *Raphanus raphanistrum* (runch) there are available products of MCPB in which small amounts of MCPA have been included. Mixing of MCPB and MCPA products is possible but the amount of MCPA (acid equivalent) should not exceed one part in six of MCPB (acid equivalent). The manufacturer of the products should be consulted before mixing to ensure that they are compatible. Such additions of MCPA do not materially affect the safety of the herbicides to cereals.

2,4-DB-SALT AND MIXTURE OF 2,4-DB-SALT AND MCPA-SALT OR 2,4-D-AMINE

14. 2,4-DB-salt may be applied on spring oats and barley from the 1 leaf stage until the start of 'shooting' or 'jointing' but application on spring wheat should be made only between the 5 leaf stage and the start of 'shooting' or 'jointing'. Winter wheat, barley and oats should be sprayed when fully tillered until the start of 'shooting' or 'jointing'. If sprayed earlier than recommended, 2,4-DB-salt is likely to cause some ear malformities, although these are likely to be less than those given by MCPA under similar circumstances. To improve the control of certain weeds, notably *Sinapis arvensis* (charlock) and *Raphanus raphanistrum* (runch) there are available products of 2,4-DB in which small amounts of MCPA have been included. Mixing of 2,4-DB and MCPA products is possible but the amount of MCPA (acid equivalent) should not exceed one part in six of 2,4-DB (acid equivalent). The manufacturers of the products should be consulted before mixing to ensure that they are compatible. Such additions of MCPA do not materially affect the safety of herbicides to cereals. Small amounts of 2,4-D may be added in a similar way but such mixtures or products containing 2,4-DB and small amounts of 2,4-D should be applied to winter wheat and barley when fully tillered until the start of 'shooting' or 'jointing' and to spring wheat and barley from the 5 leaf stage until the start of 'shooting' or 'jointing'.

MECOPROP

15. Mecoprop-salt may be applied to spring barley and oats and to the varieties Jufy I and Koga II spring wheat from the 1 leaf stage until the start of 'shooting' or 'jointing'. Spring wheat varieties other than Koga II and Jufy I must not be sprayed with mecoprop until at least the 4 leaf stage has been reached. Mecoprop-salt may be sprayed on winter-sown wheat, barley and oats when the plants are fully tillered, but before 'shooting' or 'jointing'.

16. Mecoprop may be applied at 32 oz per acre to winter wheat, barley and oats before the end of the year for the control of *Stellaria media* (chickweed). Where the crop is late and the chickweed is still germinating, spraying may be delayed to the end of January at the latest. After this time, winter cereals become more susceptible to damage from mecoprop until once again a safe (the fully tillered) stage is reached (see paragraph 15). Mecoprop used in this way for the control of chickweed is not influenced by cold weather.

DICHLORPROP-SALT

17. Dichlorprop-salt may be applied to spring barley and oats from the 1 leaf stage, until the start of 'shooting' or 'jointing' and to spring wheat from the 5-leaf stage until the start of 'shooting' or 'jointing'. Dichlorprop-salt may be sprayed on winter wheat, oats and barley in the spring when the plants are fully tillered, but before 'shooting' or 'jointing'.

MCPA PLUS 2,3,6-TBA

18. Mixtures containing 12 oz MCPA and 4 oz 2,3,6-TBA per acre may be applied to spring wheat, barley and oats from the 5 leaf stage until the start of 'shooting' or 'jointing', and on winter wheat, barley, oats and rye when fully tillered until the start of 'shooting' or 'jointing'. Where grain quality is not important, earlier spraying of winter wheat, spring wheat and spring barley is possible, as described for MCPA in paragraphs 9 and 10. The mixture does not appear to be adversely influenced by cold weather.

MCPA PLUS 2,6-DICHLORO-3-METHOXYBENZOIC ACID

19. Mixtures containing 18 oz MCPA and 1·3 oz 3,6-dichloro-2-methoxybenzoic acid per acre may be applied to spring wheat, barley and oats from the 5 leaf stage until the start of 'shooting' or 'jointing' and on winter wheat, barley, oats and rye, when fully tillered until the start of 'shooting' or 'jointing'.

DNOC AND DINOSEB (SPRING APPLICATION)

20. DNOC and dinoseb-ammonium or-amine may be sprayed on cereals in the spring between the 3 leaf stage and the start of 'shooting' or 'jointing' and treatment during the earlier part of this period is frequently preferable in order to obtain a greater degree of weed control. If treatment is delayed until the weeds are more advanced in growth it may be necessary to increase the dose of DNOC up to 25 per cent above the recommended maximum in order to obtain good weed control, even though this increases the risk of scorching the cereal. During very cold weather in spring it may also be ncessary to increase the dose of DNOC by 25 per cent. These increased doses should not be applied to oats. Dinoseb-ammonium and -amine are less selective than DNOC for the control of weeds in cereals, and may cause appreciable scorch at doses approaching 2 lb per acre, but the crop recovers and the yield is not decreased. The maximum safe amount of dinoseb varies according to weather conditions, as indicated in Table 4. Under normal conditions oats should not be harrowed or rolled during the ten days before or seven days after spraying DNOC or dinoseb; nor should cereal crops be sprayed when wet or when frost is imminent. The winter oat varieties S147 and S172 are more susceptible to damage from DNOC than are other oat varieties. Normally four hours freedom from rain following spraying is sufficient for DNOC to give satisfactory weed control.

DNOC AND DINOSEB (WINTER APPLICATION)

21. [Tentative] DNOC and dinoseb-ammonium and -amine may be applied to winter wheat during the winter at doses up to three-quarters of the maxima given in Table 4, providing the soil is dry enough to allow the spraying equipment on the field without mechanical damage to the crop and that continuous frost is not likely to be experienced immediately afterwards. Severe frost, although aiding weed control, may lead to the treatment causing serious damage to the wheat. The period of freedom from rain following spraying needs to be considerably longer than that following normal spring applications of DNOC to achieve satisfactory weed control.

SULPHURIC ACID

22. Sulphuric acid may be applied to all spring cereals from the 5 leaf stage until the start of 'shooting' or 'jointing'. Treatment with sulphuric acid causes considerable scorch to the crop which is transient. Crop damage is generally least where high volume rates are used.

The doses given in Table 4 are for 100 per cent pure acid and conversion is required for the acid content of the product used; for example the doses should be multiplied by 1·3 for B.O.V. containing 77 per cent v/v sulphuric acid.

BARBAN FOR THE CONTROL OF *Avena fatua* AND *Avena ludoviciana* (WILD OATS)

23. Barban at 5 oz per acre in 10 to 20 gallons of water may be applied at any stage of growth to winter wheat (with the exception given below), spring wheat and the following barley varieties: Bonus, Carlsberg II, Craigs Triumph, Delta, Earl, Elsa, Gateway, Gazelle, Hafnia, Hasia II, Hillmarsh, Ingrid, Kenia, Maythorpe, Pallas, Pioneer, Rika, Spratt-Archer, Swallow, Topper, Union, Vada, Volla, Wisa and Ymer. Winter wheat, particularly Hybrid 46 and Professeur Marchal, sometimes suffers a temporary check following barban treatment in March, but it recovers when growth commences in spring. Winter wheat should not be sprayed between mid-January and the end of February. The herbicides should be applied when the majority of wild oats (*Avena fatua* or *Avena ludoviciana*) have between 1 and 2·5 leaves, independent of the stage of growth of the crop. The satisfactory control of wild oats depends upon competition from the crop smothering out weakened but surviving wild oat plants. For this reason barban should not be used in a poor crop. Barban cannot be used on oat crops.

Spraying MCPB simultaneously with barban is satisfactory but other herbicides may be applied only after an interval of 3 days after using barban.

See pages 173–176 for further details.

BARBAN FOR THE CONTROL OF *Alopecurus myosuroides* (BLACKGRASS)

24. Barban at 5 oz per acre may be applied in 10 to 20 gallons of water to winter wheat in November or December for the control of blackgrass. The blackgrass should have at least 2 leaves on the majority of plants.

DREDGE CORN: CEREAL MIXTURES

25. Dredge corn which contains cereals only may be treated in the same way as a normal cereal crop, provided that the permissible maximum dose and safe stage of growth are observed for the most susceptible cereal present.

B. CEREAL LEGUME MIXTURES

MCPB-SALT ON MIXTURES OF CEREALS AND PEAS

26. MCPB-salt at doses up to 32 oz may be applied to mixtures of cereals and peas when the peas have developed between three and six leaves: MCPB-salt should not be used on dredge corn containing beans or vetches. The dose is dictated by the presence of the peas and is less than the maximum dose permissible on some cereals. As cereals may be sprayed with MCPB-salt at any time after the 1 leaf stage until the start of 'shooting' or 'jointing', the peas also determine the time of spraying.

MCPA-SALT AS DUST ON MIXTURE OF CEREALS AND PEAS

27. [Tentative] MCPA-salt may be applied as a dust at up to 24 oz per acre to mixtures containing peas provided the peas are about 8 ins. high.

DINOSEB ON MIXTURES OF CEREALS AND PEAS

28. Dinoseb-amine and ammonium may be applied to mixtures of cereals and peas provided that the dose is not higher than is recommended for the most susceptible cereal in the mixture (see Table 4) or for peas (see paragraphs 7 and 72). Conditions specified for the use of dinoseb on cereals and on peas should be complied with.

DINOSEB ON MIXTURES OF CEREALS AND BEANS OR VETCHES

29. [Tentative] Dinoseb-amine at doses up to a maximum of 1·5 lb per acre may be applied at high volume rates to mixtures of cereals and beans or vetches (see Table 4 for the maximum safe dose and stages of growth at which dinoseb-amine may be used on cereals) provided the legume has not grown too rapidly and is protected to some extent from the spray by the cereals and the weeds.

C. CEREALS UNDERSOWN WITH GRASS
AND CLOVER OR LUCERNE

30. The presence of grass, grass and clover or lucerne seedlings beneath a cereal crop restricts the herbicides that may be used to those that are suitable for both the cereal and the undersown crop. Paragraphs 1 to 25 describe the use of herbicides on cereal crops, and paragraphs 90 to 99 the use of herbicides on seedling clover, grasses and lucerne. The recommendations in paragraphs 31 to 35 below, summarize the use of herbicides in undersown cereals. Stages of growth of legume seedlings are described in paragraph 88 (page 63). Most frequently the stage of growth and type of legume will decide the choice of herbicide and the time of spraying. Where the legumes are sown very early, however, e.g., at or soon after the sowing of a cereal, or alternatively where sowing of the legumes has had to be delayed to a very late stage, then susceptibility of the cereal growth stage must be considered. In the latter case the effect of physical damage by tractor wheel marks in the crop must also be borne in mind.

MCPB-salt and Mixtures of MCPB-salt and MCPA-salt on Cereals Undersown with Clover (and Grass)

31. MCPB-salt may be used at up to 32 oz per acre on cereals undersown with grass and clover mixtures containing red or white clover, provided most of the clovers have reached the first trifoliate leaf stage. Where the mixture contains both red and white clovers care should be taken to verify that both species have reached the resistant stage. The cereal must have reached the stage of growth specified in paragraph 13 before spraying. To improve the control of certain weeds notably *Sinapis arvensis* (charlock) and *Raphanus raphanistrum* (runch) there are available commercial products of MCPB in which small amounts of MCPA have been included. Mixing of MCPB and MCPA products is possible but the amount of MCPA acid equivalent should not exceed one part in six of MCPB acid equivalent. The manufacturer of the products should be consulted before mixing to ensure that they are compatible. Such additions of MCPA do not affect the safety of the herbicide to the cereal or undersown grass and clover.

2,4-DB-salt and Mixtures of 2,4-DB-salt and MCPA-salt or 2,4-D-amine on Cereals Undersown with Clover (and Grass)

32. 2,4-DB-salt may be used at up to 32 oz per acre on cereals undersown with mixtures containing red or white clover, provided most of the clovers have reached the first trifoliate leaf stage. On red clover 2,4-DB is slightly more toxic than MCPB and may cause leaf deformities, but these do not persist for more than six to eight weeks. Where the mixture contains both red and white clover care should be taken to verify that both species have reached the resistant stage. The cereal must have reached the stage of growth specified in paragraph 14 before spraying. To improve the control of certain weeds, notably *Sinapis arvensis* (charlock) and *Raphanus raphanistrum* (runch), there are available commercial products of 2,4-DB in which small amounts of MCPA or 2,4-D have been included. Mixing of 2,4-DB with MCPA or 2,4-D products is possible but the amount of MCPA or 2,4-D acid equivalent should not exceed one part in six of 2,4-DB acid equivalent. The manufacturer of the products should be consulted before mixing to ensure that they are compatible. Such additions of MCPA or 2,4-D do not affect the safety of the herbicide to the undersown grass and clover but paragraph 14 should be consulted concerning the type and stage of growth of cereal such mixtures may be used on.

2,4-DB-SALT ON CEREALS UNDERSOWN WITH LUCERNE (AND GRASS)

33. 2,4-DB-salt may be used at up to 32 oz per acre on cereals undersown with lucerne or lucerne/grass mixtures, provided most of the lucerne seedlings have reached the first trifoliate leaf stage. The least check to the lucerne is given by treatment between the first and fourth trifoliate leaf stages (see paragraph 63). The cereal must have reached the stage of growth specified in paragraph 14 before spraying.

DNOC AND DINOSEB

34. DNOC and dinoseb-ammonium or -amine are safe, as used for cereals, if the undersown seeds are drilled (not broadcast), and spraying takes place at least seven days before the grass and clover seeds are drilled, or during the three days following drilling.

35. Dinoseb-ammonium or -amine may be applied to cereals at the stage of growth specified in paragraph 20 and after the clovers have developed two trifoliate leaves (see paragraph 88). Cereals undersown with lucerne may be treated in a similar manner.

SULPHURIC ACID

36. Sulphuric acid can be used for cereals, either before the seeds are drilled or after drilling and before germination (see paragraph 22).

MCPA-SALT AND 2,4-D-AMINE and -ESTER

37. MCPA and 2,4-D are not recommended for routine use because seedling clovers are very susceptible to these herbicides. In an emergency, the application of low doses of liquid or dust preparations (e.g. 12 oz MCPA-salt or

2,4-D-amine, 6 oz of 2,4-D-ester or 24 oz MCPA-salt in dust form) may be made to control susceptible weeds (see Table 5) which have made sufficient growth to shield the legume seedlings partially. Safety to the seedling clovers is greatly dependent upon the shielding effect of the cereal cover crop and the weeds, but age of the seedling clover is also a factor and both red and white clover should have developed at least two trifoliate leaves before the spray is applied. On red clover, but not on white clover, MCPA is safer than 2,4-D. Insufficient evidence is available to indicate whether high- or low-volume application is safest. On cereals undersown with lucerne MCPA and 2,4-D must not be used.

BARBAN FOR THE CONTROL OF WILD OATS (*Avena Fatua* AND *A. Ludoviciana*) OR BLACKGRASS (*Alopecurus Myosuroides*)
38. Where barban has been applied to cereals (see paragraphs 23 and 24), grasses and clover may be sown after an interval of three days from spraying.

SECTION (ii) ARABLE CROPS OTHER THAN CEREALS

BEAN (FIELD)

39. Dinoseb-amine may be applied to winter-sown crops of field beans at doses up to 1·5 lb per acre at high volume. The beans should be sprayed only when they are about three inches high and while growth is still 'hard', i.e. before rapid growth starts.

40. Simazine at 0·75 to 1 lb per acre may be applied in medium or high volume, within 10 days after drilling, for the control of annual weeds. No cultivations should be carried out between spraying and the emergence of the crop. The lower dose should be used in medium or light soils. It is important that the seed-bed should be good and that the beans are drilled to an even depth, as deeply as is consistent with good agricultural practice. If the beans are sown shallowly or if heavy rain follows spraying, marginal blackening of the leaf may occur. This effect should be mild and should not affect the yield of beans.

41. Chlorpropham at 1 lb per acre plus fenuron at 0·25 lb per acre may be applied at high or medium volume, within a few days after sowing spring-sown beans, for the control of annual weeds. It is important that the seed-bed should be good and the beans drilled to an even depth, as deeply as is consistent with good agricultural practice. If the beans are sown shallowly or heavy rain follows spraying, some marginal blackening or distortion of the leaf may occur. This effect should be mild and should not affect yield.

42. Chlorpropham at 1 lb per acre plus diuron at 0·25 lb per acre may be applied at high or medium volume, within a few days after sowing spring beans, for the control of annual weeds. It is important that the seed-bed should be good and the beans drilled as deeply as is consistent with good agricultural practice. If the beans are sown shallowly or heavy rain follows spraying, some marginal blackening or distortion of the leaf may occur. This effect should be mild and should not affect yield.

43. Barban at 10 oz per acre may be applied to control *Avena* spp. (wild oats). The wild oats must be at the 1 to 2·5 leaf stage at the time of spraying. The crop may be scorched but will later recover. The control of wild oats will not be complete, because crop competition at the time of spraying will not be very vigorous. Control will be improved if the beans are drilled in narrow rows to give better competition. [**For Information**] A pre-emergence application of simazine does not appear to make beans any more sensitive to barban.

44. [**For Information**] Di-allate at 1·5 lb per acre may be applied to the soil at medium or high volume rates not sooner than two days before drilling spring-sown beans, for the control of *Avena fatua* (wild oats). As soon as possible after spraying the chemical should be incorporated into the soil by means of straight-toothed harrows on which the lateral distance of the tines is not greater than four inches. In order to incorporate the chemical as evenly as possible the depth of penetration of the tines should be as near four inches as practicable. Two passes of the harrow at right angles to each other are normally necessary to get adequate incorporation. On very fine, soft tilths only one pass of the harrow should be carried out and care should be taken that penetration is not greater than four inches. The treatment is likely to be unsatisfactory on cloddy seedbeds. Drilling should take place at right angles to the direction of the first harrowing. After application drilling should not be delayed longer than three weeks in order to obtain satisfactory wild oat control. Field experience indicates that simazine may be satisfactorily used on beans treated with di-allate. Di-allate used for the control of wild oats in beans has given a good control of *Alopecurus myosuroides* (blackgrass).

45. [**Tentative**] Dinoseb-amine may be used on spring-sown beans in the manner recommended for winter beans in paragraph 39, but there is more risk of scorching the crop, especially when early growth has been rapid.

BEET (FODDER AND SUGAR)

46. Pentachlorophenol in an emulsifiable oil formulation (in which the oil is not persistent) may be applied as a pre-emergence treatment at doses up to 3 lb per acre in medium or high volume. Where natural seed has been used spraying may be delayed until the first plants are just emerging but with other seed the crop should not be sprayed later than 3 days before the estimated emergence of the beet and application must not be made once any of the beet have come through. It has been suggested that, as a rough guide, beet may be expected to emerge three days after the seedling has developed a root half an inch long. This herbicide acts primarily as a contact killer and the treatment is of little value when few or no weeds have appeared.

47. **[Tentative]** Propham plus endothal may be applied as a medium volume pre-emergence spray on sugar beet and fodder beet. The dose has to be adjusted according to the soil type, as indicated below.

Very light sand 1·5 lb endothal plus 1·125 lb propham per acre
Sand   2·0 ,,   ,,   ,, 1·5 ,,   ,,   ,,   ,,
Light loam   3·0 ,,   ,,   ,, 2·25 ,,   ,,   ,,   ,,
Medium loam   4·0 ,,   ,,   ,, 3·0 ,,   ,,   ,,   ,,

The mixture is not recommended for use on heavy soils and soils high in organic matter. Best results are obtained with applications made before the middle of April. With later applications it is important that rain falls within a week of spraying. As the mixture of herbicides is expensive treatment may be confined to a band along the row, reliance being placed on cultivations for controlling weeds between the rows. The mixture will, under favourable conditions, give a satisfactory control of the following weeds: *Anagallis arvensis, Capsella bursa-postoris, Chrysanthemum segetum, Echium vulgare, Galeopsis tetrahit, Geranium* spp., *Lamium amplexicaule, Papaver rhoeas, Poa annua, Polygonum aviculare, Polygonum convolvulus, Polygonum lapathifolium, Polygonum persicaria, Ranunculus arvensis, Senecio vulgaris, Solanum nigrum, Stellaria media, Urtica urens.* Weeds which are less readily controlled include *Fumaria officinalis, Galium aparine, Silene alba, Sonchus oleraceous,* and *Veronica* spp. The response of *Chenopodium album* is variable and this weed generally exhibits some resistance.

48. **[Tentative]** Sodium or ammonium trichloroacetate (TCA) may be applied at 7 lb acid equivalent per acre for the control of *Avena fatua* (wild oats). Spraying may be at medium or high volume, preferably on to a level seed-bed rather than on the plough furrow, about two weeks before drilling. The duration of the interval between spraying and drilling is not critical, the primary purpose being to allow time for rain to carry the herbicide into the soil. It should also be worked in before drilling as thoroughly and as deeply as possible without risking any damage to the tilth. As an alternative to spraying, this herbicide may be applied as a mixture with fertilizer. The preparation of such a mixture is a specialized operation and should not be attempted on the farm. Treatment with TCA should not be expected to eliminate wild oat completely but on average it will reduce the population by about three-quarters.

It will only kill those seeds of *Avena* spp. which germinate and dormant seeds are not affected. The treatment therefore should not be expected to reduce substantially the infestation in a subsequent year.

49. [Tentative] Propham may be applied to the soil before sowing beet for the control of *Avena fatua* (wild oats). A dose of 3 lb per acre may be used on heavy loam soils but this can damage the crop on sandy soils where the dose should be reduced to 2 lb per acre. Conversely on some heavy clay soils a dose of 4·5 lb. per acre may be necessary to achieve satisfactory weed control. Spraying may be at low or high volume rate 1 to 5 days before drilling the crop. Propham is volatile and must be worked into the soil soon after spraying but it appears to spread more rapidly in the soil than sodium or ammonium trichloracetate (TCA) and requires less cultivations for mixing-in; in practice the normal seedbed preparations have been adequate. The control of wild oats is generally less reliable than with TCA. The crop may be stunted in the early stages and although this is normally quickly outgrown it can be serious on light land. As with TCA, only germinating wild oats are affected but propham has the advantage of killing also a number of broad-leaved weeds in particular, *Polygonum aviculare* (knotgrass) and *Stellaria media* (chickweed).

50. [For Information] Di-allate at 1 to 1·5 lb per acre may be applied to the soil at medium or high volume rates not sooner than two days before drilling sugar beet for the control of *Avena fatua* (wild oats). The higher dose should be used where the maximum control of wild oats is required. The lower dose will give an inferior control but may be judged sufficient where manual singling is to be carried out. As soon as possible after spraying the chemical should be incorporated into the soil by means of straight-toothed harrows on which the lateral distance of the tines is not greater than four inches. In order to incorporate the chemical as evenly as possible the depth of penetration of the tines should be as near four inches as practicable. Two passes of the harrow at right angles to each other are normally necessary to get adequate incorporation. On very fine tilths only one pass of the harrow should be carried out and care should be taken that penetration should not be greater than four inches. The treatment is likely to be unsatisfactory on cloddy seed-beds and, after spraying, too much working of the soil may lead to poor wild oat control. Drilling should take place at right angles to the direction of the first harrowing. After application drilling should not be delayed longer than three weeks in order to obtain satisfactory wild oat control. Di-allate used for the control of wild oats in sugar beet has given a good control of *Alopecurus myosuroides* (blackgrass).

51. [For Information] Sodium nitrate may be applied at the rate of 2·5 cwt in 100 gallons of water per acre when the beet have at least two true leaves expanded. The addition of a wetting agent to the spray solution is essential. Proprietary wetting agents vary considerably in their suitability for this pur-

5

pose and many are wholly unsuitable in that they cause cloudiness and precipitation in the spray solution. The effectiveness of the wetting agent in increasing the weed-killing power of the spray also varies and suitability in this respect can only be determined as a result of experience. Manufacturers should be approached for assistance in selecting an efficient proprietary wetting agent and for advice as to the exact amount needed. The rate usually required is 0·5 to 1 gallon per 100 gallons of spray solution but this varies according to the product used. The most rapid results from this treatment are obtained under warm humid conditions and it is important that there should be 12 to 24 hours of fine weather after spraying. The larger the weeds the more difficult they are to kill, and some, notably grasses and species of *Chenopodiaceae* are unharmed by the spray, although *Chenopodium album* (fat hen) may be killed in the very early stages of growth. The beet may show temporary wilting, scorching or yellowing after spraying, but these symptoms soon disappear and the crop derives manurial benefit from the sodium nitrate.

This treatment is not reliable, especially in the drier eastern counties but may be useful as an emergency measure. It does not eliminate the need for mechanical or manual cleaning operations but may facilitate them. For the response of weeds to sodium nitrate spray see Table 10.

52. [**For Information**] Formulations of cresylic acid marketed specifically for weed control, have been successfully used in recent years as contact pre-emergence herbicides for beet. These formulations contain mixtures of chemical compounds and it is not possible to relate doses to any particular active ingredient (see also paragraphs 151–158).

CARROT

See paragraphs 185 to 189 on pages 93 and 94.

FLAX

53. MCPA-salt may be applied at doses up to 12 oz per acre in a high volume of spray or 24 oz per acre as a dust. Application should be made when the flax is between 2 and 6 inches high.

54. DNOC-sodium may be applied at up to 6 lb per acre in about 100 gallons of water when the flax is between 2 and 6 inches high.

KALE

55. Sulphuric acid may be applied to marrow-stem and thousand-head kale by a high-volume spraying machine at up to 100 gallons per acre of an 8 per cent v/v solution. The crop should be sprayed when it has between two and six leaves. Application during the early part of this period may cause some reduction in plant density of the crop but customary seed rates are so liberal that this is not usually important. Some crop scorch generally occurs and this is offset by the better weed control obtained by early spraying. The crop must be in a vigorous growing condition when sprayed so as to benefit from the control of weeds, and application of a nitrogenous fertilizer aids recovery. After the 4 leaf stage the concentration of sulphuric acid may be increased to 10 per cent v/v and up to the same quantity of concentrated sulphuric acid (e.g. 13 gallons of B.O.V.) may be applied at low volume if an acid-resistant machine is available. Crop scorch may be less from the later application but control of the more fully-grown weeds is much poorer and as the crop has already suffered considerably from their competition the net beneficial effect is generally less. Where the kale is sown in rows, inter-row cultivations will remove any weeds surviving between the rows. This is not possible with broadcast crops and early spraying to ensure good weed control is particularly necessary in such situations.

Table 10 shows the susceptibility of some common annual weeds to sulphuric acid.*

56. Sodium monochloroacetate at 20 lb in not less than 20 gallons of water per acre may be applied to marrow-stem kale between the 1 leaf and the 5 leaf stages. The dose should be increased to 25 lb in not less than 25 gallons of water per acre where the weed growth is 'hard'. Damage to the crop increases markedly after the 5 leaf stage. Yield increases have been greatest when the chemical has been applied in 100 gallons per acre even though weed control has been better at lower volume rates. Thousand-head kale should be sprayed between the 2 and 5 leaf stages. Table 10 shows the susceptibility of a number of common weeds to sodium monochloroacetate.*

57. Contact pre-emergence weedkillers such as pentachlorphenol at 3 to 4 lb per acre, diquat at 0·375 to 0·75 lb per acre formulated with a wetter, paraquat at 0·5 to 1·0 lb per acre formulated with a wetter, sulphuric acid 10 per cent solution at 100 gallons per acre, and cresylic acid preparations (see paragraphs 151–158 for fuller details of these treatments) may be used on kale provided a delayed seed-bed technique (see page 8) is employed to encourage the weeds to germinate before the crop. The seed-bed should be prepared 7 to 10 days in advance of drilling which should be carried out with minimum disturbance of the seed-bed. Spraying may be carried out within 2 days before or after sowing to kill emerged weeds. When spraying is delayed until after sowing it should be remembered that the weather could prevent spraying; leading as a consequence to an acute weed problem. Spraying before sowing may be preferable provided the weeds have germinated well by this time.

* Readers are reminded that all references are to chemicals without 'wetters' and 'spreaders' and these should not be added to sprays unless specifically recommended.

Under dry conditions weeds may not, in any case, germinate satisfactorily and the grower must judge the feasibility of this treatment in the light of his own experience. The treatment is useful more particularly where the crop is sown in narrow drills and where crop competition prevents later weeds becoming established. It is not suitable for broadcast crops.

58. [Tentative] The methyl mercapto triazine G.34360 (desmetryne) (see page 273) may be applied at 4 to 6 oz per acre, in medium volume, for the control of *Chenopodium album* and certain other weeds. The lower dose should be applied when the kale is growing vigorously. The kale should not be sprayed before it has at least 2 fully expanded true leaves. Later applications will not reduce the yield of kale but control of *Chenopodium album* is unreliable if flower buds are forming.

59. [Tentative] Sodium or potassium cyanate may be applied at a dose of 10 lb per acre between the 1 and 5 leaf stages. This treatment is of limited value.

60. [For Information] Gas liquor, available from some Regional Gas Boards, is used as a post emergence treatment in kale which is at the 2 to 5 leaf stages for the control of annual weeds. As the weed-killing principle in gas liquor is unknown and may vary from batch to batch no specific recommendation for its use can be made.

LINSEED

61. M CPA-salt can be used at doses up to 32 oz per acre as liquid sprays or 48 oz per acre as dusts. Sprays must be applied in high volume and the crops must be not less than 1 to 2 inches and not more than 8 to 10 inches high. This recommendation applies to the varieties Royal, Redwing, Valuta and Dakota. Other varieties may be more susceptible.

62. D N O C-sodium can be applied at 6 lb per acre in about 100 gallons of water when the crop is not less than 1 to 2 and not more than 8 to 10 inches high.

LUCERNE

63. Dinoseb-ammonium at doses up to 1·5 lb per acre or dinoseb-amine at doses up to 2 lb per acre may be applied in high volume to seedling lucerne. Where good growing conditions have prevailed during the days preceding spraying and temperature is high on the day of spraying, it may be necessary to reduce the dose (e.g. by 0·5 lb per acre at over 70°F). The seedlings should have developed two trifoliate leaves before spraying (see paragraph 88). Spraying of lucerne-grass mixtures in this way may alter the balance between the two components of the mixture.

64. 2,4-D B-salt may be applied at doses up to 48 oz per acre to seedling lucerne, provided that most of the seedlings have reached the first trifoliate leaf stage (see paragraph 88). The optimum time of treatment is between the first and fourth trifoliate leaf stages, as this is the period of maximum sensitivity to weed competition. Treatment after development of the fourth trifoliate leaf may produce deformity in subsequent lateral and tiller growth. Although this deformity will disappear within 6 to 8 weeks of spraying, it will affect the ability of the lucerne to compete with semi-resistant weeds, particularly if the crop is late summer-sown. The herbicide should not be applied to lucerne direct-sown in late summer where *Stellaria media* (chickweed) is abundant.

65. [Tentative] Chlorpropham may be applied at 2 lb per acre at high volume to seedling lucerne which has reached the fourth trifoliate leaf stage. This treatment is primarily of value for the control of *Stellaria media* (chickweed). Chlorpropham is slow in action on established plants and the full effect may not be evident for several weeks. Grasses sown with the lucerne are likely to be damaged by this treatment.

66. [Tentative] Dalapon-sodium may be applied to established lucerne for the control of grasses at doses up to 5 lb per acre at medium or high volume. The crop should be sprayed when dormant either in the spring after the grasses have begun to grow but before the growth of the lucerne has started, or in the autumn in the period between the cessation of growth of the lucerne and of the grasses. In general better control of grasses results from spring application. Such treatment should result in comparative freedom from competition from grasses during the ensuing season, but the killing of the grasses may result in much ground being bare when the lucerne becomes dormant in the following autumn. This bare ground may then become recolonized by grasses or broad-leaved weeds.

MAIZE (Fodder and grain)

67. Atrazine can be applied as a residual pre-emergence spray for the control of annual weeds. The dose should be 1 lb per acre on light soils and 1·5 lb per acre on heavy soils. Weed control may be unsatisfactory on soils high in organic matter. Where the crop fails for some reason (e.g. bird damage) it will not be possible to plant another crop until the atrazine has disappeared from the soil. Under normal conditions it should be possible to sow or plant a crop in the autumn. Atrazine controls the same range of weeds as simazine (see Table 11).

68. Simazine can be applied as a residual pre-sowing or pre-emergence spray for the control of annual weeds (see Table 11). The dose should be 1 lb per acre on light soils and 1·5 to 2 lb per acre on heavy soils or soils high in organic matter. Weed control is least satisfactory under dry conditions where atrazine is to be preferred. The reliability of simazine can be improved, where the soil tilth is satisfactory, by harrowing-in with light chain harrows. Weed control may be unsatisfactory on soils high in organic matter. Where the crop fails for some reason (e.g. from bird damage) it will not be possible to plant another crop until the simazine has disappeared from the soil. Under normal conditions it should be possible to sow or plant a crop in autumn.

69. [Tentative] 2,4-D-amine may be used at up to 16 oz per acre at the time the crop is 3 to 6 inches high. As this treatment might check the crop to some extent it is recommended only where the weed situation demands it.

70. [Tentative] 2,4-D-ester at 24 to 32 oz per acre may be applied at the time of crop and weed emergence to control weeds susceptible to 2,4-D. The treatment will kill weeds present at the time of spraying and persist for some time to kill further weeds as they germinate. At the 'spearing' stage (first shoot) maize, although it exhibits considerable resistance to 2,4-D, is not completely tolerant. The treatment should not be applied where the weed infestation does or is likely to include weed species that are resistant or even moderately resistant to 2,4-D-ester.

71. [For Information] Atrazine has been satisfactorily applied as a combined contact and soil-acting herbicide for the control of annual weeds which are not bigger than 1 inch in height. The stage of growth of maize appears to be immaterial.

PEA (Field, drying and vining)

72. Dinoseb-ammonium may be used on peas for drying, at doses up to 2 lb per acre applied at high volume when the temperature is not below 55°F and the maximum of the day will not rise above 80°F. Above and below these limits spraying should not be carried out. Where good growing conditions have prevailed before spraying and pea growth is 'soft' it is necessary, particularly at higher temperatures, to reduce the maximum dose to avoid undue scorch to the crop. At over 70°F, in these conditions, 1 lb per acre should be regarded as the maximum. Peas should be sprayed after three leaves have expanded (generally when about 3 inches high) but before the plants reach a height of 10 inches. The crop should not be sprayed when wet. When the crop has been damaged by high winds or blowing soil, spraying should not take place until a week after the occurrence of damage. If the field has been treated with sodium or ammonium trichloroacetate (TCA) as a pre-sowing application not more than half the normal dose of dinoseb-ammonium should be applied, as excessive damage may occur at higher doses; however, there should also be an increase in susceptibility of the weeds and a satisfactory control should be achieved. On vining or picking peas, dinoseb-amine is preferable to dinoseb-ammonium as it causes less scorch and should therefore generally be chosen (see paragraph 72).

73. Dinoseb-amine may be used on drying peas and certain varieties of picking and vining pea at doses up to 2·5 lb per acre at 40 gallons per acre and above, when the temperature is between 45 and 85°F. If good growing conditions precede spraying and the temperature at the time of application is higher than 65°F, doses between 1·5 and 2 lb. per acre should be used. If spraying follows a period of dry cool weather, and the weed growth is 'hard', a dose of more than 2 lb per acre may be required. The crop may be sprayed at any time after the first leaf has expanded but before it attains a height of 10 inches. Spraying should not be attempted when the crop foliage is wet or when rain is expected within twelve hours. The warnings given in paragraph 71 regarding crops damaged by wind or treated with TCA also apply. The amine salt of dinoseb is somewhat less effective than the ammonium salt in killing weeds, but as the risk of damage to the crop is considerably reduced, the selectivity is greater. Thus the crop may be sprayed earlier when the weeds are younger and more susceptible, and in practice the weed control obtained with dinoseb-amine is as effective as with dinoseb-ammonium. Experience has shown that whilst most varieties of pea grown for picking green or vining can be sprayed with dinoseb-amine the following varieties tend to be susceptible and should not be treated. Duplex, Foremost, Early Bird, Exquisite, Gregory's Surprise, Morse's Market, Pilot, Sharpe's Vedette, Sharpe's Miracle, Kelvedon Triumph and Thomas Laxton.

74. MCPB-salt may be applied at doses up to 32 oz per acre in high, medium or low volume when the peas have from 3 to 6 expanded leaves. This treatment may be applied safely to the following varieties: Alaska, Canner's Perfection, Charles I, Clipper, Dark-skinned Perfection, Early Bird, Harrison's Glory, Lincoln, Onward, Perfected Freezer, Rondo, Servo and Zelka. With these varieties marked bending and distortion may appear within a day or two of spraying but this is outgrown within about two weeks; there is no marked depressing effect on yield nor is maturity delayed. Some doubt exists as to the safety of this treatment on the varieties Gregory's Surprise, Kelvedon Wonder, Meteor, Thomas Laxton and Shasta. The treatment is of most use in pea crops where *Chenopodium album* (fat hen) or *Cirsium arvense* (creeping thistle) is the dominant weed. For effective control of the latter species, hoeing should stop for at least ten days before spraying.

75. Sodium or ammonium trichloroacetate (TCA) may be applied to the soil, 2 to 4 weeks before sowing peas, but not before the last week in February, at 7 lb acid equivalent per acre for the control of *Avena fatua* (wild oat). Spraying may be at medium or high volume rate, preferably after the plough furrows have been levelled. The chemical should be worked into the soil, as deeply and thoroughly as is consistent with avoiding damage to tilth, during

the preparation of the weed-bed. Treatment should not be expected to eliminate wild oat completely but on average will reduce the population in the year of treatment by three-quarters. It will kill only those seeds of wild oat which germinate and will not therefore substantially reduce infestation in a subsequent year. Peas may be affected by the treatment and yields are sometimes reduced by up to 20 per cent. The nature of the waxy surface of the leaf is also altered and if dinoseb-amine or -ammonium is subsequently used, the dose of dinoseb should be reduced (see paragraphs 71 and 72). Pre-sowing treatment with TCA is consequently recommended only on heavily infested fields.

76. Propham at 3 lb per acre may be applied to the soil before sowing peas, but not before the beginning of March, for the control of *Avena fatua* (wild oat). Spraying may be at low or high volume rate, preferably after the plough furrows have been levelled. Sowing may take place four days or more after spraying. Propham is volatile and must be worked into the soil soon after spraying but it appears to spread more rapidly in the soil than sodium or ammonium trichloroacetate (TCA) and requires less cultivations for mixing in. The control of wild oats is generally less reliable than with TCA; it does not affect the growth of peas but may retard emergence. As with TCA, only germinating wild oats are affected but propham has the advantage of killing also a number of broad-leaved weeds, in particular *Polygonum aviculare* (knotgrass) and *Stellaria media* (chickweed).

77. Chlorpropham at 1 lb plus fenuron at 0·25 lb per acre or chlorpropham at 1 lb plus diuron at 0·2 to 0·4 lb per acre may be applied as a medium or high volume spray after drilling, but before any weeds have emerged and at least a week before crop emergence, for the control of annual weeds in springsown peas. It is important that the seed-bed should be left with a fine, even tilth and that the peas should be sown not less than one inch below the soil surface. This treatment should not be used on very light, sandy or silt soils deficient in clay and organic matter, as on such soils crop damage may result.

78. [Tentative] Barban at 10 oz per acre may be applied to control *Avena fatua* (wild oat). The wild oats must be at the 1 to 2·5 leaf stage at the time of spraying. The crop may be scorched but will later recover. The control of wild oats will not be complete, because crop competition at the time of spraying will not be very vigorous. Control will be better if the peas are drilled in narrow rows to give maximum competition.

79. [Tentative] Dinoseb-amine may be applied at the rate of 3 to 4 lb per acre as a medium or high volume pre-emergence spray for the control of broadleaved annual weeds in spring-sown peas. The lower dose should be used on the lighter soils and the peas should be sown not less than an inch below the soil surface. The spray can be applied at any time after sowing until about three days before the crop is expected to emerge.

POTATO

80. [Tentative] MCPA-salt at up to 16 oz per acre may be applied in high or low volume as a post-emergence spray before the haulm is fully grown on crops not to be certified for seed. Varietal differences in susceptibility to MCPA-salt exist but there is little information available. Majestic appears less susceptible than King Edward and Arran Banner. Twisting of foliage and some leaf deformity, such as crowding of the lateral veins, will follow treatment. Yield may be affected.

81. [For Information] Paraquat at 16 oz per acre, in medium volume, has been successfully applied, pre-emergence, to kill weed seedlings that have germinated before the crop has emerged.

See also the notes on the triazines, linuron and N-(3,4-dichlorophenyl)-propion-amide in Chapter XIII regarding some other herbicides being tested for use in potatoes.

SECTION (iii) GRASSLAND AND GRASS SEED CROPS

THE NEWLY SOWN SWARD

82. The sowing of a new sward may follow an arable crop or replace an old sward which has become unproductive. In both situations care must be taken that perennial weeds do not survive to infest the new sward. At the end of a period of arable cropping the troublesome weeds are likely to be grasses such as *Agrostis* spp. (bent grass) and *Poa* spp. (meadow grass), because most broad-leaved perennial weeds may be controlled in the previous cereal crops by spraying. Where one grass sward is to be replaced immediately by another, there may be regeneration of all the species that were in the old sward.

DESTROYING A SWARD

Ploughing and cultivating

83. Techniques of ploughing are well known and are described in many books elsewhere. There are however certain points about the operation of ploughs that are recognized as influencing the survival of perennial weeds. When turning over grassland, skim coulters should be used and work should be at such a depth as will allow complete inversion of the furrow. This will help to prevent grasses growing up between the furrow slices, particularly where the opening and finishing of plough work takes place. The reversible plough allows continuous level work, without opening and finishing, and a better degree of weed control may be achieved. Where soil conditions permit, a heavy roller or furrow press may help to reduce weed grass regeneration. Discs are commonly used after ploughing old turf, and there is a danger of them turning up the old sward if they are driven too fast or in the wrong direction or are set wrongly. The first pass should be in line with the ploughing, at a slow speed with the discs set at a narrow angle to the line of draught.

Rotary cultivation

84. Rotary cultivation is becoming increasingly popular especially on wet or shallow soils where it may have certain advantages over normal ploughing and cultivation. At least two rotary cultivations are generally necessary. If re-seeding is to take place in the spring, the first rotary cultivation should be in the autumn to allow the subsequent winter frosts to assist in killing the sward and the second cultivation should be in the spring. For mid- or late-summer reseeding the two cultivations should take place in the same year with a gap of 2 to 4 weeks between them, according to the weather. The conventional operations of final seed-bed preparation and sowing then follow. An important aspect of this method of sward destruction is the judgement of the depth of setting the implement. If the rotors run deep the old sward may become in-corporated too deeply into soil which may then be difficult to consolidate in dry weather, whilst in wet weather the cut slices of the old sward may tend to regenerate. The more shallow the penetration, the less the deep-rooted plants are disturbed and the more they are able to survive and invade the new sward. It is also important to adjust the rotor speed relative to the forward speed for the correct tilth that is required.

Herbicides

85. [**Tentative**] Where difficulties are encountered in destroying the old sward by cultivation, chemical herbicides may be used. According to the nature of the sward, dalapon at 5 to 10 lb per acre, amino triazole at 2 to 4 lb per acre, or paraquat at 1 to 2 lb per acre will give a substantial but not complete kill of grasses, which may be assisted by surface cultivations during the prepara-tion of the seed-bed. Amino triazole is also effective in controlling a number of broad-leaved weeds. The method of dealing with the old sward may vary according to its type. In the case of dalapon and amino triazole care must be taken that the interval between spraying and sowing allows time for the chemical to disappear from the soil (see page 169). Examples of techniques employing herbicides in reseeding a sward containing a mixture of grasses and broad-leaved weeds are:

(a) The operation to start in early summer when MCPA or 2,4-D is used to control the broad-leaved weeds. In late September or early October dalapon is applied to kill the grasses. The following March or April the surface is burnt over, if necessary, and then cultivated shallowly with discs, pitch-pole or rotary cultivator. Seeds and fertiliser are then broadcast, harrowed in and rolled. This technique may be suitable for certain lowland and hill swards.

(b) The old sward is killed with paraquat in July or early August. About two weeks later, at a time when soil moisture is adequate for the seeds to be sown, the surface is rotary cultivated and seeds and fertiliser are broadcast and harrowed in; the surface being rolled well after sowing. This technique has been used most successfully on lowland swards.

(c) Where normal reseeding methods by ploughing or rotary cultivation is contemplated, an application of one of these herbicides at least two weeks beforehand will greatly reduce the risk of perennial grass plants in the old sward surviving through into the new sward.

Chemical destruction prior to reseeding is the subject of much experimentation and as yet too little experience is available to allow firm recommendations. Farmers wishing to try any technique of this nature should obtain technical advice before starting

86. [For Information] Sward destruction by chemical herbicides to be followed by oversowing without cultivations is a promising but difficult technique which has succeeded best in high rainfall areas.

CONTROLLING WEEDS IN THE YOUNG SWARD

87. It may be necessary to control weeds in the young sward for two main reasons. Sufficient annual weeds are present to compete seriously with the grass and legume seedlings or, in the case of undersown crops, with the cereal cover crop; seedling perennial weeds are present, notably *Rumex* spp. (docks), *Ranunculus.* spp (buttercups), *Plantago* spp. (plantains) which if allowed to become established are very difficult to control by any means. Seedling *Rumex* spp., for example, can be readily killed in young leys with MCPB or 2,4-DB without injury to the grass and clover seedlings and a potential infestation of *Cirsium arvense* (creeping thistle) can also be dealt with at this time before the root system has become established.

Growth stages of legume and grass seedlings

88. The response of seedling legumes and grasses to selective herbicides is influenced by their stage of growth. Treatment at too early a growth stage – or too high a dose – may result in reduction in plant stand, as well as stunting and distortion of survivors. Determination of the correct growth stage is therefore of great importance. The development of legume seedlings in undersown crops of cereals, or when direct-sown is given in terms of the number of expanded leaves. On emergence two small round or oval cotyledons are apparent. These are sometimes called 'seed' leaves but are not true leaves. They are followed by a single simple leaf which is the unifoliate leaf or 'spade' leaf. All subsequent leaves have three leaflets — these typical 'clover' leaves are called trifoliate leaves. Seedlings of white clover and lucerne at the first trifoliate leaf stage are illustrated in Fig. 4. The growth stage of seedling grasses

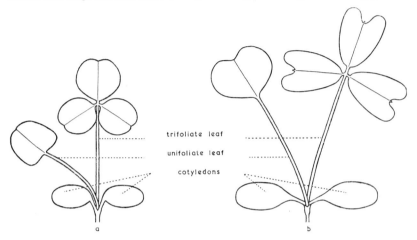

trifoliate leaf

unifoliate leaf

cotyledons

a   b

FIG. 4. Legume seedlings at first trifoliate leaf stage: (a) white clover; (b) lucerne. ×2½. (Drawn by R. J. Chancellor.)

may be described by the number of leaves or tillers as with cereals. The relation between these stages of growth and subsequent damage is not clearly understood, although resistance generally increases with age. Ear damage is only relevant in crops grown for seed, and then only in the year following sowing, see paragraph 110. Generally, the legume seedlings are more likely to be permanently damaged than the grass seedlings, and where both are present in the young sward the stage of growth of the legume seedlings should be the limiting factor.

Cutting and grazing

89. In a young sward undersown in cereals, the only method of control in the crop is by use of herbicides, but in direct sown seedling swards the control of annual weeds is sometimes attempted by mowing. Mowing is only effective, however, against annual weeds of upright habit. Many weeds of prostrate habit such as *Polygonum aviculare* (knotgrass) or *Stellaria media* (chickweed) are not affected by mowing and are often encouraged by the removal of the competition given by the tall growing species. The prostrate species are usually the most serious from the point of view of competition with the seedling sward. Similarly as most of the perennial seedlings are in the rosette stage during the year of sowing, these are also unaffected by mowing and may indeed be encouraged. Early grazing to control weeds suffers from similar limitations as mowing and may be more inclined to favour the successful establishment of perennial weeds.

Tolerance of seedling grasses to herbicides

90. [Tentative] Table 6 shows the earliest safe stage of growth of seedling grasses at which herbicides may be applied and the maximum recommended dose of herbicides. The recommendations are for the spraying of seedling grasses without reference to other associated crop plants such as clover, cereal cover crops, rape, etc. The appropriate paragraphs should also be consulted when such associated crops are present. Crops should not be sprayed within 10 days after or before rolling. Growth regulator herbicides may be applied at low to high volume and dinoseb in 40 to 100 gallons per acre. In the absence of sufficient critical data the recommended safe stages of growth of grass species and doses of herbicide are all given tentatively.

Tolerance of seedling clover to herbicides

91. MCPA-salt at up to 16 oz per acre in low or high volume may be applied where red clover is the only species of clover present if the ley has become dominated by a susceptible weed. In order to reduce to a minimum the possible damage to the clover, spraying should be delayed as long as possible to allow the clover to become established, and also to permit the weed to form a canopy to protect the clover from much of the spray. It is important, on the other hand, not to delay spraying so long that the weed becomes resistant to the herbicide or the ley begins to suffer from the competition. Careful balancing of these factors is necessary in deciding upon spraying.

Only under exceptional circumstances should this treatment be applied to leys containing white clover as appreciable reduction in the clover content of the sward can result. If the ley is completely dominated by a susceptible weed, an application of low doses of liquid or dust preparations (e.g. 12 oz MCPA-salt or 2,4-D-amine, 6 oz of 2,4-D-ester or 24 oz MCPA-salt in dust form) may be made to control susceptible weeds (see Table 9) which have made sufficient growth to shield the seedlings partially. Safety to the seedling clovers is greatly dependent upon the shielding effect of the cereal cover crop, if any, and the weed, but age of the seedling clover is also a factor and both red and white clover should have developed at least two trifoliate leaves before the spray is applied. MCPA is safer than 2,4-D for use on red clover but not on white

TABLE 6. EARLIEST SAFE STAGE OF GROWTH OF SEEDLING GRASSES AT WHICH HERBICIDES MAY BE APPLIED AND THE MAXIMUM RECOMMENDED DOSES OF HERBICIDES (TENTATIVE)

Species	Stage of growth	Maximum permissible dose in oz per acre						
		MCPA-salt	2,4-D-amine	MCPA/2,3,6-TBA MCPA+TBA	MCPB-salt	2,4-DB-salt	Mecoprop-salt	Dinoseb-amine
Ryegrass Cocksfoot Meadow fescue	3–4 inches high, beginning to tiller	16	12	12 + 4	48	48	40	16*
Timothy	1–2 inches high, beginning to tiller	12	8	12 + 4	48	48	40	16*
Red fescue		16	12	12 + 4	48	48	40	16*

*Dinoseb-amine may be applied once the grasses have reached the three-leaf stage.

clover. Insufficient evidence is available to indicate whether high- or low-volume application is safest.

92. MCPB-salt and 2,4-DB-salt are much less toxic to red and white clover than MCPA-salt and 2,4-D-salt and are therefore generally to be preferred for use on seedling leys when these varieties of clover are present. The following maximum doses may be used at any time after the clovers have developed their first trifoliate leaf:

MCPB-salt (on white and red clover)	32 oz per acre
2,4-DB-salt (on white clover)	48 oz per acre
2,4-DB-salt (on red clover)	32 oz per acre

2,4-DB is slightly more toxic than MCPB to red clover and may cause leaf deformities, but these do not persist for more than six to eight weeks. Where the mixture contains both red and white clover care should be taken to verify that both species have reached the resistant stage. On red clover MCPB is to be preferred unless *Polygonum* species are predominant.

93. Mixtures of MCPB or 2,4-DB with very small amounts of MCPA or 2,4-D have been introduced to improve the range of weed species controlled without losing selectivity towards clovers. Such mixtures are of particular value for the control of Cruciferous weeds, many of which are moderately resistant or resistant to MCPB and 2,4-DB but can be readily killed by very low doses of MCPA or 2,4-D (4 to 6 oz per acre).

94. Dinoseb-ammonium or -amine may be applied to red and white clover, provided the plants have developed two trifoliate leaves. Application should be made in high volume at doses up to a maximum of 1·5 lb per acre for the ammonium salt or 2 lb per acre of amine formulations. Where good growing conditions have prevailed during the days preceding spraying and temperature is high on the day of spraying, it may be necessary to reduce the dose (e.g. by 0·5 lb per acre at over 70°F). Dinoseb is liable to cause some leaf scorch and should be applied only where justified by a dense weed stand.

95. Where seedling grasses are present with the clover paragraph 90 should be consulted. See paragraphs 30–38 for recommendations on cereals undersown with grass and clover.

Tolerance of seedling lucerne to herbicides

96. Dinoseb-ammonium at doses up to 1·5 lb per acre or dinoseb-amine at doses up to 2 lb per acre may be applied in high volume to seedling lucerne. Where good growing conditions have prevailed during the days preceding spraying and temperature is high on the day of spraying, it may be necessary to reduce the dose (e.g. by 0·5 lb per acre at over 70°F). The seedlings should have developed two trifoliate leaves before spraying (see paragraph 88). Spraying of lucerne-grass mixtures in this way may alter the balance between the two components of the mixture.

97. 2,4-DB-salt may be applied at doses up to 48 oz per acre to seedling lucerne, provided that most of the seedlings have reached the first trifoliate leaf stage (see paragraph 88). The optimum time of treatment is between the first and fourth trifoliate leaf stages, as this is the period of maximum sensitivity to weed competition. Treatment after development of the fourth trifoliate leaf may produce deformity in subsequent lateral and tiller growth. Although this deformity will disappear within six to eight weeks of spraying, it will affect the ability of the lucerne to compete with semi-resistant weeds, particularly if the crop is late summer-sown. The herbicide should not be applied to lucerne direct-sown in late summer where *Stellaria media* (chickweed) is abundant. This weed is resistant to 2,4-DB, and if cold wet conditions follow spraying, it will grow away vigorously and smother the crop. MCPA MCPB and 2,4-D should not be used on seedling lucerne.

98 [Tentative] Chlorpropham may be applied at 2 lb per acre at high volume to seedling lucerne which has reached the fourth trifoliate leaf stage. This treatment is primarily of value for the control of *Stellaria media* (chickweed). Chlorpropham is slow in action on established plants and the full effect may not be evident for several weeks.

Tolerance of seedling sainfoin to herbicides

99 [Tentative] MCPB salt may be applied at up to 32 oz per acre to seedling sainfoin which has developed at least one trifoliate leaf (see paragraph 88).

100 [Tentative] Dinoseb-ammonium or -amine may be applied to seedling sainfoin which has developed two trifoliate leaves (see paragraph 88) in the same way as to lucerne (see paragraph 96).

GRASSES AND LEGUMES UNDERSOWN IN CEREALS

101. The presence of grass, grass and clover or lucerne seedlings beneath a cereal crop restricts the herbicides that may be used to those that are suitable for both the cereal and the undersown crop. Paragraphs 1–25 describe the use of herbicides on cereal crops, and paragraphs 90, 91–95, 96–98 and 99–100 the use of herbicides on seedling grasses, clover, lucerne and sainfoin respectively. Stages of growth of legume seedlings are described in paragraph 88. Paragraphs 30 to 38 (pages 48–50) summarize recommendations on the use of herbicides in undersown cereals.

ESTABLISHED LEYS AND PERMANENT GRASSLAND

102. (a) A **ley** may contain a single grass or a mixture of grasses and clover; it is sown as a crop and should be kept free of weeds. Due partly to the widespread use of herbicides in cereals, leys in a cereal and grass rotation do not usually become infested with broad-leaved perennial weeds, such as buttercups or thistles. Where this does happen the control measures described in paragraphs 103 and 104 can be used. More widespread, but less easily seen and appreciated, are the grass weeds. These may arise from seed in the soil, as for example the *Poa* spp. (meadow grass) or they may have been present during arable cropping and survive to invade the new sward, as *Agrostis* spp. (bent grass) may do.

(b) A **permanent pasture** is a long-established mixture of species which has reached dynamic equilibrium, the balance of which is decided by the climate, the soil and the management given by the farmer. Any alteration in these environmental factors may lead to a change in the composition of the sward. A long-established pasture usually contains twenty or more species, though a smaller number will occupy most of the area; both grasses and broad-leaved plants are commonplace. All these species vary in their productivity and nutritional value, and are regarded as desirable plants or weeds accordingly. With the broad-leaved plants the decision as to their desirability is fairly clear cut, such species as *Ranunculus* spp. (buttercups), *Cirsium* spp. (thistles), etc undoubtedly being weeds. With the grasses the distinction is not so easy; *Holcus lanatus* (Yorkshire fog) and *Agrostis* spp. (bents) may be regarded as weeds on land capable of satisfactorily growing ryegrass; but they may be desirable on hill land where poorer species of grass only are present. The improvement of permanent pasture involves the establishment and increase of more productive and nutritious species of grass at the expense of less desirable species. Established leys and permanent pasture almost invariably contain a proportion of weed grasses. Apart from pure lucerne (see paragraph 105) there are no herbicides which may be recommended for the control of these weeds. Many broad-leaved weeds however can be controlled by chemicals, and weed control can be a key that opens the door to the more efficient use of fertilizers, to better utilization of the herbage and thus to more efficient and cheaper grass production.

MCPA, 2,4-D, MCPB AND 2,4-DB

103. The chemicals used for the control of broad-leaved perennial weeds are MCPA, 2,4-D, MCPB and 2,4-DB. As their application will inevitably entail spraying grass and clover as well as the weed, it is important that the risks involved are clearly understood. Established grasses have such a degree of resistance to these chemicals that they are unlikely to suffer damage, except where seed production is involved. Legumes, particularly white clover and lucerne, are much more susceptible to damage. MCPA and 2,4-D are generally more toxic to weeds and cheaper than are MCPB and 2,4-DB, but they are also much more toxic to clover and it is necessary to take this into account when choosing the herbicide. Pasture in this country can be divided into two types:

(a) There are pastures in which the sown or indigenous clover population is sparse and not contributing much to the sward. Little will be lost if the clover is suppressed by MCPA or 2,4-D, so these herbicides may be used in controlling broad-leaved perennial weeds at the times and doses, up to the maximum dose, required for efficient control of the weed, as described in paragraphs 113 to 130. Low to high volume rates may be used.

(b) There are leys and permanent pastures where white clover is an abundant and highly valued constituent because it contributes both to the herbage and to the nitrogen supply of the grasses. On these swards it is important that herbicide treatment should not depress the clover. The maximum dose that may be applied if there is a risk of clover depression is 8 oz per acre of MCPA-salt or 2,4-D-amine or 4 oz per acre of 2,4-D-ester. Such doses are, however, inadequate for a substantial control of most broad-leaved weeds, and MCPB or 2,4-DB should be used if clover depression is to be avoided; MCPB-salt and 2,4-DB-salt may be applied at up to 48 oz per acre in low to high volume rates.

Management in relation to spraying

104. Where grass is to be cut for hay the herbicides can be applied either in early spring e.g. for the control of *Ranunculus* spp. (buttercup) or delayed until regrowth of the weed after mowing, e.g. for the control of *Cirsium arvense* (creeping thistle). Any suppression of clover from spraying may be exaggerated where a hay crop is taken. Where grassland is grazed the time of treatment should be at the optimum time for the control of the weed. Where a treatment is used which is liable to suppress the clover, spraying as early in the season as possible can provide a longer growing season in which to encourage recovery of the clover. Grazing about a week before spraying will reduce the amount of clover leaf present and so minimize the risk of suppression. Good grazing management and fertilizer practice is important to encourage a competitive sward that will help to prevent recovery of the weeds.

DALAPON

105. [Tentative] Dalapon-sodium may be applied to established lucerne for the control of grasses at doses up to 5 lb per acre at medium or high volume. The crop should be sprayed when dormant either in the spring after the grasses have begun to grow but before the growth of the lucerne has started, or in the autumn in the period between the cessation of growth of the lucerne and of the grasses. In general better control of grasses results from spring application. Such treatment should result in comparative freedom from competition from grasses during the ensuing season, but the killing of the grasses may result in much ground being bare when the lucerne becomes dormant in the following autumn. This bare ground may then become recolonized by grasses or broad-leaved weeds.

106. [For Information] Investigations are being made into the use of sub-lethal doses of dalapon and paraquat as an aid to changing the balance of the grass constituents of a sward. No recommendations are yet possible on this aspect of the use of herbicides for sward improvement.

ROUGH GRAZING

107. Very large areas of the British Isles are classified as rough grazing because, as the name implies, the plant species growing on them are coarse and have low feeding value for livestock. Usually the vegetation is the result of adverse climate or soil but these two factors are not always the sole cause. Common land near to centres of population is often infested with *Ulex* spp. (gorse) or *Rubus* spp. (brambles) and these are regarded as having amenity value to townspeople visiting the area. Similarly, many upland areas covered by *Calluna vulgaris* (heather) provide not only grazing for sheep but a home for grouse, the shooting of which is highly valued. Rough grazings often have uses other than agricultural which may influence the extent and means by which they can be improved. There are, nevertheless, many on which the stock-carrying capacity could be increased. Even where improvement is not contemplated, the owner (or public authority where common land is concerned) has a statutory duty under the Weeds Act 1959 (see Chapter IX) to control and prevent the spread of injurious weeds. The dominant species on rough grazing vary greatly according to climate, soil and topography. *Rubus* spp. (brambles), *Ulex* spp. (gorse) and *Pteridium aqualinum* (bracken) have virtually no feeding value for stock, whereas *Calluna vulgaris* (heather), *Nardus stricta* (moor mat grass), *Molonia caerulea* (flying bent) and *Juncus* spp. (rushes) can for periods of the year provide valuable grazing, though of poor productivity by lowland standards.

108. Where improvement is contemplated specialist advice should be obtained, not only because of the financial assistance that may be obtained from the Ministry of Agriculture, Fisheries and Food, but because a detailed assessment of the drainage, soil and economic situation is usually necessary to indicate the best method of improvement. Herbicides have a part to play, either in preventing the degeneration of herbaceous vegetation into scrub or in schemes for improving the grazing value of the land. Information on these two aspects may be found in Chapter IV, Section (ii) and in the notes on individual weed species in paragraphs 113 to 130.

GRASSES AND CLOVER FOR SEED PRODUCTION

109. The weeds which are important in grass and clover seed crops and general measures for their control are discussed in Chapter XI. The use of herbicides in newly sown seedling grasses and clover are dealt with in the preceding paragraphs 82 to 102. The following recommendations concern the use of herbicides in the year of harvest of the seed.

GRASSES FOR SEED PRODUCTION

110 [Tentative] Not more than 24 oz MCPA-salt, 16 oz 2,4-D-amine, 8 oz 2,4-D-ester, 40 oz of mecoprop or dichlorprop or 12 oz MCPA plus 4 oz. 2,3,6-TBA per acre in low or high volume should be used on established grass in the season of seed production. They should not be sprayed earlier than 4 to 5 weeks before ear emergence is expected nor later than ear emergence itself. Species and varieties of grasses differ appreciably in their time of emergence and the habit of the particular grass concerned should be taken into account, no one time being likely to be suitable for spraying all crops.

Table 24 on page 259 shows the approximate safe periods for using growth regulators on Aberystwyth varieties of grass based on the normal time of ear emergence in Cambridgeshire. These times vary according to the season and should also be adjusted for other parts of the country. At the risk of inducing some ear deformity, earlier spraying of timothy may be necessary to control weeds before they become resistant.

CLOVER FOR SEED PRODUCTION
Red Clover

111. No recommendation can be made for treatment of established red clover intended for seed.

White Clover

112. [Tentative] MCPB may be used in established white clover intended for seed at doses up to 32 oz per acre particularly for the control of *Cirsium arvense* (creeping thistle), *Plantago* spp. (plantains) and *Rumex crispus*, *R. sanguineus* and *R. conglomeratus* (docks), provided that it is applied before mid-May. This will usually only be possible where grazing is practised before shutting up for seed. Application made after taking a hay crop, or after the end of May may cause loss of seed yield.

NOTES ON SOME COMMON WEEDS OF GRASSLAND

The following notes are concerned with aspects of the biology and control of weeds as they occur in grassland. General notes on some of these weeds, together with information on their control on arable land, are also to be found in Chapter **V**.

CIRSIUM ARVENSE (creeping thistle)

113. Creeping thistle is one of the most persistent and troublesome perennial weeds of grassland. It spreads by rhizomes which may remain dormant for many years if deeply buried under a vigorous sward but which may, under the right conditions, readily produce new shoots. Seedlings of this weed are uncommon. Creeping thistle is usually most troublesome in pastures that are mainly grazed, particularly where there is a tendency to overgraze in winter or early spring and undergraze in summer. The control of creeping thistle on pasture is often attempted by cutting in the flower-bud stage, but unless cutting is done regularly eradication is seldom achieved. In grassland which is mainly used for hay or silage the weed is usually less evident. Changes in management can reduce the incidence of creeping thistle.

114. Chemical treatment is usually a much more satisfactory means of control, but the success is influenced by the situation. On reseeded grassland the disturbance of the rhizomes by the cultivations used in preparing the seed-bed usually leads to an abundant emergence of shoots and the number of shoots to the amount of rhizomes is high. In this condition the weed may be particularly vulnerable to herbicides. In established grassland the ratio of shoots to rhizomes may be low and control of the weed less readily achieved. The herbicides MCPA, 2,4-D, MCPB and 2,4-DB can all be used on creeping thistle in pasture. They will produce a good control of top shoots in the first and perhaps second year after spraying; but the chemicals do not achieve a complete kill of the root system and gradual reinfestation is likely to occur. The choice of chemical will depend on considerations of clover safety (see paragraph 103). The optimum time to spray on grazed pastures is the early flower-bud stage, but application may be made in the late summer/early autumn, providing the thistles are growing actively, as for example after a hay crop. Further applications in subsequent years are often necessary. Recommended doses of MCPA, 2,4-D, MCPB and 2,4-DB-salts are: 24 to 32 oz per acre for maximum suppression. A useful degree of control can be achieved by lower doses of about 16 oz per acre.

See also M.A.F.F. Advisory Leaflet No. 51.

EQUISETUM SPP. (horsetail)

115. The two most important weed species are *Equisetum arvense* and *E. palustre*, both of which are poisonous to stock and constitute a considerable hazard when present in hay, dried grass or silage. *E. palustre* is the more important species in grassland and thrives in damp situations. The two species can be distinguished by the number of grooves on the sterile stems, *E. palustre* having four to eight, while *E. arvense* usually has more, up to nineteen. The shoots of both species are readily killed by MCPA, MCPB, 2,4-D and 2,4-DB but there is generally strong regrowth from the underground rhizomes the year following treatment. A partial kill of the root system of *E. arvense* may be obtained by a single application; but with *E. palustre* a single application is unlikely to produce any permanent effect. Available evidence suggests that some long-term reduction of *E. palustre* is most likely to follow spraying if competition from the grass components of the sward is increased by suitable grazing or cutting management and fertilizer treatment. In general, the aerial shoots should be treated when they have made maximum growth.

Recommended doses:

(*a*) for kill of aerial shoots only, 12 to 20 oz MCPA, MCPB, 2,4-D or 2,4-DB-salt per acre; 8 to 12 oz 2,4-D-ester.

(*b*) for kill of aerial shoots and for partial suppression of regrowth, 32 oz MCPA or 2,4-D-salt or -ester per acre: MCPB and 2,4-DB at 32 oz are reported to give similar results.

For the control of *E. palustre* in grassland required for hay or silage, MCPA or 2,4-D applied a week or more before the grass is to be cut will successfully kill *Equisetum* shoots thus allowing a crop to be taken.

JUNCUS SPP. (rushes)

116. The rushes which are most commonly regarded as weeds can be quite easily identified despite their similarity. The eight species listed in Table 9 can be divided into two groups according to whether the flowering stems bear leaves with green blades or not. Those that do *not* are *Juncus inflexus*, *J. conglomeratus* and *J. effusus*. *J. inflexus* is blue-green, and has a discontinuous pith throughout the stem, unlike the other two which have a continuous pith (at least at the base) and are green in colour. *J. conglomeratus* has a deeply ridged stem especially near the top, but *J. effusus* is hardly, or only slightly, ridged. Those rushes that have green leaf blades on the flowering stem can be separated as follows: *J. maritimus* has the flowers borne on the side of the stem, unlike the others, which have them at the end; in addition the stem leaves have stiff points. *J. squarrosus* can be separated from the remaining species by the leaves being solid whereas the leaves of *J. subnodulosus*, *J. acutiflorus* and *J. articulatus* are divided up internally into hollow compartments.

The divisions are both across and along the leaf in *J. subnodulosus*, but are only across in the leaves of the other two species. The leaves of *J. articulatus* are definitely compressed laterally, but those of *J. acutiflorus* are hardly compressed at all.

117. Only one of these species, *Juncus effusus*, the soft rush, has so far been found to be readily killed by MCPA and 2,4-D. *J. conglomeratus* is closely allied to *J. effusus* but little information is available regarding the effect of herbicides. Species which are generally resistant to applications of MCPA and 2,4-D at doses up to 32 oz per acre are *J. articulatus* (jointed rush), *J. inflexus* (hard rush) and *J. squarrosus* (heath rush). There are indications that *J. inflexus* may be moderately susceptible to MCPA when cutting is carried out 3 to 4 weeks after treatment. The reaction of other species of *Juncus* to herbicides is not known. Spraying of *J. effusus* should take place preferably before flowering when the rushes are growing vigorously. It is strongly recommended that the rushes are cut about four weeks after treatment; this not only improves the kill obtained but helps the sward to develop over the dead rush clumps. If desired, cutting may take place a month before spraying with equally good results, but if this is done the cut litter must be removed before spraying. Spraying uncut rushes can also give good results, particularly when the rushes have been cut in previous years. Higher doses than those given below may be required for a complete kill. Cutting immediately before or after spraying is not recommended. The soil on which rushes grow almost always contains dormant seed which will germinate if provided with air and light. To prevent this poaching should be avoided and a vigorous tight sward must be achieved by the use of fertilizers and controlled grazing. Recommended doses for established *J. effusus* are: MCPA-salt and 2,4-D-amine, 32 oz per acre; 2,4-D-ester, 16–24 oz per acre.

118. The ploughing of rush infested pasture involves a considerable risk of regeneration from incompletely buried roots. Spraying at least three weeks before ploughing will prevent regrowth in the new sward. The soil disturbance caused by ploughing is likely to stimulate the germination of *J. effusus* seedlings and MCPA or 2,4-D at 16 oz per acre applied in the year after sowing will control the seedlings but clover may be severely checked. There is little information concerning MCPB or mixtures of 2,4-D or MCPA with MCPB. The aim must be to achieve a tight vigorous sward as quickly as possible to avoid successive germinations of rush.

See also M.A.F.F. Advisory Leaflet No. 433.

PLANTAGO SPP. (plantains)

119. *Plantago major*, *P. media* and *P. lanceolata* are the three species most commonly occurring as perennial weeds of grassland. *P. major* has a stalked leaf and tends to be distributed in gateways, on cattle paths and on areas severely disturbed by animals. *P. media* has hairy leaves and tends to be confined to old calcareous grassland becoming particularly common on close grazed areas on chalk. *P. lanceolata* is a ubiquitous weed in all types of lowland grass. Although *P. lanceolata* is sometimes thought desirable for its high mineral content, there is no doubt that the presence of these rosette plants reduced the amount of light available for more desirable and productive herbage. Old pasture is particularly prone to carry large populations of *P. lanceolata* and *P. media*. The only possible means of cultural control is to prevent the entry of the species as seedlings by maintaining a tight sward and avoiding the production of 'breaks' in the sward where the seedlings establish. The three species are easily controlled by a wide range of herbicides being killed, normally, by a single application of 12 oz per acre MCPA-salt or 2,4-D-amine or 24 oz per acre of MCPB-salt or 2,4-DB-salt.

PTERIDIUM AQUILINIUM (bracken)

120. Bracken is a dominant plant over considerable areas, generally on light acid soils, in both woods and grassland. It is a very persistent and troublesome weed, because not only is it normally avoided by grazing animals, but it is also capable of spreading very extensively by means of its underground rhizomes. Control measures at the present time are almost entirely based on mechanical treatments. Details of these, together with valuable guidance for those concerned with bracken eradication, are given in the Ministry of Agriculture Advisory Leaflet No. 190. In brief, the problem can be divided into bracken on ploughable land, and bracken on unploughable land. The former is relatively easily dealt with by ploughing in the summer, followed by heavy discing and application of lime and fertilizers. The land is sown to a pioneer crop such as rape, turnips or Italian ryegrass in the late summer, and this, after grazing in the autumn, is disced in during December. The followng spring the land should be fit for potatoes, rye or oats or for direct reseeding. On unploughable land, bracken can be greatly reduced in quantity and vigour, but not eliminated, by cutting or bruising the fronds twice a year for a number of years. A subsidy is available in England, Wales and Scotland to encourage this treatment (see page 267).

121. [For Information] Herbicides have been tested extensively on bracken in recent years but no chemical has so far achieved large scale control. Amino triazole and 4-CPA-ester at doses in the range of 5 to 10 lb per acre, applied just prior to maturity of the fronds have on occasions achieved successful control but there have also been instances where the results have been unsatisfactory.

RANUNCULUS SPP. (buttercups)

122. Buttercups are commonly found in permanent pastures but they may also invade old leys. They are unpalatable plants which stock will not readily eat and their presence may lead to a reduction in the grazing of neighbouring grasses. There are three distinct species that are most important as grassland weeds and as they differ in their reactions to MCPA, MCPB, 2,4-D and 2,4-DB it is necessary to identify the type of buttercup correctly before treatment. *R. bulbosus*, the earliest flowering of the three, can be distinguished by the swollen stem base found just underground (except in the early spring) and by the sepals which are bent downwards away from the open flower. *R. repens* can be distinguished from the other species during the summer months by its creeping habit; during the winter this may not be a useful distinguishing feature. It has furrowed flower stalks and the apical lobe of the basal leaves is long-stalked and projects beyond the other two lobes, unlike *R. acris*, of which the flower stalks are not furrowed and the three lobes of the basal leaves all radiate from a simple point. The sepals of *R. repens* and *R. acris* are spreading and not bent downwards during flowering.

123. *R. repens* is easily controlled by MCPA, MCPB, 2,4-D and 2,4-DB. The best time for treatment is in spring or early summer up to flowering, during which period 12 to 24 oz. per acre of MCPA or 2,4-D-salt or 24 to 32 oz per acre of MCPB or 2,4-DB-salt are recommended. Successful treatment may, however, be made at any time of the year during active growth of the weed, but the dose should be increased. *R. acris* is slightly less susceptible than creeping buttercup. The recommendations for treatment are similar, but long term control is not so certain. *R. bulbosus* is much more resistant than the other species. Treatment in spring will usually prevent flowering the same season but may not result in a significant reduction in the population the year after treatment. After flowering the leaves die back and the plant is dormant in the summer, but new leaves appear again in the autumn; as germination of the seed occurs also at this time, it is suggested that treatment might be more effective in autumn than in spring. When a field is to be sprayed for buttercup control it is advisable to exclude stock for 10 days before and after spraying.

RUMEX SPP. (docks)

124. The two most widespread species of *Rumex* occurring as weeds of grassland are *R. crispus* (curled dock) and *R. obtusifolius* (broad-leaved dock). In the seedling stage, before a large taproot has formed, both species are readily killed by MCPA, 2,4-D, MCPB and 2,4-DB. When a young clover-grass ley is observed to be infested with dock seedlings, it is very desirable to kill these before they become established, MCPB and 2,4-DB should be used at the highest dose that is harmless to the clovers as soon as the majority of the dock seedlings are considered to have emerged; MCPA or 2,4-D can also be used under the conditions specified in paragraphs 91 and 92.

125. Established plants are much more difficult to kill and *R. obtusifolius*, particularly, may be completely resistant to these herbicides when well established in grassland. Repeated spraying in grassland will often reduce and eventually eliminate docks, but the expense and also the damage to the clovers is unlikely to be justified. A method of control that has given good results is to plough and sow down to a one-year ley of Italian ryegrass, followed by spraying as necessary during the summer to kill the docks without loss of production. The ley is followed by a cereal, so that any surviving docks can be sprayed again. The recommended doses for use in established grassland are: *Rumex crispus* MCPA-salt and 2,4-D-amine 24 to 32 oz per acre; MCPB and 2,4-DB-salts 32 to 48 oz per acre; 2,4-D-ester 16 to 24 oz per acre (see paragraph 103).

See also M.A.F.F. Advisory Leaflet No. 46.

SENECIO JACOBAEA (ragwort)

126. Ragwort is poisonous to cattle and horses and is scheduled as an injurious weed under the Weeds Act of 1952. Power is given under the Act to serve on the occupier of the land on which the weed is growing a notice in writing requiring him to 'cut down or destroy the weed in the manner and within the time specified in the notice.' Effective spraying with herbicides is generally recognized as meeting the requirements of this Act. Ragwort is a weed most commonly found on neglected or overgrazed pastures, but it may also rapidly invade young leys, particularly after direct reseeding. There are three main phases in its life cycle: (i) the germination of the seed and establishment of the seedling, (ii) the formation and development of a rosette, and (iii) flowering and seed production. The rosette stage may be indefinitely prolonged by cutting or trampling and the plant may then become branched and considerably enlarged. If undisturbed, ragwort is a biennial. Seed production is prolific and vegetative propagation may also take place by means of shoots arising from root fragments. Seeds germinate very quickly under suitable conditions but can remain viable for several years if buried in the soil.

127. The most common method of control is cutting the flowering shoots when in full flower. Provided the cut shoots are removed from the field, seeding is prevented, but otherwise the treatment has no beneficial effect on the population present and indeed may encourage the plants to perennate. Crowding sheep on to the land for short periods will effectively reduce a ragwort infestation. Old ewes are favoured for this practice. Seedling establishment is the most vulnerable phase in the life history of ragwort and a high level of grassland husbandry resulting in a dense sward will on its own prevent the weed from becoming a menace. The most effective method of cultural control of an established infestation is to plough and introduce an arable rotation before sowing down again to grass under a cover crop. Direct reseeding should be avoided. On much ragwort infested land, control by management and rotational cropping is not feasible and herbicides offer the most effective means of control.

128. MCPA and 2,4-D at the recommended doses will normally kill ragwort plants (all stages of growth) present at the time of spraying, but results may be masked because: (i) the flowering shoots may continue to produce flowers and viable seed in the season of spraying, and (ii) new seedlings or regrowth from roots may appear under favourable conditions soon after spraying. The success of a spray treatment depends therefore to a large extent on whether or not the field becomes recolonized following spraying. A single treatment may or may not be successful and repeat applications must be allowed for in any programme of chemical ragwort control.

Recommended doses:

MCPA-salt and 2,4-D-amine 24 to 32 oz per acre; 2,4-D-ester 16 to 24 oz per acre. 2,4-D has generally given better results than MCPA. Ragwort is resistant to MCPB and 2,4-DB.

The best time for treatment appears to be in June or early July in southern counties, when the flowering shoot is developing rapidly and seedlings and rosettes are growing strongly. Spraying should not be deferred until the flower buds are well formed. As ragwort may become more palatable after spraying, it is advisable to prevent stock from having access to treated fields until after the ragwort plants are dead.

See also M.A.F.F. Advisory Leaflet No. 280.

TARAXACUM OFFICINALE (dandelion)

129. Dandelion is a very common plant in many types of grassland. The fresh green leaves arise in a rosette from a long tap root, and the deep yellow flowers may be seen in early summer. Because of its strong root system and ability to regrow from below shallow ploughing, dandelion can cause trouble by regenerating in direct reseeded swards. Dandelion may be well controlled by 2,4-D or MCPA, but 2,4-D gives more consistently good results than MCPA. The best time to spray is in spring at the flower-bud stage, but good results may be obtained at any time providing the weed is growing strongly. Recommended doses are: 2,4-D-amine 16 to 24 oz per acre, MCPA-salt 32 oz per acre. Dandelion is resistant to both MCPB and 2,4-DB. On pastures where it is wished to avoid depression of white clover, some supression of dandelion may be achieved by 2,4-D-amine at 8 oz per acre, but spraying may have to be repeated in subsequent years.

URTICA DIOICA (stinging nettle)

130. Regular cutting will eliminate stinging nettle and where this weed occurs sporadically over pastures that have been continuously grazed, this is the most practical method of control unless heavy controlled stocking is possible. The presence of nettles generally indicates a loose soil structure and trampling by cattle will often eliminate the weed provided it is done systematically. Ploughing and an arable rotation before reseeding will also eliminate nettles.

Spraying with MCPA, 2,4-D, or MCPB at the maximum dose recommended for grassland (see paragraph 103) will quickly kill the top growth, but new shoots will soon appear and eradication involves repeated spraying and possibly severe damage to clovers unless it is feasible to spray only the nettle clumps. Where the weed occurs in isolated clumps or pure stands, herbicides offer a practical method of control and eradication can be achieved by repeated applications of MCPA, 2,4-D mecoprop or 2,4,5-T, or by one or two applications of sodium chlorate. The most economical method of using sodium chlorate is to spray a 5 per cent w/v solution (5 lb in 10 gallons water) on to fully developed nettle clumps, so that they are completely wetted. A wetting agent should preferably be added to the solution. Grass will be scorched but seldom killed by this treatment, which should be repeated if any shoots appear a few weeks later. Mecoprop, MCPA, 2,4-D or 2,4,5-T applied as 0·5 per cent sprays in the same way will kill the top growth, but repeated applications over two or three years are likely to be necessary before eradication is achieved; 2,4,5-T and mecoprop appear to be more effective than MCPA or 2,4-D. They are also more toxic to clover. The best results will be obtained by spraying in early June when the nettles are beginning to flower, followed by an autumn application to the regrowth, repeating in subsequent years until the nettles have been eliminated.

See also M.A.F.F. Advisory Leaflet No. 47.

SECTION (IV) PRE-HARVEST DESICCATION

Chemical desiccants are primarily used to facilitate the harvesting of crops. The two main requirements in British agriculture, at present, are the desiccation of forage legumes grown for seed to aid harvesting, and the destruction of potato haulm to permit mechanical lifting of the tubers.

FORAGE LEGUMES GROWN FOR SEED

131. Dinoseb, specially formulated for crop desiccation, may be applied at 1·35 to 1·8 lb in 40 to 50 gallons of water per acre.

132. Diquat, formulated with a wetter, may be applied at 6 to 8 oz in 20 to 30 gallons of water per acre, for red and white clover.

133. DNOC may be applied at 2 to 4 lb per acre. For crop desiccation, this compound is formulated in oil as an emulsifiable concentrate and prepared for spraying by dilution with water to a volume of 20 gallons or more per acre. The addition of 1 to 2 gallons of tractor fuel oil to the concentrate before dilution may improve the results, particularly where the lower doses of the chemical are applied.

134. Sulphuric acid as an 8 to 9 per cent v/v solution with a wetting agent, may be applied at the rate of 100 gallons per acre, or as a 77 per cent v/v solution (i.e. undiluted B.O.V.) without a wetting agent, at 15 to 20 gallons per acre. In diluting sulphuric acid, the acid must always be added slowly to the water and not vice-versa. Acid is corrosive to many metals.

135. Pentachlorophenol may be applied at 5 lb per acre as an oil emulsion in 20 gallons of water per acre. The use of tractor fuel oil as the diluent in place of water leads to better results, and the volume rate may then be reduced to 10 to 15 gallons per acre. Even in fuel oil however, this chemical is slower in action than the first four mentioned above.

136. Sodium monochloroacetate may be applied at 15 lb in 20 to 100 gallons of water per acre with added wetting agent. This chemical is generally slower to act than the first four mentioned above.

NOTES ON TECHNIQUE

137. It is important that the spray should penetrate the crop and best results follow the use of high spraying pressures. The effect of a chemical desiccant is to arrest any further development of the seed and it is important not to spray too soon, otherwise there may be a large proportion of immature seed in the harvested crop. The crop should be sprayed, other conditions permitting, when the maximum yield of mature seed can be expected. If sprayed too early, the crop may yield a very high proportion of unripe seed, which can result in a worthless sample. Efficient harvesting of clover by the combine-harvester depends upon correct setting of the machine and maintaining a slow forward speed to avoid overloading. Desiccated clover will require a different setting from that for leafy crops. (For details of the use of combine-harvesters for harvesting clover seed see the National Institute of Agricultural Botany's Herbage Seed Growers' Leaflet No. 4, 'Harvesting and Threshing Grass and Clover Seed'.)

138. [For Information] In all crops there seems to be advantages in using a quick-acting chemical which shows its effects within a few hours of application. The technique is rarely successful in wet weather, when re-growth can occur to make harvesting more difficult. The maximum benefit may be obtained in hot dry weather by allowing harvest to proceed quickly before the weather breaks. It is therefore advisable to make use of the long-range forecast service, and to time spraying to coincide with a 48-hour dry spell. In general, there is a period of about 10 days during which clover seed crops have reached the right stage for cutting, and spraying and harvesting should if possible be within this period. *Red clover* can usually be combined direct, and the aim should be to combine-harvest within two to three days of spraying. Under good conditions, this may be less. *White clover* must usually be cut first and then threshed with a combine-harvester fitted with a pick-up attachment. In many cases it is possible to spray one day and to cut the next, when the combine-harvester may start picking up the crop two to three hours after cutting. In really good weather it has been possible to spray in the morning, cut in the afternoon, and combine later the same day. If harvest is delayed too long after spraying, white clover heads will fall to the ground and be lost. When the crop is very short desiccation is not necessary and may even make the problem of harvesting more difficult. *Lucerne* is not grown for seed to any great extent in this country. Experience suggests, however, that treatment may be similar to red clover. Germination tests have indicated that the viability of clover seed taken from chemically desiccated drops is not impaired, but the proportion of 'hard' seed is occasionally increased.

WARNING REGARDING HERBICIDES TOXIC TO LIVESTOCK

139. Where dinoseb, diquat, DNOC or pentachlorophenol have been used, on no account should any part of the crop be fed to stock after threshing. Stock should not be allowed to enter the harvested field until at least 10 days after harvesting in the case of dinoseb, DNOC and pentachlorophenol and 21 days after spraying in the case of diquat, to give time for spray residues to disappear.

POTATO HAULM

140. Dinoseb, specially formulated for crop desiccation, can be applied at 1·8 to 2·7 lb in 40 to 100 gallons of water per acre, the higher dose being used on vigorous haulm.

141. Diquat can be applied at 8 to 11 oz in 20 to 40 gallons of water per acre by land sprayer, or in 2½ to 5 gallons of water per acre from the air. Not more than 8 oz per acre should be used on the variety King Edward. Leaf kill with diquat is rapid (3 to 4 days), while kill of stems takes place rather more slowly (10 to 14 days).

142. DNOC, formulated in oil as an emulsifiable concentrate, can be used at the rate of 3 lb of DNOC per acre, at a volume rate of 25 gallons or more per acre.

143. Sulphuric acid as a 12 per cent v/v solution may be applied at 100 gallons per acre (i.e. 12 gallons of 100 per cent acid in 88 gallons of water, or 15 gallons of B.O.V. in 85 gallons of water). B.O.V. may be used undiluted at the rate of 20 gallons per acre. In diluting sulphuric acid, the acid must always be added slowly to the water and not vice-versa. Acid is corrosive to many metals.

144. Fluid Coal Tar Oils containing not less than 20 per cent of phenols, of which not less than 80 per cent distil within the range of 220° to 330°C can be applied without dilution at 25 to 30 gallons per acre for normal conditions and 30 to 35 gallons on vigorous haulm in the early season (e.g. in seed production). The sprayed foliage appears oil-soaked within an hour or two of the application and the leaves are killed within about five days. Tar oil fractions are non-corrosive to metals but can cause smarting and reddening of the skin.

145. Sodium chlorate should be applied at 15 lb per acre in areas of low autumn rainfall, increasing to 30 lb where rainfall is high. A high or medium volume rate should be used. Increasing the dose above 15 lb in low rainfall areas does not generally increase its efficiency, and may be harmful to the succeeding crop especially where this is winter sown. Sodium chlorate is only moderately effective as a potato haulm destroyer as it does not readily kill the stems. Warning of the fire hazard connected with the use of sodium chlorate is given in Chapter I.

NOTES ON TECHNIQUE

146. The destruction of potato haulm may be carried out to stop the growth of tubers, to facilitate the mechanical lifting of potatoes or to prevent the spread of blight from foliage to tubers. All recommended methods of haulm destruction, including mechanical means, are effective for stopping growth and/or making harvesting easier, provided the treatments are carried out 10 to 14 days prior to lifting. With mechanical haulm destruction a full 14 days should be allowed, as the blight fungus may continue to produce spores on the cut debris in the drills until this dries up. For the prevention of the spread of blight to the tubers it is necessary to spray with a haulm destroyer before the blight has spread to any extent through the crop (such early treatment may reduce yield), and the spray used should produce a quick kill. For the prevention of tuber infection in the soil, good soil cover, blight preventive spraying of the foliage and the use of the more blight resistant varieties are important, but the correct timing of the application of haulm killing chemical can help to reduce to a minimum the risk of tuber infection by blight spores. It is important with all sprays that the foliage should be thoroughly covered. With the exception of diquat and sulphuric acid, fine weather is essential for some time following spraying. Sulphuric acid may give better results when applied during damp or misty weather, and diquat, being readily absorbed into plant foliage, can be applied with success even if light rain falls immediately after application.

147. Normally haulm destruction has no adverse effect on tuber quality, but instances have occurred of discoloration of the tubers following the treatment of actively growing foliage with some of the herbicides recommended. The conditions leading to this damage are not fully understood, but drought appears to be a predisposing factor.

EFFECT ON WEEDS

148. *Stellaria media* (chickweed) and other low growing weeds in the potato rows can be effectively killed, where the spray penetrates the foliage, by all these chemicals. *Stellaria media* which is 'spongy' and wet may prove difficult to kill.

WARNING REGARDING HERBICIDES TOXIC TO LIVESTOCK

149. Where dinoseb and DNOC have been used, stock must be kept out of treated areas for a period of at least 10 days, and a period of 10 days must elapse between spraying and lifting of the tubers. Where diquat has been used stock must be kept out of treated areas for at least 3 weeks.

CHAPTER III

RECOMMENDATIONS FOR THE USE OF HERBICIDES IN HORTICULTURE

The use of herbicides for weed control in horticultural crops is rapidly expanding, and as a result of experimental work and field experience during the past two years, it has been possible to amplify considerably the recommendations and information presented in the previous edition of this *Handbook*. Notes are included on the factors which affect the successful use of residual soil-acting herbicides in horticulture. The technique of contact pre-emergence spraying is one which is applicable to many different crops, and is dealt with in paragraphs preceding the recommendations for individual crops. Weed control methods for use in vegetable crops (page 88), fruit crops (page 100), flower crops and ornamentals (page 110) and lawns and sports turf (page 116) are then described.

USE OF RESIDUAL HERBICIDES IN HORTICULTURE

150. Residual soil-applied herbicides used in horticulture include chlorpropham, monuron, diuron, simazine, atrazine, dinoseb-amine, 2,4-DES and mixtures of chlorpropham plus fenuron, chlorpropham plus diuron and endothal plus propham. Recommendations for their use can be found in the paragraphs relating to particular crops. For maximum effectiveness, residual herbicides should be applied to weed-free ground, and they then kill weed seedlings which germinate during a period of weeks following application. The degree of weed control which is obtained, and the risk of crop damage which is entailed, depend to a considerable extent on soil and climatic conditions, of which the following are among the more important.

Soil type. In general, herbicidal activity is greatest on light mineral soils such as sands and silts which are deficient in clay and in organic matter. On heavier soils and on those with a high content of organic matter, part of the herbicide which is applied is rendered non-available to the plants, so that on these soils weeds are less effectively controlled. This is especially true of black fen soils, where such herbicides as chlorpropham may be entirely ineffective at normal doses. The downward movement of residual herbicides under the influence of rainfall is also affected by soil type, and is greatest on light, sandy or silt soils. It is often necessary therefore to vary the dose according to the type of soil, and in the paragraphs for individual crops a range of doses is given in these instances. Some residual pre-emergence treatments, though safe on loams, cannot be recommended for use on very light soils because of the risk that downward movement and subsequent crop damage may occur, should heavy rain follow application.

Soil moisture. For maximum effectiveness, adequate soil moisture is essential, and the best results are usually obtained when the herbicide can be applied to moist soil during a showery period. If applied during a period of dry weather, the herbicide may remain on the soil surface and weed seedlings may then become established before the herbicide has become active, so that poor control is obtained. With 2,4-D E S, soil moisture is necessary so that the conversion to 2,4-D can take place in the soil.

Temperature. With most residual herbicides, best results are obtained when the soil is warm and moist, so that conditions are favourable to rapid weed germination. These conditions are, however, most favourable to rapid disappearance of the herbicides from the soil. With chlorpropham especially, high temperatures lead to rapid disappearance, and this herbicide is more effective under cool conditions.

151. When used correctly, residual herbicides can be of great value to horticulture. It is stressed, however, that the doses and times of application recommended for individual crops should be adhered to, otherwise there may be a risk of incurring crop damage. When used as pre-emergence treatments, in most instances crop safety depends to some extent on the protection afforded by the layer of soil above the crop seed. It is therefore important that the drilling should be even and the seed sown as deeply as possible, consistent with the requirements for good germination.

CONTACT PRE-EMERGENCE SPRAYING

152. This technique consists essentially of applying just before crop emergence a spray of a contact herbicide in order to kill the seedling weeds that have emerged before the crop. A general description of the technique will be found on page 8. The following notes give further details of the herbicides available for this purpose and of their method of use, and indicate the scope for their employment in horticulture. It must be stressed that worthwhile results will only be obtained when circumstances are such that an appreciable number of weed seedlings appears before the crop emerges, and that the control achieved is usually only temporary.

VAPORIZING OIL

153. Ordinary tractor vaporizing oil applied undiluted at doses of from 40 to 80 gallons per acre effectively kills a wide range of seedling weeds (see Table 10) and is especially useful where *Poa annua* (annual meadow grass) and

Stellaria media (chickweed) predominate. Applications made just before the first crop seedlings emerge have given good results on many vegetable and sown flower crops. Vaporizing oil can also be used on anemones, just before the first fronds emerge, and on daffodils and tulips before shoot emergence has begun.

SULPHURIC ACID

154. For contact pre-emergence work, sulphuric acid is usually applied in a concentration of 10 to 12·5 per cent v/v at 100 gallons per acre. A suitable wetting agent, preferably of the sulphonated oil type, should be incorporated at the rate of 1 pint per 100 gallons of spray, as this gives better control of those weeds that are difficult to wet (see Table 10). Sulphuric acid is an effective herbicide, although *Poa annua* (annual meadow grass) is not usually killed, and has been used as a contact pre-emergence treatment on many crops, particularly on onions and leeks. It can also be applied before shoot emergence of daffodils and tulips. Sulphuric acid tends to be unpopular, however, because of the need for special resistant spraying machinery and because it is unpleasant to handle. The undiluted acid can also be used as a pre-emergence spray at doses of 15 to 18 gallons of B.O.V. per acre, employing a machine which gives good coverage at these volume rates. Concentrated acid is less corrosive to metals than is dilute acid, but extreme care is required both in handling and in the actual spraying.

CRESYLIC ACIDS

155. Proprietary preparations containing cresylic acids are now available for contact pre-emergence use. These consist of mixtures of chemicals and it is therefore not possible to relate doses to any one active ingredient. When applied according to the manufacturers' instructions, cresylic acids give good control of broad-leaved weed seedlings and such formulations have been used extensively in recent years for pre-emergence weed control in a wide range of vegetable and flower crops.

PENTACHLOROPHENOL

156. Proprietary formulations containing pentachlorophenol in a non-persistent, emulsifiable oil have now been on the market for a number of years. For pre-emergence use on sown crops, the usual dose is equivalent to 3 to 4 lb per acre of pentachlorophenol, applied in from 30 to 100 gallons of water. These formulations have given good results when used on large-seeded crops such as runner and broad beans, but ther have been instances of damage to onions and red beet, usually when the crop has been grown on a light, sandy soil and heavy rain has followed spraying. At doses of 1 to 3 lb per acre, pentachlorophenol has also been used on annual flower crops, but even at these low doses there appears to be some risk of damage to crops that have very small seeds and are therefore sown shallowly. Manufacturers of individual products containing pentachlorophenol list the crops for which their products can be used as a pre-emergence spray, and their directions should be followed. At higher doses, pentachlorophenol is used as a pre-emergence treatment on bulb crops (see paragraph 282), and at these doses some residual effect is obtained.

DIQUAT

157. Proprietary formulations of diquat which include a wetter have given good results as a contact pre-emergence treatment for killing seedling broad-leaved weeds in a wide variety of sown crops. The normal dose is equivalent to 6 oz diquat per acre, but where the weeds have passed the seedling stage, 12 oz per acre may be required. Diquat acts very rapidly and rainfall a short time after application has little effect on its performance. On reaching the soil, diquat is inactivated, so that applications can be made immediately before the crop begins to emerge. Diquat is also useful for removing weed vegetation prior to the emergence of bulb crops.

PARAQUAT

158. Paraquat, formulated with a wetter, may be used as an alternative to diquat as a contact pre-emergence treatment, and is more effective than diquat against seedling grasses. The normal dose is equivalent to 8 oz per acre, or 16 oz per acre where the weeds have passed the seedling stage.

SECTION (i) VEGETABLES

ASPARAGUS (established beds)

159. Contact sprays (see paragraphs 152 to 158) may be applied before the first 'spears' emerge to control seedling weeds that have appeared during early spring.

160. Granular calcium cyanamide may be applied to the beds at doses of 3–6 cwt per acre before 'spear' emergence to control germinating weeds.

161. Monuron or diuron may be applied for the control of seedling annual weeds at 0·70 to 1·5 lb per acre on light, sandy soils and 1·5 to 3 lb per acre on soils with a high clay or organic matter content. The spray may be applied at medium or high volume, as a band or overall treatment, after the beds have been finally worked, during the period beginning four weeks before the 'spears' emerge and ending during the early cutting period. A second application may be made immediately following completion of cutting, provided that the dose per application does not exceed 2·5 lb per acre. Monuron and diuron are formulated as wettable powders and continuous agitation of the suspension is necessary to prevent settling out in the spray tank. Monuron and diuron persist in the soil for several months and kill weeds as they emerge. Most annual species are susceptible (see Table 11), but *Fumaria* spp. (fumitory) and *Veronica* spp. (speedwell) are resistant.

162. Simazine can be applied at a dose of 1·5 lb per acre for the control of seedling annual weeds. The spray may be applied at medium or high volume, as a band or overall treatment, after the beds have been finally worked but before 'spear' emergence. Simazine is formulated as a wettable powder and continuous agitation of the suspension is necessary to prevent settling out in the spray tank. Simazine persists in the soil for several months and kills weeds as they emerge. Most annual species are susceptible (see Table 11), but the degree of control obtained may be poor under dry conditions and where the soil has a high organic matter content.

163. MCPA-salt may be applied during summer, after the cutting season is over, as a high volume directed spray at doses of up to 32 oz per acre for the control of susceptible perennial weeds (see Table 9). It is desirable that the weeds should be well grown and the spray should be directed by hand lance on to the weed foliage, avoiding contact with the asparagus stems and fern. This method has proved particularly useful as a spot treatment for the control of *Convolvulus arvensis* (field bindweed), but repeated treatments in subsequent years may be necessary to secure eradication.

164. Dalapon can be used for the control of perennial grasses such as *Agropyron repens* (couch). If shoots of these grasses are present in spring, before the first 'spears' emerge, dalapon may be applied at a dose of 7·5 lb per acre as a medium volume spray. It can also be applied in summer, after the cutting season is over and the fern is well grown, but the spray must then be directed by hand lance on to the grass foliage and contact with the asparagus fern must be avoided, otherwise damage will result. At a concentration of 0·75 lb in 10 gallons of water, dalapon is useful for the spot treatment of *Agropyron repens* in asparagus beds.

ASPARAGUS (seed-beds)

165. Asparagus seed germinates very slowly, and contact pre-emergence treatments (see paragraphs 152 to 158) can give useful control of seedling weeds that emerge before the crop.

166. [Tentative] Monuron at 1 lb per acre may be applied as a medium or high volume spray shortly after sowing for the control of annual weeds (see Table 11). It is important that this dose should not be exceeded, as on light soils under conditions of heavy rainfall, higher doses have caused severe crop damage.

BEANS (broad)

167. Contact pre-emergence sprays (see paragraphs 152 to 158) may be used to kill seedling weeds that emerge before the crop.

168. Simazine at 0·75 to 1 lb per acre may be applied as a medium or high volume spray within a few days after sowing for the control of annual weeds (see Table 11) in spring-sown broad beans. The lower dose should be used on light or medium soils. Agitation is necessary in order to prevent the suspension settling out in the spray tank. It is important that the seed-bed should be left with a fine, even tilth and that the beans should be sown not less than one inch below the soil surface. If heavy rain follows application, some marginal blackening of the leaves may occur, but this should not affect yield.

169. Chlorpropham 1 lb plus fenuron 0·25 lb per acre or chlorpropham 1 lb plus diuron 0·2 to 0·4 lb per acre may be applied as a medium or high volume spray after drilling, but before any weeds have emerged and at least a week before crop emergence, for the control of annual weeds in spring-sown broad beans. It is important that the seed-bed should be left with a fine, even tilth and that the beans should be sown not less than one inch below the soil surface. This treatment should not be used on very light, sandy or silt soils deficient in clay and organic matter, as on such soils crop damage may result.

170. Dinoseb-amine may be applied at a dose of 3 to 4 lb per acre as a medium or high volume pre-emergence spray for the control of broad-leaved annual weeds in spring-sown broad beans. The beans should be sown not less than one inch below the soil surface, and the spray can be applied at any time after sowing until about three days before the crop is expected to emerge.

BEANS (french)

171. Contact pre-emergence sprays (see paragraphs 152 to 158) may be used to kill seedling weeds that emerge before the crop.

172. Dinoseb-amine may be applied at a dose of 3 to 4 lb per acre as a medium or high volume pre-emergence spray for the control of broad-leaved annual weeds. The beans should be sown not less than one inch below the soil surface, and the spray can be applied at any time after sowing until about three days before the crop is expected to emerge. Where the crop rows are widely spaced, a saving in the cost of material can be made if the spray is applied as a band treatment over the rows only, and cultivation relied on to keep the alleys free from weeds. There is some evidence that the climbing variety Blue Lake may be rather more susceptible than other varieties, and until further information is available, treatment of this variety cannot be recommended.

BEANS (runner)

173. Contact pre-emergence sprays (see paragraphs 152 to 158) may be used to kill seedling weeds that emerge before the crop.

174. Dinoseb-amine may be applied at a dose of 3 to 4 lb per acre as a medium or high volume pre-emergence spray for the control of broad-leaved annual weeds. The beans should be sown not less than one inch below the soil surface, and the spray can be applied at any time after sowing until about three days before the crop is expected to emerge. Where the crop rows are widely spaced, a saving in the cost of material can be made if the spray is applied as a band treatment over the rows only, and cultivation relied on to keep the alleys free from weeds.

BEET (red)

175. Contact pre-emergence sprays (see paragraphs 152 to 158) may be used to kill seedling weeds that emerge before the crop.

176. Sodium nitrate at a dose of 2·5 cwt in 100 gallons of water per acre may be applied as a post-emergence spray when the beet have at least two true expanded leaves for the control of annual weeds (see Table 10). If the weeds are small in relation to the size of the beet, it is preferable to wait until the beet have four true leaves, since scorching of the crop is less likely to occur at this stage. The addition of a wetting agent to the spray is important. The usual quantity of wetting agent required is 0·5 to 1 gallon per 100 gallons of spray, but proprietary wetting agents vary both in their suitability and the amount required, and the manufacturers should be approached for their advice. The most rapid results from this treatment are obtained under warm, humid conditions, and it is important that there should be a period of 12 to 24 hours of fine weather after spraying. The beet may show temporary wilting, scorching or yellowing after spraying, but these symptoms soon disappear and the crop derives manurial benefit from the sodium nitrate. This treatment has given very variable results in practice, being less reliable in the drier eastern counties than in the northern and western regions of the British Isles. *It should therefore be regarded only as an emergency measure for use when a crop is in danger of being swamped by a dense stand of susceptible weed species.*

177. **[Tentative]** A mixture of endothal plus propham may be applied immediately after drilling as a medium volume spray for the control of annual weeds. It is important that the dose should be adjusted according to the type of soil, as follows:

Very light sand 1·5 lb endothal plus 1·125 lb propham per acre
Sand   2·0 ,,   ,,   ,, 1·5 ,,   ,,   ,,   ,,
Light loam   3·0 ,,   ,,   ,, 2·25 ,,   ,,   ,,   ,,
Medium loam   4·0 ,,   ,,   ,, 3·0 ,,   ,,   ,,   ,,

This treatment does not give good results on heavy clays, nor on black fen or other soils with a high organic matter content. In order that the herbicide may become active before weed seedlings establish, some rain is necessary within a week after application for maximum efficiency. Most annual weeds are susceptible, but *Atriplex patula* (orache), *Chenopodium album* (fat hen), *Galium aparine* (cleavers) and *Sinapis* spp. (charlock, white mustard) are relatively tolerant.

BRUSSELS SPROUTS (seed-beds)

178. Contact pre-emergence sprays (see paragraphs 152 to 158) may be used to kill seedling weeds that emerge before the crop.

179. Sodium monochloroacetate at a dose of 20 lb per acre may be applied as a medium or high volume spray when the sprouts have 2 to 4 true leaves for the control of some annual broad-leaved weeds (see Table 10). Some scorch may occur, but this is not usually serious. Wetting agents must not be added to the solution*, otherwise crop damage will result, and a coarse, low-pressure spray is desirable. A period of at least 12 hours of fine weather after spraying is essential.

BRUSSELS SPROUTS (transplanted)

180. Sodium monochloroacetate at a dose of 20 lb per acre may be applied as a medium or high volume spray 7 to 10 days after planting out, when a flush of seedling weeds has appeared. Some common weeds, such as *Chenopodium album* (fat hen), are not killed by this treatment (see Table 10). The crop may suffer some scorch, but this is not usually serious. Wetting agents must not be added to the solution*, otherwise crop damage will result, and a coarse, low-pressure spray is desirable. A period of at least 12 hours of fine weather after spraying is essential.

CABBAGE (spring, seed-beds and direct-drilled)

181. Contact pre-emergence sprays (see paragraphs 152 to 158) may be used to kill seedling weeds that emerge before the crop.

* N.B. All references in the Handbook are to chemicals without added 'wetters' and 'spreaders'. These should not be added to sprays unless specifically recommended.

182. Sodium monochloroacetate at a dose of 20 lb per acre may be applied as a medium or high volume spray when the cabbage have 2 to 4 true leaves for the control of some annual broad-leaved weeds (see Table 10). Some scorch may occur, but this is not usually serious. Wetting agents must not be added to the solution*, otherwise crop damage will result, and a coarse, low-pressure spray is desirable. A period of at least 12 hours of fine weather after spraying is essential.

183. [For Information] A mixture of endothal plus propham applied as a medium volume spray immediately after drilling, as described for red beet (paragraph 177) is reported as having given good results. Further experience of this method is required before any recommendation can be made.

CABBAGE (spring, transplanted)

184. Sodium monochloroacetate at a dose of 20 lb per acre may be applied as a medium or high volume spray 7 to 10 days after planting out, when a flush of seedling weeds has appeared. Some common weeds, such as *Chenopodium album* (fat hen), are not killed by this treatment (see Table 10). The crop may suffer some scorch, but this is not usually serious. Wetting agents must not be added to the solution*, otherwise crop damage will result, and a coarse, low-pressure spray is desirable. A period of at least 12 hours of fine weather after spraying is essential.

CARROTS

185. Contact pre-emergence sprays (see paragraphs 152 to 158) may be used to kill seedling weeds that emerge before the crop.

186. Certain mineral oils may be used for the selective post-emergence control of many annual weeds (see Table 10) in carrot crops. Proprietary selective mineral oils are approved by the Agricultural Chemicals Approval Scheme which requires that they shall have a distillation range of between 140 and 210°C and an aromatic content of not less than 15 per cent and not more than 25 per cent of the oil. These oils are used at doses of 40 to 80 gallons per acre (or lower doses per acre if applied as band treatments over the crop rows only) and should be applied after the carrots have fully developed their cotyledons and while the weeds are still small. Spraying should not be attempted after the carrots reach 'pencil thickness'. Frame-grown carrots can be similarly treated provided that adequate ventilation can be given during the period following treatment and there is no risk of frost.

187. Most tractor vaporizing oils can be used in a similar manner on maincrop carrots, provided it is not intended to market the thinnings, but these oils

* N.B. All references in the Handbook are to chemicals without added 'wetters' and 'spreaders'. These should not be added to sprays unless specifically recommended.

should not be applied before the carrots have two true leaves. Because different brands and batches of vaporizing oils vary in their effects on plants, a test should be carried out first to verify that the particular oil is satisfactory. Late spraying should be avoided so as not to incur a risk of tainting the crop, and vaporizing oils should not be used on carrots grown for bunching, either outdoors or in frames.

188. [Tentative] Chlorpropham at 2 lb per acre may be applied within three days after drilling as a medium or high volume spray for the control of many annual weeds (see Table 11). The seed should be drilled as deeply as possible consistent with obtaining good germination, and the treatment should not be used on very light, sandy or silt soils deficient in clay and organic matter, as on such soils crop damage may result.

189. [For information] Chlorpropham 1 lb plus diuron 0·2 lb per acre applied as a medium or high volume spray within three days after drilling has given good results on light or medium loams. This treatment should not be used on very light, sandy or silt soils deficient in clay and organic matter, as on such soils crop damage may result.

CELERY

190. [For information] Proprietary selective mineral oils (see paragraph 186) applied at 50 gallons per acre have been successfully used for weed control in seed-beds. Good results have been obtained with sprays applied at any time from the cotyledon stage until the crop has 4 to 5 true leaves.

191. [For information] Chlorpropham at 1 to 2 lb per acre has given good results when applied as a post-planting spray on pricked-out celery. The application should be made within a week after pricking out; if delayed beyond this time, crop damage may result.

LEEKS (seed-beds and direct-drilled)

192. Contact pre-emergence sprays (see paragraphs 152 to 158) may be used to kill seedling weeds that emerge before the crop.

193. Sodium monochloroacetate at a dose of 20 to 30 lb per acre may be applied as a medium or high volume spray for the control of some annual broad-leaved weeds (see Table 10). It should be applied after the plants have passed the crook stage but before they have four leaves. Wetting agents must not be added to the solution, otherwise crop damage will result. A period of at least 12 hours of fine weather after spraying is essential, and spraying should not be attempted if frost is imminent.

194. [For Information] Chlorpropham at 2 lb per acre, chlorpropham 1 lb plus fenuron 0·25 lb per acre and chlorpropham 1 lb plus diuron 0·2 lb per acre have all given good results on light and medium loams when applied as medium or high volume sprays within three days after drilling. The seed should be drilled at a depth of one inch, and the treatments should not be used on very light, sandy or silt soils deficient in clay and organic matter, as on such soils crop damage may result.

LEEKS (transplanted)

195. Sulphuric acid may be used as a post-planting spray for the control of broad-leaved annual weeds that appear shortly after planting. It should be applied within a month after planting and the strength of the spray will depend on the weed species present (see Table 10), but is usually from 5·5 to 10 per cent v/v applied at 100 gallons per acre.

196. [Tentative] Chlorpropham 2 lb per acre, chlorpropham 1 lb plus fenuron 0·25 lb per acre or chlorpropham 1 lb plus diuron 0·2 lb per acre may be applied as a medium or high volume spray after the leeks have become established for the control of annual weeds. These treatments should not be used on very light, sandy or silt soils, as on such soils crop damage may result.

LETTUCE (seed-beds and direct-drilled)

197. [For Information] Chlorpropham at 1 lb per acre, applied as a medium or high volume spray immediately after drilling, has given good control of susceptible annual weeds (see Table 11) both in frames and in the open. The treatment should not be used on very light, sandy or silt soils, as on such soils crop damage may result.

LETTUCE (transplanted)

198. [Tentative] Chlorpropham at 1 lb per acre may be applied as a high volume spray to weed-free soil a few days before planting out lettuce under glass for the control of susceptible annual weeds (see Table 11). Watering after application should be avoided. Some instances of injury to frame lettuce have been reported when sunny periods, leading to high temperatures under the glass, have followed planting.

ONIONS (bulb, direct-drilled)

199. Contact pre-emergence sprays (see paragraphs 152 to 158) may be used to kill seedling weeds that emerge before the crop.

200. Sulphuric acid may be applied as a post-emergence spray after the onions have passed the crook stage and are straightening up. The strength of the spray will depend on the weed species present, but is usually from 5·5 to 10 per cent v/v applied at 100 gallons per acre (see Table 10).

201. Sodium monochloroacetate at a dose of 20 to 30 lb per acre may be applied as a medium or high volume post-emergence spray for the control of some annual broad-leaved weeds (see Table 10). The onions should have passed the crook stage and have straightened up. Wetting agents must not be added to the solution, otherwise crop damage will result. A period of at least 12 hours of fine weather after spraying is essential, and spraying should not be attempted if frost is imminent.

202. [Tentative] Chlorpropham 1 to 2 lb per acre or chlorpropham 1 lb plus diuron 0·2 lb per acre may be applied as a medium or high volume spray within three days after drilling for the control of annual weeds. The seed should be drilled at a depth of one inch, and the treatments should not be used on very light, sandy or silt soils, as on such soils crop damage may result.

ONIONS (bulb, grown from sets)

203. [For Information] Chlorpropham 2 lb per acre, chlorpropham 1 lb plus fenuron 0·25 lb per acre and chlorpropham 1 lb plus diuron 0.2 lb per acre have all given good control of susceptible weed species when applied as medium or high volume sprays to planted onion sets prior to shoot emergence.

ONIONS (salad, spring or green)

204. Contact pre-emergence sprays (see paragraphs 152 to 158) may be used to kill seedling weeds that emerge before the crop.

205. Sulphuric acid may be applied as a post-emergence spray after the onions have passed the crook stage and are straightening up if a heavy infestation of susceptible weeds develops. The strength of the spray will depend on the weed species present but is usually from 5·5 to 10 per cent v/v applied at 100 gallons per acre (see Table 10). The leaf scorch which may occur is more serious with salad onions than with bulb onions, as it detracts from the appearance of the produce.

206. Sodium monochloroacetate at a dose of 20 to 30 lb per acre may be applied as a medium or high volume post-emergence spray for the control of some broad-leaved annual weeds (see Table 10). The onions should have passed the crook stage and have straightened up. Wetting agents must not be added to the solution, otherwise crop damage will result. A period of at least 12 hours of fine weather after spraying is essential, and spraying should not be attempted if frost is imminent or if the temperature is likely to rise above 80°F. If crops sown for over-wintering have not reached the required stage of growth before mid-August, spraying is not advisable as recovery from the check received may not be complete.

207. [**Tentative**] Chlorpropham 1 to 2 lb per acre, chlorpropham 1 lb plus fenuron 0·25 lb per acre or chlorpropham 1 lb plus diuron 0·2 lb per acre may be applied as a medium or high volume spray within three days after drilling for the control of annual weeds. The seed should be drilled at a depth of one inch, and the treatments should not be used on very light, sandy or silt soils, as on such soils crop damage may result.

PARSLEY

208. Contact pre-emergence sprays (see paragraphs 152 to 158) may be used to kill seedling weeds that emerge before the crop.

209. Mineral oils may be applied as post-emergence sprays as described for carrots (paragraph 186). This crop is rather more susceptible than carrots and should not be sprayed until two true leaves have developed.

210. [**For Information**] Chlorpropham at 1 to 2 lb per acre and chlorpropham 1 lb plus diuron 0·2 lb per acre have given good control of susceptible annual weeds when applied as medium or high volume sprays within three days after drilling on light or medium loams. These treatments should not be used on very light, sandy or silt soils, as on such soils crop damage may result.

PARSNIPS

211. Contact pre-emergence sprays (see paragraphs 152 to 158) may be used to kill seedling weeds that emerge before the crop.

212. Mineral oils may be applied as post-emergence sprays as described for carrots (paragraph 186). This crop is rather more susceptible than carrots and should not be sprayed until two true leaves have developed.

213. [**For Information**] Chlorpropham at 1 to 2 lb per acre and chlorpropham 1 lb plus diuron 0·2 lb per acre have given good control of susceptible annual weeds when applied as medium or high volume sprays within three days after drilling on light or medium loams. These treatments should not be used on very light, sandy or silt soils, as on such soils crop damage may result.

PEAS (market-garden, for picking green)

For field, drying and vining peas see paragraphs 71 to 78 in Chapter II.

214. Contact pre-emergence sprays (see paragraphs 152 to 158) may be used to kill seedling weeds that emerge before the crop.

215. Dinoseb-amine at doses of up to 2·5 lb per acre in a volume of 40 gallons of water or above may be used on most varieties of peas as a post-emergence spray for the control of annual weeds (see Table 10). Spraying should not be attempted when the temperature is lower than 45°F or higher than 85°F. If good growing conditions precede spraying and the temperature at the time of application is higher than 65°F, doses of between 1·5 and 2 lb per acre should be used. If spraying follows a period of dry, cool weather, so that the weed growth is 'hard', a dose of more than 2 lb per acre may be required. The crop may be sprayed at any time after the first leaf has expanded, but before the plants attain a height of 10 inches. Best results are usually obtained by spraying at an early stage of growth, after all the weeds have emerged but while they are still small seedlings. Spraying should not be attempted when the crop foliage is wet nor when rain is expected within 12 hours. If the crop has been damaged by high winds or blowing soil, spraying should not take place until a week after the occurrence of the damage. Experience has shown that whilst most varieties of peas grown for picking green can be sprayed with dinoseb-amine, the following varieties tend to be susceptible, and spraying of these varieties is not recommended except as a last resort: Duplex, Foremost, Early Bird, Exquisite, Gregory's Surprise, Morse's Market, Pilot, Sharpe's Vedette, Sharpe's Miracle, Thomas Laxton and Kelvedon Triumph. Dinoseb-amine is preferable to dinoseb-ammonium for use on market-garden peas, since the latter causes a greater amount of scorch and check to growth.

216. M C P B-salt may be applied at doses up to 32 oz per acre for the control of annual and some perennial weeds (see Table 9). High, medium or low volume may be used, and the spray should be applied when the peas have from 3 to 6 expanded leaves. This treatment can be applied to a number of varieties including: Alaska, Canner's Perfection, Charles I, Clipper, Dark-skinned Perfection, Early Bird, Lincoln, Onward and Perfected Freezer. With these varieties marked bending and distortion may appear within a day or two of spraying but this is outgrown within about two weeks; there is no marked depressing effect on yield, nor is maturity delayed. Some doubt exists as to the safety of this treatment on the varieties Gregory's Surprise, Kelvedon Wonder, Meteor, Thomas Laxton and Shasta. The herbicide is of most use in pea crops where *Chenopodium album* (fat hen) or *Cirsium arvense* (creeping thistle) is the dominant weed. For effective control of the latter species, hoeing should stop for at least 10 days before spraying.

217. Chlorpropham at 1 lb plus fenuron at 0·25 lb per acre or chlorpropham at 1 lb plus diuron at 0·2 to 0·4 lb per acre may be applied as a medium or high volume spray after drilling, but before any weeds have emerged and at least a week before crop emergence, for the control of annual weeds in spring-sown peas. It is important that the seed-bed should be left with a fine, even tilth and that the peas should be sown not less than one inch below the soil surface. This treatment should not be used on very light, sandy or silt

soils deficient in clay and organic matter, as on such soils crop damage may result.

218. [Tentative] Dinoseb-amine may be applied at a dose of 3 to 4 lb per acre as a medium or high volume pre-emergence spray for the control of broad-leaved annual weeds in spring-sown peas. The lower dose should be used on the lighter soils and the peas should be sown not less than one inch below the soil surface. The spray can be applied at any time after sowing until about three days before the crop is expected to emerge.

RHUBARB

219. Dalapon may be applied at a dose of 7·5 lb per acre for the control of perennial grasses such as *Agropyron repens* (couch). Spraying should be carried out in autumn, when grass foliage is still present but after the rhubarb foliage has died down and the crowns have become dormant. The spray should be directed on to the grass foliage, avoiding the rhubarb crowns. The same treatment can also be used in early spring, again as a directed spray, avoiding the crowns and the young rhubarb leaves.

220. Chlorpropham at 2 lb plus fenuron at 0·5 lb per acre or chlorpropham at 2 lb plus diuron at 0·4 lb per acre may be applied as a medium or high volume spray when the crowns are dormant for the control of annual weeds. Treatment may be carried out in late autumn or late winter, but should not be applied after bursting of the pink membrane.

221. Simazine at 1·5 to 2 lb per acre in early spring or 2 to 2·5 lb per acre in autumn or early winter may be applied as a medium or high volume spray for the control of annual weeds (see Table 10).

SWEET CORN (direct-drilled)

222. Simazine may be applied as a residual pre-emergence spray for the control of annual weeds (see Table 10). On light soils, a dose of 1 lb per acre should be used; on heavy or more highly organic soils, 1·5 to 2 lb per acre may be required to secure adequate weed control. Weed control is least satisfactory under dry conditions. It should be borne in mind that in the event of crop failure due to bird attack or other causes, it would not be possible to sow or plant any other kind of crop in the sprayed field until the simazine had disappeared from the soil. Under normal conditions it should be possible to sow or plant another crop in autumn.

223. Atrazine may be applied as a medium or high volume spray for the control of annual weeds at any time after sowing until the weeds are 1·5 inches high. On light soils a dose of 1 lb per acre should be used; on medium or heavy soils, 1·5 lb per acre may be required. Atrazine has been found to give better results than simazine under dry conditions. It should be borne in mind that in the event of crop failure due to bird attack or other causes, it would not be possible to sow or plant any other kind of crop in the sprayed field until the atrazine had disappeared from the soil. Under normal conditions it should be possible to sow or plant another crop in autumn.

SECTION (ii) FRUIT

INTRODUCTION

224. During the past few years much progress has been made in the use of chemical methods of weed control in fruit crops. Safe and effective treatments are now available for use in orchards and it is possible to control most common weeds in bush and cane fruits by chemical means, provided that the ground is not already infested with deep-rooted perennial species.

Although weeds do not usually present as great a problem in apple and pear plantations as in soft fruit crops, herbicides are useful for controlling weed growth around recently planted trees and also in established arable and grass orchards. With young trees, where weed competition for nutrients and moisture is particularly severe, it is now possible to obtain good weed control from the time of planting. In established arable or grass orchards, ground not reached by the cultivating implement or mower may be sprayed with herbicides to eliminate expensive hand-hoeing or cutting. While the competition by shallow-rooted grass and broad-leaved weeds around established trees is unlikely to be severe, the damage due to certain pests, notably dock sawfly, and to such diseases as collar rot (*Phytophthora cactorum*) may be reduced by controlling weed growth; in addition the risk of damage to the surface roots and stems by field mice and voles will be lessened.

While the use of herbicides can greatly reduce the cost of weed control operations in apple and pear orchards, it may not always be necessary or desirable to control completely the vegetation around the trunks. Complete weed kill may allow the invasion of less desirable species, for example high doses of herbicides such as dalapon, amino triazole and paraquat may result in a grass sward being replaced by broad-leaved weeds. In many cases, therefore, it may be preferable to use a sub-lethal dose to check the vegetation rather than to kill it. Moreover, where weed growth is eradicated on soils liable to surface compaction, infiltration of rain may be prevented and water may collect around the trunk, increasing the risk of fungal infection and harm to the roots through lack of aeration. More information is needed, therefore, to determine the most suitable herbicides and doses for top fruit under different systems of management and on different soil types.

Soft-fruit growers are showing particular interest in chemical means of weed control because of the shortage of suitable workers and the high cost of hand labour. In these crops the use of herbicides possesses many advantages over cultivation in addition to reducing production costs and avoiding mechanical injury to shallow roots. For example, spraying can often be carried out in the winter when labour is more freely available, or in unsettled weather during the growing season when cultivation is impossible due to wet soil conditions. The use of a persistent soil-applied herbicide, such as simazine, enables ground to be kept weed-free for many months and sprayed plantations need less attention during the growing season than those under cultivation.

In recent years simazine has been outstanding as a herbicide in bush and cane fruits when applied under suitable conditions (see page 104). Simazine is more effective when used at relatively low doses of about 1 to 2 lb per acre on clean ground to suppress germinating weeds over a long period rather than at higher doses in an attempt to control established weeds. It is preferable therefore to take advantage of the persistent properties of simazine by planting on clean ground initially and by using this herbicide to maintain the ground in a weed-free condition from the start.

In spite of the advantages of chemical methods of weed control it is not yet certain to what extent cultivation may be reduced or eliminated in soft fruit crops. On soils liable to surface compaction, such as those with a high silt content, some cultivation may be necessary to maintain satisfactory aeration conditions and to allow better penetration of rain into the soil. Under conventional systems of planting, occasional cultivation between the rows may also be necessary to eliminate tracks left by machinery. However, recent experiments in Northern Ireland, conducted over a period of years on blackcurrants and gooseberries growing in a medium loam soil, have shown that a spray programme based on a number of herbicides can be effective in replacing cultivation for the control of weeds without any adverse effect on the crop. In these experiments a hard surface crust formed under rain impact and resulted in run-off and erosion on sloping sites, but it was found that a satisfactory soil structure in the surface layers could be maintained by means of a mulch of well-rotted farmyard manure. A straw mulch also effectively prevented erosion but sometimes resulted in increased frost damage at blossom time.

Where weeds have been controlled by herbicides alone over a period of years, it has usually been necessary to vary the spraying programme according to the weed species present and the kind and age of the fruit crop. A herbicide programme which has been used effectively in a number of bush and cane fruit plantations is one based on simazine applied at 2 lb per acre in the early spring followed by paraquat at 1 lb per acre in the early winter. Provided the ground was not infested with deep-rooted perennial weeds this programme has maintained the ground in a clean condition for a year at a total cost of approximately £12 per acre, compared with an annual cost of cultivation ranging from about £11 to £50 per acre. Wherever weeds are controlled completely by chemical means for several years, the weed seed population in the surface soil is reduced; consequently lower doses of herbicides are adequate to maintain the ground in a weed-free condition and the cost of weed control may be further decreased.

Long-term experiments are being conducted at a number of research stations to determine how weed control by herbicides may best be integrated with fruit-growing practice. While no definite recommendations on this subject can be made at present, it seems likely that the use of herbicides will result in considerable changes in present-day methods of soft fruit production.

TREE FRUITS

225. Paraquat formulated with a wetter may be applied as a directed spray at 1 to 2 lb per acre at any time of the year to control the aerial parts of grasses and broad-leaved weeds. Regrowth will occur from perennial weeds with large underground storage systems. The spray must not come into contact with the tree foliage as otherwise severe injury will occur.

226. Diquat formulated with a wetter may be applied as a directed spray at 1 to 2 lb per acre at any time of the year to control the aerial parts of grasses and broad-leaved weeds. Regrowth of grasses and perennials will occur. The treatment must be repeated once or twice for a season's weed control, but is particularly useful where a short-term control is desired or where broad-leaved annuals only are present. Care must be taken to avoid wetting the tree foliage as otherwise severe injury will occur.

227. D N O C or tar oil winter washes at normal fruit-tree spraying concentrations may be used during the summer to kill annual weeds and check broad-leaved perennials and grasses growing around the base of the fruit trees. Pentachlorophenol in miscible oil formulation may also be used for this purpose at doses of 3 to 6 lb in 100 gallons of final spray solution. These sprays should be applied at a volume rate sufficient to wet the weeds thoroughly and care must be taken to see that the spray does not come into contact with the tree foliage.

228. Mixtures of equal parts of tractor vaporizing oil and diesel oil may also be used in a similar manner. The spraying should be carried out after the weeds have started to grow in the spring, and preferably on hot sunny days. Care should be taken to avoid wetting the tree trunks as bark injury can occur, and with young trees it is safer to protect the trunks with a guard.

APPLES AND PEARS

229. Simazine at 1 to 2 lb per acre may be used annually to control germinating weeds (see Table 11). Established weeds are not usually killed and the ground should be clean cultivated before spraying. The treatment may be applied in established orchards or around newly planted trees provided the ground is well firmed. Application may be made at any time of the year when the soil is moist and good results will generally be obtained from treatment made in the late winter or early spring.

[For Information] Simazine has caused injury to stone fruits on some occasions. There is evidence of differences in the sensitivity of different varieties and root-stocks, and until further information is available, simazine cannot be recommended for these fruits.

230. MCPA or 2,4-D may be used, up to a maximum dose of 32 oz per acre, for the control of susceptible weeds in apple orchards, but great care is necessary to ensure that the spray does not come into contact with the trees. Owing to the possibility of vapour damage, ester formulations should not be used for orchard work. Every effort should be made to avoid drift, as both MCPA and 2,4-D can cause serious damage to fruit trees. The use of these materials is, therefore, best limited to spot treatments by means of knapsack or other low pressure sprayer. Booms of crop sprayers should not be used owing to the grave danger from drift, and the use of fruit tree spraying machinery should also be avoided because of the risk of contaminating subsequent pesticide sprays. Provided that spraying is not carried out at blossom time, MCPA and 2,4-D may be used at any period during the growing season. Apple varieties differ in their sensitivity to 2,4-D, Bramley's Seedling, Emneth Early and Miller's Seedling being particularly susceptible to damage. Pears are known to be more susceptible than apples to 2,4-D and MCPA, whilst for other tree fruits there is insufficient evidence on which to base recommendations.

231. Dalapon at 6 lb per acre applied round the trunks will effect a substantial reduction in *Agropyron repens* (couch) and other grasses. The trees should be well established and have been planted out for more than four years. The herbicide should be applied in just sufficient water to wet the grass foliage thoroughly but to avoid excessive run-off on to the soil. There is evidence of differences in response to dalapon by different varieties and rootstocks, and Cox's Orange Pippin may be less tolerant than most varieties. Repeated applications are necessary to obtain complete eradication of *Agropyron repens*.

[For Information] Dalapon has caused injury to stone fruits on some occasions and no recommendations for its use on plums, cherries or peaches can be made at present.

232. Amino triazole (activated) at 4 lb per acre may be applied around the trunks to suppress many broad-leaved weeds and grasses including *Agropyron repens* (couch). The treatment should only be used around trees that have been planted out for at least four years and are well established. Trees with injured bark should not be treated as severe leaf chlorosis may result. Application should be made before petal-fall in the spring or after picking in the autumn when the weeds are growing actively. Treatment during the dormant season is not effective.

233. [Tentative] Simazine at 5 lb per acre may be used around the base of established trees to control annual weeds and shallow-rooting perennial species. The trees should have been planted out for at least one year before this treatment is used. To be effective, simazine must reach the soil and consequently the presence of heavy weed growth at the time of spraying is undesirable. The most suitable time for application is in early spring, preferably during a showery period. Because of the possibility of a build-up of simazine in the soil, only one application at 5 lb per acre should be made each year.

234. [Tentative] Diuron at 5 lb per acre may be used to control established shallow-rooted grasses and broad-leaved annual weeds and to suppress germinating seedlings. The trees should have been planted for four years or more before this treatment is used. The most suitable time for application is in the late winter or early spring, preferably during a showery period.

235. [Tentative] A mixture of diuron at 4 lb and amino triazole (activated) at 4 lb per acre may be used to control existing weed growth and to suppress germinating weeds around the trunks of established trees which have been planted out for four years or more. Trees with injured bark should not be treated as severe leaf chlorosis may result. Application should be made in the spring before petal-fall or in the autumn after picking, while the established weeds are growing actively.

BLACKCURRANTS

236. Simazine at 1 to 2 lb per acre may be used annually from the time of planting to control germinating weeds (see Table 11). Established weeds are not usually killed and the ground should be clean cultivated before spraying. Application may be made at any time of the year when the soil is moist. Best results are generally obtained from treatment made in the late winter or early spring.

237. Chlorpropham at 2 lb per acre may be applied in the winter for the control of many germinating weeds (see Table 11). The soil should be clean at the time of treatment as established weeds are not normally controlled by this dose. *Senecio vulgaris* (groundsel) is tolerant to chlorpropham and weed control is usually less satisfactory than that obtained with simazine at 2 lb per acre.

238. Dalapon at 4 to 8 lb per acre may be applied as a directed spray to control grasses. Application may be made between autumn and early spring but to avoid crop injury, spraying should be completed before bud-burst. Dalapon at 4 lb per acre will control *Poa annua* (annual meadow grass) and seedling grasses, and may be used on bushes planted out for at least one year. A dose

of 8 lb per acre will substantially reduce perennial grasses but repeated application in successive years will usually be necessary to control *Agropyron repens*
(couch). This high dose should only be used on well-established bushes
(planted out for at least three years) and the herbicide should be applied in
just sufficient water to wet the grass foliage thoroughly but to avoid excessive
run-off on to the soil.

239. 2,4,5-TB or MCPB at 32 to 48 oz per acre may be used for the control
of *Convolvulus arvensis* and *Calystegia sepium* (bindweeds). These herbicides
should be applied in August after the crop has been picked and the growth of
the bushes has slowed down; MCPB is more liable to cause damage than
2,4,5-TB if applied before the bushes have stopped growing, but it is less expensive and will also control broad-leaved weeds such as *Cirsium* spp. (thistles)
and *Ranunculus repens* (creeping buttercup). Provided application is timed
correctly, both herbicides may be applied over the bushes. If practicable,
however, the spray should be directed on to the weed foliage avoiding the
crop as much as possible.

240. Paraquat formulated with a wetter may be applied as a carefully directed
spray at 0·5 to 1 lb per acre at any time of the year to control established
shallow-rooted grasses, annual broad-leaved weeds and creeping buttercup.
There is no danger of crop injury due to root uptake *but precautions must be
taken to avoid wetting the bushes*, as paraquat may cause serious damage to
the top growth of blackcurrants even when the crop is dormant.

241. Diquat formulated with a wetter may be applied as a carefully directed
spray at 0·5 to 1 lb per acre at any time of the year to control established annual
broad-leaved weeds and creeping buttercup. There is no danger of crop
injury due to root uptake *but precautions must be taken to avoid wetting the
bushes*, as diquat may cause serious damage to the top growth of blackcurrants even when the crop is dormant.

242. [Tentative] Diuron at 2·5 lb per acre may be applied annually to the soil
to control germinating annual weeds. The application should be made in
late winter or early spring before bud-burst and after established weeds have
been eliminated by cultivation or other means. The treatment should not be
applied to bushes planted out for less than one year.

243. [For Information] Simazine at 1 to 2 lb per acre has given good control
of germinating weeds in newly planted blackcurrant cuttings. No crop injury
occurred provided the soil was firm at the time of treatment.

244. [For Information] Simazine at 5 lb per acre has been applied to established
bushes for three successive years without any adverse effect. This treatment
gave good control of annual weeds and shallow-rooted perennials. Doses
above 5 lb per acre have occasionally caused injury and blackcurrants appear
to be more susceptible than raspberries or gooseberries to high doses of
simazine.

245. [For Information] Chlorpropham at 2 lb plus fenuron at 0·5 lb per acre applied to clean ground between mid-November and late December has given good control of winter annual weeds. At 4 lb and 1 lb per acre respectively the same mixture of herbicides has been used to suppress existing weed growth.

GOOSEBERRIES

246. Simazine at 1 to 2 lb per acre may be applied annually to clean ground to control germinating weeds (see Table 11). Best results are obtained if application is made when the soil is moist and early spring is a suitable time.
247. Paraquat formulated with a wetter may be applied as a directed spray at 0·5 to 1 lb per acre at any time of the year to control established shallow-rooted grasses, *Ranunculus repens* (creeping buttercup) and annual broad-leaved weeds. There is no risk of crop injury due to root uptake and slight wetting of dormant buds during the winter is unlikely to have any adverse effect. After bud-burst, spray drift may cause severe damage and strict precautions must be taken to avoid wetting the foliage.
248. Diquat formulated with a wetter may be applied as a directed spray at 0·5 to 1 lb per acre at any time of the year to control established *Ranunculus repens* (creeping buttercup) and annual broad-leaved weeds. There is no risk of crop injury due to root uptake and slight wetting of dormant buds during the winter is unlikely to have any adverse effect. During the growing season precautions must be taken to avoid wetting the foliage as otherwise severe injury can occur.
249. Dalapon at 4 lb per acre may be applied as a directed spray in November or December to control *Poa annua* (annual meadow grass) and seedling grasses.
250. 2,4-DES at 3 to 5 lb per acre may be used as a high volume spray during the growing season for the control of germinating weeds. The spray must be applied to clean ground, and best results will be obtained under warm, moist conditions (see paragraph 150). Weed control is usually less satisfactory than that obtained with simazine at 1 to 2 lb per acre.
251. Chlorpropham at 2 lb per acre may be applied in the winter for the control of many germinating weeds (see Table 11). The soil should be clean at the time of treatment as established weeds are not normally controlled by this dose. *Senecio vulgaris* (groundsel) is tolerant to chlorpropham and weed control is usually less satisfactory than that obtained with simazine at 2 lb per acre.
252. [Tentative] Dalapon at 8 lb per acre applied as a directed spray during November or December will effect a substantial reduction in annual and perennial grasses, but repeated applications in successive years are necessary to obtain a complete eradication of *Agropyron repens* (couch). Gooseberries

are more sensitive than blackcurrants to dalapon and this treatment may cause temporary injury. The treatment should only be used on well established bushes (planted out for at least three years) and the herbicide should be applied in just sufficient water to wet the grass foliage thoroughly but to avoid excessive run-off on to the soil.

253. [**Tentative**] Simazine at up to 5 lb per acre may be applied when the bushes are well established (at least two years after planting out) to control annual and shallow-rooted perennial weeds. Best results are obtained if the spray is applied when the soil is moist and early spring is a suitable time. Because of the possibility of a build-up of simazine in the soil, only one treatment per year should be given and application should not be made during the year before grubbing the bushes.

254. [**Tentative**] Diuron at 2·5 lb per acre may be applied annually to the soil for the control of germinating annual weeds. The application should be made in late winter or early spring before bud-burst and after established weeds have been eliminated by cultivation or other means. The treatment should not be applied to bushes planted out for less than one year.

255. [**For Information**] Simazine at 1 to 2 lb per acre has given good control of germinating weeds without injury to newly planted gooseberry cuttings. It is important that the soil around the cuttings should be firm before applying this treatment.

256. [**For Information**] MCPB at 32 to 48 oz per acre has been used in August and early September to control *Convolvulus arvensis* and *Calystegia sepium* (bindweeds). Provided application was made after the gooseberries had stopped growing, no injury occurred even when the bushes were wetted by the spray.

257. [**For Information**] Chlorpropham 2 lb plus fenuron 0·5 lb per acre applied to clean ground between mid-November and late December has given good control of winter annual weeds. At 4 lb and 1 lb per acre respectively the same mixture of herbicides has been used to suppress existing weed growth.

RASPBERRIES

258. Simazine at 1 to 2 lb per acre may be applied annually to clean ground to control germinating weeds (see Table 11). Best results are obtained when the soil is moist and early spring is usually the most suitable time.

259. Paraquat formulated with a wetter may be applied as a carefully directed spray at 0·5 to 1 lb per acre at any time of the year to control established shallow-rooted grasses, *Ranunculus repens* (creeping buttercup) and annual broad-leaved weeds. There is no risk of crop injury due to root uptake but, after bud-burst, spray drift may cause severe damage and strict precautions must be taken to avoid wetting the foliage and young suckers.

260. Diquat formulated with a wetter may be applied as a carefully directed spray at 0·5 to 1 lb per acre at any time of the year to control established

Ranunculus repens (creeping buttercup) and annual broad-leaved weeds. There is no risk of crop injury due to root uptake, but, after bud-burst, spray drift may cause severe damage and strict precautions must be taken to avoid wetting the foliage and young suckers.

261. 2,4-D E S at 3 to 5 lb per acre as a high volume spray may be applied during the growing season to control germinating weeds in cane nurseries and fruiting plantations. The soil must be clean at the time of application and best results will be obtained in warm, moist conditions (see paragraph 150). Weed control is usually less satisfactory than obtained with simazine at 1 to 2 lb per acre.

262. Tar oil winter wash at a concentration of 8 per cent v/v may be applied during the late winter at a volume of 150 to 300 gallons of water per acre to control many annual weeds. The spray should be directed towards the ground and application may be timed to coincide with the tar oil treatment to control the raspberry moth.

263. [Tentative] Diuron at 2·5 lb per acre may be applied annually to the soil for the control of germinating annual weeds. The application should be made in the late winter or early spring before bud-burst and after established weeds have been eliminated by cultivation or other means. The treatment should not be applied to canes planted out for less than one year.

264. [Tentative] Simazine at up to 5 lb per acre may be applied when the canes are well established (at least two years after planting) to control annual and shallow-rooted perennial weeds. Best results are obtained if the spray is applied when the soil is moist and early spring is a suitable time. Because of the possibility of a build-up of simazine in the soil, only one treatment per year should be given and application should not be made during the year before grubbing the canes.

265. [Tentative] Dalapon at 4 lb per acre may be applied as a directed spray between mid-November and mid-January to control *Poa annua* (annual meadow grass) and seedling grasses. This treatment is not effective against broad-leaved weeds.

266. [For Information] Dalapon at 8 lb per acre applied as a directed spray between November and bud-burst has given temporary control of *Agropyron repens* but occasionally this treatment has caused crop injury. When applied during the growing season, dalapon has damaged the young cane growth of some varieties and application in September and October on the variety Lloyd George injured the following year's fruiting canes. Dalapon has also suppressed the emergence of suckers in cane nurseries.

STRAWBERRIES

267. Dinoseb-amine may be applied at 1 to 2 lb per acre in the autumn or early winter for the control of *Stellaria media* (chickweed) and other broad-leaved annual weeds. The ideal time of application is as soon as the weeds have emerged following autumn cultivation of the crop. February applications are inadvisable as a higher dose is required to achieve results and the risk of damage to the strawberries is greater. Dinoseb-ammonium is more likely to cause crop injury than dinoseb-amine, but it is more effective against weeds and can be used at doses up to 1·25 lb per acre. Strawberries should not be treated in the same year as they are planted, as experience has shown that they may be severely checked. There is some evidence that Cambridge Favourite may be more susceptible to injury than other varieties.

268. 2,4-DES at 3 to 5 lb in 50 to 200 gallons of water per acre may be applied to strawberry fruiting beds to control germinating weeds. It is essential to spray the whole of the soil surface evenly in order to obtain satisfactory results and the higher volumes of 100 to 200 gallons per acre are therefore preferable. Application may be made at any time during the growing season, but cultivation should be carried out a few days in advance of spraying to ensure that no growing weeds are present. As applied 2,4-DES is inactive as a herbicide but is converted to the active 2,4-D under warm, moist soil conditions. Under such conditions a reasonable control of germinating seedlings may be expected for about a month. If the soil is cold and dry, the conversion to 2,4-D takes place only slowly and weed seeds may germinate and become established, so that results are poor. The herbicide gives adequate control of germinating seedlings of many annual weeds, but in general the control of *Poa annua* (annual meadow grass) and *Stellaria media* (chickweed) tends to be variable. When 2,4-DES is applied to fruiting beds in early summer, before strawing down, satisfactory control of weeds may be obtained throughout the cropping period. Further application can then be made when cleaning up the beds after picking. Most varieties of strawberry show no damage following treatment with 2,4-DES, although Huxley Giant appears to be the most sensitive. The treatment of runner beds with 2,4-DES is not recommended as, in addition to temporary epinasty of the runners, it is possible to reduce runner production, nor should 2,4-DES be used on strawberries grown under cloches, in frames or in glasshouses.

269. [**Tentative**] Simazine may be used as an overall spray at 0·5 to 1 lb per acre (1 to 1·5 lb on heavy soil) between July and December on the varieties Cambridge Vigour, Cambridge Favourite, Royal Sovereign, Redgauntlet and Talisman. There is evidence of varietal differences in susceptibility and, until further information is obtained, other varieties should be treated solely on an experimental basis. Doses of 0·5 to 1·5 lb per acre will normally kill germinating seedlings only and the ground should be cultivated before spraying. Satisfactory results will not be obtained if the soil is dry at the time of application. Treatments made in the spring or on newly planted beds have occasionally caused injury.

270. [**Tentative**] Chlorpropham at 1 to 2 lb per acre can be applied to the soil following autumn cultivation for the control of germinating weeds (see Table 11). Established weeds, with the exception of *Stellaria media* (chickweed) will not be killed. If chlorpropham is applied at any time of the year other than in autumn or early winter, damage to the strawberry plants may result. Chlorpropham is not suitable for use in milder districts where there is little or no dormancy of the crop, and damage has been noted in England and in Northern Ireland, particularly with the variety Cambridge Vigour, where the spray was applied in the period November–December. Chlorpropham should only be used on plants which are well established.

271. [Tentative] Paraquat formulated with a wetter may be applied as a carefully directed inter-row spray at 0·5 to 1 lb per acre at any time of the year to control runners, established shallow-rooted grasses and annual broadleaved weeds growing in the alleys. There is little danger of injury due to root uptake but strict precautions must be taken to avoid wetting the crop foliage. Very slight chlorosis may occur on the foliage of parent plants as a result of translocation from treated runners but this is unlikely to be serious.

272. [Tentative] Diquat formulated with a wetter may be applied as a carefully directed inter-row spray at 0·5 to 1 lb per acre at any time of the year to control runners and annual broad-leaved weeds growing in the alleys. There is no risk of injury due to root uptake but strict precautions must be taken to avoid wetting the crop foliage. Very slight chlorosis may occur on the foliage of parent plants as a result of translocation from treated runners but this is unlikely to be serious.

273. [For Information] Mixtures of chlorpropham and fenuron will control a wider range of weeds than chlorpropham alone. Chlorpropham 1 lb plus fenuron 0·25 lb per acre applied to clean soil in early winter has given good results in a number of trials without injury to established strawberries. Occasionally, however, some damage has resulted and further information on the reliability of this treatment under different soil and weather conditions is desirable.

274. [For Information] Simazine has been applied as an overall spray at 0·5 to 1 lb per acre (1 to 1·5 lb on heavy soil) in late June and July to control germinating weeds in runner beds. These doses have had no adverse effect on the parent plants or on young runners which rooted normally during the summer and autumn.

SECTION (iii) FLOWER CROPS AND ORNAMENTAL SHRUBS
INTRODUCTION

275. The use of herbicides for the control of weeds in flower crops and ornamentals is still in a preliminary stage and, at present, only a limited number of recommendations can be made. It must be stressed that most flowers and ornamentals are grown in a large number of species and varieties under a wide range of soil and climatic conditions. A great deal more information about their response to herbicides will therefore be needed before more recommendations can be made.

ANEMONES

276. Contact pre-emergence sprays of vaporizing oil, cresylic acid formulations, diquat or paraquat (see paragraphs 152 to 158) can be applied to kill seedling weeds that appear before the first fronds emerge.

277. Pentachlorophenol at 6 lb per acre, may be applied not later than four days before the fronds begin to emerge for the control of seedling weeds.

278. [For Information] Simazine at 1 lb per acre applied to clean soil before the crop emerges has given promising results in a number of trials. The treatment is most effective if the ground is moist at the time of application or if rain falls within a few days.

279. [For Information] A mixture of chlorpropham 0·5 lb plus fenuron 1 lb per acre, applied to clean soil before crop emergence, has given good results in a number of trials but there have also been cases of damage, especially on light soils.

ANNUAL AND BIENNIAL FLOWERS

280. [Tentative] Contact pre-emergence sprays of vaporizing oil, cresylic acid formulations, dimexan, diquat or paraquat (see paragraphs 152 to 158) may be used in a number of annual and biennial flower crops, including calendula, clarkia, cornflower, godetia, typsophila, larkspur, stock, sweet william and wallflower.

BULBS (Daffodils, tulips and bulbous iris)

281. Contact pre-emergence herbicides (see paragraphs 152 to 158) may be applied to kill seedling weeds that appear before the first shoots have emerged. The usefulness of these treatments is increased if the beds are harrowed late in the season, thus ensuring that only small weeds are present at the time of treatment.

282. Pentachlorophenol at 8 lb per acre, as an emulsifiable oil formulation diluted with water to 100 gallons per acre, may be applied, not later than a week before the first shoots of the crop are expected to appear, for the control of seedling and germinating weeds. The usefulness of this treatment is increased if the beds are harrowed late in the season. When applied at this dose, pentachlorophenol gives some control of germinating weeds in addition to its contact action on the weeds already present.

283. Chlorpropham at 4 lb in 100 gallons of water per acre may be applied as a residual pre-emergence spray not later than a week before the first shoots are expected to emerge for the control of annual weeds (see Table 11). The land should be clean at the time of application as, with the exception of *Stellaria media* (chickweed), established weeds are not controlled by this chemical.

284. Chlorpropham at 2 lb per acre in a high volume of water may be applied to clean soil as a post-emergence spray provided that, in the case of daffodils, the spray is applied before the crop is 2 inches high or, in the case of tulips, before the leaf unfolds. This treatment should not be used where chlorpropham has also been applied as a pre-emergence spray but can be used after earlier treatment with pentachlorophenol or other contact pre-emergence materials.

285. Chlorpropham 2 lb plus fenuron 0·5 lb per acre may be applied to clean land as a high volume residual spray. The application can be made at any time from soon after planting in the autumn, until just before crop shoots emerge.

286. Chlorpropham 2 lb plus diuron 0·4 lb per acre may be applied to clean land as a high volume residual spray. The application can be made at any time, from soon after planting in autumn (on established beds after late summer cleaning) until just before the crop shoots emerge. The treatment is most effective when used in combination with an earlier contact pre-emergence treatment.

287. [For Information] Dalapon at 4 lb per acre has often been used for the control of annual grasses in established beds and appears safe *as long as the old crop foliage is completely dead, the new shoot has not started to grow and the stand of weed is thick enough to keep most of the spray from reaching the ground.* Where these conditions do not exist, or higher doses are used, damage is caused which appears in the flowers 15 to 18 months later. The risk of damage is especially serious when the crop is being grown for bulb production.

CHRYSANTHEMUMS

288. Proprietary formulations based on cresylic acids may be used as directed sprays for the control of annual weeds among chrysanthemums grown in the open and under glass. Application must be delayed until the base of the stem has become woody, and great care must be taken not to apply the spray over the plants, otherwise serious damage will result. The lower leaves are not easily avoided, and may be scorched, but this loss of foliage on a well-established plant does not affect subsequent growth.

289. 2,4-DES at 4 to 6 lb in at least 100 gallons of water per acre can be applied to clean ground among chrysanthemums which have been planted out for ten days or more in the open. The herbicide is most effective when applied to soil which is moist and warm, but under prolonged dry soil conditions results are poor. It can be applied as an overhead spray and the work can therefore be carried out more rapidly than when directed sprays of cresylic acids are used. Of the large number of varieties on which 2,4-DES has been tested only two, Pauline Shepherd and New Princess have been injured (the injury consisting of a growth distortion typical of the effects of growth-regulators) and these two varieties should not be treated.

DAHLIAS

290. Proprietary preparations based on cresylic acids may be used as directed sprays for the control of annual weeds among dahlias. Because of the soft growth of these plants, very great care must be taken that the spray does not come into contact with the foliage.

291. [For Information] 2,4-DES at 4 lb per acre applied as an overhead high volume spray ten days after planting out rooted cuttings, has given promising results on a number of varieties. The land should be clean at the time of treatment and the best results are obtained under moist, warm soil conditions.

GLADIOLI (under glass)

292. [Tentative] Chlorpropham at 1 lb per acre may be applied as a high volume residual pre-emergence spray immediately after planting for the control of annual weeds (see Table 11). Because of the risk of damage from volatilization of the herbicide, this treatment should not be used if crops other than gladioli are being grown in the same house or in the same block of houses.

GLADIOLI (in the open)

293. [Tentative] Chlorpropham at 4 lb per acre may be applied as a high volume spray immediately after planting for the control of germinating annual weeds in flowering size corms.

294. [Tentative] Chlorpropham at 2 lb plus fenuron at 0·5 lb per acre may be applied as a high volume spray immediately after planting for the control of germinating annual weeds in flowering size corms.

295. [Tentative] Chlorpropham at 2 lb plus diuron at 0·4 lb per acre may be applied as a high volume spray from immediately after planting until just prior to crop emergence for the control of germinating annual weeds in flowering size corms.

296. [Tentative] 2,4-DES at 4 lb plus fenuron at 0·5 lb per acre may be applied as a high volume post-emergence spray to crops grown in the open. The land should be clean at the time of treatment and the best results are obtained under moist, warm soil conditions.

297. [For Information] Simazine and monuron have been used experimentally for weed control in gladioli, and doses up to 2 lb per acre are worthy of further trial.

PERENNIAL FLOWERS

298. [For Information] Chlorpropham at 1 lb, 2,4-DES at 4 lb and simazine at 1 lb per acre applied as high volume sprays to established plants growing in clean ground have all given promising results in preliminary trials on asters (perennial), chrysanthemum maximum, paeony, pyrethrum and scabious. At 4 lb per acre 2,4-DES also shows promise in phlox and on established violet plants. Further information on the reliability of these treatments under different soil and weather conditions is required before specific recommendations can be made. The chance of injury is greater on light, inorganic soils and when there is heavy rain after spraying. With some species, such as paeony and pyrethrum, there is evidence that applications of simazine directed so as to avoid the crop foliage are safer than overhead sprays.

ROSES AND ROSE STOCKS

299. 2,4-DES at 4 lb per acre may be applied as a high volume directed spray in spring. The land should be clean at the time of treatment and the best results are obtained under moist, warm conditions. Of the many varieties treated only two, Ena Harkness and Masquerade, have occasionally been slightly affected by this treatment, the effect consisting of a temporary distortion of growth.

300. Simazine may be applied at up to 1·5 lb per acre, or 2 lb on heavy soils, as an overhead spray at medium or high volume to established rose stocks or budded roses at any time of the year for the control of annual weeds (see Table 11). The most convenient times for treatment are in summer or autumn after budding and in spring when the bushes are headed back, at both of which times the land is normally clean. The treatment will not be fully effective unless the soil is moist or rain falls shortly afterwards. If two or more applications are made during the year the dose used should not exceed 1 lb per acre per application because of the risk of a build up of chemical in the soil.

301. [Tentative] Simazine at 1 lb per acre can be used as an overhead spray at medium or high volume immediately after planting out stocks. Normally at this time the land is clean and soil conditions are suitable for the action of the chemical. The soil should be made firm round the base of the plants before treatment.

SHRUBS

302. 2,4-DES at 3 to 5 lb per acre may be applied as a directed spray in spring, using at least 100 gallons of water per acre. The land must be clean at the time of spraying and under favourable conditions, when the soil is warm and moist, establishment of annual weeds is prevented for a period of 5 to 6 weeks.

303. [For Information] Simazine at up to 1·5 lb per acre as a medium or high volume spray has been used commercially for the control of annual weeds in a wide range of nursery stock, including both broad-leaved and coniferous species. The majority of subjects appear to be unaffected by the above doses when established, but damage has been caused to some species of the following: chaenomeles, larix, lonicera, prunus, spiraea, symphoricarpus and syringa; deutzia and euonymus are regarded as especially sensitive. Less information is available about the results of spraying immediately after planting but good results have been obtained on a number of species. The chance of injury is greater on light inorganic soils and when there is rain after spraying. With many of the genera listed above there is evidence that applications directed so as to avoid the crop foliage are safer than overall sprays.

304. [For Information] 2,4-DES or mixtures of 2,4-DES plus fenuron as spring and summer applications, combined with autumn or winter applications of chlorpropham or chlorpropham plus fenuron, have shown promise for the control of annual weeds in nursery stock.

305. [For Information] Dalapon has been used as a directed spray to check the growth of *Agropyron repens* (couch) and other perennial grasses among a number of established trees and shrubs at the rate of 8 lb per acre. The susceptibility of woody plants to dalapon varies greatly, some, such as *Prunus* species (and roses) being relatively susceptible. The risk of damage is minimized by spraying in autumn or early spring when the crop is dormant but the weeds are still growing. A dense stand of weed growth also reduces the risk by preventing the spray solution reaching the soil. With 4 lb per acre, which is sufficient to kill annual grasses, litttle damage has been reported as long as the treatment is confined to established plants during the dormant season.

306. [For Information] Diquat or paraquat at 0·5 to 1 lb per acre may be applied as a directed spray during the dormant period to control established annual broad-leaved weeds, *Ranunculus repens* (creeping buttercup) and, with paraquat, shallow-rooted grasses. There is no risk of crop injury due to root uptake but care must be taken to avoid the plants as much as possible. On most deciduous species slight wetting of dormant buds is unlikely to have any adverse effect but after bud-burst or on evergreens spray drift may cause severe damage. Unopened buds of some *Ribes* spp. have also been damaged.

SECTION (iv) LAWNS AND SPORTS TURF
INTRODUCTION

307. The control of weeds is an essential part of the management of lawns and sports turf. Apart from their general unsightliness, weeds can often be a positive obstruction to the sporting activities for which the turf is grown. The use of the synthetic growth-regulators MCPA and 2,4-D is now an established practice in the maintenance of weed-free lawns and sports turf, while mecoprop is being increasingly used for certain specific problems. The response of common turf weeds to these herbicides is given in Table 7. There are, however, some weed problems which cannot be resolved by the use of these herbicides, and other methods of control are necessary. The use of herbicides is but one aspect of turf management, and does not replace the normal essential operations in the groundsman's calendar. In fact the application of herbicides cannot be expected to achieve desired results unless drainage, aeration, feeding, cultivation and propagation are correctly carried out as circumstances direct.

ESTABLISHED TURF

308. MCPA, 2,4-D and mecoprop may be applied to fully established turf at up to the following maximum doses:

MCPA-salts	80	oz per acre		
2,4-D-salts	64	,,	,,	,,
2,4-D-ester	40	,,	,,	,,
Mecoprop-salts	64	,,	,,	,,

MCPA and 2,4-D should normally be applied at doses between 16 and 32 oz and mecoprop at 32 to 48 oz per acre, when spraying equipment is used. Because of the reduced efficiency of application by watering-can and the difficulties of measuring the small quantities of herbicide required, higher doses are usually recommended for this method of application. For the more resistant weeds, several sprayings at doses which should never exceed half the maximum, given at 4 to 6 week intervals, are likely to be more satisfactory than a single large dose. Weeds which are normally susceptible but which have developed resistance because they have grown under 'hard' conditions, will require higher doses or repeated dressings. When treating local patches of weeds, great care should be taken to avoid overdosing, otherwise the grass may be scorched and scorching of the weeds may result in decreased translocation of the herbicide. See Table 7 for information on weed susceptibility. (See also paragraphs 315–318.)

FERTILIZERS

309. MCPA, 2,4-D and mecoprop are most effective if the weeds are growing vigorously. For this reason it is often worth while to apply a special dressing of nitrogenous fertilizer 10 to 14 days before spraying. If such a treatment is not made, then a dressing applied shortly after spraying will help the grass to fill in the gaps left by the dying weeds. Dressings rich in phosphate or lime should be avoided because these encourage the establishment and growth of *Trifolium repens* (white clover).

MOWING

310. Herbicide treatment should be arranged so as to leave at least three days between mowing and spraying, in order to allow for some regrowth of the weeds. This is particularly necessary for *Trifolium repens* (white clover). The timing of the spray depends to a large extent on the height of cut, weed habit and weather conditions. After spraying, at least one day should elapse before mowing, and preferably three days where possible, to allow translocation of the herbicide into the root systems of the weeds to take place.

SEED-BEDS

311. [For Information] The treatment of seed-beds is not recommended, as the 'take' of grass seeds is likely to be reduced if the seed is sown within 6 to 8 weeks following application of 2,4-D or 8 to 12 weeks following application of MCPA. It is known that under some circumstances seed may be sown within considerably shorter periods than these, but the effect on the grass is influenced by several factors and it is generally accepted that the periods recommended are safe for the country as a whole. An exception may be made in the reseeding of bare patches in an established sward, but a higher seeding rate than normal should be used to compensate for impaired germination. It is particularly important that mecoprop should not be used for seed-beds prior to sowing the seed, because of its high pre-emergence activity against some grass species. Re-seeding of large areas sprayed with mecoprop should not be carried out in the same season.

NEWLY-SOWN TURF

312. Grass mixtures containing fine grasses, i.e. bents and fescues, should not be treated for 6 months after sowing. Even after this interval it is unwise to use doses approaching those given in paragraph 308 until the sward is well established.

313. Grass mixtures containing mainly ryegrass and/or other coarse grasses may be sprayed at an earlier stage than recommended in paragraph 312 if

9

domination by annual weeds susceptible to MCPA and 2,4-D is threatened (see Table 7). For the control of *Stellaria media* (chickweed), *Trifolium repens* (white clover) and some other weed seedlings, mecoprop at 24 to 32 oz per acre may be used in preference to MCPA and 2,4-D. Spraying should be delayed until the majority of the grasses have at least 2 to 3 expanded leaves.

NEWLY-LAID TURF

314. Newly-laid, good-quality turf should not be treated with selective herbicides until at least 6 months after laying, unless conditions for establishment are particularly favourable. After 6 months it may be treated as described in paragraphs 308 to 310.

ROUGH GRASSLAND ON GOLF COURSES ETC.

Attention is drawn to the relevant information on road verges and woody weeds in Chapters VI and IV respectively.

APPLICATION OF HERBICIDES TO LAWNS AND SPORTS TURF

315. Selective herbicides are best applied as aqueous sprays, using any appropriate spraying equipment. The volume of spray applied may be from 50 to 100 gallons per acre; volume rates lower than 20 gallons per acre are generally less effective. When a watering-can is used to treat limited areas it is necessary to apply a higher dose of herbicide than if the treatment is applied with a spraying machine (see paragraph 308). To ensure maximum efficiency, economy and safety in the application of herbicides by hand-sprayer or watering-can, some method of marking out is recommended. Dust applications are less effective than sprays, and the storage of herbicide dusts may present hazards. Their convenience for the spot treatment of local areas may, however, outweight these disadvantages.

TIMING OF APPLICATION

316. Herbicides can be applied at any time of the year when weeds are in active growth, the best time being during late spring and early summer. Good results may be obtained by spraying in the autumn but at this time of the year turf fills in very slowly.

EFFECT OF WEATHER

317. Fine warm weather, moist soil and active growth are conducive to the best results. Unsatisfactory results are most likely to be obtained during cold periods or during drought, although if the drought is not prolonged the weeds will quickly respond to the herbicide with the advent of rain. Application during drought when temperatures are high may cause serious damage to the grass. Regular watering during summer drought is particularly important after herbicide treatment to ensure maximum weed effect and grass recolonization. Light showers of rain following application are not likely to cause appreciable loss in efficiency but it is inadvisable to spray in rainy weather.

PRECAUTIONS

318. Great care should be taken that no drift is allowed to reach vegetables, flowers, fruit trees, bushes or shrubs, as many of these are extremely suscept-ible to MCPA, 2,4-D and mecoprop. Spraying near greenhouses should be particularly avoided, even though the doors and ventilators are closed. When treating the edges of lawns which tend to be overhung by herbaceous plants it is advisable to use a protective barrier such as a board, but it is essential to avoid touching the plants with the contaminated surface. Where valued plants surround a small, confined lawn, application by watering-can rather than by sprayer is recommended. The first cut of mowings after the herbicide has been applied should not be used for mulching purposes, and if com-posted, should be allowed to rot down completely before use.

319. Wherever possible, spraying equipment should be reserved solely for the application of herbicides. After use, all equipment should be washed out thoroughly and stored separately from general horticultural appliances. Pre-cautions concerning the use of field sprayers are dealt with in Chapter VII, Section (iii) and Chapter VIII, Section (ii). Care should be taken that green-house and other garden water supplies are not contaminated by watering-cans and other equipment used for the application of herbicides. Containers in which herbicides, particularly dusts, are packed should be stored away from fertilizers, other garden preparations, seeds and planting materials. Storage of either full or empty containers of herbicides in greenhouses should be avoided; the vapour hazard is serious.

SPECIAL WEED PROBLEMS

LEGUMES (CLOVERS AND TREFOILS)

320. The following species commonly occur in turf:

Lotus corniculatus (birdsfoot trefoil)
Medicago lupulina (black medick)
Trifolium dubium (yellow suckling clover)
Trifolium pratense (red clover)
Trifolium repens (white clover).

Mecoprop at doses between 32 and 40 oz per acre, is particularly useful for the control of *Trifolium repens* (white clover). Application should not be made until early summer when the clover is growing vigorously. With an application at this time no further treatment should be necessary during the season. Some regrowth may occur during the following year particularly if no steps are taken to encourage the grass by the application of a nitrogenous fertilizer. White clover flourishes on soils rich in phosphate and is discouraged by acid soils and by application of nitrogenous fertilizers. As a long-term measure unfavourable conditions for its growth can be maintained by regular use of ammonium sulphate and ferrous sulphate (sulphate of iron).

321. Repeated application of mecoprop may achieve some measure of control of *Medicago lupulina* (black medick) but none of the other legumes are reliably controlled by MCPA, 2,4-D or mecoprop. Consistently good control of many turf weeds, notably members of the Compositae such as *Taraxacum officinale* (dandelion), *Leontodon* spp. (hawkbits) and *Bellis perennis* (daisy), may not be obtained where mecoprop is used even at the maximum permissible dose (paragraph 308). Where such species are present the addition of MCPA or 2,4-D at 10 to 12 oz per acre to mecoprop is desirable.

SAGINA PROCUMBENS (pearlwort)

322. This weed is a widespread problem in turf and can be controlled by the use of lawn sand or MCPA. The former is the conventional method and is generally to be preferred where pearlwort is the dominant weed and the infestation is heavy. Where pearlwort occurs with other weeds and the infestation is relatively light, MCPA can be used (see Table 7). A typical lawn sand mixture for broadcast application at up to 1,200 lb per acre (4 oz per square yard), is:

    3 parts ammonium sulphate
    1 part calcined ferrous sulphate
    10 parts carrier.

For spot treatment of isolated patches of pearlwort the same mixture without the carrier may be applied at 1 oz per square yard. Lawn sands should ideally be applied on a dewy morning when the soil is moist and the weather fine and warm. They may be applied at any time during the growing season, but late spring or early summer is preferred. If application is followed by drought, artificial watering should be given after a few days. Scarifying the turf in spring is a useful cultural method of control for this weed.

MOSS

323. Chemical control methods, which are of a temporary nature unless combined with cultural improvements, are given below. Methods involving the use of mercury products are in extensive use and are the most reliable.

324. Mercurous chloride (calomel) is effective in controlling moss. Because of its insolubility, particle size is important; with finely divided material a dose of 0·6 to 1·0 g per square yard is usually sufficient to eradicate moss and give protection against re-infestation for several months. The best time for treatment is in early autumn. Because of the small quantities involved, calomel is formulated with a carrier for easier measurement and distribution. Calomel has been most frequently applied as a powder, but special formulations are now available which can be applied as suspensions in a coarse spray. The addition of calomel to calcined ferrous sulphate and/or ammonium sulphate will increase the duration of control normally obtained with these materials.

325. Mercuric chloride (corrosive sublimate), which is effective as a fungicide in turf, can also be used in conjunction with calomel for the control of moss. Corrosive sublimate is particularly effective as an eradicant, while calomel gives protection against re-infestation. A total dose of 0·3 g per square yard of a 2 : 1 mixture of calomel and corrosive sublimate is adequate for the control of most mosses. Corrosive sublimate is a scheduled poison (see page 236), and both the powder and spray fluid should be handled with extreme care and kept away from food and out of the reach of children and animals. Because of its extremely poisonous nature corrosive sublimate should not be used on domestic lawns and public areas.

326. Lawn sand as for pearlwort (see paragraph 322). The addition of calomel (see paragraph 324) to this treatment will increase the duration of control.

327. Where the presence of moss is thought to be due to infertility, calcined ferrous sulphate should be applied in late March or early April after the first mowing, at a dose of 0·25 to 0·5 oz in 3 oz sand, or 1 gallon of water, per square yard. This should be followed by application of a general fertilizer.

328. Potassium permanganate applied at 1 oz per square yard, either dry, with sand, or in 1 gallon of water, gives a fair control but some species of mosses are resistant to this treatment. Potassium permanganate tends to oxidize partly-decayed matter in the turf, thereby increasing aeration and fertility.

329. Cultural methods for the control of moss include:
    (i) Avoidance of too frequent rolling.
    (ii) Improvement of drainage.
    (iii) Improvement of grass vigour by
        (a) increasing depth of soil where necessary;
        (b) watering in dry periods;
        (c) application of fertilizer in spring and autumn;
        (d) aeration.
    (iv) Reduction of shade.
    (v) Control of weeds, worms, pests and diseases.
    (vi) Care in mowing
        (a) not too close in summer;
        (b) use of the grass box to collect spores.
    (vii) Raking in late winter.
    (viii) Avoidance of lime and calcareous fertilizers unless pH is below 5·5.

TABLE 7. THE RESPONSE OF COMMON TURF WEEDS TO MCPA, 2,4-D AND MECOPROP

Doses given below are applicable only when spraying equipment is being used (see paragraph re watering-can use).

VS – Very susceptible	Consistently killed by 16 to 24 oz MCPA or 2,4-D or by 32 to 40 oz mecoprop per acre.
S – Susceptible	Often killed by 16 to 24 oz MCPA or 2,4-D or by 32 to 40 oz. mecoprop per acre, but a second application sometimes necessary.
MS – Moderately susceptible	Often killed by 32 to 48 oz MCPA or 2,4-D or by 40 to 48 oz mecoprop per acre, but a second application sometimes necessary.
MR – Moderately resistant	Some useful effect by repeated applications under favourable conditions.
R – Resistant	No useful effect with up to maximum permitted doses.

Weed	MCPA -salt	2,4-D-amine and -ester	Mecoprop -salt
1. *Achillea millefolium* (yarrow)	MR	MR	MR
2. *Aphanes arvensis* (parsley piert)	R	R	
3. *Armeria maritima* (sea pink)	S	S	
4. *Bellis perennis* (daisy)	MS	S	MS
5. *Centaurea nigra* (knapweed)	MS	MS	
6. *Cerastium holosteodes* (mouse-ear chickweed)	MS	MS	MS
7. *Cirsium acaulon* (stemless thistle)	MS	MS	
8. *Cirsium arvense* (creeping thistle)	S	S	S
9. *Convolvulus arvensis* (field bindweed)	MS	MS	MR
10. *Crepis* spp. (hawk's beard)	S	S	
11. *Erodium cicutarium* (common storksbill)	MS	MS	
12. *Erodium maritimum* (sea storksbill)	MS	MS	
13. *Erodium moschatum* (musk storksbill)	MS	MS	
14. *Galium saxatile* (heath bedstraw)	MS	MS	
15. *Geranium molle* (dove's foot cranesbill)	MR	MR	MS
16. *Glaux maritima* (sea milkwort)	MS	MS	
17. *Hieraceum pilosella* (mouse-ear hawkweed)	S	S	MS
18. *Holcus lanatus* (Yorkshire fog)	R	R	R
19. *Holcus mollis* (creeping softgrass)	R	R	R
20. *Hypochaeris radicata* (cat's ear)	S	S	MS
21. *Leontodon autumnalis* (autumnal hawkbit)	MS	MS	MR
22. *Lotus corniculatus* (birdsfoot trefoil)	MR	MR	MR

TABLE 7— *continued*

Weed	MCPA -salt	2,4-D-amine and -ester	Mecoprop -salt
23. *Luzula campestris* (field woodrush)	MR	R	MS
24. *Medicago lupulina* (black medick)	MR	MR	MR
25. *Montia chondrosperma* (water chickweed)	MR	MR	
26. *Plantago coronopus* (starweed)	S	S	S
27. *Plantago lanceolata* (ribwort)	VS	VS	S
28. *Plantago major* (greater plantain)	VS	VS	S
29. *Plantago maritima* (sea plantain)	VS	VS	
30. *Plantago media* (hoary plantain)	VS	VS	S
31. *Polygonum aviculare* (knotgrass)	*MS	*MS(E)	R
32. *Potentilla anserina* (silverweed)	MS	MS	
33. *Potentilla erecta* (common tormentil)	MR	MR	
34. *Potentilla reptans* (cinquefoil)	MR	MR	
35. *Poterium sanguisorba* (salad burnet)	MR	MR	
36. *Prunella vulgaris* (self-heal)	MS	MS	MS
37. *Ranunculus acris* (crowfoot)	S	MS	MS
38. *Ranunculus bulbosus* (bulbous buttercup)	MR	MR	MR
39. *Ranunculus ficaria* (lesser celandine)	MR	MR	
40. *Ranunculus repens* (creeping buttercup)	VS	S	S
41. *Rumex acetosa* (sorrel)	S	S	S
42. *Rumex acetosella* (sheep's sorrel)	S	S	S
43. *Sagina procumbens* (pearlwort)	MS	MR	MS
44. *Senecio jacobaea* (ragwort)	MS	MS	
45. *Spergula arvensis* (corn spurrey)	MS	MS	MS
46. *Stellaria media* (chickweed)	MR	MR	VS
47. *Taraxacum officinale* (dandelion)	MS	S	MR
48. *Trifolium dubium* (yellow suckling clover)	MR	MR	MR
49. *Trifolium repens* (white clover)	MR	MR	VS
50. *Tussilago farfara* (coltsfoot)	MR	MR	R
51. *Veronica arvensis* (wall speedwell)	MR	MR	
52. *Veronica chamaedrys* (germander speedwell)	MR	MR	MS
53. *Veronica filiformis*	MR	MR	MR
54. *Veronica serpyllifolia* (thyme-leaved speedwell)	MR	MR	

* MS for seedlings, MR when established.
(E) Ester formulations recommended.

CHAPTER IV

RECOMMENDATIONS FOR THE USE OF HERBICIDES IN FORESTRY

SECTION (i) FOREST NURSERIES

INTRODUCTION

330. Chemical treatments for the control of weeds in forest nurseries may be divided into five classes:

Pre-sowing treatment of seed-beds.
Pre-emergence treatment of seed-beds.
Post-emergence treatments:
  (a) Seed-beds;
  (b) Transplant lines;
  (c) Poplar and willow.

Treatment of fallow land.
Treatment of uncultivated land.

Recommendations and general information concerning each method are given below.

PRE-SOWING TREATMENT OF SEED-BEDS

331. Soil sterilizing chemicals, notably formalin (as a soil drench containing 22 gallons of commercial 38 per cent formalin per acre), or chloropicrin (applied by means of a soil injector at 30 gallons per acre), applied to the seed-bed several weeks before sowing, frequently result in a marked improvement of tree seedling growth, particularly on light-medium loam soils which are neutral or only slightly acid. Such treatments also appreciably reduce the emergence of weeds during the season of treatment.

332. Vaporizing oils applied at 40 to 60 gallons per acre at any time to within 4 or 5 days of sowing can effectively control most weeds which have emerged. The seed-bed should be prepared early in the season, several weeks in advance of sowing.

333. Diquat at 0·5 lb in 20 gallons water per acre may be used in a similar way to vaporizing oils (paragraph 332).

PRE-EMERGENCE TREATMENT OF SEED-BEDS

334. Vaporizing oil applied by spray as a contact herbicide prior to crop seedling emergence will kill most annual weeds that have emerged; the treatment may be applied to any tree species at a dose of 60 gallons per acre. The vaporizing oil used should meet the following specifications: Specific gravity 0·82; boiling range, 145–250°C; aromatic hydrocarbons 12–35 per cent.

The herbicide should be applied to newly emerged weeds not later than 3 to 4 days before tree seedlings begin to emerge above ground level. As a guide, it can be assumed that if, on excavation, germinating seeds are found to have radicles 0·5 inches long, they will probably begin to emerge in 3 to 4 days. This simple test gives a guide to the latest safe date for spraying. In many cases earlier spraying will be justified, and in general, spraying should be done as soon as an appreciable number of weeds has emerged. It is quite safe to apply two or more mineral oil sprays as long as the last one is applied no later than 3 to 4 days before crop seedling emergence.

335. Simazine at 2 lb per acre may be applied to seed-beds of oak, beech and sweet chestnut, (i.e. big-seeded hardwood species which are covered with 1 to 2 inches of soil following sowing). The herbicide must be applied before seedlings emerge.

336. [**For Information**] Cresylic acid (4 to 5 lb tar acids per gallon) applied at 5 to 10 gallons in 40 gallons of water per acre as a pre-emergence contact spray has given good control of annual weeds without serious crop injury.

POST-EMERGENCE TREATMENTS

SEED-BEDS

337. Light mineral oils of the type similar to those used for spraying carrots, (conforming to the specification: Boiling range 150 to 250°C, aromatic hydrocarbons 18 to 20 per cent), can be used for the control of annual weeds in seed-beds of several conifer species. Tree species can be grouped according to their resistance to mineral oil, and the dose should be adjusted accordingly as indicated below:

Group I. Resistant (dose: 25 gallons per acre):

Abies nobilis	Noble fir
Abies grandis	Giant fir
Chamaecyparis lawsoniana	Lawson cypress
Picea abies	Norway spruce
Picea sitchensis	Sitka spruce
Pinus mugo	Mountain pine
Pinus nigra var. *calabrica*	Corsican pine
Pinus sylvestris	Scots pine
Thuja plicata	Western red cedar

Group II. Moderately resistant (dose: 15 gallons per acre):

Larix decidua	European larch
Larix leptolepis	Japanese larch
Pinus contorta	Lodgepole pine
Pseudotsuga taxifolia	Douglas fir
Tsuga heterophylla	Western hemlock

Group III. Sensitive (should not be sprayed):
Hardwood spp.

The first application may normally be made 3 to 4 weeks after germination is complete. Generally, the resistance of the trees increases with age, although the most resistant trees can be safely sprayed while the cotyledons are enclosed in their testas. While the testas are being shed and immediately afterwards, there is a period of extreme susceptibility, but this will pass in three or four weeks, as the tree develops, depending on growing conditions; freshly acquired resistance is usually accompanied by a slight darkening in colour. If damage occurs it usually consists of scorched leaves, or may be merely slight stunting of growth without scorch. This must be considered before applications are repeated. Seedlings must not be sprayed in times of drought or very bright, hot sun. Soil moisture should be high, (natural or by watering), though the foliage should be dry. If the foliage of crop and weed seedlings is wet, the treatment will be somewhat less effective than under cool, dry conditions, but it will not damage the crop species.

It is important that normal hand weeding is not neglected during the period when sprays cannot safely be applied, as the first permissible spray will only be effective against newly germinated weeds. Frequency of spraying will be governed by the development of the weed population, and sprays should be applied as required up to a maximum of 6 in one season. Weeds surviving two spray treatments should be regarded as resistant and be removed by hand. The doses recommended will give a satisfactory control of most annual weeds but only while they are young, the best control being obtained when they are in the cotyledon (seed-leaf) stage. Older annual weeds, and the aerial parts of perennial weeds, may be scorched and checked in growth but will survive.

338. White spirit may be applied to growing seed-beds in their second year at the same doses as for first year beds (see paragraph 337) at any time except in the four weeks following budbreak. Sprays are likely to be ineffective if there is a dense cover of seedling foliage to prevent the spray reaching the young weeds.

339. Simazine may be applied to seed-beds in their second year of growth subject to the same provisions that are made for transplants (see paragraph 340).

TRANSPLANT LINES

340. Simazine may be applied at 2 lb in 60 to 100 gallons of water per acre to most transplants and to seedlings in their second year of growth (whether undercut or not). Sprays may be applied at any time in late winter or spring until late May when the soil surface is moist. The ground should be free from weeds at the time of spraying. (See Chapter I for general recommendations for the use of simazine.) A second spray may be applied in July, August or September to ground carrying crops that will not be disturbed until the following spring, provided that a minimum period of 4 months has elapsed from the first spray. Simazine may be applied as late as October or November to crops which are to remain undisturbed in the succeeding year. A second spray should only be applied when it is clear that young weeds have recently germinated and have become established. Existence of a few healthy large weeds, especially of deep-rooted species is no indication that simazine has disappeared.

The following species may be sprayed:

Norway and Sitka spruce, Scots, Corsican, and Lodgepole pine, Douglas fir, Lawson cypress, Western red cedar, Western hemlock, Hybrid and Japanese larch, *Abies nobilis*, *Abies grandis*, oak, birch, beech and Sweet chestnut.

European larch and *Picea omorika* are more susceptible than most species and should be sprayed at 1 lb in 60 to 100 gallons water per acre.

The following must *not* be sprayed:

(i) Ash, rooted cuttings of poplar.
(ii) *All* plants less than 2 inches tall at the time of spraying.

341. Mineral oils as inter-row sprays, i.e. sprays restricted to the spaces between the rows of plants, may be applied to most common conifer species. Hardwood species may only be sprayed in the dormant season. In all cases it is important to direct the oil on to the ground between the lines and to minimise the amount coming into contact with young tree foliage. It is, of course, also important to spray weeds at an early stage of development. A week or a fortnight after an inter-row spray, the area should be weeded by hand or machine to remove any surviving large weeds. Thereafter, if subsequent spray applications are properly timed, little hand weeding should be necessary.

White spirits or vaporizing oils may be used as inter-row sprays as follows:

Season	Bud break to mid-June	Mid-June to end of season	Dormant season
Hardwoods	Not safe	Not safe	Vaporizing oil, 40 gal/acre
Douglas fir Larches Pine Tsuga Firs	White spirit, 25 gal/acre	White spirit, 40 gal/acre or Vaporizing oil, 25 gal/acre	Vaporizing oil, 40 gal/acre
Spruces Lawson cypress Thuja	White spirit or Vaporizing oil, 25 gal/acre	White spirit or Vaporizing oil, 40 gal/acre	Vaporizing oil, 40 gal/acre

N.B. – Plants of any species less than 5 inches in height should not be sprayed at doses exceeding 25 gallons per acre during the growing season.

POPLAR AND WILLOW

342. In cutting beds and transplant lines of poplar, good control of annual weeds can be obtained using either vaporizing oil at 60 gallons per acre, or pentachlorphenol at 2 to 4 lb per acre, as a contact herbicide and repeating the treatment monthly, or as often as weed growth requires, during the growing season.

343. In stool-beds of poplar and willow, annual weeds can be controlled by application of simazine at 3 to 4 lb per acre in the spring. Where perennial grasses are the main weed species, good control can be obtained with dalapon as a directed spray at 8 to 10 lb in 20 to 40 gallons of water per acre applied shortly before bud break of the crop.

TREATMENT OF FALLOW LAND

344. The fallow area in the nursery rotation provides a useful stage for attacking the weed population by combination of cultivation and chemical control. *Agropyron repens* (couch grass) and *Ranunculus repens* (creeping buttercup) present in the nursery can be eradicated using dalapon, TCA, or sodium chlorate for the former, and MCPA or 2,4-D for the latter, following the recommendations given in Chapter V, p. 143 *et seq.* for these particular species. Where dalapon is used, seed sowing or transplanting should normally be deferred for 8 weeks after application and if exceptionally dry, for 12 weeks after application. Other perennials, for example *Rumex acetosella* (sorrel), also can be controlled by sodium chlorate applied at a dose of 2 cwt per acre as spray. This treatment will control any established annual weeds present at the time of spray. Notes on the use of sodium chlorate and the relative susceptibility of weeds to it are given in Chapter VI and Table 13. Six months should be left between application of the chlorate and seed sowing or transplanting. Where only annual weeds are present, these may be controlled most cheaply by regular cultivation. Other effective, but more expensive methods of control, include sprays of vaporizing oil at 60 gallons per acre, diquat at 1 lb per acre and fortified mineral oils (see Chapter VI).

TREATMENT OF UNCULTIVATED LAND

345. Weeds on uncultivated land, notably paths, fence lines, and the surrounds of buildings, are often overlooked as important sources of weed seed infection in forest nurseries. Weeds in such situations are frequently difficult to control by cutting or cultivation, and non-selective, persistent herbicides can be used with advantage in early spring to control most annual weeds and keep the sites free from seeding weeds for 12 months or more. Such chemicals can be applied close to the boundaries of cultivation without risk to crops, as there is little or no lateral movement of the chemical in the soil. Fuller details of treatments employing simazine, monuron and other materials to control weeds of uncropped land are given in Chapter VI.

SECTION (ii) FOREST: THE CHEMICAL CONTROL OF WOODY WEEDS

INTRODUCTION

346. In forestry the growth of unwanted woody species can give rise to difficult problems, particularly when preparing areas of hardwood scrub or neglected woodland for planting and when controlling coppice sprouts and other woody growth throughout the period of establishment of the new tree crop. Manual and mechanical methods of controlling woody growth are well known, and include cutting by hand, burning, and the use of heavy machinery for cutting, grubbing or removal of growth. Following such methods, re-sprouting from severed stumps or roots may be vigorous, requiring repeated cutting to maintain the control achieved. The use of chemical methods of control, by which vigorous re-sprouting can be reduced, has attracted much attention in recent years, and chemicals such as 2,4-D, and particularly 2,4,5-T and ammonium sulphamate, have proved very effective against many woody species, both for initial control and prevention of re-sprouting. The choice of control methods will vary according to the situation, size and mode of growth of the species concerned, but there are many circumstances in which chemical methods can be used with advantage to replace, or supplement, normal manual or mechanical methods of control. They can assist in controlling woody growth at several stages in forest management, viz. complete or partial control of vegetation prior to planting, weeding in the early stages of crop establishment and in cleaning and thinning operations including stand improvement by treatment of unwanted trees.

347. Whilst woody weeds are a particular problem in forestry they may encroach on agricultural land and on to roadsides, fence lines, ditches, firebreaks, railway embankments and the surrounds to buildings or industrial installations. In agriculture the most important problems are in preventing encroachment of woody growth from hedges, scrub, etc. into field verges and drainage channels, and in removing cover for vermin, particularly rabbits. This section therefore deals with woody weeds as a general problem and does not limit itself entirely to forestry aspects. It first gives a short account of the principles involved when using chemicals for improvement of land occupied by unwanted woody species, then briefly describes the chemicals and recommends methods of using them, and finally provides a table indicating the susceptibility of the more important woody species to treatment with 2,4-D or 2,4,5-T in the recommended manner.

GENERAL PRINCIPLES

348. It is not always appreciated that the destruction of woody plants by chemical or other means does not in itself necessarily produce an acceptable change in the vegetation. If, for instance, a dense stand of scrub or brambles is killed *in situ*, the bare ground under the treated bushes is rapidly colonized by herbaceous plants and possibly seedlings of woody species, and unless steps are taken to control these, the treatment is unlikely to be considered successful. It is essential when contemplating the use of chemicals to decide on the long-term objective of the treatment and to plan how this can be attained with the facilities and budget available. Three points, particularly, should be borne in mind. First, it is unusual for a single chemical treatment to be so completely successful that no regrowth at all occurs from the roots or stems of treated plants; second, the dead woody vegetation may remain for some time and may be considered unsightly, and may impede access or prevent grazing of herbaceous growth by stock; and third, any bare ground may be invaded by undesirable species, replacing one type of weed problem by another. To avoid disappointing results it is essential to regard chemical treatment as one part only of a reclamation project, which has as its object the establishment of a desirable and reasonably stable plant community, such as a grass sward or a forest crop. In practice, several stages are usually involved:

(1) Treatment with the chemical, preceded if necessary by preparation, usually cutting, which may be followed by heaping or burning of the cut growth, e.g. practical or complete clearance where dense stands of woody growth make access and applications to the stems or foliage impracticable, or where control can best be obtained by treatment of cut stumps.

(2) Removal of the dead woody plants by burning *in situ*, or collecting into heaps by hand or mechanical means followed by burning, or by trampling by livestock. With adequate advance preparation, this stage is seldom necessary before planting a forest crop.

(3) Encouraging the establishment of the desired crop or vegetation in the treated area. Where the object is to obtain a productive sward, intensive grazing or mowing may suffice, provided areas of bare ground are not large and the existing herbaceous vegetation is of a desirable nature; otherwise it may be necessary to carry out suitable cultivations to produce a tilth followed by broadcast sowing of, for instance, grass and clover. In forestry, the tree crop is usually planted shortly after control of the initial woody growth has been secured.

(4) Application of additional treatment with the chemical as required to deal with any regeneration that occurs. Whereas the original chemical treatment may have been on a large scale involving mechanical spraying equipment and considerable cost, follow-up treatments may often be carried out at low cost using a knapsack sprayer for 'spot' application to any shoots or woody plants that have appeared. In some situations, quite different weed problems may arise following the control of woody growth. Thus, in forestry, growth of grasses or herbaceous species may become a problem and require cutting-back or spraying with appropriate herbicides.

These remarks apply to projects where it is intended that the land be put to a productive use and should not be allowed to revert to its former state. They would not necessarily be applicable where only a short-term removal of woody growth is required, e.g. for rabbit control, or where control of individual stumps or large trees is required.

CHEMICALS

Many different chemicals are effective to some degree on woody species, but the most generally useful compounds available at present are 2,4,5-T, 2,4-D and ammonium sulphamate.

2,4,5-T AND 2,4-D

349. These growth regulators are effective for the control of many woody species when applied by several methods as detailed below. They are effective at relatively low doses, are of low toxicity to man or animals, and do not corrode spraying equipment. Generally, for woody species, ester formulations of these compounds are superior to water-soluble metallic salt or amine derivatives. The specific ester may vary from product to product, and low volatile esters should be used to reduce the hazard of vapour drift on to susceptible crops. Although 2,4,5-T is more effective than 2,4-D on the majority of woody plants, 2,4-D is relatively cheap and effective for certain woody species (see Table 8) and is particularly useful against herbaceous weeds. Commercial products often contain a mixture of 2,4-D and 2,4,5-T esters, usually in the proportion 2 : 1, and these are economical and valuable, notably for foliage spraying where mixed stands of woody and herbaceous weeds are encountered. Choice of the type of herbicide to use should be governed by the species composition of the growth to be controlled and the cost of chemical. If the species are susceptible to 2,4-D, this herbicide should be used. If most species are resistant to 2,4-D, then 2,4,5-T should be used. Mixtures of 2,4-D and 2,4,5-T should be used where there are only a few species present which are resistant to 2,4-D. Products based on 2,4,5-T or 2,4-D esters, and mixtures of 2,4-D plus 2,4,5-T esters, are available formulated as emulsifiable concentrates which can be emulsified in water for foliage spraying, or dissolved in mineral oil for application to the bark of stems or cut-stumps. Cheaper unformulated esters of these compounds are also available for use in oil-solution. Diesel oil, paraffin, gas-oil, or vaporizing oil are suitable oil diluents for formulated and unformulated ester products.

350. [For Information] A recent development has been the introduction of invert-emulsions of esters of 2,4-D and 2,4,5-T. Unlike the normal 'oil-in-water' emulsions in which water forms the continuous phase, an invert emulsion consists of water droplets suspended in a continuous oil phase. Such emulsions are of special interest as they are 'thicker' than 'oil-in-water' types and are less liable to spray-drift. A further advantage is that the spray droplets are visible on plant surfaces for a short time after application which helps as a marker in control of spraying operations. The 'thick' nature of the emulsion necessitates special care in preparation and mixing. It has also been claimed that in some circumstances, herbicides applied as invert-emulsions are more effective than the same herbicide applied as an ordinary emulsion. No firm recommendations can be made at present.

FENOPROP

351. [For Information] Fenoprop has been found promising in the U.S.A. when applied as a foliage spray for the control of woody plants and is reported to be superior to 2,4,5-T notably on oak species. No firm recommendations can be made at present.

AMMONIUM SULPHAMATE

352. This chemical is effective against a wide range of woody plants, including several important species which are relatively resistant to 2,4,5-T and 2,4-D. It is a very soluble crystalline solid, which absorbs moisture readily when exposed to damp air. It is of low toxicity to animals, and a point to stress is that in solution it is highly corrosive to some metals, particularly brass, brass alloys and galvanized material in spraying equipment. It can act both as a contact and translocated herbicide, and is mainly used in concentrated aqueous solution or in dry solid form for application to cut-stumps, or notches or 'frill-girdles' cut in the stems of standing trees.

METHODS OF APPLICATION AND USES

353. Five methods of applying herbicides for controlling woody growth are in common use. These are:

(1) Summer foliage sprays.
(2) Winter sprays to dormant shoots.
(3) Basal-bark sprays to standing stems.
(4) Treatment of cut girdles or notches on standing trees.
(5) Treatment of cut-stumps.

The choice of method depends on many factors, including the type of vegetation, season, accessibility and available equipment.

SUMMER FOLIAGE SPRAYS

CHOICE OF CHEMICALS

354. 2,4,5-T, 2,4-D, or mixtures of the two compounds (see above) may be used very effectively at this stage for controlling seedlings, low shrubs and thickets, coppice and tree growth, and regrowth following cutting. An emulsifiable concentrate should be used, diluted with water to produce an emulsion for application as an overall spray to foliage. Addition of oil to the emulsion may increase the effectiveness of treatments against more resistant species.

METHODS AND EQUIPMENT

355. Foliage sprays give the best results when applied during the time between maximum leaf expansion and the end of the period of shoot growth, i.e. June–August. This treatment has proved very effective against brambles, heather and seedling woody species. It is rather less effective against coppice sprouts developing from stools with well established root systems, and fresh sprouts may develop requiring a further treatment for complete kill. In all cases it is essential that a reasonably large leaf area is exposed to treatment, and coppice

10

sprouts should not normally be treated with foliage sprays until they are two or three years old. After spraying, it is an important general rule that treated growth should not be cut until it is dead, or resprouting from the stump will occur.

356. In foliage spraying, the aim must always be complete and uniform coverage of leaf-surfaces and shoots, and the volumes of spray per acre required to achieve this will depend on the type of growth, and the spraying equipment used. Broadly, sprays may be applied as 'high-volume' (50 to 150 gallons per acre), or 'low-volume' (5 to 20 gallons per acre) using the same amount of active ingredient per acre. In practice, high-volume treatments have usually given more consistent results than low-volume sprays. The main types of application are briefly described in paragraphs 357 to 361 below.

Low Growth

357. For low weed-growth, i.e. less than 4 feet high, there is a choice between high-volume spraying, using powered pressure sprayers or knapsack sprayers, and low-volume spraying using aircraft or powered 'mist-blowers'. For *high-volume* spraying, dilute the equivalent of 2 to 4 lb (acid equivalent)* of the herbicide in the volume of water judged necessary to cover all leaf surfaces per acre. This will require 50–150 gallons of water per acre depending on the height and density of growth. On easy ground, with uniformly low growth, a tractor-mounted sprayer with a raised spray-boom is effective and cheap. However, this may be impossible under many conditions, and the best method will be to use a power-sprayer mounted on a tractor, trailer or other vehicle, to supply one or more long hoses fitted with spray-lances, which can be controlled by hand within the treatment area. Power sprayers permit speedy treatment of large areas, and should be used at fairly high pressures, around 60 lb per square inch, to ensure efficient spray distribution and coverage. The large volumes of liquid required for this treatment make it impractical for treating areas where water supplies are limited or where vehicle-mounted spray-tanks cannot be taken. Knapsack sprayers are valuable for localized treatments but are impractical for overall spraying except in small areas.

358. [Tentative] *Low-volume* spraying is a relatively recent development in this application, and requires a tractor-mounted or knapsack-type 'mist-blower', capable of delivering a finely divided spray uniformly over a swathe 10 to 15 feet wide. Good coverage can be achieved on most low growth types at about 15 gallons spray per acre, using this method. This technique is still somewhat experimental, but merits practical scale trial as it greatly reduces the problem of transporting and handling large volumes of liquid. In suitable circumstances, aerial spraying may be an efficient and cheap method for

* Readers are reminded that all doses refer to the acid equivalent or active ingredient of the herbicide as appropriate.

treatment of low growth. Low volume spraying using mist blowers or aircraft may give rise to a considerable risk of damage to adjoining susceptible crops through drift of fine spray droplets unless special precautions are taken (see paragraph 382). For low-volume spraying use 2 to 4 lb of the herbicide in 10 to 20 gallons of spray per acre. This may be applied in water or a 1 : 4 mixture of oil and water. If the latter, the emulsifiable concentrate should be dissolved in oil, and an emulsion prepared by slowly adding the herbicide and oil solution to the water, stirring to ensure a fine emulsion.

High Growth

359. It is usually impractical to apply foliage sprays to growth higher than about 4 feet using ground equipment, although isolated shrubs, etc. can be treated up to 6 to 8 feet using a power spray-lance or mist-blower. Recent experience has shown that helicopters can be used effectively and cheaply for foliage spraying of high cover, notably birch, oak, aspen, chestnut and black-thorn. For helicopter spraying, 2 to 4 lb of herbicide in 5 gallons diesel oil or 10 gallons 1 : 4 diesel oil and water emulsion may be used. Spray-swathe markers, usually two men with poles and flags, *must* be used to ensure accurate work in areas of woody growth. Helicopter operations are rapid, the machine normally operating at about 40 m.p.h. some 4 to 6 feet above the canopy and covering a swathe width of about 60 feet. A well planned ground organization is essential to exploit this feature to the full (see paragraph 358).

360. [**For Information**] Aerial spraying of herbicides is a relatively new departure, and sites for aerial applications must be carefully selected with an eye to amenity considerations and the risk of spray drift on to susceptible agricultural or horticultural and garden crops. Spraying should not normally be done when the wind speed exceeds 5 m.p.h. or within 400 yards of a susceptible crop.

Uses

361. Foliage sprays can be usefully employed for woody weed control in several situations, viz:

(a) Preparation of ground for tree planting.

(b) [**Tentative**] Weed control after tree planting. Recent experience has shown that 2,4,5-T or 2,4-D + 2,4,5-T mixtures can be used for selective control of broad-leaved woody weeds in young *conifer* crops, providing spraying is *confined to the period August to October, when conifer shoots have ceased elongation and terminal buds have formed.* The following species appear to be resistant to sprays applied at this stage – Scots pine, Corsican pine, *Pinus contorta*, Norway spruce, Sitka spruce, Douglas fir, *Thuja* and Lawson cypress. The dose should not exceed 2 lb (acid equivalent) per acre, and the treatment should be applied only as a water emulsion. Oil must *not* be used as a diluent. The sprays can be applied overall at low-volume or high-volume (see paragraphs 357 and 358), but low-volume spraying, may be preferable on many sites due to the reduced weight of liquid for transport. With knapsack-type sprayers and mistblowers, the sprays can be directed to ensure that heavier patches of weed growth are well covered, and to minimize the volume reaching the crop. Although this recommendation is **tentative**, results show promise and practical-scale trial is justified.

(c) Release of underplantings of conifer species by control of high hardwood cover where amenity considerations permit.

(d) Reclamation of agricultural land on which scrub is encroaching.

(e) Removal of cover as part of vermin control programmes.

(f) Control of woody growth on uncropped land, e.g. roadsides, power-lines, fence-lines and fire-breaks.

WINTER SPRAYING OF DORMANT SHOOTS

362. Some species are more susceptible to overall treatment with 2,4,5-T or 2,4-D in winter than in summer, e.g. hawthorn and buckthorn. However, dormant season treatments must be applied at a somewhat higher concentration in *oil*; water is not a suitable carrier at this stage.

CHOICE OF CHEMICALS

363. As oil solutions are involved, unformulated esters or esters formulated as emulsifiable concentrates may be used (see also paragraphs 349 and 350).

METHODS AND EQUIPMENT

364. All shoots must be thoroughly wetted, but with the exception of evergreen species the volume required for coverage will be low compared with summer foliage spraying. The requirement of an oil diluent will normally mean that the cost per acre will be higher than foliage sprays. The herbicide should be applied at a minimum of 4 lb per acre in the volume of oil required to wet all shoot surfaces. The remarks in paragraph 357 above regarding equipment for high-volume spraying also apply. Little information is available on the use of low-volume sprays at this season.

USES

365. Dormant shoots sprays are effective against a wide variety of woody species. However, they must not be applied to conifers or other forest plantations, as all crops are liable to damage by oil sprays (see paragraph 361).

BASAL BARK SPRAYS

366. This method can be used for controlling standing shrubs and small trees, and is particularly useful where foliage spraying is dangerous on account of drift, where it is desired to extend the season of treatment, and where it is unnecessary to incur the expense of cutting and clearance of growth.

CHOICE OF CHEMICALS

367. Basal sprays are prepared by dissolving esters of 2,4,5-T or 2,4-D in oil. For most species, 2,4,5-T is the best chemical, but 2,4-D or mixtures of 2,4-D and 2,4,5-T may be suitable on certain kinds of growth. Unformulated esters or emulsifiable concentrates may be used.

METHODS AND EQUIPMENT

368. The method involves spraying or painting a concentrated solution of the herbicide in oil on to the bark around stem bases. The solution should be applied to saturate the bark to the point of run-off over the full circumference of the stem from a height of 12 inches to ground level. The main target is the bark at, and immediately below, ground level and spraying should be done to ensure run-down and thorough wetting of this region. Oil solutions are necessary to ensure adequate penetration of the bark. Smaller trees and shrubs, i.e. less than 4 to 6 inches diameter are the most susceptible, probably because of their thinner bark and easier penetration of the herbicide. The required concentrations for spraying are 10 to 20 lb per 100 gallons of oil (usually diesel oil or vaporizing oil), a general satisfactory strength being 15 lb per 100 gallons. The volume of spray required per acre to ensure thorough wetting of the root-collar region varies greatly with size and density of growth, but will usually be in the region of 20 to 60 gallons per acre. As a guide, the volumes required will be about 30 ml (1/20th pint) spray per inch of stem diameter (i.e. 1 gallon of spray will treat about 150 inches of stem diameter. Most hardwoods are susceptible to treatment at any season, the most consistent results having been obtained in the period January to August. It is important that the stems be dry at the time of spraying. Power sprayers with long hoses, or knapsack sprayers, operated at low pressures to avoid wasteful and dangerous drift, are suitable for this work. Both types should be fitted with instantaneous trigger type 'on–off' taps to avoid wastage of material. Narrow-angle cone jets facilitate accurate and economical spraying.

USES

369. In forestry, basal bark spraying has been found an effective and economical method for opening up the top-cover of unmerchantable species before or after underplanting. In the latter case, there is no serious risk to the planted crop providing treatments are applied in the dormant season (January to March) and care is taken to prevent drift on to crop trees.

CUT-BARK TREATMENTS ON STANDING TREES

370. These treatments involve application of herbicides to freshly cut surfaces, usually in the form of frill-girdles or notches cut into the bark and sapwood near the base of the standing stems. They are most applicable to stems larger than 4 to 6 inches in diameter, for which they may be better than basal bark sprays because of better penetration and economy of chemicals.

CHOICE OF CHEMICALS

371. Depending on species, 2,4,5-T, 2,4-D or a mixture of esters may be used in oil solution. Unformulated esters or emulsifiable concentrates can be used. For species resistant to these growth-regulators, ammonium sulphamate may be applied as dry crystals or in concentrated aqueous solution.

METHODS AND EQUIPMENT

372. If 2,4,5-T or 2,4-D is used, a 'frill' girdle may be prepared, as near ground level as possible, consisting of a series of downward-sloping and overlapping cuts made with a light axe. The herbicide solution containing 20 lb per 100 gallons of oil should then be poured or sprayed into the *fresh* cuts to flood the whole length of the frill girdle. The volume applied must be sufficient to wet the full circumference of the girdle, and it may be easier to spray the bark at the top edge of the girdle, allowing the solution to run down into the cuts. As a general rule about 5 ml solution will be required per inch of stem diameter, (i.e. 1 gallon will treat about 900 inches stem diameter).

373. If 2,4,5-T or 2,4-D is used, 'notches' may be cut with a small axe near the ground level, each notch being made by two slanting strokes of the axe to produce a downward sloping notch penetrating at least to the cambium, and preferably into the outer sapwood. Notches should be spaced not wider than 4 inches edge to edge. The notches should be treated with the herbicide in oil solution, using 5 to 10 ml solution per notch. Notching is the cheapest and easiest method, but frilling usually gives the most consistently good control.

374. Ammonium sulphamate, when applied to stem cuts, is effective against the majority of woody species including several, notably hawthorn, ash and Rhododendron, which are resistant to 2,4,5-T and growth regulators. This compound can be used very conveniently applied as dry crystals to notches (see paragraph 373), at about 0·5 oz crystals per notch. Alternatively, frill girdles may be treated with a solution containing 4 lb of the chemical per gallon of water.

375. With the methods described in paragraphs 370 to 374 the best results should be obtained by treatment very shortly after the cuts are made, preferably after full leaf development in the period July to September. Knapsack or small hand-sprayers are suitable for treatment of girdles using low spray-pressures. Alternatively, a simple spouted-can may be used. Ammonium sulphamate solution is corrosive to some metals and should normally be handled in plastic containers or corrosion-resistant sprayers. A suitable measuring spoon and plastic bucket are suitable for dry application of this salt.

USES

See paragraph 369. Treatments can be used in planted areas if care is taken to prevent drift.

TREATMENT OF CUT-STUMPS

376. This method involves felling of unwanted shrubs and trees followed by application of herbicide to prevent regrowth.

CHOICE OF CHEMICALS

See paragraph 371.

METHOD AND EQUIPMENT

377. 2,4,5-T or 2,4-D in oil at 15 lb per 100 gallons of oil is the most satisfactory treatment. As for basal-bark spraying (paragraph 368), the bark at the ground line is the main target for treatment and in practice, sprays should be applied to wet the periphery of the cut-surfaces, and the whole of the bark surface of the stump to the point of run-off. Treatment can be applied effectively at any season, January to March being the best period for winter treatment. At any season spraying of rain-wet stumps should be avoided. Stumps which have re-sprouted producing coppice shoots, can also be killed by spraying the bark of the stump and bases of the young shoots. This is also recommended as a 'spot' treatment of any sprouts appearing in the season following spraying of newly-cut stumps.

378. Ammonium sulphamate is effective as a stump treatment for most woody species, including Rhododendron, laurel, hawthorn and ash, which are resistant to 2,4,5-T. For stumps and stools with many stems, the best method is treatment of freshly cut stumps using ammonium sulphamate at 4 lb per gallon of water plus a wetting agent, applied liberally to the stump, particularly the cut-surfaces. Alternatively, if the number of stems is not too large, it will be easier and cheaper to apply dry crystals to the cut surface at the rate of about 0·5 oz per inch of stump diameter. In this case retention of crystals will be improved if the cutting is done to produce a level or vee-shaped cut-surface.

379. Killing of large stumps, i.e. 10 inches in diameter and over, can be a problem in some circumstances. Surface application of 2,4,5-T or ammonium sulphamate may not be sufficient in these cases, particularly if the stump has been cut for some time before treatments can be applied. In such cases, it may be necessary to apply the herbicide to a frill girdle or a series of notches cut into the bark and sapwood as low as necessary on the stump in order to expose living tissues. Ammonium sulphamate as dry crystals or in aqueous solution or 2,4,5-T oil solution can then be applied as described in paragraphs 337 and 338. For cut-stump treatment, low-pressure spraying is required for accurate placement and avoidance of wasteful drift. The simplest knapsack sprayers are suitable for this purpose (see paragraph 368). As ammonium sulphamate solution is highly corrosive to metal parts of spraying equipment, special resistant sprayers, or a plastic watering-can with *fine* rose should be used.

USES

380. Treatment of cut-stumps to prevent coppice-sprout production on hardwoods is easy to apply, and, in forest areas, can result in considerable saving in costs of subsequent weeding. Also, costs of cleaning operations at the time of brashing and first thinning will be reduced. The treatment can also be applied to stumps among a young tree crop providing treatments are applied in the dormant season and care is taken to avoid drift on to crop trees.

PRECAUTIONS

PROTECTION OF OPERATORS

381. All the herbicides mentioned have a very low level of toxicity to man and animals, but prolonged exposure, notably to oil solutions, may cause skin or eye irritation to some individuals. Plastic gloves and light goggles should be available for personnel mixing spray materials. Also, for some types of mist-spraying, a face mask may be desirable to avoid prolonged breathing in of oil droplets.

SPRAY DRIFT

382. Both 2,4-D and 2,4,5-T can cause serious damage if spray is allowed to drift on to nearby susceptible crops. The risk is greatest with low-volume overall sprays, i.e. 'mist-blower' or aerial sprays, but precautions must be taken during any spraying operation. The main points to observe are discussed generally in Section (iii) of Chapter VII. In forests avoid spraying in areas adjoining susceptible agricultural or other crops. When aerial spraying, do not spray within at least 400 yards of a susceptible crop. This distance may need to be greater in adverse conditions. The actual distance must be determined by individual judgement. Always use low volatile ester formulations to reduce the risk of damage by vapour drift.

CLEANING OF EQUIPMENT

383. Great care must be taken to clean spraying equipment thoroughly after use for 2,4-D or 2,4,5-T spraying before it is used for any other purpose. Cleaning should be done immediately after spraying by pouring a volume of diesel oil into the tank and recirculating through the sprayer, pump and spray lines, into the tank. This oil should then be sprayed out and replaced by a large volume of water containing a wetter, circulated through the sprayer, followed by washing in clean water, Equipment which has been used for ammonium sulphamate solution should be washed and sprayed out thoroughly with clean water, and metal parts treated with light oil.

THE RESPONSE OF WOODY WEEDS TO 2,4,5-T-ESTER AND 2,4-D-ESTER

384. Table 8 summarizes the information available on the response of some common woody weeds to 2,4,5-T-ester and 2,4-D-ester when applied in the manner recommended in the preceding paragraphs.

TABLE 8. THE RESPONSE OF COMMON WOODY WEEDS TO ESTER FORMULATIONS OF 2,4,5-T AND 2,4-D

Recommended ranges of doses for esters of 2,4,5-T and 2,4-D are:

(1) Overall Summer Foliage Sprays – 2 to 4 lb (a.e.) per acre in water.
(2) Overall Winter Shoot Sprays – 4 to 6 lb. (a.e.) per acre in oil.
(3) Basal Bark and Cut-stump Treatments – 10 to 20 (a.e.) per 100 gallons of oil.

The categories of response for these doses are as follows:

S Consistently good control by suggested technique with little resprouting.
MS Good control of aerial growth by suggested technique but generally requiring a higher concentration than for 'S' category.
MR Some useful effect from the higher concentrations, but recovery rapid.
R No useful effect at the highest doses quoted.

Species	Water				Oil				Remarks
	Overall sprays								
	Summer foliage		Dormant shoot		Basal bark		Stump		
	2,4-D	2,4,5-T	2,4-D	2,4,5-T	2,4-D	2,4,5-T	2,4-D	2,4,5-T	
Acer campestre (Maple)		MS		MS	MS	S		S	
Acer pseudoplatanus (sycamore)		MS				MS		MS	
Aesculus hippocastanum (horse chestnut)		MS				S		S	
Alnus spp. (alder)	MS	S		S	MR	MS		S	
Betula spp. (birch)	MS	S		S	MS	S	S	S	
Buxus sempervirens (box)		MS		S					

TABLE 8—*contiued*

Species	Water				Oil				Remarks
	Overall sprays				Basal bark		Stump		
	Summer foliage		Dormant shoot						
	2,4-D	2,4,5-T	2,4-D	2,4,5-T	2,4-D	2,4,5-T	2,4-D	2,4,5-T	
Calluna vulgaris (heather)	S*	MR							*Apply June/Aug. at 5 lb. (a.e.) in 60 gallons per acre.
Carpinus betulus (hornbeam)		MR		MS		MS		S	
Castanea sativa (spanish chestnut)		MS			MS	S	MS	S	
Thelycrania sanguinea (dogwood)		S		MS				MS	
Corylus avellana (hazel)	MR	MS		MS	MR	MS	MS	S	
Crataegus monogyma (hawthorn)	R	MR		S	R	MR		MR	Ammonium sulphamate to cut stumps (see text).
Fagus sylvatica (beech)		MS		S					
Fraxinus excelsior (ash)	MR	MR		MS	R	MR	MR	MS	
Hedera helix (ivy)	R	MR		S					
Ilex aquifolium (holly)	R	R			MR			MS	
Juniperus communis (juniper)	R	R							
Ligustrum vulgare (privet)		MS		MS			MR	MS	
Pinus sylvestris (scots pine)	R	MR			MR	MS			
Populus spp. (poplar)	MS	S		S	MS	S		S	
Prunus spinosa (blackthorn)		S		MS	R	MS	MR	S	
Pyrus communis (wild pear)		MS						S	
Quercus spp. (oak)	R	MR		MS	MS	S		MS	
Rhamnus cartharticus (buckthorn)		MS		S				MS	
Rhododendron ponticum (rhododendron)	R	MR		MS	R	MR	R	MR	Ammonium sulphamate to cut stumps (see text).
Rosa spp. (briar)	MR	S†		S				S	
Rubus spp. (blackberry etc.)	MR	S†		S				S	Old canes more susceptible than young growth. † Good control at 1–2 lb (a.e.) per acre.
Salix spp. (willow)	S†	S†		S		MS		MS	
Sambucus nigra (elder)	MS	S†		S	S	S		S	
Sarothamnus scoparius (broom)	S	S				MS		MS	
Sorbus aucuparia (rowan)	MS	MS				MS		MS	
Tilia spp. (lime)		MS						S	
Ulex spp. (gorse)	MR	S	MS††				MR	S	†† Applied in water.
Ulmus spp. (elm)	MR	MS		S			MS	S	
Vaccinium spp. (bilberry)	MS								

CHAPTER V

THE EFFECT OF HERBICIDES ON WEEDS OF AGRICULTURE, HORTICULTURE AND FORESTRY

SECTION (i) THE RESPONSE OF HERBACEOUS WEEDS TO GROWTH REGULATOR HERBICIDES

EXPLANATORY NOTES

385. Table 9 indicates the susceptibility or resistance of annual, biennial or perennial weeds (other than woody and aquatic species, and weeds in lawns and sports turf) to growth regulator herbicides applied at doses commonly recommended in agricultural and horticultural practice. It is intended to serve as a comprehensive reference list and a guide for the reader who wishes to choose the appropriate herbicide for any particular weed or group of weeds. Detailed information on the susceptibility of weeds of importance in cereals is given in Table 5, on page 38. The response of weeds in lawns to MCPA, 2,4-D and mecoprop is given in Table 7 on page 122, and the susceptibility of woody weeds to 2,4-D and 2,4,5-T will be found in Table 8 on pages 141–2.

When selecting a herbicide it should be remembered that crop tolerance should be taken into consideration and the appropriate paragraph(s) in the preceding chapters should be consulted. Once a particular herbicide has been selected and a product based on it obtained, the manufacturers' instructions should be carefully followed.

Table 9 is based on the results of experimental and practical applications of typical commercial products containing the active ingredient(s) specified at the head of each column and without any special additives such as wetting agents. The doses chosen for the chemicals are typical of those currently recommended for many purposes but should not be taken as indicating either the maximum tolerated by any particular crop or the relative activity in general of the various herbicides.

386. Several commercial mixtures of some herbicides are available as branded products. The two appearing in Table 9 are included because information on the susceptibility of weeds to one component in each mixture is not presented elsewhere in the Handbook. The other commercial mixtures contain herbicides for which there are categories of response shown in Table 9. The purpose of mixtures of two or more herbicides is to extend the range of weeds controlled. It is not possible however to deduce from this table the susceptibility of weeds to commercial mixtures. As a practical guide the potential value of a mixture may be estimated by combining the list of species classified as generally susceptible to one constituent with those similarly classified with regard to the other constituent, except where the dose of one of the constituents is appreciably lower than the dose shown in the table. The Agricultural Chemicals Approval Organization (see Chapter VIII, Section (iv)) has approved a number of mixtures. A list of Approved Products may be obtained from the Ministry of Agriculture, Fisheries and Food (Publications), Ruskin Avenue, Kew, Surrey.

TABLE 9. THE RESPONSE OF HERBACEOUS WEEDS TO GROWTH REGULATOR HERBICIDES

Definition of categories

	Annual and seedling biennials and perennials	*Established biennials and perennials*
S – **Susceptible**	Consistently good control at all stages of growth up to the beginning of flowering.	Consistently good control (both shoot and roots) when treated at the recommended time.
MS – **Moderately susceptible**	Good control in seedling stage (cotyledon to 2 or 3 leaves) and possibility of useful suppression at later growth stages.	Aerial growth usually killed and a useful measure of long term control obtained under suitable conditions.
MR – **Moderately resistant**	Checked in seedling stage only (cotyledon to 2 or 3 leaves).	Variable effect on aerial growth—appreciable long term control unlikely from a single application.
R – **Resistant**	No useful effect.	No useful effect.

Chemical and dose; oz acid equivalent per acre Weed	MCPA -salt 24	2,4-D -amine 20	MCPB -salt 32	2,4-DB -salt 32	Meco-prop -salt 40†	Dichlor-prop -salt 40†	MCPA plus 2,3,6- TBA -salts 12+4	MCPA plus 3,6-dichloro-2-methoxy-benzoic acid-salts 18+1·3	Cross reference (page no.)
1. *Achillea millefolium* (P) (yarrow)	MR	MR	—	—	—	—	—	—	
2. *Aegopodium podagraria* (P) (ground elder)	R	R	R	R	—	—	—	—	167
3. *Aethusa cynapium* (A) (fool's parsley)	MS	—	—	—	—	—	—	—	
4. *Agrimonia eupatoria* (P) (common agrimony)	R	R	R	R	—	—	—	—	
5. *Agropyron repens* (P) (couch grass)	R	R	R	R	R	R	R	R	167
6. *Agrostemma githago* (A) (corncockle)	R	R	R	—	—	—	MR	—	

TABLE 9 (*continued*)

Chemical and dose; oz acid equivalent per acre / Weed	MCPA -salt 24	2,4-D -amine 20	MCPB -salt 32	2,4-DB -salt 32	Meco-prop -salt 40†	Dichlor-prop -salt 40†	MCPA plus 2,3,6-TBA -salts 12+4	MCPA plus 3,6-dichloro-2-methoxy-benzoic acid-salts 18+1·3	Cross reference (page no.)
7. *Agrostis gigantea* (P) (common bent-grass)	R	R	R	R	R	R	R	R	167
8. *Agrostis stolonifera* (P) (creeping bent-grass)	R	R	R	R	R	R	R	R	167
9. *Ajuga reptans* (P) (bugle)	R	R	R	R	R	—	R	—	
10. *Allium ursinum* (P) (ramsons)	R	R	—	—	—	—	—	—	
11. *Allium vineale* (P) (wild onion)	MR	MR	—	—	—	—	—	—	171
12. *Alopecurus myosuroides* (A) (blackgrass)	R	R	R	R	R	R	R	R	172
13. *Amsinckia intermedia* (A)	R	MR	—	—	MR	—	R	MS	
14. *Anagallis arvensis* (A) (scarlet pimpernel)	MS	MS	MS	MS	MR	MR	MS	S	
15. *Anchusa arvensis* (A or B) (bugloss)	MR	MR	—	—	—	—	MS	—	
16. *Anthemis arvensis* (A) (corn chamomile)	MR	MR	R	R	MR	MR	MS	—	
17. *Anthemis cotula* (A) (stinking mayweed)	MR	MR	R	R	MR	R	MS	—	
18. *Anthriscus sylvestris* (P) (cow parsley)	MR	MR	—	—	—	—	—	—	
19. *Aphanes arvensis* (A) (parsley piert)	R	R	R	R	—	R	R	—	
20. *Arctium lappa* (B) (greater burdock)	MR	MR	—	—	—	—	—	—	

TABLE 9 (*continued*)

Weed — Chemical and dose; oz acid equivalent per acre	MCPA -salt 24	2,4-D -amine 20	MCPB -salt 32	2,4-DB -salt 32	Meco- prop -salt 40†	Dichlor- prop -salt 40†	MCPA plus 2,3,6- TBA -salts 12+4	MCPA plus 3,6-dichloro- 2-methoxy- benzoic acid-salts 18+1·3	Cross reference (page no.)
21. *Arctium minus* (B) (lesser burdock)	MS	MS	—	—	—	—	—	—	
22. *Arenaria serpyllifolia* (A or B) (thyme-leaved sandwort)	S	S	—	—	—	—	—	—	
23. *Armoracia rusticana* (P) (horse-radish)	MS	MS	—	—	MS	—	—	—	
24. *Arrhenatherum elatius* (P) (onion couch)	R	R	R	R	R	R	R	R	173
25. *Artemisia vulgaris* (P) (mugwort)	MS	MS	—	—	—	—	—	—	
26. *Atriplex patula* (A) (common orache)	S	S	MS	MS	S	MS	S	S	
27. *Avena fatua* (A) (wild oat)	R	R	R	R	R	R	R	R	173
28. *Avena ludoviciana* (A) (wild oat)	R	R	R	R	R	R	R	R	173
29. *Bellis perennis* (P) (daisy)	MS	MS	MR	MR	MS	—	MS	MS	
30. *Brassica juncea* (A) (Indian mustard)	S	S	—	—	—	—	—	S	
31. *Brassica napus* var. *arvensis* (A) (rape)	S	S	—	—	—	—	S	S	

† Total mecoprop or dichlorprop in terms of active and inactive isomers in ratio 50/50.
(A), (B), (P) – Annual, biennial, perennial respectively.

TABLE 9 (continued)

Weed	MCPA -salt 24	2,4-D -amine 20	MCPB -salt 32	2,4-DB -salt 32	Meco- prop -salt 40†	Dichlor- prop -salt 40†	MCPA plus 2,3,6- TBA -salts 12+4	MCPA plus 3,6-dichloro- 2-methoxy- benzoic acid-salts 18+1·3	Cross reference (page no.)
32. Brassica nigra (A) (black mustard)	S*	S*	S	S	S	S	S	S	
33. Brassica rapa ssp. campestris (A) (wild turnip)	S	S	S	—	S	MS	S	S	
34. Calystegia sepium (P) (bellbine)	MS	MS	MS	MS	—	—	—	—	
35. Capsella bursa-pastoris (A) (shepherd's purse)	S	S	S	S	S	MS	S	S	
36. Cardamine hirsuta (A) (hairy bittercress)	—	—	—	—	—	—	MS	—	
37. Cardaria draba (P) (hoary pepperwort)	S	S	MS	—	—	—	—	—	
38. Carduus nutans (P) (musk thistle)	MS	MS	MS	—	—	—	—	MS–MR	176
39. Carex spp. (P) (sedges)	R	R	R	—	—	—	—	—	
40. Centaurea cyanus (A) (cornflower)	S	S	—	—	—	—	—	MS	
41. Centaurea nigra (P) (knapweed)	MS	MS	—	—	—	—	—	—	
42. Centaurea scabiosa (P) (greater knapweed)	MR	MR	—	—	—	—	—	—	
43. Cerastium arvense (P) (field mouse-ear chickweed)	R	R	R	—	MS	—	MS	—	
44. Cerastium glomeratum (A) (sticky mouse-ear chickweed)	MR	MS	R	—	MR	—	MS	—	

Weed	MCPA -salt 24	2,4-D -amine 20	MCPB -salt 32	2,4-DB -salt 32	Meco- prop -salt 40†	Dichlor- prop -salt 40†	MCPA plus 2,3,6- TBA -salts 12+4	MCPA plus 3,6-dichloro- 2-methoxy- benzoic acid-salts 18+1·3	Cross reference (page no.)
45. *Cerastium holosteoides* (A or P) (mouse-ear chickweed)	MS	MS	—	—	MS	MS	MS	—	
46. *Chaenorhinum minus* (A) (small toadflax)	—	—	—	—	MR	—	—	—	
47. *Chaerophyllum temulentum* (B) (rough chervil)	—	—	—	—	—	—	—	—	
48. *Chamaenerion angustifolium* (P) (rosebay willow-herb)	R	MR	—	—	—	—	—	—	
49. *Chenopodium album* (A) (fat hen)	S	S	S	S	S	S	S	S	
50. *Chrysanthemum leucanthemum* (P) (ox-eye daisy)	MR	MR	R	—	MR	—	MR	—	
51. *Chrysanthemum segetum* (A) (corn marigold)	R	R	R	R	R	R	MR	—	
52. *Chrysanthemum vulgare* (P) (tansy)	MR	MR	—	—	—	—	—	—	
53. *Cichorium intybus* (P) (chicory)	MS	MS	R	MR	—	—	MS	S	
54. *Cirsium acaulon* (P) (stemless thistle)	MR	MR	—	—	—	—	MR	—	

† Total mecoprop or dichlorprop in terms of active and inactive isomers in ratio 50/50.

(A), (B), (P) – Annual, biennial, perennial respectively.

*Susceptible to 5 oz.

11

TABLE 9 (continued)

Weed; Chemical and dose; oz acid equivalent per acre	MCPA -salt 24	2,4-D -amine 20	MCPB -salt 32	2,4-DB -salt 32	Mecoprop -salt 40†	Dichlorprop -salt 40†	MCPA plus 2,3,6-TBA -salts 12+4	MCPA plus 3,6-dichloro-2-methoxy-benzoic acid-salts 18+1·3	Cross reference (page no.)
55. *Cirsium arvense* (P) (creeping thistle) Sd, Sh	S	S	S	S	S	S	S	S	177
EP(a)	S	S	S	S	S	—	MS	MS	
EP(g)	MS	MS	MS	MS	MS	—	MS	—	
56. *Cirsium vulgare* (B) (spear thistle) Sd	S	S	S	S	—	—	MS	—	
EP	MS	MS	MS	MS	—	—	MR	—	
57. *Colchicum autumnale* (P) (autumn crocus)	MR	MR	—	—	—	—	—	—	
58. *Conium maculatum* (B) (hemlock)	MR	MR	—	—	—	—	—	—	
59. *Conopodium majus* (P) (pignut)	R	R	—	—	—	—	—	—	
60. *Convolvulus arvensis* (P) (field bindweed) Sh	S	S	S	S	R	—	MS	S	177
EP	MR	MR	MR	MR	R	—	MS	MS	
61. *Conyza canadensis* (A) (Canadian fleabane)	S	S	—	—	—	—	—	—	
62. *Coronopus didymus* (A) (lesser swine-cress)	S	S	MS	S	S	—	S	S	
63. *Coronopus squamatus* (A or B) (swine-cress)	MR	MR	MR	MR	S	—	—	S	
64. *Crepis biennis* (B) (rough hawk's beard)	S	S	—	—	—	—	MS	—	
65. *Crepis capillaris* (A) (smooth hawk's beard)	—	MS	—	—	—	—	MS	—	
66. *Cuscuta epithymum* (A) (common dodder)	—	—	—	—	—	—	—	—	

TABLE 3 (continued)

Weed — Chemical and dose; oz acid equivalent per acre	MCPA -salt 24	2,4-D -amine 20	MCPB -salt 32	2,4-DB -salt 32	Meco-prop -salt 40†	Dichlor-prop -salt 40†	MCPA plus 2,3,6-TBA -salts 12+4	MCPA plus 3,6-dichloro-2-methoxy-benzoic acid-salts 18+1·3	Cross reference (page no.)
67. *Datura stramonium* (A) (thorn apple)	MS	MS	MR	MS	—	—	MS	—	
68. *Daucus carota* (B) (wild carrot)	MR	MR	R	MR	MR	—	MR	MR	
69. *Descurainia sophia* (A) (flixweed)	S	S	—	—	—	—	—	—	
70. *Echium vulgare* (B) (viper's bugloss)	MR	MR	—	—	—	—	MS	—	
71. *Epilobium* spp. (P) (willow herb)	MR	MR	R	R	—	—	MS	—	
72. *Equisetum arvense* (P) (horsetail) **Sh**	S	S	S	S	—	S	S	S	
72. *Equisetum arvense* (P) (horsetail) **EP**	R	R	R	R	R	—	R	—	
73. *Equisetum palustre* (P) (marsh horsetail) **Sh**	S	S	S	S	—	—	—	—	
73. *Equisetum palustre* (P) (marsh horsetail) **EP**	R	R	R	R	—	—	—	—	
74. *Erodium cicutarium* (A) (common storksbill)	MR	MR	—	—	—	—	—	—	
75. *Erysimum cheiranthoides* (A) (treacle mustard)	S	S	S	S	—	—	S	S	
76. *Euphorbia exigua* (A) (dwarf spurge)	—	—	—	—	—	—	—	—	

† Total mecoprop or dichlorprop in terms of active and inactive isomers in ratio 50/50.

(A), (B), (P) – Annual, biennial, perennial respectively.

Sd – seedlings   Sh – shoots.
EP – established plants.
(a) – in arable land.
(g) – in grass land.

TABLE 9 (continued)

Weed / Chemical and dose; oz acid equivalent per acre	MCPA -salt 24	2,4-D -amine 20	MCPB -salt 32	2,4-DB -salt 32	Meco- prop -salt 40†	Dichlor- prop -salt 40†	MCPA plus 2,3,6- TBA -salts 12+4	MCPA plus 3,6-dichloro- 2-methoxy- benzoic acid-salts 18+1·3	Cross reference (page no.)
77. *Euphorbia helioscopia* (A) (sun spurge)	MS	MR	—	—	—	—	—	—	—
78. *Euphorbia peplus* (A) (petty spurge)	MR	R	—	—	—	—	—	—	—
79. *Filipendula ulmaria* (P) (meadow sweet)	MR	MR	R	R	—	—	—	—	—
80. *Fumaria officinalis* (A) (fumitory)	MS	MS	MS	MS	S	MS	MS	S	—
81. *Galeopsis speciosa* (A) (large flowered hempnettle)	S	MS	—	—	—	—	S	S	—
82. *Galeopsis tetrahit* (A) (common hempnettle)	S	MR	MS	MR	MS	MS	S	S	—
83. *Galinsoga parviflora* (A) (gallant soldier)	S	S	—	—	—	—	S	S	—
84. *Galium aparine* (A) (cleavers)	R	R	R	R	S	MS	MR	MR	—
85. *Galium saxatile* (P) (heath bedstraw)	MR	—	—	—	—	—	MR	—	—
86. *Galium mollugo* (P) (hedge bedstraw)	—	—	—	—	—	—	MR	—	—
87. *Galium verum* (P) (ladies' bedstraw)	R	R	R	R	—	—	MR	—	—
88. *Geranium dissectum* (A) (cut-leaved cranesbill)	MR	MR	—	—	—	—	MR	—	—
89. *Geranium molle* (A) (dove's foot cranesbill)	MR	MR	—	—	MS	—	MR	—	—
90. *Geranium pratense* (P)	MR	MR	—	—	—	—	—	—	—

Weed / Chemical and dose; oz acid equivalent per acre	MCPA -salt 24	2,4-D -amine 20	MCPB -salt 32	2,4-DB -salt 32	Meco-prop -salt 40†	Dichlor-prop -salt 40†	MCPA plus 2,3,6-TBA -salts 12+4	MCPA plus 3,6-dichloro-2-methoxy-benzoic acid-salts 18+1·3	Cross reference (page no.)
91. *Geranium pusillum* (A) (small-flowered cranesbill)	—	—	—	—	—	—	—	—	
92. *Gnaphalium uliginosum* (A) (marsh cudweed)	—	—	R	—	—	—	—	—	
93. *Heracleum sphondylium* (P) (hogweed)	MR	MR	—	—	—	—	—	—	
94. *Hieraceum pilosella* (P) (mouse-ear hawkweed)	MS	MS	—	—	—	—	—	—	
95. *Holcus lanatus* (P) (Yorkshire fog)	R	R	R	R	R	R	R	R	
96. *Holcus mollis* (P) (creeping softgrass)	R	R	R	R	R	R	R	R	
97. *Hyoscyamus niger* (A or B) (henbane)	MR	MR	—	—	—	—	—	—	
98. *Hypericum perforatum* (P) (common St John's wort)	MR	MR	—	—	—	—	—	—	
99. *Hypochoeris radicata* (P) (cat's ear)	MS	MS	—	—	—	—	—	—	
100. *Iris pseudacorus* (P) (yellow flag)	MR	MR	R	R	—	—	—	—	
101. *Juncus acutiflorus* (P) (sharp-flowered rush)	—	—	—	—	—	—	—	—	
102. *Juncus articulatus* (P) (jointed rush)	R	R	R	R	—	—	—	—	

† Total mecoprop or dichlorprop in terms of active and inactive isomers in ratio 50/50.
(A), (B), (P) – Annual, biennial, perennial respectively.

TABLE 9 (continued)

Weed — Chemical and dose; oz acid equivalent per acre	MCPA -salt 24	2,4-D -amine 20	MCPB -salt 32	2,4-DB -salt 32	Meco-prop -salt 40†	Dichlor-prop -salt 40†	MCPA plus 2,3,6-TBA -salts 12+4	MCPA plus 3,6-dichloro-2-methoxy-benzoic acid-salts 18+1·3	Cross reference (page no.)
103. Juncus conglomeratus (P)	MS	—	MS	MS	—	—	—	—	
104. Juncus effusus (P) Sd, Sh EP (soft rush)	S MS	S MS	S MR	—	—	—	—	—	
105. Juncus inflexus (P) (hard rush)	MR	R	R	MR	—	—	—	—	
106. Juncus maritimus (P) (sea rush)	MR	MR	—	—	—	—	—	—	
107. Juncus squarrosus (P) (heath rush)	R	R	R	R	—	—	—	—	
108. Juncus subnodulosus (P) (blunt-flowered rush)	—	R	—	—	MR	—	—	—	
109. Knautia arvensis (P) (field scabious)	MS	MS	—	—	R	—	R	—	
110. Lamium album (P) (white deadnettle)	R	R	R	—	R	—	R	—	
111. Lamium amplexicaule (A) (henbit)	MS	MR	R	R	R	—	MS	—	
112. Lamium purpureum (A) (red deadnettle)	MR	MR	R	—	R	—	MR	—	
113. Lapsana communis (A) (nipplewort)	R	R	R	R	—	—	R	S	
114. Legousia hybrida (A) (Venus's looking glass)	MS	MR	—	—	—	—	MS	—	
115. Leontodon autumnalis (P) (autumnal hawkbit)	MS	S	MS	S	—	—	—	—	

Weed	MCPA -salt 24	2,4-D -amine 20	MCPB -salt 32	2,4-DB -salt 32	Meco-prop -salt 40†	Dichlor-prop -salt 40†	MCPA plus 2,3,6-TBA -salts 12+4	MCPA plus 3,6-dichloro-2-methoxy-benzoic acid-salts 18+1·3	Cross reference (page no.)
116. *Leontodon hispidus* (P) (rough hawkbit)	MR	MS	—	—	—	—	—	—	
117. *Linaria vulgaris* (P) (toadflax)	R	R	—	—	—	—	—	—	
118. *Lithospermum arvense* (A) (corn gromwell)	MS	MS	—	—	—	R	MS	—	
119. *Lotus corniculatus* (P) (birdsfoot trefoil)	MR	MR	—	—	—	—	—	—	
120. *Luzula campestris* (P) (field woodrush)	R	R	R	R	—	—	—	—	
121. *Lythrum salicaria* (P) (purple loosestrife)	—	MS	—	—	—	—	—	—	
122. *Matricaria recutita* (A) (wild chamomile)	R	R	R	R	R	R	MS	—	
123. *Matricaria matricarioides* (A) (pineapple weed)	R	R	R	R	R	—	MS	S	
124. *Medicago lupulina* (A or P) (black medick)	MR	MR	R	—	MR	—	S	—	
125. *Mentha arvensis* (P) (corn mint)	MR	MR	R	R	MR	R	R	MR	178
126. *Montia perfoliata* (A)	—	—	—	—	—	R	—	—	
127. *Myosotis arvensis* (A) (common forget-me-not)	MS	MS	MR	R	R	R	MS	—	

† Total mecoprop or dichlorprop in terms of active and inactive isomers in ratio 50/50.
(A), (B), (P) – Annual, biennial, perennial respectively.
Sd – seedlings. Sh – shoots.
EP – established plants.

TABLE 9 (continued)

Chemical and dose; oz acid equivalent per acre — Weed	MCPA -salt 24	2,4-D -amine 20	MCPB -salt 32	2,4-DB -salt 32	Meco-prop -salt 40†	Dichlor-prop -salt 40†	MCPA plus 2,3,6-TBA -salts 12+4	MCPA plus 3,6-dichloro-2-methoxy-benzoic acid-salts 18+1·3	Cross reference (page no.)
128. *Odontites verna* (A) (red bartsia)	MS	MS	R	—	—	—	—	—	
129. *Oenanthe crocata* (P) (hemlock water dropwort)	MS	—	—	—	—	—	—	—	
130. *Ononis repens* (P) (restharrow)	R	R	R	R	R	—	R	—	
131. *Orobanche minor* (A) (lesser broom-rape)	—	—	—	—	—	—	—	—	179
132. *Oxalis* spp. (P)	R	R	R	R	—	—	—	—	
133. *Papaver argemone* (A) (long prickly-headed poppy)	—	—	—	—	MS	—	MR	—	
134. *Papaver dubium* (A) (long-headed poppy)	—	—	—	—	MS	—	MR	—	
135. *Papaver rhoeas* (A) (corn poppy)	S	S	MS	MS	S	MS	MS	S	
136. *Petasites hybridus* (P) (butterbur)	R	MR	—	—	—	—	—	—	
137. *Picris echioides* (A or B) (bristly ox-tongue)	—	MS	—	—	—	—	MR	—	
138. *Plantago coronopus* (A, B or P) (starweed)	MS	MS	—	—	—	—	MS	—	
139. *Plantago lanceolata* (P) (ribwort)	S	S	S	S	S	—	—	S	
140. *Plantago major* (P) (greater plantain)	S	S	S	S	S	—	—	S	
141. *Plantago media* (P)	S	S	S	S	S	—	—	S	

TABLE 9 (continued)

Weed / Chemical and dose; oz acid equivalent per acre	MCPA -salt 24	2,4-D -amine 20	MCPB -salt 32	2,4-DB -salt 32	Meco-prop -salt 40†	Dichlor-prop -salt 40†	MCPA plus 2,3,6-TBA -salts 12+4	MCPA plus 3,6-dichloro-2-methoxy-benzoic acid-salts 18+1·3	Cross reference (page no.)
142. *Poa annua* (annual meadowgrass)	R	R	R	R	R	R	R	R	
143. *Polygonum amphibium* (P) (amphibious bistort)	MR	MR	—	—	—	—	—	—	
144. *Polygonum aviculare* (A) (knotgrass)	MR	MS	MR	MS	MR	MR	MS	S	
145. *Polygonum bistorta* (P) (bistort)	R	R	R	R	—	—	—	—	
146. *Polygonum convolvulus* (A) (black bindweed)	MR	MS	MR	MS	MR	S	MS	S	
147. *Polygonum lapathifolium* (A) (pale persicaria)	MR	MS	MR	S	S	S	MR	S	
148. *Polygonum persicaria* (A) (redshank)	MR	MS	MR	S	MR	S	MS	S	
149. *Potentilla anserina* (P) (silverweed)	MR	MR	—	—	—	—	—	—	
150. *Potentilla reptans* (P) (cinquefoil)	R	R	—	—	—	—	MR	—	
151. *Pteridium aquilinum* (P) (bracken)	R	R	R	R	R	—	R	—	
152. *Pulicaria dysenterica* (P) (fleabane)	MS	MS	—	—	—	—	—	—	
153. *Ranunculus acris* (P) (crowfoot)	S	S	S	S	S	S	—	S	

† Total mecoprop or dichlorprop in terms of active and inactive isomers in ratio 50/50.
(A), (B), (P) – Annual, biennial, perennial respectively.

TABLE 9 (*continued*)

Weed / Chemical and dose; oz acid equivalent per acre		MCPA-salt 24	2,4-D-amine 20	MCPB-salt 32	2,4-DB-salt 32	Mecoprop-salt 40†	Dichlorprop-salt 40†	MCPA plus 2,3,6-TBA-salts 12+4	MCPA plus 3,6-dichloro-2-methoxy-benzoic acid-salts 18+1·3	Cross reference (page no.)
154. *Ranunculus arvensis* (A) (corn buttercup)		S	S	S	S	S	MS	S	S	
155. *Ranunculus bulbosus* (P) (bulbous buttercup)	Sd, Sh	S	S	S	S	—	—	—	MR	
	EP	MR	MR	MR	MR	—	—	—	MR	
156. *Ranunculus repens* (P) (creeping buttercup)		S	S	S	S	S	—	S	S	
157. *Ranunculus sardous* (A) (hairy buttercup)		S	S	S	—	—	—	S	—	
158. *Raphanus raphanistrum* (A) (wild radish)		S	S	MR	R	S	S	S	S	
159. *Rhinanthus minor* (A) (yellow rattle)		MR	MR	—	—	—	—	MR	—	
160. *Rorippa sylvestris* (P) (creeping yellow-cress)		—	—	—	—	—	—	—	—	
161. *Rumex acetosa* (P) (sorrel)	Sh	MS	MS	—	—	—	—	—	—	
	EP	MR	MR	—	—	R	—	—	—	
162. *Rumex acetosella* (P) (sheep's sorrel)	Sh	MR	MS	—	—	—	—	—	—	
	EP	MR	MR	—	—	R	—	—	—	
163. *Rumex conglomeratus* (B or P) (sharp dock)		MS	MS	—	—	—	—	—	—	180
164. *Rumex crispus* (P) (curled dock)	Sd, Sh	S	S	S	S	S	S	S	S	180
	EP(a)	S	S	MS	MS	MS	—	MR	MS	
	EP(g)	MS	MS	MS	MS	—	—	—	—	
165. *Rumex obtusifolius* (P) (broad-leaved dock)	Sd, Sh	S	S	S	S	S	S	S	S	180
	EP(a)	S	S	MR	MR	MS	—	—	MR	
	EP(g)	MR	MR	R	R	—	—	—	—	

TABLE 9 (*continued*)

Weed / Chemical and dose; oz acid equivalent per acre	MCPA -salt 24	2,4-D -amine 20	MCPB -salt 32	2,4-DB -salt 32	Meco-prop -salt 40†	Dichlor-prop -salt 40†	MCPA plus 2,3,6-TBA -salts 12+4	MCPA plus 3,6-dichloro-2-methoxy-benzoic acid-salts 18+1·3	Cross reference (page no.)
166. *Scandix pectenveneris* (A) (shepherd's needle)	MR	MR	R	R	—	—	MR	MS	
167. *Scleranthus annuus* (A or B) (annual knawel)	MS	MS	—	—	—	—	MS	—	
168. *Senecio aquaticus* (B) (marsh ragwort)	MS	MS	—	—	—	—	—	—	
169. *Senecio jacobaea* (B or P) (ragwort)	MS	MS	R	R	—	—	—	—	
170. *Senecio squalidus* (A) (Oxford ragwort)	—	—	—	—	—	—	—	—	
171. *Senecio viscosus* (A) (stinking groundsel)	—	—	—	—	—	—	—	—	
172. *Senecio vulgaris* (A) (groundsel)	MR	MR	R	MR	MR	MR	MR	S	
173. *Sherardia arvensis* (A) (field madder)	—	—	R	—	—	—	—	—	
174. *Silene album* (A, B or P) (white campion)	R	R	R	—	MS	—	S	S	181
175. *Silene dioica* (B or P) (red campion)	—	R	—	—	MS	—	—	—	
176. *Silene noctiflorum* (A) (night-flowering campion)	R	R	—	—	—	—	—	—	

† Total mecoprop or dichlorprop in terms of active and inactive isomers in ratio 50/50.
(A), (B), (P) – Annual, biennial, perennial respectively.

Sh – shoots. Sd – seedlings.
EP – established plants.
(a) – in arable land.
(g) – in grass land.

TABLE 9 (*continued*)

Weed	Chemical and dose; oz acid equivalent per acre	MCPA -salt 24	2,4-D -amine 20	MCPB -salt 32	2,4-DB -salt 32	Meco- prop -salt 40†	Dichlor- prop -salt 40†	MCPA plus 2,3,6- TBA -salts 12+4	MCPA plus 3,6-dichloro- 2-methoxy- benzoic acid-salts 18+1·3	Cross reference (page no.)
177. *Silene vulgaris* (P) (bladder campion)		R	R	R	—	MS	—	—	—	
178. *Sinapis alba* (A) (white mustard)		S	S	S	S	S	S	S	S	
179. *Sinapis arvensis* (A) (charlock)		S*	S*	S	S	S	S	S	S	
180. *Sisymbrium officinale* (A) (hedge mustard)		S	S	—	—	—	—	S	S	
181. *Solanum dulcamara* (P) (woody nightshade)		MR	MR	—	—	—	—	—	—	
182. *Solanum nigrum* (A) (black nightshade)		MR	MR	—	—	MR	—	MR	—	181
183. *Sonchus arvensis* (P) (perennial sowthistle)	Sh	MS	MS	MS	MS	MR	—	—	—	
	EP	MR	MR	—	—	—	MR	S	—	
184. *Sonchus asper* (A) (spiny sowthistle)		S	S	S	S	MS	MR	S	—	
185. *Sonchus oleraceus* (A) (annual sowthistle)		S	S	S	S	MS	MS	S	MS	
186. *Spergula arvensis* (A) (corn spurrey)		MR	MR	R	R	MR	MS	MS	MR	
187. *Stellaria media* (A) (chickweed)		MS	MS	R	R	S	S	MS	S	
188. *Symphytum officinale* (P) (comfrey)		MR	MR	R	R	—	—	—	—	
189. *Taraxacum officinale* (P) (dandelion)	Sd, Sh	MS	S	R	MR	MR	—	—	—	
	EP	MR	MS	R	MR	MR	—	—	—	

TABLE 5 (continued)

Weed — Chemical and dose; oz acid equivalent per acre	MCPA -salt 24	2,4-D -amine 20	MCPB -salt 32	2,4-DB -salt 32	Meco-prop -salt 40†	Dichlor-prop -salt 40†	MCPA plus 2,3,6-TBA -salts 12+4	MCPA plus 3,6-dichloro-2-methoxy-benzoic acid-salts 18+1·3	Cross reference (page nc.)
190. *Thlaspi arvense* (A) (field pennycress)	S	S	S	S	S	MS	S	S	—
191. *Tragopogon pratensis* (A, B or P) (goat's beard)	MS	MS	—	—	—	—	—	—	—
192. *Tripleurospermum maritimum* ssp. *inodorum* (A) (scentless mayweed)	MR	MR	R	R	MS	MR	MS	MR	182
193. *Tussilago farfara* (P) (coltsfoot) **Sh**	MS	MS	—	—	R	MR	MS	MR	182
193. *Tussilago farfara* (P) (coltsfoot) **EP**	MR	MR	—	—	S	—	MR	MR	
194. *Urtica dioica* (P) (stinging nettle) **Sd, Sh**	S	S	S	—	—	—	—	—	
194. *Urtica dioica* (P) (stinging nettle) **EP**	MR	MR	MR	—	S	—	S	—	
195. *Urtica urens* (A) (annual nettle)	S	S	S	S	S	S	S	S	
196. *Valerianella locusta* (A) (lamb's lettuce)	—	—	—	—	—	—	—	—	
197. *Veronica agrestis* (A) (procumbent speedwell)	MR	MR	R	R	R	—	MR	—	
198. *Veronica anagallis-aquatica* (P or A) (water speedwell)	—	—	—	—	—	—	—	—	
199. *Veronica arvensis* (A) (wall speedwell)	MR	MR	—	—	MR	—	MR	—	

* Susceptible to 5 oz.

† Total mecoprop or dichlorprop in terms of active and inactive isomers in ratio 50/50.

(A), (B), (P) – Annual, biennial, perennial respectively.

Sd – seedlings.
Sh – shoots.
EP – established plants.

TABLE 9 (continued)

Weed / Chemical and dose; oz acid equivalent per acre	MCPA -salt 24	2,4-D -amine 20	MCPB -salt 32	2,4-DB -salt 32	Meco-prop -salt 40†	Dichlor-prop -salt 40†	MCPA plus 2,3,6-TBA -salts 12+4	MCPA plus 3,6-dichloro-2-methoxy-benzoic acid-salts 18+1·3	Cross reference (page no.)
200. *Veronica chamaedrys* (P) (germander speedwell)	MR	MR	—	—	R	—	—	—	
201. *Veronica hederifolia* (A) (ivy-leaved speedwell)	MR	MR	R	R	—	—	MR	—	
202. *Veronica persica* (A) (buxbaum's speedwell)	MR	MR	MR	R	MR	MR	MR	—	
203. *Veronica serpyllifolia* (P) (thyme-leaved speedwell)	MR	MR	—	—	—	—	—	—	
204. *Vicia cracca* (P) (tufted vetch)	MS	MS	—	—	—	—	MS	—	
205. *Vicia hirsuta* (A) (hairy tare)	S	S	—	—	—	—	S	S	
206. *Vicia sativa* (A) (common vetch)	MS	MS	—	—	S	—	MS	S	
207. *Viola arvensis* (A) (field pansy)	MR	MR	MR	MR	R	R	MR	—	
208. *Viola tricolor* (A) (heart's ease)	MS	MR	MR	MR	R	R	MR	—	
209. *Xanthium spinosum* (spiny cocklebur)	S	S	S	S	—	—	—	—	

† Total mecoprop or dichlorprop in terms of active and inactive isomers in ratio 50/50.
(A) (B) (P) – Annual, biennial, perennial respectively.

SECTION (ii) THE RESPONSE OF ANNUAL WEEDS TO CONTACT HERBICIDES

387. The information given in Table 10 is intended as a general indication of the response of some common annual weeds to sulphuric acid, selective mineral oil, sodium nitrate, dinoseb-amine and sodium monochloroacetate.

The response to dinoseb of some weeds not shown in this table may be found in Table 5 (pages 38–41). The response of some annual weeds to DNOC may also be found in Table 5.

TABLE 10. THE RESPONSE OF ANNUAL WEEDS TO CONTACT HERBICIDES

S — **Susceptible** — Complete or nearly complete kill.
MS — **Moderately Susceptible** — Effective suppression, with partial kill.
MR — **Moderately Resistant** — Temporary suppression, the duration depending on the environment.
R — **Resistant** — No useful effect.
They refer to two stages of growth:
Sd — **Seedling Stage** — Cotyledon to the 2–3 leaf stage.
Yp — **Young Plant Stage** — 3–4 leaf stage to the early flower-bud stage.

Weed	Stage of growth	Sulphuric acid, 10% v/v, 100 gal./ acre *	Selective mineral oil 60 gal./ acre	Sodium nitrate 2½ cwt./ acre †	Dinoseb -amine 2 lb./ acre	Sodium mono-chloro-acetate 20 lb./ acre
Anthemis arvensis	Sd	MS w	—	MS	S	—
(corn chamomile)	Yp	MR w	—	R	MR	—
Anthemis cotula	Sd	MS w	—	MS	S	R
(stinking mayweed)	Yp	MR w	—	R	MR	R
Atriplex patula	Sd	S w	S	R	S	R
(common orache)	Yp	MR w	MR	R	MR	R
Capsella bursa-pastoris	Sd	S	S	S	S	S
(shepherd's purse)	Yp	MS	MS	MS	MS	MS
Chenopodium album	Sd	S w	S	MR	S	R
(fat hen)	Yp	MR w	MS	R	MR	R
Fumaria officinalis	Sd	MS w	MS	S	S	R
(fumitory)	Yp	R	R	MR	MS	R
Galeopsis tetrahit	Sd	S	S	MS	S	S
(hempnettle)	Yp	MS	MR	R	MS	MS
Galinosoga parviflora	Sd	—	S	S	—	—
(gallant soldier)	Yp	—	MR	MS	—	—
Lamium amplexicaule	Sd	S	S	MS	—	—
(henbit)	Yp	S	MS	R	—	—
Lamium purpureum	Sd	S	S	MS	—	—
(red deadnettle)	Yp	MS	MS	R	—	—

TABLE 10 (*continued*)

Weed	Stage of growth	Sulphuric acid, 10% v/v, 100 gal./acre *	Selective mineral oil 60 gal./acre	Sodium nitrate 2½ cwt./acre †	Dinoseb-amine 2 lb./acre	Sodium mono-chloro acetate 20 lb/acre
11. *Papaver rhoeas*	Sd	MS	S	S	S	R
(corn poppy)	Yp	R	MR	MS	MR	R
12. *Poa annua*	Sd	R	S	MR	R	R
(annual meadow grass)	Yp	R	S	R	R	R
13. *Polygonum aviculare*	Sd	S w	S	S	S	R
(knotgrass)	Yp	MR w	MR	MS	R	R
14. *Polygonum lapathifolium*	Sd	S	S	S	S	S
(pale persicaria)	Yp	MR	MR	MS	R	S
15. *Polygonum persicaria*	Sd	S	S	S	S	S
(redshank)	Yp	MR	MR	MS	R	S
16. *Raphanus raphanistrum*	Sd	S	MS	S	S	MS
(wild radish)	Yp	MS	MR	MR	MR	MR
17. *Senecio vulgaris*	Sd	S	MS	S	S	MS
(groundsel)	Yp	MS	R	MS	MR	MS
18. *Sinapis arvensis*	Sd	S	S	S	S	S
(charlock)	Yp	S	MS	S	S	MS
19. *Solanum nigrum*	Sd	S	S	—	S	—
(black nightshade)	Yp	MR	MR	—	R	—
20. *Sonchus asper*	Sd	S w	MS	MS	S	MS
(spiny sowthistle)	Yp	MR w	R	R	MR	R
21. *Sonchus oleraceus*	Sd	S w	MS	MS	S	MS
(annual sowthistle)	Yp	MR w	R	R	MR	R
22. *Spergula arvensis*	Sd	S	S	S	MS	S
(corn spurrey)	Yp	MS	MS	MR	MR	S
23. *Stellaria media*	Sd	S	S	S	S	S
(chickweed)	Yp	MS	S	MR	S	MR
24. *Tripleurospermum mari-*	Sd	S w	S	S	S	MS
timum ssp. *inodorum*	Yp	MR w	MR	MR	MR	R
(scentless mayweed)						
25. *Urtica urens*	Sd	S w	MS	S	S	S
(annual nettle)	Yp	MR w	MR	MS	MR	MS
26. *Veronica hederifolia*	Sd	S w	S	S	S	—
(ivy-leaved speedwell)	Yp	MR w	MR	MS	MR	—
27. *Veronica persica*	Sd	S	S	S	S	S
(buxbaum's speedwell)	Yp	MS	MR	MS	MR	S
28. *Viola arvensis*	Sd	—	MS	S	MS	—
(field pansy)	Yp	—	R	MS	MR	—

* 'w' after the response categories for sulphuric acid indicates that the effect will be improved if a wetting agent can be added to the spray.

† The spray must include a wetting agent, as described under 'Beet' on page 91.

SECTION (iii) THE RESPONSE OF ANNUAL WEEDS TO SOIL-APPLIED (RESIDUAL) HERBICIDES

388. Table 11 summarizes information at present available on the response of annual weeds to applications, made before emergence of the weeds, of some residual herbicides used selectively in crops. Because of the variety of factors influencing the degree of control achieved, the information presented in the Table must be regarded as **tentative**, and is intended only as a guide to the *relative* susceptibility of the different species to a particular herbicide.

TABLE 11. (TENTATIVE) THE RESPONSE OF ANNUAL WEEDS TO SOIL-APPLIED (RESIDUAL) PRE-EMERGENCE HERBIBIDES

S— 75–100 per cent kill.   I— Partial kill.   R— No use effect.

Weed	Monuron 1–2 lb/acre	Simazine 1–2 lb/acre	Chlor-propham 1–2 lb/acre	Propham 2–4 lb/acre
1. *Alopecurus myosuroides* (blackgrass)	—	S	S	—
2. *Anagallis arvensis* (scarlet pimpernel)	—	—	—	R
3. *Anthemis arvenis* (corn chamomile)	—	—	—	—
4. *Anthemis cotula* (stinking mayweed)	—	—	—	—
5. *Atriplex patula* (common orache)	S	S–I	I	R
6. *Avena fatua* (wild oat)	—	S–I	S	S
7. *Capsella bursa-pastoris* (shepherd's purse)	S	S	S	I–R
8. *Chenopodium album* (fat hen)	S	S	I	R
9. *Fumaria officinalis* (fumitory)	R	S–I	S–I	R
10. *Galeopsis tetrahit* (hempnettle)	—	—	—	I
11. *Galinsoga parviflora* (gallant soldier)	—	—	R	—
12. *Galium aparine* (cleavers)	—	I–R	R	—
13. *Geranium dissectum* (cut-leaved cranesbill)	—	I–R	R	—
14. *Lamium amplexicaule* (henbit)	I	S	R	—
15. *Lamium purpureum* (red deadnettle)	I	S	R	R
16. *Matricaria recutita* (wild chamomile)	S	S	R	R
17. *Medicago lupulina* (black medick)	—	S	—	—

TABLE 11 (continued)

Weed	Monuron 1–2 lb/acre	Simazine 1–2 lb/acre	Chlor-propham 1–2 lb/acre	Propham 2–4 lb/acre
18. *Papaver rhoeas* (corn poppy)	—	S	S	—
19. *Poa annua* (annual meadow grass)	S	S	S	S
20. *Polygonum aviculare* (knotgrass)	I	S	S	S
21. *Polygonum convolvulus* (black bindweed)	I	I	S	S
22. *Polygonum lapathifolium* (pale persicaria)	—	I	S	S
23. *Polygonum persicaria* (redshank)	—	I	S	S
24. *Ranunculus arvensis* (corn buttercup)	—	R	—	—
25. *Raphanus raphanistrum* (wild radish)	S	S	I	R
26. *Scandix pecten-veneris* (shepherd's needle)	—	S	—	—
27. *Senecio vulgaris* (groundsel)	I	S	R	R
28. *Sinapis arvensis* (charlock)	—	S	I	R
29. *Solanum nigrum* (black nightshade)	—	S	R	—
30. *Sonchus asper* (spiny sowthistle)	I	S	R	R
31. *Sonchus oleraceus* (annual sowthistle)	I	S	R	R
32. *Spergula arvensis* (corn spurrey)	S	S	S	S
33. *Stellaria media* (chickweed)	S	S	S	S
34. *Thlaspi arvense* (pennycress)	S	S	S	—
35. *Tripleurospermum mariti-mum* ssp. *inodorum* (scentless mayweed)	—	S	R	R
36. *Urtica urens* (annual nettle)	S–I	S	S	—
37. *Veronica hederifolia* (ivy-leaved speedwell)	R	I	S–I	I
38. *Veronica persica* (buxbaum's speedwell)	R	I	S	I
39. *Vicia hirsuta* (hairy tare)	—	I	—	—
40. *Viola tricolor* (heart's ease)	—	—	—	I

SECTION (iv) NOTES ON SOME INDIVIDUAL WEEDS

Perennial weeds important mainly in grassland are dealt with in Chapter II, Section (iii), pages 73–80.

AEGOPODIUM PODAGRARIA (ground elder)

389. Ground elder is one of the most persistent and troublesome weeds of the garden. It spreads quickly by means of brittle rhizomes which break into fragments with cultivation and rapidly produce vigorous new aerial shoots. Eradication can generally only be achieved by removing any valued plants and then repeatedly forking over the ground, removing as many pieces of rhizome as possible. Eradication in beds of established perennial plants or shrubs, or when the weed is growing in a hedge, is seldom feasible, but repeated hoeing between the plants accompanied by hand removal of all ground elder leaves as soon as they appear above the ground will do much to keep the weed under control. Only really persistent weeding will have a useful effect. Ground elder is resistant to MCPA and 2,4-D, but good control has been obtained with 2,4,5-T-amine and -ester at 16–32 oz a.e. per acre, and with MCPA/2,3,6-TBA mixtures applied as foliage sprays at 24 oz MCPA and 8 oz 2,3,6-TBA per acre. Sodium chlorate at 2 cwt per acre will greatly reduce the weed but up to 5 cwt per acre may be required for complete eradication of a dense stand. Sodium chlorate should only be used when the area is well away from any valued trees or shrubs.

AGROPYRON REPENS (Couch grass), *AGROSTIS* spp. (bent grasses)

390. *Agropyron repens* can be distinguished from the rhizomatous species of *Agrostis* with which it is sometimes confused by the presence of auricles (small pointed projections at the base of the leaf blade) which often clasp the stem, by hairs on the upper side of the leaves and by the distinctive flowering head. The latter resembles that of perennial ryegrass except that the spikelets are set with the flat face opposite the stem; it is quite unlike the much-branched, diffuse flowering head of *Agrostis* spp. The species of *Agrostis* which are particularly troublesome as weeds are *Agrostis gigantea*, which has underground creeping stems, and *Agrostis stolonifera* which has surface creeping stems. *Agrostis canina* and *Agrostis tenuis* which may have short rhizomes are less important. The methods of control for all these grasses in arable land are similar. (See also M.A.F.F. Advisory Leaflet No. 89.)

CONTROL BY CULTIVATION

391. The control of rhizomatous weed grasses has, until recently, been dependent on summer fallowing using the plough, cultivator or harrow, a procedure which can be effective in a dry season but is liable to fail when wet weather persists. Another method that can be very successful even in wet years is a programme of rotary cultivations designed first to break up the rhizomes and then to kill the resulting fragments by a process of exhaustion of their reserves both of food materials and the buds from which regrowth can take place. The first cultivation should be deep and carried out slowly to ensure maximum fragmentation. The second, which can be carried out more rapidly, should take place as soon as new shoots appear above the ground. A further cultivation should take place as soon as regrowth occurs again and the process then repeated until all the grass has been killed. The most common faults resulting in lack of control are too long an interval between regrowth and cultivation allowing new rhizomes to be formed, and failure to persist in the treatment until all fragments are dead.

CHEMICAL CONTROL
Sodium Chlorate

392. For the control of *Agropyron repens* in arable land, sodium chlorate can be used as an early autumn application at 1–2 cwt per acre. Oats, vetches, peas, potatoes and cabbage are relatively tolerant and may be sown in the spring following an autumn treatment; but barley, mangolds, beet and turnips are more sensitive and should not be sown until at least 12 months after treatment. Sodium chlorate has been largely superseded by TCA, amino triazole and dalapon.

393. TCA can be used to control *Agropyron repens*, *Agrostis stolonifera* (creeping bent grass), and with less certainty *Arrhenatherum elatius* (onion couch). Heavy soils should be treated in the autumn with two applications, each of 15–20 lb per acre. Shallow ploughing or cultivation should precede each application in order to bring the rhizomes near the surface. After spraying, light cultivations may help to maintain the chemical in close contact with the rhizomes in the soil but should be varied according to soil and weather conditions. TCA may be rapidly leached from light sandy soils and it is therefore best to treat these in the spring, either with one dose of 30 lb per acre or with two treatments each at 15 lb per acre. Normally TCA should be applied in high volume, but if it is well distributed on a moist soil surface as little as 20 gallons of water per acre can be used. Summer and autumn treatments can be followed by normal cropping in the following spring except on some fen soils and soils high in humus content, where only crops resistant to TCA should be sown. Wheat, oats, barley and rye are susceptible and should not be sown as winter crops following autumn treatment nor as spring crops following spring treatment. Winter cereals may generally be safely planted in land treated in the spring, provided at least four months have elapsed between the last application of the chemical and the sowing of the crop. The persistence of TCA in the soil is, however, influenced by rainfall and soil type and may be prolonged in soils of high humus content. Potatoes, rape, kale, turnips and linseed appear to be the crops most resistant to TCA and may be planted a month after the last spray application; peas, sugar beet and beans also show considerable resistance, but should not be sown sooner than two months after the last spray treatment.

394. Dalapon and amino triazole, in contrast to TCA, should be applied to the *foliage* of actively growing couch grass, when rain is not expected for at least 12 hours. The dose of either chemical required to ensure a complete kill of the weed under all conditions is generally uneconomic for agricultural purposes, lower doses are therefore recommended that give a high degree of control but which are unlikely to eradicate the weed completely unless careful attention is paid to timing of the application and to associated cultivations and cropping. Doses of 7·5 to 12 lb dalapon per acre and of 4 to 6 lb amino-triazole per acre (activated formulation, see page 19) are generally recommended for the control of couch in arable land. Cultivation before treatment may assist by breaking up the rhizomes and stimulating dormant buds to grow. Sufficient time should elapse between cultivation and spraying to allow a good cover of foliage to develop. Ploughing not less than 2 weeks after spraying is generally considered an essential part of treating couch with these herbicides. It is emphasized that the main object of this is to bury the couch rhizomes as deeply and completely as possible to impede regeneration from any surviving rhizome buds. Complete inversion of the plough furrow and as deep ploughing as possible should therefore be aimed at. Cultivations after ploughing should be restricted to those required to obtain a seedbed and should be as shallow as possible to avoid breaking the rhizomes or bringing them to the surface. A vigorous crop following a dalapon or amino triazole treatment will further reduce the chances of any surviving rhizome fragments re-establishing the infestation. A well-fertilized 'smother' crop such as kale is ideal. The crops that can be sown and the minimum safe interval between spraying and sowing are different for the two herbicides and the manufacturers' instructions should be carefully studied.

Stubble or fallow treatment

395. Dalapon and amino triazole can be applied at any time between mid-March and the end of October provided the couch is growing actively.

(a) *Autumn use.* Applications of 10 to 12 lb dalapon or 4 lb activated amino-triazole made in the autumn can be followed by normal cropping the following spring. In the case of dalapon, a minimum interval of 4 months should elapse between spraying and sowing if spring cereals are to be grown. If ploughing after treatment is delayed a minimum interval of 40 days should elapse between ploughing and sowing. Winter wheat or oats (not barley) can be sown following an application of amino triazole (*not* dalapon) provided there is an interval of 3 weeks between spraying and ploughing. In sandy soils the interval between spraying amino triazole and sowing or planting should be increased to 6 weeks.

(b) *Spring use*. Dalapon can be used in the spring but spring cereals cannot safely be sown afterwards. Certain other crops, e.g. carrots, kale, beet, potatoes can follow treatment provided some 6 to 7 weeks elapse between application of 8 to 10 lb dalapon per acre and sowing. Ploughing should take place 2 weeks after spraying. Precise recommendations concerning intervals between spraying and sowing various crops vary for the different products available. Amino triazole may be applied in spring at 4 lb per acre before sowing wheat, oats, potatoes or maize. Three weeks should elapse between spraying and ploughing. The crop may then be sown as soon as the cultivations are complete. In sandy soils the interval between spraying and sowing or ploughing should be increased to 6 weeks. Both dalapon and amino triazole can be used on headlands and verges to prevent couch grass spreading into the field. Where cultivations and cropping as indicated cannot be carried out, the dose applied should be increased to around 20 lb dalapon and 6 lb activated amino triazole.

(c) *Mixtures of amino triazole and dalapon*. Current investigations indicate that *Agropyron repens* tend to be more readily controlled by amino triazole than by dalapon whilst *Agrostis* spp. tend to be better controlled by dalapon. Where *Agropyron repens* and *Agrostis* spp. are growing together or where the control of broad-leaved weeds is required in addition to grass weeds there is likely to be an advantage in using mixtures of dalapon and amino triazole.

Control of couch in crops

396. Dalapon is recommended at 4 to 8 lb per acre for the control of couch in a number of established crops including apples, pears, blackcurrants, gooseberries, raspberries, asparagus, certain ornamental shrubs and lucerne. All these crops are liable to be damaged if attention is not paid to the specific instructions given elsewhere in this book or on the manufacturers' labels. Frequently, dormant season applications only are recommended and emphasis is placed on the need to ensure that the applied dalapon is retained as much as possible by the weed foliage thereby minimizing contact with the soil.

397. Amino triazole is recommended for the control of couch in established apples (see page 103) and has the advantage that it kills many broad-leaved weeds in addition to the couch grass. Amino triazole is less selective than dalapon and special care is needed while spraying to ensure that drift does not reach the foliage of the crop plants.

Persistence of dalapon and amino triazole in soil

398. After couch grass has been sprayed with dalapon or amino triazole and a crop is to be planted, it is important that any residue of the herbicides in the soil is sufficiently small not to damage the crop. When in doubt the advice should be obtained from the suppliers. It should be remembered that both herbicides tend to persist longer when the soil is exceptionally cold or dry and that the time between spraying and sowing or planting may have to be increased.

ALLIUM spp. (onions)

399. *Allium vineale* (wild onion) and *A. ursinum* (ramsons) are the two species most commonly occurring as weeds. *A. ursinum* has broad leaves and a triangular stem and prefers wooded or shady places, unlike *A. vineale* which has rounded leaves and stem and is found in more open situations. *Allium vineale* (wild onion) which causes tainted milk and flour, is an extremely persistent weed, and is particularly troublesome on heavy land.

Cultural control is possible by preventing the formation of the three types of bulb structure (main bulbs, hard offsets and aerial bulbils) which are responsible for the persistence and spread of the plant. All three structures sprout in autumn and grow until the following July when the plants die down. At this time a proportion produce a head of bulbils on the aerial shoots. Usually this is in place of the inflorescence, though sometimes flowers are carried on it together with the bulbils, which, after shedding, may lie on or in the soil for a considerable period before sprouting. At the base of the mature plant is a bulb, together with a number of offsets which can also persist for a long time in the soil. One successful programme of cultural control, described in detail in M.A.F.F. Advisory Leaflet No. 313, is based on a succession of spring-sown crops, preceded each year by a late autumn ploughing. The object of this is to disturb the weed, thereby reducing main bulb and hard offset formation and at the same time destroying young plants developing from bulbils. Autumn-sown wheat, beans and short leys should be avoided whilst bare fallows serve only to spread the weed. If wild onion occurs on wet, heavy land, it is not worth attempting to eradicate it until the land has been drained.

400. Reports from America suggest that excellent control of *Allium vineale* can be obtained with 2,4-D, but this finding has not been confirmed in this country. The doses needed appear to be higher than are generally recommended for both grass and arable crops. Spraying with MCPA or 2,4-D in cereal crops may reduce the height of wild onion so that the bulbils are formed below the cutter bar of the combine; otherwise herbicides are of little value.

401. [Tentative] *Allium ursinum* is only important because it can cause tainting of milk. Amino triazole at 6 lb per acre, applied before flowering, can give a good control.

ALOPECURUS MYOSUROIDES (blackgrass)

402. This annual grass is frequently a troublesome weed, particular on heavy soils. It is of greatest importance in autumn-sown cereals and in herbage seed crops. It is not only strongly competitive in the early stages of crop growth but its seed is difficult and expensive to separate from cultivated grass and clover seed. Blackgrass seed is most difficult to separate from seed of fescues, particularly meadow fescue (*Festuca pratensis*), ryegrasses and cocksfoot. It is much less of a problem in timothy and the clovers where it can generally be removed satisfactorily.

At the present time no firm recommendation can be made for the chemical control of blackgrass and cultural control measures must be used. These are based on the absence of any natural dormancy in blackgrass seed and are aimed at encouraging the seed to germinate by surface cultivations when the crop is off the ground or by inter-row cultivation in the case of herbage seed crops grown in wide drills. Of equal importance are measures taken (*a*) to prevent the seed from shedding, and (*b*) to avoid the sowing of crop seeds which are contaminated. Blackgrass should be treated as a farm problem and eliminated wherever it is possible rather than waiting until it is a particular problem in a crop. In autumn-sown cereals blackgrass seed is normally shed before harvest and surface cultivations of the stubble will encourage germination and allow much of the shed seed to be destroyed before sowing another crop. A succession of spring-sown crops where seed-beds are prepared thoroughly will greatly reduce a blackgrass infestation, although on the type of land on which blackgrass is often most troublesome this may not be practicable. A very heavily infested cereal crop may be cut for silage to prevent the shedding of blackgrass seed.

403. For herbage seed crops, every opportunity should be taken to eliminate blackgrass before sowing and during the seedling stage of the crop by the following methods:

    (a) *In the autumn before sowing*, stubble cultivation (perhaps with contact herbicide) and late ploughing to ensure maximum germination of seed; complete inversion in ploughing to ensure a thorough kill.

    (b) *In spring*, destruction of plants surviving at the time of seed-bed preparation.

    (c) In direct-sown herbage seed crops the possible use of the 'stale seed-bed' technique and a contact herbicide before emergence of crop grass.

(d) Topping of direct-sown crops as frequently as necessary to prevent seed being shed from any blackgrass plants growing with the crop.

(e) Inter-row cultivations, and if necessary (and possible) hand-weeding.

By this means it should be possible to prevent seed being formed and shed during the year of sowing in a crop sown direct in spring. This in turn will avoid the growth in autumn or afterwards of new plants whose seed would contaminate the crop seed. For an undersown crop, however, or one sown in autumn after a crop in which blackgrass was present and able to shed seed, such a contamination is likely. Inter-row cultivations, if possible, should be made to destroy the seedlings and young plants. Various herbicide treatments have been tested for use in the autumn and winter of the year of sowing, but no recommendations can yet be made.

If the seed crop, in the summer of the first harvest year, shows more black-grass plants than field inspection standards allow or enough to cause serious difficulty in cleaning, it is advisable to sacrifice the seed harvest and take hay or silage from the crop to prevent the blackgrass from shedding seed. Subsequent topping is then advisable from time to time to deal with the recovering blackgrass.

404. The use of barban for the control of blackgrass in winter wheat is described in paragraph 24 on page 47.

ARRHENATHERUM ELATIUS (onion-couch) (form with stems swollen at base)

Methods of control are similar to those for *Agropyron repens.*

AVENA spp. (wild oat)

405. Two species of wild oat occur: *Avena fatua* and *Avena ludoviciana*. *A. fatua* has a widespread distribution and germinates principally in the spring (March–May) but also in the autumn (September–October); the exact period being determined by the weather. Seeds of *A. fatua* rarely germinate outside these periods. *A. ludoviciana* is restricted to the south Midlands and south-east of England, and germinates in the winter between October and March. The two species in the vegetative stage are, in practice, indistinguishable one from the other, or from cultivated oats. The species of wild oat may be readily identified when ripe seed heads are present. Two main characteristics suffice to distinguish them: (*a*) the way the ripe seeds are shed, and (*b*) the presence or absence of an awn on the third seed of the spikelet. These characteristics are explained below:

How to Distinguish between *Avena fatua* and *Avena ludoviciana* by Seed Characteristics

	Avena fatua	*Avena ludoviciana*
(a) Shedding of ripe seeds	Seeds of a spikelet fall separately and base of each seed has an abscission scar	Seeds of a spikelet fall together and force is necessary to separate them. Only the first seed has an abscission scar; the second and, where present, the third seeds have upon their base the remains of the stalk.
(b) Awn on third seed of spikelet	Where third seed is present it has an awn	Where third seed is present it has no awn.

The species cannot be distinguished from each other on colour or hairiness of seed. Both are very variable and each can show all possible variants though some are more common than others. The fringe of hairs round the base of the seed distinguishes wild from cultivated oats. Both *A. fatua* and *A. ludoviciana* have variants with husks which are glabrous except for the basal hairs.

Control by Cultivation

406. On clean land care must be taken to avoid contamination. Clean seed is essential. Once wild oats are present eradication is difficult and depends upon (a) destroying germinating plants, and (b) preventing the shedding of seed. Wild oat seed can remain dormant in the soil for at least three years, and more under some conditions (e.g. under a ley) and, even assuming therefore that seed is prevented from being shed each year, eradication in less than this period of time will not be possible by cultural methods. The destruction of germinating plants of *A. fatua* can be attempted both in the autumn and in the spring. After the harvest of a cereal, shallow ploughing or broadsharing and surface cultivation can encourage the seeds to germinate; young plants will then be destroyed by subsequent ploughing. In the spring, late sown crops will allow time for a flush of young plants to be encouraged by the preparation of a seed-bed; these can then be destroyed in the final cultivation for the crop. The spring-germinating plants of *A. fatua* generally do most damage because they are more numerous than the autumn crop, and also do not suffer any check due to freezing or water-logging of the soil. Autumn germinating wild oats that do survive in mild winters are however important, but destruction of the autumn crop of seedlings, though a step in the right direction, is usually less important than a thorough clean-up in the spring. As *A. ludoviciana* is winter-germinating it usually occurs only in autumn or very early sown spring corn. A succession of spring-sown crops, sown after March, can therefore help considerably to reduce the infestation.

Normally wild oats which appear in a cereal crop will have shed most of their seed before the crop is harvested. In order to prevent seeding of wild oats a three or four year sequence of cropping should be chosen carefully. Row crops of most kinds allow cultivation, both before and after sowing, which will destroy wild oats satisfactorily. Arable silage crops of almost any kind such as mustard or kale will permit spring germination and killing of wild oats. Some farmers have tried late-sown spring cereals in wide rows which are tractor-hoed. Early sown and proud winter wheat may also help to control *A. fatua* by virtue of its smothering action in the spring. Stubble burning is unlikely to kill many *A. fatua* seeds although it may shorten the dormancy period; it may actually induce dormancy of the seed of *A. ludoviciana*.

CHEMICAL CONTROL

407. Recommendations and information on the use of herbicides for the control of wild oats are to be found under the following crops in Chapter II.

Crop	Herbicide	Paragraph	Page
Cereal	barban	23	46
Cereals to be undersown with grass and clover	barban	38	50
Field beans	barban	43	51
,, ,,	di-allate	45	51
Beet (fodder and sugar)	trichloracetic acid	48	52
,, ,, ,, ,,	propham	49	53
,, ,, ,, ,,	di-allate	50	53
Peas	trichloracetic acid	75	59
,,	propham	76	60
,,	barban	78	60

Notes on chemicals

(a) *Trichloracetic acid* (T C A) is applied to the soil, into which it must be worked thoroughly, before sowing peas or sugar beet. It kills wild oats as they germinate. At the doses recommended it will bring about a substantial reduction in the number of wild oat plants in the season of treatment.

(b) *Propham* is an alternative treatment to trichloracetic acid. It is volatile and consequently required less thorough incorporation. Peas and beet may be sown sooner after using propham than after using trichloracetic acid. It is generally not quite so reliable in controlling wild oats as trichloracetic acid.

(c) *Di-allate* is also applied to the soil and kills wild oats as they germinate. It generally gives a better control than propham or trichloracetic acid.

Diallate is available as an emulsifiable concentrate which requires complete mixing in the tank before spraying. It must be carefully incorporated into the soil as soon as possible after spraying.

(d) *Barban* is applied to the foliage of wild oats when the majority of plants have between 1 and 2½ leaves. The satisfactory control of wild oats results from a combination of the effect of the chemical on the weed and the competition from the growing crop itself. Therefore all measures contributing to a good crop, such as proper preparation of the seed bed, adequate fertilizer usage, full seed rates, etc. help to increase the competition with the weakened wild oats and so reinforce the effect of the herbicide.

In any one area, spring-germinating wild oats normally germinate over a period of several weeks, the great majority during one or two weeks. The spray should be timed to catch the main flush of wild oats at the susceptible stage. This will be between mid-March and early May.

Autumn or winter germinated *Avena fatua* and *Avena ludoviciana* in winter wheat may be sprayed with barban in winter except for the period mid-January to the end of February. The susceptible stage of growth of wild oat may be slightly less critical in winter than in spring. Winter wheat may be checked after spraying in March but it recovers after growth commences in the spring.

See also M.A.F.F. Advisory Leaflet No. 452.

CARDARIA DRABA (hoary pepperwort)

408. Hoary pepperwort is generally found on roadsides and waste places but it is a serious weed of arable land in several districts, particularly in Kent, Essex and Hertfordshire, where it has been a major problem for many years. It grows on a wide range of soil types. It is a perennial possessing an extensive system of vertical roots, which may penetrate downwards into the soil for several feet, and horizontal roots which may spread over a wide area. Flowering takes place from May to July and abundant seed is formed. The weed can be spread by introducing either seed or pieces of root into clean ground. Once established, hoary pepperwort is very difficult to control by normal methods of tillage but sowing the field to a long-term ley will give good results. Fallowing alone, unless really deep ploughing is carried out, is seldom completely effective. Winter cereal favours the early growth of the weed in the following season and should be avoided if possible. Thoroughly cultivated root crops will help to reduce infestations.

409. The chemical control of hoary pepperwort has proved very successful and is based on a spraying programme carried out in cereal crops over 2–3 years. The weed cannot be eradicated by a single treatment with MCPA or 2,4-D, but well over 90 per cent control can be obtained by treatment in a winter cereal, in two successive seasons. If this is done, MCPA and 2,4-D are equally effective and should be applied at 12 to 16 oz per acre during the period after the shoots are a few inches high up to the flowering stage. To ensure eradication of the weed after two years' spraying, it is advisable to plant a spring cereal or other crop resistant to MCPA and 2,4-D in the third year so that a spray treatment can again be made, if a few remaining shoots appear. If only a single year's treatment can be made, the dose should be increased to the maximum permissible on the crop, and MCPA used in preference to 2,4-D if treatment is made shortly after the pepperwort shoots have emerged. If the weed is treated at the flowering stage, MCPA and 2,4-D are equally effective.

CIRSIUM ARVENSE (creeping thistle)

410. Creeping thistle is one of the most persistent and troublesome perennial weeds of grassland and arable land. It spreads rapidly by means of brittle rhizomes which readily produce new shoots or may remain dormant for many years if deeply buried under a vigorous sward. Seeds are not regarded as an important means of propagation because they are rarely, if ever, shed from the flowering head, and fertile seeds are not carried by the thistle-down which blows about in great abundance. The seeds remain in the flowering head and are released when the head falls to the ground and rots; seedlings of this thistle are uncommon, spread of the weed being principally by vegetative means. Control by cultivation must aim to destroy the root system by frost or drying, otherwise it will only serve to increase the infestation. Really deep ploughing is very effective. In cereal crops, spraying should be postponed as long as possible if the main object is to control creeping thistle. Spraying will kill any shoots that have emerged, but if carried out too early may be followed by considerable regrowth. Recommended doses for MCPA and 2,4-D are 16 to 24 oz per acre; MCPB and 2,4-DB should be applied at 24 to 32 oz per acre and mecoprop at 40 oz per acre.

See page 73 regarding *Cirsium arvense* in grassland. See also M.A.F.F. Advisory Leaflet No. 57.

CONVOLVULUS ARVENSIS (field bindweed)

411. Field bindweed is an important weed of arable land and in perennial horticultural crops. It can be distinguished from the larger bindweeds (*Calystegia* spp.), which are mainly horticultural and garden weeds, by its smaller leaves and flowers, the latter being up to 3 cm across as compared with 4 cm or more for the larger bindweeds. Field bindweed sets abundant viable seed although seedlings are seldom observed in the field. The mature plants have extensive brittle rhizomes, small fragments of which can give rise to aerial shoots and soon produce vigorous plants. This makes the weed very difficult to eradicate by cultivation from wet, heavy or stony soils or when established in perennial crops such as blackcurrants and raspberries. The main period of growth is from June to September and cultural control in arable land except by inter-row cultivation or by fallowing is often impracticable.

412. Bindweed shoots are readily killed by MCPA or 2,4-D but an appreciable kill of the root system is generally only obtained if the plants are approaching the flowering stage at the time the treatment is made. In cereal crops, bindweed generally emerges too late to be much affected by MCPA and 2,4-D, although its growth may be checked. In order to obtain the maximum effect spraying should be delayed until the bindweed shoots are well developed. Under these conditions, the shoots will be killed and there may be an appreciable reduction in shoot numbers the following year. Promising results have been obtained by spraying bindweed in cereal stubble two to three weeks after harvesting when new growth has been made; the field should not be ploughed for at least two weeks after spraying.

Recommended doses are: MCPA-salt 24 to 32 oz, 2,4-D-amine 24 to 32 oz, 2,4-D-ester 16 to 24 oz per acre; 2,4-D is more effective than MCPA. Good results have also been obtained with MCPB at 32 oz per acre.

413. The selective control by MCPA or 2,4-D of bindweed in horticultural fruit plantations has not so far been successful on a commercial scale, because it is difficult to prevent the sprays from making contact with the crop and damage may result. On the other hand, bindweed can be selectively controlled in asparagus with MCPA; MCPB and 2,4,5-TB at 2 to 3 lb per acre have been used for the selective control of bindweed in blackcurrants. (See Chapter III, Section (ii).)

EQUISETUM spp. (horsetail) — see page 74.

JUNCUS spp. (rushes) — see page 74.

MENTHA ARVENSIS (corn mint)

414. Corn mint is an arable weed of mainly light soil, often somewhat acid. It multiplies principally by rhizomes and it may be increased by division following the use of implements such as disc harrows. The plant is downy, with whorls of small lilac flowers appearing in August to September. It has a characteristic smell. The normal use of MCPA, 2,4-D, mecoprop and MCPA plus 2,3,6-TBA in cereal crops is generally ineffective against this weed but MCPA plus methoxychlorbenzoic acid will suppress it if the weed has adequate foliage for uptake of the herbicide. This normally means spraying has to be delayed until as late as possible (see Chapter II, Section (i)). Good control has been reported following the use of 1 to 2 lb per acre simazine. It has also been observed that TCA-sodium at 20 to 30 lb per acre, when used for couch control, has effected a long term reduction of *Mentha arvensis*. Simazine or compounds based on boric oxide will give complete eradication of the weed in uncropped land (see Chapter VI).

OXALIS spp. (oxalis)

415. There are six species of *Oxalis* that occur as weeds in the British Isles. The most important are the bulbous species: *O. corymbosa* D.C., *O. latifolia* H.B. and K., *O. pes-caprae* L. (*O. cernua* Thunb.) and *O. tetraphylla* Cav. Of the fibrous rooted species which are not very frost hardy and may grow as annuals, *O. corniculata* L. and *O. stricta* L. (*O. europaea* Jord.) can be troublesome weeds of cultivation. The distribution varies with the species. *O. corniculata*, *O. corymbosa* and *O. stricta* are fairly widely distributed over the southern and central counties of England; *O. latifolia* is common in Devon, Cornwall and the Channel Isles; *O. tetraphylla* is occasionally found in Jersey; *O. pes-caprae* is only found in the Isles of Scilly, where it is a common weed in bulb fields. They are purely horticultural as distinct from agricultural weeds and are only found in tilled soil in flower, vegetable and market gardens, nurseries and glasshouses. They are very troublesome on account of their persistence and rapid growth. These notes are confined to the more serious species, those that multiply and spread by bulbils formed underground during the growing season: *O. latifolia*, *O. corymbosa*, *O. tetraphylla* and *O. pes-caprae*. The bulbils are easily detached from the root in late summer, and are spread through the soil by digging and cultivating. The bulbils area very persistent indeed, and destruction of the foliage only stimulates the ripening of the bulbils, the food reserves in the taproot being called on for the purpose. Thus cultivating the soil only causes the plants to increase faster. The rapid increase of *Oxalis* spp. since the war has been attributed by some to the use of rotary cultivators. The bulbils are carried over short distances by birds, and probably in mud on machinery and men's boots. They are carried over greater distances in nurserymen's goods such as plant roots and compost, and fresh infestations are thereby started. Peat in particular is often the vehicle for bulbils, and after it has been spread on the ground the plants rapidly emerge. Hygienic methods should be applied to prevent the spread of bulbils to new sites. Compost and peat should not be stacked on infested soil. In nurseries where *Oxalis* is prevalent such materials should be kept covered to keep birds out. Peat found to contain bulbils (looking like tiny hazel-nut kernels, about 0·25 in. long) should not be spread on clean soil.

Individual plants, if dug up, should be burnt in an incinerator and under no circumstances put on a compost heap. Nursery plants grown in infested ground and lifted for dispatch should be washed free of soil and examined for adhering bulbils. Cultivation, except at very frequent intervals, is only a palliative and is worse than useless for reducing the number of plants. Herbicides appear to be almost without effect. Some will destroy the foliage, but this only stimulates the growth of the bulbils. Some growers have set young pigs to forage for the bulbs, with some success. It appears that bulbils will pass through full-grown pigs unharmed. A successful method of control is to choke out the plants by grassing-over infested land. The grass must be left down for at least three years to make sure that all bulbils are dead. Unfortunately few small growers can afford this. It is important to clean out all stray plants in paths, walls and odd corners that would otherwise be a source of re-infestation.

416. Fumigation of the soil with mixtures of dichloropropene and dichloropropane has shown some promise, but this treatment is too costly to use except where the ground is very valuable. Recent trials have shown that *Oxalis corymbosa* can be controlled economically by sodium N-methyldithiocarbamate (metham-sodium) applied as a drench in autumn or summer at 60 gallons of the commercial product per acre followed by heavy watering to provide a seal.

PLANTAGO spp. (plantains) — see page 75.

PTERIDIUM AQUILINUM (bracken) — see page 76.

RANUNCULUS spp. (buttercups) — see page 77.

RUMEX spp. (docks)

417. The two most important species of Rumex occurring as weeds are *R. crispus* (curled dock) and *R. obtusifolius* (broad-leaved dock). Several other species can also be troublesome weeds, particularly *R. conglomeratus*, but as there are few records dealing with their control, these remarks will be confined to *R. crispus* and *R. obtusifolius*. The lower leaves of *R. crispus* usually have curled edges and the three corners of the perianth surrounding the seed do not have long prominent teeth. In contrast, *R. obtusifolius* has lower leaves with flat or slightly undulating margins and the three corners of the perianth surrounding the seed have up to five long, prominent teeth.

In the seedling stage, before a large taproot has formed, both species are readily killed by MCPA, 2,4-D, MCPB and 2,4-DB. Established plants are much more difficult to kill and *R. obtusifolius*, particularly, may be almost completely resistant to these herbicides when well established in grassland. In cereal crops, the flowering shoots of docks arising from pieces of old rootstock may be severely checked or killed and seeding reduced or prevented by spraying with these chemicals. A method of control that has given good results is to plough and sow down to a one-year ley of Italian ryegrass, followed by spraying as necessary during the summer to kill the docks, without loss of production. The ley is followed by a cereal, so that any surviving docks can be sprayed again.

Recommended doses:

(i) seedlings and regrowing rootstocks in cereals:

R. crispus: MCPA-salt and 2,4-D-amine 16 to 24 oz, MCPB and 2,4-DB 32 to 48 oz, 2,4-D-ester 16 oz per acre.

R. obtusifolius: MCPA-salt and 2,4-D-amine 24 to 32 oz, MCPB and 2,4-DB 32 to 48 oz, 2,4-D-ester 16 oz per acre.

Mecoprop and dichlorprop at 40 oz per acre have given good control of both species, when they have been growing actively in cereals.

(ii) established plants in grassland and waste places (see also page 77):

R. crispus: MCPA-salt and 2,4-D-amine 24 to 32 oz, MCPB and 2,4-DB 32 to 48 oz, 2,4-D-ester 16 to 24 oz per acre.

R. obtusifolius – resistant.

See also M.A.F.F. Advisory Leaflet No. 46.

418. [**For Information**] Rotary cultivation carried out in a manner similar to that described for the control of *Agropyron repens* (paragraph 39) has given good control of *Rumex obtusifolius*.

SILENE ALBA (white campion)

419. This is a weed of arable land, particularly where the soil is chalky. It can be an annual, biennial or short-lived perennial in behaviour. It is a scheduled weed under the herbage certification scheme for timothy and white clover. Its seed is a frequent contaminant of the seed of red and white clover, trefoil, kale and broccolli. White campion is susceptible at the seedling stage to 40 oz of mecoprop-salt per acre or 12 oz of MCPA plus 4 oz of 2,4,6-TBA per acre, and moderately susceptible to the latter herbicide mixture at the young plant stage. These herbicides can be used on grass seed crops in which case seed production of the weed can be prevented. They cannot be used on clover.

SENECIO JACOBAEA (ragwort) — see page 78.

SONCHUS ARVENSIS (perennial sowthistle)

420. *Sonchus arvensis* differs from the two annual sowthistles *S. asper* and *S. oleraceus* in being a perennial with creeping underground stems and in

13

having conspicuous yellow glandular hairs on the flowering heads and on their stems. The two annuals can easily be distinguished from each other by the nature of the auricles at the base of the leaf; the auricles of *S. asper* are rounded in outline and are pressed flat against the stem, whereas those of *S. oleraceus* are pointed and often project on the other side of the stem, but are not pressed flat against it. Control can be achieved by frequent cultivations, but they may not be successful unless the creeping rhizomes are fully exposed to dry or frosty conditions. The best results are obtained by combining cultural and chemical treatments.

421. The growth of aerial parts can be retarded and flowering completely suppressed if *Sonchus arvensis* is sprayed early, when growth is vigorous, with MCPA, MCPB, 2,4-D or 2,4-DB. This is unlikely to lead to permanent control with MCPA or 2,4-D; the long-term effects of MCPB and 2,4-DB are unknown. MCPA/2,3,6-TBA mixtures are reported to be more effective than MCPA for the long-term suppression of this weed.

Recommended doses for temporary suppression:

MCPA-salt and 2,4-D-amine 24 to 32 oz per acre; 2,4-D-ester 16 to 24 oz per acre; MCPB and 2,4-DB 32 to 48 oz per acre; MCPA 12 oz plus 2,3,6-TBA 4 oz per acre.

Mecoprop has given temporary control of aerial shoots at 40 oz per acre.

TRIPLEUROSPERMUM MARITIMA spp. *INODORA*
(scentless mayweed)

422. Scentless mayweed is one of the most abundant annual weeds of arable land and occurs on all soil types. It is a scheduled weed species under the herbage certification scheme in timothy seed crops, the seeds of the weed being very difficult to separate from those of the crop during seed cleaning. It can be distinguished from *Anthemis* spp. by the absence of narrow chaffy scales interspersed in the florets on the receptacle head, and from *Matricaria recutita* by having a solid receptacle, in contrast to the hollow one of this species. Germination occurs mainly in the spring, with a secondary flush in the autumn. Scentless mayweed is resistant or moderately resistant to many herbicides but is moderately susceptible to 40 oz mecoprop per acre and to 12 oz MCPA plus 4 oz 2,3,6-TBA per acre, at the *seedling* stage. These herbicides may be used in herbage seed crops and cereals. The weed is also susceptible at the seedling stage to DNOC and dinoseb (see Chapter II, Section (i)).

TUSSILAGO FARFARA (coltsfoot)

423. Coltsfoot is particularly troublesome on heavy soils, but can occur in abundance on all soil types. It spreads rapidly by means of rhizomes, which often penetrate the soil to a considerable depth, making eradication difficult by normal cultivations. It flowers and sets seed long before the leaves appear. Coltsfoot is mainly a weed of arable land and waste places, and seeding an infested arable field down to a good ley can often be an effective means of eradication.

424. Spraying with MCPA or 2,4-D in a cereal crop does little more than kill the leaves and the most effective treatment for badly infested fields appears to be sodium chlorate applied at 150 to 200 lb per acre to corn stubble. Spraying should be carried out as soon as possible, preferably at the end of July or early August. (For precautions regarding following crops, see page 168 under *Agropyron repens*.) It is resistant to mecoprop but is reported to be severely checked by MCPA/2,3,6-TBA mixtures and by 2,4,5-T.

425. [**For information**] Evidence from the continent indicates that coltsfoot is susceptible to amino triazole and to fenoprop.

URTICA DIOICA (stinging nettle) — see page 80.

CHAPTER VI

RECOMMENDATIONS FOR THE USE OF HERBICIDES ON UNCROPPED LAND AND IN WATER

SECTION (i) TOTAL WEED CONTROL

INTRODUCTION

426. Herbicides are used for the non-selective control of all vegetation in many different situations. Total weed control is, for instance, required on railway tracks, forestry fire breaks, paths, playground, petroleum installations, stockyards and around farm buildings; situations where any form of plant growth is harmful because it prevents the area from being used for the purpose for which it was intended. Examples of the type of damage caused include destruction of surface paving, drainage channels, mechanical and electrical equipment; in addition weeds sometimes cause a fire risk.

Non-selective herbicides may also be used to eradicate or control the spread of injurious weeds (Chapter IX) or other undesirable plants, along fence lines, or on waste ground.

The main advantage of chemicals, as opposed to manual or mechanical methods of weed control, is their ability to prevent weed growth for long periods and thus to maintain weed-free areas clean. They also enable weed control to be practised on obstructed areas inaccessible to mechanized equipment.

Weeds of uncropped land which has not been specially treated are often much more vigorous and diverse than those of cropped land where regular cultivations and crop competition limit the number of species that can survive. The chemicals that are used must therefore be capable of controlling a wide range of both annual and perennial species and also of preventing immediate reinfestation.

427. The chemicals available for total weed control can be broadly classified into three groups as follows:

Contact herbicides – These are used as initial 'knock-down' treatments for the control of all vegetation growth, and for killing annuals. They

184

will not prevent the regeneration of perennials and usually have little residual effect in the soil.

Translocated herbicides – These are also used for the initial control of established weeds, but have the advantage that they kill many perennial weeds as well as annuals. They are relatively non-persistent in the soil and will not prevent invasion and recolonization of the treated area.

Residual herbicides – These are used mostly as maintenance treatments of clean ground. As they are not readily leached from the surface layers of the soil they have little effect on perennial weeds.

INITIAL TREATMENTS

The first step in securing total weed control is disposal of the existing vegetation. This can be achieved as follows.

HIGH DOSE OF RESIDUAL HERBICIDE

428. Residual herbicides act through the soil and, to control weeds on infested land, they have to reach the root zones in high concentration. Hence it is necessary to apply a higher dose to weed infested land than that which would be required to prevent the growth of seedlings on clean soil. The initial dose should be approximately that necessary for the control of the most resistant of the weeds present. It is false economy to use an insufficiently high dose in the first instance as subsequent maintenance treatments cannot then give satisfactory results. This type of treatment is normally applied in very early spring before growth begins. It gives slower control of existing vegetation than contact or translocated herbicides.

CONTACT OR TRANSLOCATED HERBICIDES

429. As contact herbicides only kill existing foliage their main use in initial treatments is to give a quick kill of annual weeds. They do not prevent regeneration of perennial weeds and, therefore, are of limited use when these are present in large numbers. Translocated herbicides are suitable for controlling established weeds including susceptible perennials. As both are non-persistent they do not prevent recolonization from seed in the ground or re-invasion from outside of the treated area. Both contact and translocated herbicides are normally applied during the growing season. Mixtures of various herbicides can be used as pre-treatments before the application of a more persistent herbicide. This permits the persistent herbicide to be used at a reduced dose, but this technique involves two separate application operations.

MIXTURES OF CONTACT OR TRANSLOCATED AND RESIDUAL HERBICIDES

430. It is often an advantage to employ a combination of herbicides rather than a single chemical as an initial treatment. Such mixtures are frequently more economical and avoid the establishment of a distinctive flora of resistant weeds which may follow the use of a single chemical. Contact or translocated herbicides can be used to kill existing vegetation as described under paragraph 429 above. Residual herbicides can be applied at the same time to prevent re-infestation. However, the optimum time for applying the residual herbicide is before the weed growth begins, whereas the optimum time for translocated herbicides is after weed growth has commenced. Hence the timing of a mixture is determined by the optimum time for applying the contact or translocated component of the mixture. Choice of the particular chemicals to use will depend on the type of weeds present, and on the effect desired. Treatment at the time of maximum growth, during the summer months will leave a residue of dead weed foliage which must be cleared in order to remove the fire risk. Treatment of existing vegetation should, therefore, be carried out, as far as possible, at the beginning of seasonal growth, so that the quantity of such residues is minimal.

431. An indication of the suitability of herbicides for use as initial or long term treatments is given in Table 12, while the responses of individual species of established weeds to certain herbicides appear in Table 13. The cost of carrying out the initial treatment of established vegetation varies greatly, but may be of the order of £20 to £80 per acre. The aim should be to clear the ground of vegetation within 2 to 3 years, and thereafter to rely on less costly maintenance treatments.

CULTIVATIONS

432. In some instances it may be desirable to eliminate existing vegetation by cultivations. This method is particularly useful where dead vegetation must not be allowed becuase of the fire hazard, e.g. on firebreaks. Once the soil is free from weeds further growth can be prevented by maintenance treatments.

MAINTENANCE TREATMENTS

433. These are applied in order to prevent re-infestation once the ground has been cleared of vegetation. Under these conditions, residual herbicides will prevent weed establishment for a year or more following a single application. Maintenance treatments are best applied in early spring, before the onset of seasonal growth, but with very persistent herbicides such as monuron and simazine, it is possible to carry out treatments during the winter. It must be stressed that the performance of residual herbicides is greatly affected by the soil type and climatic conditions, so that only broad recommendations can be made. Best results are usually obtained on light or medium soils, whilst greatest persistence will be achieved in areas of low rainfall. In general, a maintenance treatment sufficient to prevent weed establishment for a period of a year might be expected to cost £10 to £20 per acre, but eventually costs should fall below £10 per acre.

APPLICATION
LIQUID APPLICATION

434. The most usual method of applying non-selective herbicides is as a spray which can be applied by a knapsack or powered machine, using a minimum of 100 gallons of water per acre. For small areas a watering can is suitable using a minimum of 2 gallons per 20 square yards. The more persistent residual herbicides are formulated as wettable powders and wherever possible a spraying machine equipped with an agitator should be used, in order to prevent the chemical from settling out in the spray tank during spraying. Dense foliage will hinder uniform application and it is advisable to cut off or burn excessive foliage before treatment.

GRANULES AND POWDER

435. Some of the residual herbicides used for total weed control are available for application in granular or powder form. By this method the amount of active ingredient applied per acre is generally the same or slightly higher than in the case of the liquid application, but the total weight of granules per acre is generally less than the weight of liquid in liquid applications. This method is particularly useful where water supplies are difficult, for small areas or for spot treatment. As chemicals generally act more slowly in granular or powder form than in the liquid form, earlier application is necessary to obtain equivalent results.

436. Chemicals used for total weed control are often applied by unskilled labour and low mammalian toxicity is therefore particularly desirable. In many situations it is also important that there should be no fire risk and that the chemical should have no corrosive effect on metals. Care should be taken to ensure that valuable plants or crops growing near treated areas are not damaged by spray drift, wash-off, or movement of chemicals through the soil into the root zone of susceptible plants.

SPECIAL PROBLEMS

437. If some species are resistant to the herbicides used they can become dominant after a period. Also when treatment from a residual herbicide is wearing off, weeds from resistant or partially resistant species can germinate and survive, e.g., ragwort is often one of the first weeds to colonize ground after residual herbicides have been used. Some perennial weeds have extensive root systems and can send their rhizomes deep into the ground under treated soil. As these rhizomes are below the levels where the chemical can penetrate the plants continue to survive. Horsetail and field bindweed are well known examples of this type of recolonization. The best method of dealing with these special weed problems is shown in the column 'Other effective herbicides' of Table 13, pages 192–194.

INFORMATION ON INDIVIDUAL HERBICIDES

MONURON AND DIURON

438. Monuron and diuron are sparingly-soluble, substituted-urea herbicides which are highly resistant to leaching and destruction by soil micro-organisms and therefore have long residual activity in the soil. They are formulated as wettable powders containing 80 per cent of active ingredient. Diuron is only about one-sixth as soluble in water as monuron, and has a longer activity against germinating annual weeds. The choice of chemical and the optimum dose are determined by the type of weed problem, the amount of rainfall and the soil characteristics. For initial treatments to control established vegetation, monuron or diuron is applied at 15 to 30 lb* per acre. Monuron is more satisfactory than diuron on heavy soils and where the annual rainfall is low; diuron is preferable on light or medium soils and in areas which receive heavier rainfall. The wettable powder formulations should be applied in a minimum of 100 gallons of water per acre, with continuous agitation to keep the chemical in suspension. For subsequent annual maintenance treatment to prevent re-infestation by seedlings, monuron or diuron may be applied at 5 to 10 lb per acre. If regrowth is largely from established perennials, or the soil is very heavy, monuron should be used at the dose of 10 to 15 lb per acre. Lower doses of monuron and diuron may be used in spray mixtures with other herbicides which control the more resistant species, including deep-rooted perennials. Granular formulations of mixtures of monuron with sodium chlorate and borates are available for dry application.

439. Monuron or diuron may be applied at any time of the year except when the ground is frozen, but best results are obtained if application is made shortly before weed growth begins in the spring, when ground cover is at a minimum. Both monuron and diuron are non-corrosive, non-volatile, non-inflammable and low in mammalian toxicity.

---

* Readers are reminded that all doses given in this Handbook refer to active ingredient or acid equivalent, whichever is appropriate.

SIMAZINE AND ATRAZINE

440. Simazine and atrazine are sparingly soluble herbicides. Simazine is extremely insoluble while atrazine is slightly more soluble. Both are persistent and are formulated as wettable powders. They are non-inflammable, non-corrosive to metals and of low mammalian toxicity. For initial treatments to control established vegetation they are applied at 10 to 20 lb per acre. When used as a maintenance treatment a dose of 3·5 to 5 lb per acre will prevent re-infestation for approximately a year. Simazine and atrazine are usually applied as suspensions in water at a minimum volume of 100 gallons per acre. Agitation is necessary to prevent settling-out in the spray tank. For best results simazine should be applied in January or February before the weeds start to grow. It can also be applied in October to December, though at doses of 5 lb or less per acre, there is a tendency for such early applications to become ineffective a little earlier than January or February treatments. If applied during March to September, the action may be slow, as simazine is dependent on soil moisture to carry it into the soil. Hence the more soluble atrazine is more suitable to apply during the growing season, March to September, partly because it acts more quickly through the soil but also because it acts through the foliage. Some species including most trees and shrubs, have root zones below the level to which simazine penetrates and are, therefore, not affected. Since atrazine penetrates more deeply into the soil some trees and shrubs may be affected. Soils high in organic matter can absorb these chemicals and on such soils their efficiency is reduced. Once these chemicals have been applied there is little or no lateral movement towards untreated areas.

441. Atrazine is also available as 4 per cent granules which give best results when applied in February to April, although they can also be used in the other months of the year. In this form atrazine is applied at 12 to 24 lb per acre (i.e. 300 to 600 lb of granules) to established vegetation, and at 6 lb (150 lb of granules) for maintenance treatment. For large areas it is best to use a granule distributor but for the small areas or spot treatment application by hand is satisfactory.

BORON COMPOUNDS

442. Sodium borate ores containing up to 65 per cent boric oxide (B_2O_3), borax (36·5 per cent B_2O_3) and more soluble compounds such as sodium metaborate (25 per cent B_2O_3) are used for total weed control. The phytotoxicity of sodium borates is approximately proportional to their B_2O_3 content. Sodium borates are fire retardants, corrosion inhibitors and have low mammalian toxicity. Borate ores applied dry, in granular form, at doses of 10 to 24 cwt B_2O_3 per acre, usually to prevent weed growth on ground cleared of weeds, will give good control of most species for a year or more. On light acid soils, sodium borates show high initial toxicity but leaching generally limits the effective period of control to one season under most rainfall conditions in Great Britain. On heavy soils and under alkaline conditions, sodium borates often persist for longer periods but toxicity may be reduced considerably by soil reactions which tend to fix the borates in relatively non-available forms. Applied at 12 to 13 cwt B_2O_3 per acre as a pre-surfacing treatment borate ores are commonly used to prevent weed growth under asphalt surfaces.

443. Borax and the more soluble borates are generally used in combination with other chemicals, particularly sodium chlorate and monuron. A 1 to 3 combination by weight of sodium chlorate and disodium octaborate tetrahydrate applied at 4 to 12 cwt per acre kills most weeds and prevents growth for one season. The solubility of this combination is limited to about 2 lb per gallon at working temperatures and can be increased by formulation with an alkali to give a sodium chlorate–sodium metaborate liquid formulation. Mixtures of monuron with sodium borate give increased persistence under most conditions and can be conveniently applied in granular form.

SODIUM CHLORATE

444. Sodium chlorate is available either as a powder formulation or as a liquid. It is used at doses of 2 to 6 cwt per acre against established vegetation and at doses of 1 to 2 cwt per acre against most annual weeds. At doses of over 3 cwt per acre, sodium chlorate will give persistent control for approximately six months, except in areas of high rainfall. The recommended time for application is during the spring months, after growth has commenced. Sodium chlorate will give a rapid kill of the majority of species, which show browning effects soon after application. When sodium chlorate is applied as a spray, it should be applied in a minimum of 100 gallons of water per acre. It is slowly soluble in water to the extent of about 10 lb to a gallon at 20°C. The presence of fire suppressant chemicals may reduce solubility. Sodium chlorate can be used alone but it is more often combined with fire suppressants which can considerably reduce the fire hazard. It is more usual to utilize prepared sodium chlorate mixtures than to mix on the site. By far the greater proportion of sodium chlorate-based herbicides are used in combination with calcium chloride, borate, magnesium chloride, or sodium phosphate. The fire risk can be minimized by applying the treatment in early spring when weeds are most susceptible and before the advent of high temperatures.

445. Sodium chlorate is easily leached from soils and under most conditions in Great Britain applications at the doses recommended above have little or no effect in preventing germination and root growth in the topsoil in the year following application. Chlorate toxicity in soils is decreased considerably by a high nitrate level, and to a lesser extent by alkaline conditions. Decomposition of chlorate in soils is usually rapid under warm, most conditions.

446. Mixtures of sodium chlorate with other herbicides may be used and where grasses predominate the addition of TCA (at 20 to 40 lb per acre), amino triazole (at 3 to 6 lb per acre) or dalapon (at 10 to 20 lb per acre) to a sodium chlorate spray will give improved results. Sodium chlorate can be mixed with residual herbicides in order to combine the rapid action of the sodium chlorate with the persistence of the residual herbicide. Such mixtures also control a wider spectrum of weeds than either chemical if used alone. Initial treatment for heavy weed growth would be 200 to 250 lb sodium chlorate plus 12 to 18 lb monuron or diuron, and this could be reduced to 150 to 200 lb sodium chlorate plus 8 to 12 lb monuron or diuron for moderate weed growth. A further reduction to 90 lb sodium chlorate plus 6 lb monuron could be applied until all deep rooted perennials are controlled. Granular formulations of sodium chlorate and monuron are available.

447. It is important that sodium chlorate should be handled with care and stored in closed, metal containers. When dry it is easily ignited by friction and may be explosive in contact with cloth, dust, wood and other organic materials. Clothing which has been wetted by solutions of sodium chlorate should not be allowed to dry until the chemical has been washed out. The use of sodium chlorate formulations containing a fire suppressant is recommended.

TABLE 12. THE MAIN CHARACTERISTICS OF HERBICIDES USED FOR TOTAL WEED CONTROL

Herbicide	Kill of existing vegetation		Prevention of regeneration of perennials		Prevention of seedling establishment			Usually suitable only in mixtures
	Grasses	Broad-leaved weeds	Grasses	Broad-leaved weeds	Few weeks	Few months	Year or more	
Simazine, diuron	×	×	× ×	×			× ×	
Atrazine, monuron	× ×	×	× ×	×			× ×	
Borates	×	×	×	× ×		×		
Sodium chlorate	×	× ×	×	× ×		×		
2,3,6-TBA		× ×		× ×		×		×
MCPA, 2,4-D, dichlorprop and mecoprop		× ×		× ×	×			×
Dalapon	× ×		× ×		×			×
TCA	×		× ×		×			×
Amino triazole	× ×	× ×	× ×	×	×			×
Diquat	×	× ×	×					×
Paraquat	× ×	× ×	× ×					× ×

× = some effect.
× × = marked effect.

TABLE 13. THE RESPONSE OF SOME ESTABLISHED BIENNIAL AND PERENNIAL WEEDS TO INITIAL TREATMENTS WITH SODIUM CHLORATE, BORAX, MONURON, DIURON, SIMAZINE AND ATRAZINE

The categories in this table indicate the response of perennial weeds to the doses given in the text. As the response of the weeds will vary with the degree of their establishment and with soil type, the categories are broadly defined, but they should serve as a guide to the relative susceptibilities of the weeds. Annual weeds are more susceptible than perennial weeds to these herbicides and will normally be controlled by the doses used against perennial weeds.

Definition of categories

VS – **Very susceptible,** well controlled by the lowest doses for initial treatment given in the text.

S – **Susceptible,** well controlled by intermediate doses for initial treatment given in the text.

MS– **Moderately susceptible,** requires the highest dose given in the text for initial treatment, in order to obtain satisfactory control.

R – **Resistant** (Weeds marked 'R' may be susceptible to higher doses of the herbicide than those given in the text for initial treatment, but on economic grounds the use of alternative herbicides would normally be considered first).

Where a mixture is desirable this is indicated by the appropriate letter:

X = MCPA, 2,4-D, mecoprop, dichlorprop or 2,3,6-TBA.   Y = dalapon, TCA.   Z = amino triazole.

Further information on the use of mixtures may be found on pages 195–6, and information on weed susceptibility to some of the herbicides employed in mixtures is given in Chapter V.

B = biennial.   P = perennial.

	Sodium chlorate	Boric oxide	Monuron or diuron	Simazine or atrazine	Other effective herbicides
1. *Achillea* spp. (P) (yarrow)	S		MS	S	
2. *Aegopodium podagraria* (P) (ground elder)	MS	MS (Y, Z)	R	R	
3. *Agropyron repens* (P) (couch grass)	MS (Y, Z)	MS (Y, Z)	MS (Y, Z)	MS (Y, Z)	TCA, dalapon (page 167 *et seq.*).
4. *Agrostis stolonifera* (P) (creeping bent)	MS (Y, Z)	MS (Y, Z)	MS (Y, Z)	MS (Y, Z)	TCA, dalapon (page 167 *et seq.*).
5. *Arcticum lappa* (B) (great burdock)	MS	S	R	R	

	Sodium chlorate	Boric oxide	Monuron or diuron	Simazine or atrazine	Other effective herbicides
7. *Artemisia vulgaris* (P) (mugwort)	MS	MS	MS (X)	MS (X)	2,4,5-T (page 142).
8. *Calluna vulgaris* (P) (heather)	S	S	R	R	
9. *Calystegia sepium* (P) (bellbine)	S	MS (X)	MS (X)	MS (X)	
10. *Cardaria draba* (P) (hoary pepperwort)	MS	R	MS (X)	S	MCPA, 2,4-D (page 176).
11. *Chamaenerion augustifolium* (P) (rosebay willow-herb)	VS	MS (X)	MS (X)	MS (X)	
12. *Cirsium arvense* (P) (creeping thistle)	S	MS (X)	MS (X, Z)	MS (X, Z)	MCPA, 2,4-D (page 177 et seq.).
13. *Convolvulus arvensis* (P) (field bindweed)	MS	MS (X)	R	R	MCPA, 2,4-D (page 177).
14. *Cynoglossum officinale* (B) (hound's-tongue)	S	S	MS	MS	
15. *Dactylis glomerata* (P) (cocksfoot)	MS	MS (Y, Z)	MS (Y, Z)	MS (Y, Z)	
16. *Epilobium* spp. (willow-herbs)	VS	MS (X)	MS (X)	MS (X)	
17. *Equisetum* spp. (P) (horsetails)	MS	MS (X)	R	R	MCPA, 2,4-D (page 74).
18. *Glechoma hederacea* (P) (ground ivy)	MS	R	S	S	
19. *Heracleum sphondylium* (P) (hogweed)	MS	MS (X)	MS (X)	MS (X)	
20. *Holcus lanatus* (P) (Yorkshire fog)	S	VS	S	S	Paraquat.
21. *Hypericum perforatum* (P) (common St. John's wort)	VS	VS	S	S	

TABLE 13 (*continued*)

	Sodium chlorate	Boric oxide	Monuron or diuron	Sinazine or atrazine	Other effective herbicides
22. *Juncus* spp. (P) (rushes)	S	MS (X)	MS (X)	MS (X)	MCPA, 2,4-D (page 74 et seq.).
23. *Malva sylvestris* (P) (mallow)	S	S			
24. *Mentha arvensis* (P) (corn mint)	S	S	MS	MS	MCPA, 2,4-D (page 75).
25. *Plantago* spp. (P) (plantains)	S	MS (X)	R	S	
26. *Potentilla* spp. (cinquefoil)	MS	MS	R	R	
27. *Poa pratensis* (P) (smooth-stalked meadow grass)	S	S	VS	VS	Paraquat.
28. *Polygonum cuspidatum* (P) (Japanese knotgrass)	R	R	R	R	
29. *Pteridium aquilinum* (P) (bracken)	MS	MS	R	R	See page 76.
30. *Ranunculus repens* (P) (creeping buttercup)	VS	S	S	MS (X)	Paraquat, diquat.
31. *Rumex* spp. (P) (docks)	MS	MS (X, Z)	R	R	MCPA, 2,4-D (page 180 et seq.), amino triazole.
32. *Senecio jacobaea* (B or P) (ragwort)	VS	MS (X)	R	R	MCPA, 2,4-D (page 78 et seq.).
33. *Sonchus arvensis* (P) (perennial sowthistle)	S	MS (X, Z)	MS (X, Z)	MS (X, Z)	See page 181.
34. *Symphytum officinale* (P) (comfrey)	VS				
35. *Taraxacum officinale* (P) (dandelion)	VS	MS (X)	MS (X)	MS (X)	MCPA, 2,4-D (page 79).
36. *Tussilago farfara* (P) (coltsfoot)	S	MS (X)	R	R	2,3,6-TBA (page 182).
37. *Urtica dioica* (P)	S	S	MS	MR	2,4,5-T, mecoprop (page

DIQUAT AND PARAQUAT

448. These are extremely quick-acting, non-persistent herbicides. They are therefore extremely effective as a means of removing existing vegetation, but their transitory effect limits their usefulness for total weed control when used alone. They are applied at doses of 0·5 to 3 lb per acre, according to the extent of vegetation. The addition of a cationic wetter at 0·1 per cent vol/vol concentration in the spray solution improves the effect of both materials, particularly against grasses. Paraquat is more effective than diquat for total weed control purposes and is able to kill the existing vegetation of a wide range of grasses, both annual and perennial, as well as many broad-leaved weeds. It does not prevent the regrowth of perennial weeds. Paraquat is particularly useful when applied in mixture with the substituted-ureas and substituted-triazines and quickly provides the bare-ground conditions which enable the residual materials to reach their place of activity. When paraquat and residual herbicides are applied in admixture, however, it is found that some plants are so damaged by paraquat that they become more susceptible to the residual herbicide.

MIXTURES

449. Short-term herbicides such as the growth-regulators (2,4-D, MCPA, mecoprop, dichlorprop and 2,3,6-TBA) or grass killers (TCA and dalapon) and amino triazole can only achieve total weed control for a short period. They can, however, be used with the more persistent herbicides for the treatment of established vegetation. When employed in this way they often extend the range of species controlled, speed up the initial effect on weeds and may permit the cost of treatment to be reduced. The circumstances in which particular mixtures may be valuable are shown in Table 13. Mecoprop, dichlorprop, 2,4-D, MCPA and 2,3,6-TBA are used in mixture at doses of 3 to 6 lb per acre wherever susceptible broad-leaved weeds are present. To improve the control of perennial grasses TCA at 20 to 40 lb or dalapon at 10 to 20 lb per acre, either with or without a growth-regulator, can be added. Amino triazole can be added at doses of 3 to 6 lb per acre against both grass and broad-leaved weeds.

450. The time of application of a mixture will, with the chemicals described above, depend largely on the optimum time of application for the short term herbicide. In most instances this will be in early spring, when growth has commenced. Mecoprop, dichlorprop, 2,4-D, MCPA and 2,3,5-TBA canal so be used for spot treatment during the summer months to kill broad-leaved weeds that have survived the spring application of a non-selective herbicide. The short-term herbicides must be considered as supplements to the action of more persistent chemicals. Chemicals which are dependent on foliar absorption are not effective when combined with quick-acting herbicides which have contact action. The weather at the time of application must be considered in relation to the conditions desirable for all the chemicals in the mixture, and the precautions required for all the constituents should be followed.

Woody weeds are generally resistant to most herbicides recommended in this section and treatment with 2,4,5-T is usually necessary (see Chapter IV, Section (ii)).

SECTION (ii) ROAD VERGES

INTRODUCTION

451. The maintenance of roadside verges in Great Britain is primarily the responsibility of Highway Authorities. In recent years the problem has become more acute because of the shortage of labour, increased costs, and the mechanical difficulties of regular cutting of vegetation along verges, embankments and central reservations along motorways and arterial roads. Maintenance consists mainly of the cutting and removal of grasses and weeds. These plants form an obstruction to the vision of motorists and other road users and serve as a source of weed seed for dispersal on to neighbouring farm land. Cutting is usually carried out from one to four times during the year, either manually by the lengthman or by mowing machines. Annual maintenance costs vary from £24 to £35 per acre; of this total, 65 to 80 per cent can be attributed to the picking up and removal of the dead vegetation. Shortage of labour, combined with these high costs, has made it necessary for County Councils to seek more rapid and less expensive methods.

In addition to County Councils, the Nature Conservancy has a direct interest in roadside verges because of the plants and animals that they harbour. The Conservancy started field studies on the effects of herbicides on the fauna and flora of verges in 1948. As a result of this work, it has been agreed that, subject to certain conditions, no objections will in future be raised to the use by Highway Authorities of herbicides containing substituted phenoxy-acetic acids for the control of roadside vegetation. Among the conditions laid down are the following:

(1) Spraying should be carried out only on trunk and A class roads and on certain dangerous corners of B class roads.

(2) On wide verges spraying should be limited to the 10 ft nearest the road edge except where stands of injurious weeds occur.

(3) Highway Authorities may be asked to leave unsprayed sections of A class roads where interesting species or communities of wild life occur.

Whilst chemical weed killers cannot eliminate the necessity for cutting or removal of vegetation on road verges, they can reduce the frequency of these operations by controlling (1) many of the more troublesome tall-growing dicotyledonous weeds; (2) many woody weeds; (3) grasses; (4) kerbside and footpath weeds; and (5) scheduled weeds (see Chapter IX).

DICOTYLEDONOUS WEEDS

452. Chemicals for use on road verges must be effective against a wide range of species, and must be of low volatility to avoid damage by vapour drift on to nearby garden or farm crops. Also, they do not need to be as highly selective in their effects on broad-leaved weeds and grasses as herbicides used for weed control in agricultural grassland. It is advisable, therefore, to use formulations specially prepared for road verges. A suitable herbicide is 2,4-D formulated as an acid in oil emulsion. This is non-volatile, and more effective than normal agricultural formulations particularly when dealing with some of the more resistant tall-growing roadside weed species, such as cow parsley, hogweed, broad-leaved dock, perennial nettle and coltsfoot. The normal recommended dose is 3 to 5 lb of 2,4-D in 80 gallons water per acre (i.e. approximately 1 mile of 8 feet wide verge). Sprays should be applied in the periods mid-March to May; or August to October.

453. Complete control of the more resistant species of weeds cannot be expected after a single season's treatment. Normally, treatment for two or more years will be required to reduce the stand of such weeds to negligible proportions. Weeds controlled by the lower dose of 3 lb per acre include:

> *Bellis perennis* (daisy)
> *Cirsium arvense* (creeping thistle)
> *Cardaria draba* (hoary pepperwort)
> *Convolvulus arvensis* (bindweed)
> *Hieracium pilosella* (hawkweed)
> *Hypochaeris radicata* (cat's ear)
> *Plantago* spp. (plantain)
> *Ranunculus* spp. (buttercup)
> *Taraxacum officinale* (dandelion)
> *Tragopogon pratensis* (goat's beard)

The higher dose of 5 lb per acre is required for control of the following species, and those marked with an asterisk will require more than one treatment.

> *Allium oleraceum* (garlic)
> *Allium ursinum* (ramsons)*
> *Anthriscus sylvestris* (cow parsley)*
> *Arcticum lappa* (burdock)
> *Artemisia vulgaris* (mugwort)
> *Centaurea nigra* (knapweed)
> *Chamaenerion angustifolium* (rosebay willow-herb)

14

Chrysanthemum leucanthemum (ox-eye daisy)
Conium maculatum (hemlock)
Galium mollugo (hedge bedstraw)
Heracleum sphondylium (hogweed)*
Mercurialis perennis (dog's mercury)
Pastinaca sativa (wild parsnip)
Rumex spp. (docks)
Senecio jacobaea (ragwort)
Torilis japonica (hedge parsley)
Tussilago farfara (coltsfoot)*
Urtica dioica (stinging nettle)

WOODY SPECIES

454. Methods of controlling woody species are described in Chapter IV. However, it should be noted that owing to the risk of vapour drift, ester formulations of 2,4-D or 2,4,5-T are not normally recommended for use as *foliage* sprays on roadside verges but 2,4-D acid in oil formulations can give a useful check of many species, while low-volatile esters of 2,4,5-T or 2,4-D plus 2,4,5-T in oil (see Chapter IV) may be used with discretion for 'spot' treatment of stumps to prevent coppice growth.

GRASSES

455. Grasses are often a major component of the vegetation of road verges and are little affected by 2,4-D. It is rarely desirable to eradicate grasses in these situations, and the normal requirement is the production of a short manageable sward of finer grasses. This can be achieved by repeated mowing or hand-cutting.

456. The growth of grass can be retarded by the application of maleic hydrazide. Such chemical treatment is particularly valuable on slopes or inaccessible spots which are difficult to mow. Application of an aqueous spray of maleic hydrazide at 5 lb per acre in March to early May will retard the growth of grasses for a period of 12 to 14 weeks and reduce the need for cutting. Regular treatment with maleic hydrazide tends to change the composition of grass vegetation, the finer and shorter grasses such as *Festuca* and *Poa*, increasing at the expense of coarser, taller species. If maleic hydrazide is applied alone, rain falling within 12 hours of treatment is likely to reduce its effectiveness. However, maleic hydrazide applied in mixture with an emulsifiable acid-in-oil formulation of 2,4-D is more weatherproof, and heavy rain in unlikely to reduce the effect unless it falls within 3 hours of treatment. Most broad-leaved weeds are little affected by maleic hydrazide, although the height of growth of some of the taller growing species, such as *Anthriscus sylvestris* (cow parsley) and *Heracleum sphondylium* (hogweed) may be reduced. In most situations it is advisable to apply maleic hydrazide in mixture with 2,4-D to prevent vigorous development of broad-leaved weed species. Thus, an application of 5 lb maleic hydrazide combined with 4 lb of 2,4-D (see paragraph 452) in 60 to 80 gallons of water in March to early May, will control both grasses and broad-leaved species for approximately 16 to 20 weeks, reducing the need for cutting for most of the growing season.

457. In situations where a very high standard of sward maintenance is required maleic hydrazide at 3 to 4 lb plus 2,4-D at 3 lb in 60 to 80 gallons water per acre should be applied in March to May, followed by a cut about 12 days later, to remove uneven winter growth. A further application of maleic hydrazide alone 8 to 10 weeks later will give a further 10 to 12 weeks of control.

TOTAL WEED CONTROL ON KERBS AND FOOTPATHS

458. Another aspect of road-verge maintenance is the control of weed growth on kerb-faces, channels and footpaths. In such situations, total weed control is necessary, and is time consuming and difficult to achieve by manual methods. Frequently, labour requirements can be reduced by application of non-selective herbicides or suitable mixtures of selective herbicides. Suitable herbicides include simazine (10 to 20 lb per acre), monuron (10 to 30 lb per acre), sodium chlorate (50 to 400 lb per acre), borax (10 to 30 cwt per acre), pentachlorophenol (20 to 30 lb per acre), or dalapon (20 to 40 lb per acre) plus 2,4-D. These herbicides should be applied at high-volume using hooded spray-jets. (See section (i) of this chapter.)

APPLICATION OF HERBICIDES

459. Application of sprays to roadside verges presents special problems. Normal agricultural sprayers are unsuitable, and it is ncessary to use equipment designed to deal with special conditions, including variation in verge width; obstructions such as telegraph poles, markers and stay wires; varying height and density of vegetation, and the special dangers of spray drift. In general the most effective and safe method of applying the chemicals is to spray at high volume rates (80 to 100 gallons per acre) and low pressures. This ensures a uniform coverage with large droplets which are not liable to serious drift. Every care must be taken to avoid spray drift and vapour drift on to hedges and neighbouring crops and gardens by following these instructions and those in Chapter VII, Section (iii). Herbicides that volatilize under field conditions should never be used.

SECTION (iii) AQUATIC WEEDS AND ALGAE
INTRODUCTION
460. The control of aquatic weeds presents a special aspect of the weed problem and so far no completely satisfactory solution has been found. In general, techniques with herbicides have not yet progressed beyond the experimental or development stage. The Inter-Departmental Advisory Committee on Poisonous Substances used in Agriculture and Food Storage considers chemicals used for the control of aquatic weeds. Readers are referred to the 'Loose-leaf dossier sheet' (see page 232) issued by this Committee.

Water plants can be divided into three categories:
  (i) emergent (e.g. reeds, grasses, water plantains, bulrush, etc.).
  (ii) submerged and floating (e.g. *Callitriche, Myriophyllum, Elodea, Potamogeton, Lemna minor,* etc.).
  (iii) algae (scums, slimes, etc.).

The situations in which they may be found are:
  (A) Ponds and lakes.
  (B) Large rivers, drainage and navigation channels. Depth of water 3 ft or more.
  (C) Small rivers, drainage channels and farm ditches always containing water. Depth of water less than 3 ft.
  (D) Farm ditches, flood overflow channels and marshy places which may dry out in summer.
  (E) Irrigation and other channels where the flow of water is regulated.
  (F) Reservoirs.

(The letters above are used to indicate the situations in the following paragraphs.)

THE PURPOSE OF WEED CONTROL
461. Dense masses of weeds obstruct the flow of water and, in drainage channels, may cause summer flooding. If the dead weeds are not removed they will collect mud and other debris during the winter, the result being a gradual silting up of the channel and loss of efficiency. Weeds must also be controlled to make room for fish and to facilitate fishing, boating and other activities. Other minor purposes are to improve the appearance of ornamental waters, allow water mills to work properly, enable cattle to drink without damaging the banks, and so on. It may not be desired to kill all vegetation completely; a little root growth may be necessary to hold the sides of the watercourse and prevent erosion.

SAFEGUARDS
462. Precautions must be taken to ensure that all interests concerned with watercourses are not detrimentally affected by any treatment adopted. Such interests include:

(1) Fisheries. Fish may not only be killed or rendered inedible by a chemical but also by the deoxygenation of the water resulting from killing the weeds.

(2) Users of water for cattle drinking, irrigation, domestic or industrial purposes. There must be no contamination that would be detrimental to these users.

(3) Riparian owners. Adjacent crops, trees, etc., can be damaged by spray drift and possibly by percolation of the chemical through the soil.

METHODS OF CONTROL

463. The traditional and still the most usual method of dealing with all forms of water weed is cutting followed by raking out. This has the advantage of dealing equally with all species. The only practicable and economic method of mechanical cutting is by boat. This method is extensively used for situation (B) and to a lesser extent for situation (A). After the weeds are cut they are removed by mechanical elevators.

Emergent weeds can be dealt with by herbicides which are being developed. Amino triazole, 2,4-D, dalapon and other chemicals may be used according to the type of weed. This method, though not yet widely used, appears to be satisfactory for situation (D) and has been used with some success for situation (A). It has obvious possibilities for dealing with the edges of watercourses and preventing weed encroachment in situation (B), but for situation (C) and to a lesser extent for situations (A) and (B) there is the danger that the benefits of removing emergent growth will be at least partially nullified by the additional growth of submerged weeds. This will be a long-term effect and there has not yet been time to judge its importance in practice.

Submerged weeds present a more difficult problem. Various chemicals which will control them have to be applied through the water and present the problem of distribution in the water. They have been used for situation (A) but the only large-scale operations in situation (E) have been abroad.

Algae can cause trouble in situations (A), (C) and (F). Some herbicides, effective against submerged weeds, may also be effective against algae. Various herbicides may be acceptable for the control of algae if fish are not important or if the water is not wanted for immediate use.

Althouth some of the chemicals employed for water weed control have selective herbicidal effects, none of them can be recommended as suitable for selective treatment among ornamental water plants.

APPLICATION OF HERBICIDES TO SUBMERGED SPECIES

464. When treating submerged weeds it is often important to obtain a reasonably accurate estimate of the volume of water that is present so that the correct amount of herbicide can be applied. In aquatic weed control doses may be given in terms of parts per million (p.p.m.). This means that for every million parts of water a certain number of equivalent parts of herbicide are used, e.g. if copper sulphate is to be used at a concentration of 1 p.p.m., then for every 1,000,000 lb (100,000 gallons) of water, 1 lb of copper sulphate is needed. The weight of water can be calculated as follows:

Area in square feet × depth in feet × 62·3 = weight of water in lb.

(6·23 gallons = 1 cubic foot; 1 gallon of water = 10 lb.)

EMERGENT SPECIES

465. These are characteristic of situations having a water table ranging from just below ground level to about half the maximum height of the plant. They are generally large and erect, and several of them which have long narrow leaves are commonly called reeds, while others do not differ markedly in form from ordinary land plants. Examples of the former are the *Typha* spp. (reedmaces), *Sparganium* spp. (bur-reeds), *Phragmites communis* (common reed), *Schoenoplectus lacustris* (bulrush), *Juncus* spp. (rushes and *Carex* spp. (sedges). Those that resemble land plants include *Epilobium hirsutum* (great hairy willow-herb), *Lythrum salicaria* (purple loosestrife) and *Rumex hydrolapathum* (great water dock). The term 'emergent' covers a great variety of plants but it is a convenient grouping to make when considering chemical control, because the treatment can be applied directly on to the leaves as opposed to making an area of fresh water into a dilute chemical solution as is still generally required for the treatment of submerged species.

DALAPON

466. Dalapon is absorbed by the leaves and translocated to the roots. It is particularly suitable for emergent water weeds because the great majority are grasses or closely allied to them and dalapon is very effective against these groups of plants. Doses of 10 to 40 lb per acre (acid equivalent) have given good control of most emergent species. Common species that have proved resistant are *Iris pseudacorus* (yellow flag), *Lythrum salicaria* (purple loosestrife), *Alisma plantago-aquatica* (water plantain), *Sagittaria sagittifolia* (arrowhead), *Schoenoplectus lacustris* (bulrush) and *Rumex hydrolapathum* (great water dock). *Iris* however, is markedly affected by 40 lb per acre and *Schoenoplectus* is apparently less susceptible only because it is hard to wet adequately with the spray. When stands of plants are tall and dense, spraying at high volumes with added wetting agents gives improved coverage. Results are liable to vary and repeated application in subsequent years may be necessary. Dalapon is not toxic to fish when used at these doses; but care should be taken, as with any chemical, to spray as little into the water as possible and to spray up-stream when treating the banks of flowing water.

2,4-D

467. 2,4-D-amine at 1 to 2 lb per acre can be used for susceptible species such as *Sparganium* spp. (bur-reeds) or for species that are resistant to dalapon i.e. *Lythrum salicaria* (purple loosestrife), *Alisma plantago-aquatica* (water plantain) and *Sagittaria sagittifolia* (arrowhead). A number of other emergent plants are also controlled by 2,4-D, but the majority are unimportant. The amine salt of 2,4-D should be used because the oils of ester formulations are likely to be toxic to fish. In addition great care must be taken to prevent pollution of flowing water because it may be used for overhead irrigation of sensitive crops. Occasionally 2,4-D is mixed with dalapon to increase the range of plants controlled.

Sodium Chlorate

468. Sodium chlorate has been used to control emergent species for a considerable time, but is now relatively little used. Thorough wetting of the plants with a 2·5 per cent solution of the chemical is recommended. If regrowth occurs a further spraying should be made. It is not toxic to fish when used in this way. There is a danger of fire when using this chemical (see page 14).

Amino Triazole

469. [For Information] Amino triazole is recommended in North America for the control of emergent water weeds at doses between 5 and 20 lb per acre of active ingredient. It will kill a wider range of plant species than dalapon. It has not been widely tested in Great Britain. Amino triazole is not toxic to fish when used at the doses given above.

Diquat and Paraquat

470. [For Information] Diquat and paraquat are at present under test for use on emergent water weeds and appear promising. A great asset in this type of situation is the rapid inactivation of these herbicides by absorption.

SUBMERGED AND FLOATING SPECIES

471. The submerged water plants, or true aquatics, are always found where the water table is permanently above ground level. They are commonly rooted in the mud and examples of these are the *Myriophyllum* spp. (water milfoils), *Potamogeton* spp. (pondweeds), *Ceratophyllum* spp. (hornworts) and *Ranunculus* spp. (water buttercups). Others are free-floating such as the *Urticularia* spp. (bladderworts). Surface floating plants include the *Lemna* spp. (duckweeds) and *Wolffia arrhiza*; but there are also a number of submerged plants which have floating leaves whose upper surface is dry. They may be the only leaves produced, e.g. *Nymphaea alba* (white water lily), and the last leaves in a series, e.g. *Callitriche* spp. (starworts) or completely different from the normal submerged leaves, e.g. *Potamogeton natans* (broad-leaved pondweed), and some *Ranunculus* spp. (water buttercups). The only method of treating submerged weeds is by making the water in which they grow into a dilute chemical solution. The chemical control of submerged and floating aquatic plants is at present, of very limited practicability because of the hazards involved in such a method of treatment with currently available herbicides.

CHOICE OF HERBICIDE ACCORDING TO SITUATION

472. The variety of situations in which submerged weed grow can be clearly divided into (a) areas of static water that are completely self-contained, (b) static water such as ponds and lakes that have an outflow and (c) all types of flowing water. In situation (a) where a body of water does not flow anywhere either above or below ground, then within the limits of other factors, i.e. toxicity to fish, trees, ornamentals etc., any suitable chemicals can be used. In situation (b) where ponds and lakes have an outflow it is possible to treat these with chemicals if the outflow can be dammed up or inflow diverted for sufficient time to allow all the chemical to be dispersed or inactivated. It is essential then to select treatments which will not persist for long in the water. Acrolein (paragraph 475) is undoubtedly suitable for this type of situation and paraquat and diquat (paragraph 477) might be suitable if they are not too rapidly absorbed. The use of other chemicals depends upon the length of time that water can be dammed up. In flowing water (c) generally there is no suitable treatment, not only because of the hazards to other water users downstream, but also because of the very large quantities of chemical required to maintain even a low concentration for any period of time. The treatment is usually only effective for a short way downstream from the point of application.

MONURON

473. [For Information] Monuron at 20 to 50 lb per acre may be employed for total weed destruction, but it should not be used where there are trees growing near to the treated water because these are likely to be killed. The safe distance from treated water depends upon the permeability of the local soils and rocks.

COPPER SULPHATE

474. [For Information] Copper sulphate may be used at 1 to 2 p.p.m., but some species are resistant to this treatment, notably the *Callitriche* spp. (starworts). Copper sulphate is generally toxic to fish used in this way.

ACROLEIN

475. [For Information] Acrolein is a very volatile liquid which requires mixing with the water and so requires special apparatus for application. It has an intense smell and is lachrymatory. It destroys the plant tops rapidly, but re-growth is liable to occur and the additional use of monuron might be useful for more persistent effect. Acrolein is also effective against algae. It is very toxic to fish which is liable to make it of limited use, although the toxic effects are reputed to disappear within 48 hours.

2,4-D

476. [For Information] 2,4-D may be applied at 5 to 10 p.p.m. or as pellets at 20 to 50 lb per acre. It is less efficient in water than on land and is best used only where notably susceptible species such as *Ranunculus* spp. (water butter-cups) and *Zannichellia palustris* (horned pond-weed) are present.

DIQUAT AND PARAQUAT

477. [For Information] Diquat and paraquat are at present being tested for the control of submerged weeds.

ALGAE

478. Algae are plants of simple form which are classified botanically accord-ing to the colour of the pigment they contain. The 'green' algae are usually the most troublesome, and they form scums on water surfaces, slime on rocks or stones, or grow in characteristic entangled mats which are called 'blanket-weeds'. Fishery owners and waterworks managers are especially concerned with the control of algae, and since the rate of reproduction of algae is ex-tremely rapid it is important that eradication be as complete as possible. There is, however, no generally satisfactory method of controlling algae and often only careful management of the water will prevent severe in-festations.

COPPER SULPHATE

479. Copper sulphate has been used at concentrations of 0·5 to 1·0 p.p.m., with varying success, since the beginning of this century. The effectiveness varies considerably with the type of water and the environmental conditions and its action is considerably diminished in hard water. Copper sulphate may be toxic to fish at the above concentrations, especially in soft water, and if fish are a primary consideration the use of copper sulphate as an algicide will be somewhat limited. A lime-wash containing 10 per cent copper sulphate is useful for keeping down algal growths on the side of swimming baths and other underwater structures.

CHLORINE

480. Chlorine and allied compounds are often used to kill bacteria and to oxidize organic matter, sulphides, and other compounds, but in addition they may be used to destroy certain algae. Their use is usually confined to reservoirs. Chlorine can be applied as a gas or gaseous solution, as the relatively stable compound chloramine, as calcium hypochlorite (bleaching powder) or as sodium hypochlorite. Bleaching powder has been used to control blanket-weed in nutrient culture solutions used in horticulture. A concentration of 0·5 to 1 p.p.m. controls the weed, but there is a danger of damage to irrigated crops. This can be overcome by passing the chlorinated water through straw filters enclosed in wire mesh which remove free chlorine by reduction.

DICHLONE

481. Dichlone (2,3-dichloro-1,4-naphthoquinone) is a recent introduction from North America. Doses required are small; 0·05 p.p.m. will prevent the growth of many algae, and some species of 'blue-green' algae are susceptible to even lower doses. Toxocity to fish lies in the region of 0·5 to 1 p.p.m. and some selectivity between algae and fish can be obtained.

SIMAZINE

482. [**For Information**] Simazine appears promising as an algicide and it may be found to be more suitable than lime-wash for swimming pools and certain other situations. It has a low mammalian toxicity and will not affect bacteria. The wettable powder formulation applied at 0·5 to 5·0 p.p.m. (active ingredient) has proved satisfactory in preliminary tests.

TABLE 14.   THE TOXICITY TO FISH OF HERBICIDES USED FOR THE CONTROL OF AQUATIC WEEDS

The toxicity of herbicides to fish depends on many factors but the chemicals likely to be used for aquatic weed control can be broadly classified as follows:

1 Sodium chlorate Dalapon Amino triazole	Safe at any concentrations less than 250 p.p.m. As no technique is likely to produce a concentration higher than this, the chemicals can be considered harmless to fish provided reasonable precautions are taken.
2 Monuron 2,4-D Diquat Paraquat	Dangerous concentration ranges from 50 to 150 p.p.m. Therefore should only be used after checking the likely concentration to be produced and consulting the manufacturers. The rate at which the chemical decomposes or is absorbed is important.
3 Copper sulphate Acrolein	Very dangerous to fish – see notes on individual chemicals.

A detailed review of the methods, particularly chemical, that are available for the control of aquatic weeds was prepared by Aylwin P. Chancellor whilst with the A.R.C. Unit of Experimental Agronomy. It is published as a bulletin by the Department of Fisheries, Ministry of Agriculture, Fisheries and Food, entitled 'The Control of Aquatic Weeds and Algae'. This bulletin is soon to be revised.

Bulletin 183 of the Ministry of Agriculture, Fisheries and Food identifies the common water weeds.

CHAPTER VII

THE MECHANICAL APPLICATION OF HERBICIDES

SECTION (i) TYPES OF MACHINES

If a herbicide is to work efficiently it must be distributed uniformly over the area that is to be treated. There are many methods by which a uniform distribution of the chemical can be obtained and these depend mainly on the physical characteristics of the active ingredient.

DUSTING MACHINES

There are many types available from hand-operated dusters carried on the chest or back to tractor-mounted and trailed machines. In the absence of specially made dusting machines, a fertilizer distributor is sometimes used for applying herbidical dusts, e.g. dusts of MCPA or 2,4-D.

Most tractor-drawn dusting machines are designed to apply from 30 to 40 up to 200 lb of dust per acre. Lower rates can be achieved by some machines but more usually hand-operated knapsack dusters are used for this purpose. There are two types — bellows type and the rotary fan type — and they may hold from 5 to 10 lb of dust. The bellows are excellent for spot treatment of individual plants since they produce a small cloud of dust for each constriction of the bellows. The rotary fan type produces a steady cloud of dust when the handle is turned at an even speed while the operator walks through the crop.

BAND SPREADERS

The introduction of herbicides in solid finely pelleted form has led to the development of machines capable of applying a band of such material over the drill rows of crops immediately after sowing. These band applicators are usually mounted as an integral part of the space drill used for sowing the crop.

SPRAYING MACHINES

Most herbicides are formulated for application as liquids and as such are generally more effective on the basis of active ingredient than dusts. The volume of liquid needed per acre will be determined by the type of herbicide that it is intended to use, the density of the foliage of the crop and weeds that are to be sprayed. With the growth regulating herbicides it is possible to achieve satisfactory weed control at 5 gallons per acre although better results are usually obtained with a minimum of 10 gallons per acre particularly with the higher doses of herbicide. With contact herbicides, e.g. DNOC and dinoseb, high volume application gives the best results because to achieve satisfactory control the maximum amount of coverage should be obtained. With these chemicals there is loss in selectivity when applied at medium or low volume rates (see also page 33).

In order to standardize the nomenclature, the following definitions of volume rates have been adopted:

Very low volume applications — 1 to 5 gallons per acre
Low volume applications   — 5 to 20 gallons per acre
Medium volume applications — 20 to 60 gallons per acre
High volume applications   — Over 60 gallons per acre.

Some sprayers are capable of operating effectively in one or two of these ranges, while others can operate effectively over the range of low to high volume.

The terms 'low volume', 'medium volume' and 'high volume' are sometimes applied to the machines themselves, and the following brief descriptions indicate the general characteristics of machines capable of operating within the various ranges.

KNAPSACK SPRAYERS

Sprayers that are carried by the operator are produced in various shapes and sizes.

The conventional knapsack sprayer comprises a 2 to 4 gallon tank shaped to fit the operator's back, a built-in pump and a small air chamber for pressure stabilization. They are normally designed to operate at 50 to 80 lb per square inch. A small boom fitted with fan jets can be used for low volume weed killing and for this purpose the unit is quite easy to work, but when using nozzles with a high output, in order to achieve a drenching spray, it is a rather laborious method. A cheaper version of the knapsack sprayer consists of a tank connected to an independent single- or double-acting hand pump.

Pneumatic sprayers have airtight containers from 2 to 4 gallons capacity and are supplied with straps so that they can be slung over the shoulders or carried on the back. The container is filled to a maximum of three-quarters full and air pumped into the remaining space by means of a fitted air pump. These machines are normally designed to work at pressures up to 120 lb per square inch. The advantages of the pneumatic sprayer over the conventional knapsack is that when spraying one hand is left free and some people feel that it is much easier to pump periodically rather than continuously. Pressure regulating valves are available which can be fitted between the lance and the pump or pressure container to achieve an even nozzle pressure.

A development of the pneumatic sprayer is the pressure retaining knapsack. With this, air is pumped into the container to a pressure of 30 to 40 lb per square inch and this is followed by the liquid, bringing the total pressure up to about 120 lb per square inch. When the liquid is discharged, the air is retained and this makes recharging operations simpler and quicker.

SMALL HAND-PROPELLED EQUIPMENT

These machines are used generally for lance spraying in small orchards, for whitewashing walls, disinfecting buildings and many odd jobs about the farm. For these requirements it is necessary to have a high pressure pump capable of handling abrasive materials. The majority have either hand-operated plunger pumps or a piston pump powered by a small engine. Their outputs range from 1 to 5 gallons per minute at maximum pressures of between 150 and 350 lb per square inch. An air stabilizing chamber and pressure regulating valve are usually fitted between the pump and lance or spray boom to maintain an even spray output at the required setting. There is one machine produced which has a 10-gallon tank constructed to withstand pressures up to 300 lb per square inch and which has a compressor in place of a pump for pressurizing the spray. The object of this is to avoid corrosive or abrasive materials coming into contact with moving parts. For spraying, the pressure tank is used as the liquid container and air is pumped in under pressure thus forcing the spray out.

TRACTOR MOUNTED OR TRAILED MACHINES

Low Pressure Sprayers

The small and more inexpensive low pressure sprayers are mounted on the tractor 3-point linkage with the pump fitted to, and driven by, the p.t.o. shaft. Pressures from 25 to 60 lb per square inch are preferred for this work — the lower the pressure the less the drift and risk of damaging neighbouring crops. Low pressure sprayers can be put into three classes.

Low Volume. These have tank capacities up to 50 gallons and pump outputs up to 300 gallons per hour, making them suitable for application rates of up to 20 gallons per acre at tractor speeds of between 4 and 5 m.p.h.

Low/Medium Volume. These have tank capacities of 40 gallons or more and pump outputs up to 750 gallons per hour. They are capable of applying spray at the rate of up to 60 gallons per acre. Like the low volume sprayers they are mainly used for applying translocated weed killers, but the greater output enables them to be used for several other farm operations on small acreages.

Low/High Volume. These are similar to low/medium volume sprayers but are capable of spraying at rates up to 100 gallons per acre.

The majority of these machines have booms which cover a swathe of 20 to 25 feet and are fitted with nozzles giving a flat fan spray but as a result of recent developments, machines are available with a hollow cone nozzle which operates with much less risk of drift than the flat fan type. Agitation in low pressure sprayers is usually provided by recirculating a proportion of the spray liquid back into the tank; effective agitation is particularly important when spraying such materials as DNOC or dispersible powders.

High Pressure Sprayers

Machines in this class are used by the contractor or by farmers with a large acreage, requiring to spray DNOC and other products which necessitate high volume rates. They are trailed, have tank sizes ranging from 100 to 300 gallons and are usually capable of applying any agricultural spray except sulphuric acid which needs to be used through machines constructed of materials capable of resisting corrosion.

Pump outputs vary between 750 and 1500 gallons per hour and the maximum pressures run from 150 to 600 lb per square inch depending on the type of pump employed. Centrifugal or piston pumps may be used for pressures up to 150 lb per square inch but beyond that piston pumps are necessary. Booms capable of swathe widths between 25 feet and 35 feet are commonplace. Either flat fan nozzles or hollow cone nozzles can be used.

With all the machines good filtration is most important. There should be a strainer in the filler-hole, at least one filter in the spray line, preferably on the suction side of the pump, and some means of filtration at the nozzle; all filters should be easily removable for cleaning. Suction hoses are normally available either as a standard fitting or as an extra so that the tanks can be filled from ponds or streams, either by means of the spray pump or through a simple injector.

AIRBLAST MACHINES

So far, only the hydraulic sprayers have been described but, before leaving the subject of liquid applicators, mention should be made of air atomizers and airblast machines although they are not very often used in this country for weed control. With these, the liquid is atomized by a nozzle or spinning disc and a powerful airblast is used to blow the spray into the crop. In this system the air supplements the water as the carrier and, consequently, allows very low rates of spray per acre to be applied. Tractor-mounted, trailed, portable and shoulder-mounted machines of this type of apparatus are available.

BAND SPRAYERS

Specially designed sprayers are now available for use in conjunction with space drills for applying bands of spray material over the drill rows of crops immediately after sowing.

SPECIAL SPRAYERS

Sprayers have also been specially designed for application of weed killers to roadsides, railway tracks, ditches and canals. Other special designs cover such uses as directed application between rows of crops by means of shielded nozzles.

Aircraft are occasionally used for applying herbicides but this practice is not very extensive owing to the dangers of spray drift of growth regulating herbicides.

PUMPS

The principal types of pumps used in spraying machines are: gear, roller vane, centrifugal, and piston. Gear pumps fitted with stainless steel shafts and phosphor bronze pinions were, until a few years ago, the standard fitting on low pressure sprayers and have given satisfactory service. The normal working pressures should not exceed 60 p.s.i. otherwise excessive wear can occur with certain chemicals, i.e. wettable powders. The rollervane and fibrevane pump are a more recent development and can work at pressures of up to 120 p.s.i. quite satisfactorily. Other claims for them, as compared with gear pumps, are that for equal performance they cost less, have a longer life and, when the rollers or blades wear, they can be replaced very cheaply.

Gear pump: a cheap and efficient low volume pump which tends to lose efficiency fairly rapidly when used to pump some agricultural sprays at pressures much above 60 p.s.i. It is not really suitable for use with wettable powders.

Roller vane pump: this will work at higher pressures than the gear pump (120 p.s.i.) and can be used with wettable powders if rather rapid wear is accepted. Like the gear pump it is cheap to replace.

Centrifugal pump: a type of pump which can be used for medium or high volume work. These pumps will generally give their best performance at low pressure and high volume. If higher pressures are required the volume of liquid passed is considerably reduced.

Piston pump: reliable and adaptable for all types of spraying, especially work demanding high pressures, but usually more costly than the other types.

NOZZLES

The most commonly used nozzles in farm sprayers are: flat fan nozzle and swirl or hollow cone nozzle.

Flat fan nozzle: this is essentially a low pressure (30 to 50 p.s.i.) nozzle and is most suitable for low or medium volume work. The spray from this type of nozzle is usually more forceful than that produced from a hollow cone nozzle of similar output. At low/medium volume rates it is thus better able to penetrate dense foliage.

Swirl or hollow cone nozzle: the liquid is forced through a swirl plate and enters a small chamber tangentially. The rotating liquid escapes through a central hole in the nozzle disc and its rotation causes it to expand to form a cone of liquid which then breaks up into droplets. Swirl plate design and chamber depth can alter performance. In practice the common method is to change the nozzle disc and vary the pressure. There is now a range of specially designed low-pressure hollow cone spray nozzles which are suitable for low volume machines. They operate at pressures of 10 to 15 lb per square inch, and are capable of delivering 10 to 35 gallons per acre at 5 miles per hour. A feature of these nozzles is that at no point is there a sudden drop in pressure, and the reduction in pressure occurs within the nozzle so that any ultra-fine droplets are absorbed before leaving the orifice. This has resulted in the production of a high degree of uniformity of droplet size, and has almost eliminated the very small drift-prone droplets which are a weakness of both flat fan nozzles and high pressure hollow cone nozzles.

British Standard 2968 : 1958 suggests standards for spray nozzles of the fan and the cone types, the main purpose being to provide for interchangeability, both physical and functional, of nozzles of like size and type made by different manufacturers. The specification relates only to performance and to the means of attachment of nozzles. Performance requirements concern rate of discharge and uniformity of distribution for ground crop spraying. Recommendations for materials and workmanship are given.

The following permissible variations of discharge rate are specified:

Fan and cone nozzles for ground crop spraying —

± 10 per cent up to and including 30 Imperial gallons per hour.

± 5 per cent above 30 Imperial gallons per hour.

The included angle of spray for fan and cone nozzles is specified as 65 degrees for general purposes or 80 degrees for special wide angle spray, both within a tolerance of ±3 degrees.

Standards for the uniformity of distribution of the spray with recommendations for overlap are given and a test procedure described.

PRESSURES

For any particular nozzle the output is proportional to the square root of

15

the pressure. An increase in pressure will therefore increase the output but will also decrease the average droplet size. High pressures which produce too many fine droplets are undesirable because they increase the danger of spray drift and with certain herbicidal treatments, such as dinoseb on peas, there is a loss in selectivity. The correct nozzle should therefore be chosen for the job in hand, and where different volumes per acre are required, different sets of nozzles or nozzle parts will usually be needed.

SECTION (ii) SPRAYING PROCEDURE

PREPARATION OF THE SPRAYING MACHINE FOR SPRAYING

The following routine should be observed when starting a new machine or commencing a season:

(1) Assemble all parts according the manufacturer's directions, up to assembly of booms, which at this stage should be omitted.

(2) Thoroughly clean all solids from the bottom of the tank.

(3) Turn the pressure regulator screw or knob so that the pressure on the valve is released — this is usually done by turning in an anti-clockwise direction.

(4) Half fill the tank with clean water and pump out.

(5) Assemble the booms according to manufacturer's directions, but do not fit the tips (or discs and swirl plates), nozzle filters, or nozzles.

(6) Half fill the tank with clean water.

(7) With the spray booms at the correct height, spray for a few seconds to clear out any dirt in the boom assembly.

(8) Fit the nozzle tips (or discs and swirl plates) and filters and start spraying. Adjust the pressure regulator to give the pressure recommended by the manufacturers. Check that all nozzles are working properly, and if fan nozzles are being used they should all be spraying in line with the spraybar. Any nozzle giving a poor spray should be removed and washed in clean water and faulty or damaged nozzles should be replaced.

CALIBRATION

Whatever type of sprayer may be chosen, it is always advisable to check before beginning to spray that the the machine is applying liquid at the correct rate. The rate of application for a given nozzle spacing depends on three factors, namely, the speed of the tractor, the operating pressure and the size of nozzle. Most manufacturers supply a table correlating these factors to the quantity of spray liquid applied per acre.

In Table 15 volume rate is related to the discharge rate of different sizes of nozzles set 18 inches apart and operating at 40 lb per square inch. In practice the discharge rate of individual nozzles of the same size and type varies considerably; also different spraying pressures may be desired. It is, therefore, important to calibrate each machine individually using the tables as a guide for selecting jet sizes pressure and tractor speed. Methods of calibration are described below.

Many manufacturers provide a dipstick for the tank containing the spray liquid as an aid to calibration, but if they do not, one can easily be made. If the tank is a vertical cylinder or rectangle in shape, measure its total capacity in gallons of water and mark the total depth on the stick. The rest of the stick then needs to be divided into equal sections representing 2 gallons, or 5 gallons in the case of larger tanks. If the tank is not of such a regular shape, a dipstick can be made by pouring in water from a bucket at 2 or 5 gallons at a time and marking the level on the stick each time; but this is a rather more tedious process.

Having obtained a suitable dipstick, the calibration procedure is as follows:

(i) Half fill the tank with water and measure the quantity with the dipstick.

(ii) Pace out 200 yards. This is the distance which has to be sprayed with an 18-ft boom to cover a quarter of an acre (100 yards for a 36-ft boom).

(iii) Start spraying and continue to spray until 200 yards has been travelled.

(iv) Stop spraying and measure the quantity of water in the tank. The difference between this and the first reading will indicate the amount used.

(v) Since the sprayer has covered a quarter of an acre, multiply the amount of water used by four. This will give the application rate per acre.

If the boom width is other than 18 feet, a simple calculation will give the distance necessary to travel to spray an acre. Where the nozzle spacing is 18 inches, as on most low volume sprayers, a simple rule to remember is that 4840 divided by the number of nozzles gives the distance in yards to travel to spray half an acre.

Another method of calibrating the sprayer which is useful if no dipstick is available requires a little arithmetic and makes use of the following formula:

$$\frac{\text{Amount of water in tank (gallons)} \times 4840}{\text{Distance travelled (yards)} \times \text{Boom length (yards)}} = \frac{\text{Rate of application}}{\text{in gallons per acre.}}$$

TABLE 15. VOLUME OF SPRAY PER ACRE AT DIFFERENT SPEEDS AND NOZZLE SIZES

Based on standard discharge rates for nozzles at 18 inch spacing, working at a pressure of 40 pounds per square inch as specified in British Standard 2968 : 1958.

Discharge rate in Imperial gallons per hour		Volume rate in gallons per acre		
		Tractor speed		
		4 m.p.h.	3 m.p.h.	2 m.p.h.
Fan nozzles	3·5	5	6·6	10
	5·25	7	9·3	14
	7	10	13·3	20
	10·5	15	20·0	30
	14	20	26·7	40
	21	30	40·0	60
	28	40	53·3	80
	42	60	80·0	120
	70	100	133·3	200
Cone nozzles	6·5	9	12·0	18
	10	14	18·7	28
	15	21	28·0	42
	20	28	37·3	56
	33	45	60·0	90
	39	54	72·0	108
	56	77	102·6	154
	75	103	137·3	206
	84	115	153·3	230
	100	138	184·0	276

To do this:

(i) Put a known quantity of water in the tank.

(ii) Pace out 200 yards or a convenient set distance.

(iii) Drive the sprayer up and down the set distance until the spray tank is empty and estimate the total distance travelled.

(iv) Check that the sprayer is working at the maker's recommended pressure.

(v) Measure the length of the spraying boom in yards.

Example:

$$\frac{10 \text{ (gallons)} \times 4840}{600 \text{ (yards)} \times 3 \text{ (yards)}} = \frac{48,400}{1,800} = 27 \text{ gallons per acre (approx.)}.$$

Of the three factors affecting sprayer output, i.e. speed, pressure and nozzle size, the only one likely to be unknown is the speed. Here a tractor speedometer is a great advantage but, without this, the tractor can be timed over a distance of 500 feet and the gear and throttle setting noted. Divide 500 by the number of seconds and multiply by 0·7 to get miles per hour. Another method is to pace the tractor for 20 seconds. The number of 1 yard steps in 20 seconds divided by 10 gives miles per hour.

The calibration by one of the above methods will probably have to be repeated two or three times until the required application rate is determined.

Calibration should never be attempted by collecting the output of a single nozzle because of the wide variation that can occur between nozzles.

A satisfactory method, however, is to measure the discharge rate of each nozzle while the machine is spraying at the desired pressure; this is done by holding a container for one minute under each nozzle in turn, the tractor being stationary, and measure the volume of water collected. The average discharge rate per nozzle per hour can then be calculated and related to volume rate by means of Table 15, an adjustment being made if the nozzle spacing is other than 18 inches, or if spraying is to be carried out at a tractor speed of other than 2, 3 or 4 m.p.h.

CALCULATION OF APPLICATION RATES AND DILUTIONS

The content of active ingredient in a herbicide may be expressed in different ways depending on the nature of the formulation.

Weight/weight (*wt/wt or w/w*). For solid formulations such as dusts or wettable powders the active ingredient (a.i.) is usually expressed as a percentage of the weight, e.g. 2 per cent wt/wt = 2 lb in each 100 lb of material = 2·24 lb per cwt of material. The following formula may be used to calculate the quantity of a commercial product required to give a specific dose of the active ingredient.

$$\text{Commercial product (lb)} = \frac{\text{dose of active ingredient required (lb)} \times 100}{\text{per cent wt/wt active ingredient in commercial product}}$$

Volume/volume (*v/v*). When a liquid formulation has a liquid active ingredient the latter is usually given as a percentage of the volume and is written as a per cent volume/volume. The chief herbicide to which this refers is sulphuric acid. For example, 15 per cent v/v B.O.V. = 15 gallons B.O.V. + 85 gallons of water = 15 gallons B.O.V. in each 100 gallons of solution.

Weight/volume (*wt/vol or w/v*). This term is used for liquid formulations which have a solid active ingredient. It is an abbreviation for weight per unit volume as grammes per cubic centimetre. However as one Imperial gallon of water weights approximately 10 lb a concentrate of 25 per cent w/v of active ingredient contains 2·5 lb of active ingredient in each gallon. Some herbicides, particularly the growth regulators, are compared on an acid equivalent (a.e.) basis, which is the content of active ingredient in the concentrate expressed as the free acid. The acid equivalent of a concentrate is always less than its content of active ingredient unless the active ingredient is itself an acid, and the extent of the difference depends on the molecular weights of the acid and salts in the concentrate, e.g.:

Molecular weight of MCPA = 200·5
Molecular weight of MCPA-sodium = 222·5
Molecular weight of MCPA-potassium = 238·5.

If, therefore, we have a sodium MCPA formulation containing 22·2 per cent weight/volume of sodium MCPA, this formulation would contain 20 per cent weight/volume of acid equivalent. Alternatively, this could be expressed as 2 lb (or 32 oz) of acid equivalent per gallon. Similarly, in a formulation with a potassium MCPA content of 23·8 per cent weight/volume the acid equivalent content would be 20 per cent weight/volume or 2 lb (32 oz) per gallon.

The recommendations in this handbook concerning the amount of herbicide to apply are given in ounces of acid equivalent per acre whilst those of manufacturers are usually given in pints per acre of their particular product. These two different methods can be related by a simple calculation. When the required amount of acid equivalent per acre is known, then the quantity of the weed killer formulation in pints per acre can be calculated as follows:

$$\frac{\text{Dose of formulation}}{\text{(pints per acre)}} = \frac{8 \times \text{oz of a.e. required per acre}}{\text{oz of a.e. in 1 gallon of concentrate}}$$

For example, on page 147 *Bellis perennis* (daisy) is shown to be moderately susceptible to 24 oz acid equivalent of MCPA (salt) per acre. Suppose we have a sodium MCPA formulation containing 30 per cent weight/volume acid equivalent (3 lb or 48 oz per gallon) the dose of the formulation required

$$= \frac{8 \times 24}{48}$$

$$= 4·0 \text{ pints per acre.}$$

Using this formula, Table 16 has been drawn up to show the amount of formulated product required for the most commonly recommended doses of acid equivalent per acre.

The volume of spray applied may vary from 5 gallons per acre upward. Spray tank sizes also very considerably. Table 17 shows the number of acres which can be treated with various tank sizes for the most usual volume application rates. From this table the number of acres which can be treated with a particular sprayer at a particular application rate can be determined. This figure multiplied by the figure from Table 16 gives the number of pints of the formulated weed killer required per sprayer load.

Example: A farmer wants to control charlock in cereals using a 25 per cent

TABLE 16. THE RELATIONSHIP BETWEEN OUNCES OF ACID
EQUIVALENT PER ACRE AND PINTS PER ACRE FOR FORMU-
LATED WEED-KILLERS CONTAINING DIFFERENT AMOUNTS OF
ACTIVE INGREDIENT

Oz of a.e. required per acre	Equivalent dose in pints* per acre for the following a.e. concentrates						
	10% (16 oz/ gal)	15% (24 oz/ gal)	20% (32 oz/ gal)	25% (40 oz/ gal)	30% (48 oz/ gal)	35% (56 oz/ gal)	40% (64 oz/ gal)
5	2·5	1·7	1·2	1·0	0·8	0·7	0·6
10	5·0	3·3	2·5	2·0	1·7	1·4	1·2
12	6·0	4·0	3·0	2·4	2·0	1·7	1·5
20	10·0	6·2	5·0	4·0	3·4	2·8	2·5
24	12·0	8·0	6·0	4·8	4·0	3·4	3·0
32	16·0	10·7	8·0	6·4	5·3	4·6	4·0
40	20·0	13·3	10·0	8·0	6·7	5·7	5·0
48	24·0	16·0	12·0	9·6	8·0	6·8	6·0

* Figures given to the nearest tenth of a pint.

TABLE 17. THE RELATIONSHIP BETWEEN TANK SIZE AND
THE NUMBER OF ACRES THAT CAN BE SPRAYED AT DIFFERENT
VOLUME RATES

Tank size in gallons	Number of acres* that can be treated at the following application rates						
	5 g.p.a.	10 g.p.a.	15 g.p.a.	20 g.p.a.	25 g.p.a.	30 g.p.a.	40 g.p.a.
30	6·0	3·0	2·0	1·5	1·2	1·0	0·8
40	8·0	4·0	2·7	2·0	1·6	1·3	1·0
45	9·0	4·5	3·0	2·3	1·8	1·5	1·1
50	10·0	5·0	3·3	2·5	2·0	1·7	1·3
60	12·0	6·0	4·0	3·0	2·4	2·0	1·5
70	14·0	7·0	4·7	3·5	2·8	2·3	1·8
80	16·0	8·0	5·3	4·0	3·2	2·7	2·0
90	18·0	9·0	6·0	4·5	3·6	3·0	2·3
100	20·0	10·0	6·7	5·0	4·0	3·3	2·5

* Figures given to the nearest tenth of an acre.

weight/volume a.e. MCPA-sodium in a 45-gallon sprayer. He decides to use 12 oz a.e. per acre and from Table 16 he should therefore use 2·4 pints per acre of the MCPA-sodium. He then decides to apply the spray at 10 gallons per acre and from Table 17 finds that a 45-gallon sprayer will do 4·5 acres at this rate. On multiplying 2·4 by 4·5 he finds that he requires 10·8 pints of the concentrate for each sprayer load.

PROCEDURE IN THE FIELD

Filling

Use a clean water supply, preferably soft, because with some herbicides more chemical is needed to obtain the same results from hard water. It is better partly to fill the sprayer with water before adding the chemical and the filters should always be used even if it takes longer to get chemical washed through. Preferably the herbicide should be properly diluted or dissolved *before* being put into the tank.

Timing

Spray when the crop and weed are at the correct stage. Spray during good growing conditions and only during suitable weather, not in strong winds, or when rain or frost is imminent. Due regard must be made for the climatic conditions when applying weed killers such as dinoseb which are influenced by the temperature.

Spray Technique

A well proven method for cereals is to spray the headlands first, once in the case of tractor mounted or small trailer sprayers, and a second bout inside the first in the case of large trailer machines. The remainder of the field should be sprayed along the drill rows starting on the leeward side.

Matching Up Work

Slight overlap is usually desirable. An inexperienced operator should at first use a marker or marking device to prevent misses or to much overlap. When mixing is done in the sprayer, spraying should be continued until it is empty (or nearly so) before refilling, as otherwise the concentration of chemical may increase above that recommended. When the sprayer becomes empty during a bout the machine should immediately turn into the previous bout and proceed to the filling station. After filling it should proceed down the partly sprayed last bout and commence spraying near where the wheel marks turn into the previous bout.

Nozzle Blockage

If the chemical or water being used is liable to block the nozzles, the filters should be cleaned frequently and repaired or replaced if damaged. A quick spraying test should be done on the headland (off the crop) or on waste ground near the filling place. Blocked or partially blocked nozzles should be replaced by clean nozzles or parts. The blocked nozzles can then be cleaned near the water supply. This applies especially when poisonous chemicals are used. If a single nozzle gets blocked during spraying, it is sometimes preferable to wait until the headland is reached before replacing. This applies particularly to dangerous chemicals and to contact weed killers being used on a machine without an anti-drip device.

STATUTORY REQUIREMENTS

For scheduled herbicides the Regulations made under the Agriculture (Poisonous Substances) Act 1952 must be followed (see Chapter VIII).

RUNNING MAINTENANCE

Correct attention to running maintenance will save much time during the season and prolong the life of the machine. The following simple routine should be adopted.

(1) As soon as possible after completion of the day's spraying wash out the sprayer with clean water.

(2) Remove nozzle tips (or discs and swirl plates) and filters, leaving them in a bucket of clean water.

(3) The gear pump should be greased daily, but care should be taken neither to over-grease nor use dirty grease. If either is done filter blockage or pump leakage may result.

(4) Lubricate all moving parts such as lifting gear and operating links periodically with a medium oil.

PREPARING THE MACHINE FOR STORAGE

As soon as the spraying machine has completed its work for the season it is important that it should be cleaned and stored away carefully. The following six points need special attention.

(1) Both the inside and outside of the machine should be thoroughly washed, first with water and detergent, then with water alone.

(2) All hoses should be removed and stored in a cool, dark place, hanging vertically, not over a nail.

(3) All parts of the machine should be drained.

(4) The tank should be dry before final storage. It should be kept under cover with the filter basket and lid in position.

(5) If the machine has an engine or gear box that uses oil, this should be renewed with the recommended oil up to the correct level.

(6) All nuts and bolts and other parts should be checked and spares obtained before storing for the winter.

SECTION (iii) DRIFT OF HERBICIDES

Many valuable crops can be destroyed or damaged by drift from herbicidal sprays and dusts. This problem has become more widespread in recent years partly owing to the more extensive use of herbicides, but also due to the application of herbicides as concentrated solutions in low volumes per acre. Spray drift is likely to be more troublesome in areas where there is a mixture of agricultural and horticultural crops. It is, therefore, important that all who apply these chemicals should understand how drift occurs so that they can take measures to prevent damage to susceptible crops

Drift may occur in three ways:

Spray drift: This is the result of the smaller droplets in the spray being carried away from the target by wind or convection currents.

Vapour drift: This occurs when the vapour from a volatile herbicide is carried away from the target area during or after spraying. It is most likely to occur in hot weather and can take place even if the air is apparently still.

'Blow off': This is the movement, by high wind, of dried spray particles or soil impregnated with the herbicide, away from the area originally treated.

Spray drift. This is by far the most important. It can be reduced or prevented by one or more of the following methods:

(1) Spray only when there is no movement of air (wind, convection current, etc.) towards a susceptible crop. In practice it is difficult to spray only on days when there is no air movement and other precautions are given below.

(2) Have the spraybar as near the target as is consistent with obtaining an adequate distribution of the chemical on the weeds. In this respect close spacing of nozzles and/or the use of wide angle nozzles enable the spraybar to be brought close to the target. To avoid 'streaky' effects it is suggested that the nozzles are tilted at an angle of 45 degrees from the vertical away from the tractor.

(3) Use as high a volume of spray per acre and as low a pressure as are consistent with good weed control and sound economics of the spraying operation.

(4) The spraying of herbicides near to susceptible crops, should, if possible, be carried out before these crops appear above the soil. For

example, oats growing near root crops may be sprayed at the 1 leaf stage before the root crops emerge above the soil.

(5) Where a susceptible crop is above the ground and is on the downwind side of a crop requiring treatment, the operator should leave an untreated strip along the edge. This should never be less than 10 yards wide and preferably much wider when conditions are adverse. The actual width must be determined by individual judgment. This untreated area should be sprayed later when there is no wind or when it is blowing away from the susceptible crop.

(6) Spraying downwind causes slightly less drift than spraying upwind or crosswind, and will reduce widespread drift when treatment is necessary in windy weather or in exposed positions. This method, however, must not be used when spraying hazardous materials, such as DNOC or dinoseb, as the toxic risks to the operator are greatly increased.

(7) Where there is any air movement, boom shields can reduce the risk of spray drift. Drag sheets, however, are not satisfactory and are not recommended.

Application from aircraft is much more hazardous than from ground spraying machines.

Nozzle design and chemical formulation are being studied in order to reduce the formation of small droplets liable to drift.

Vapour drift. This is not particularly important in the cool summer climate of Great Britain. The ester formulations of the growth regulator herbicides are the most volatile and care should be taken to use the formulations prepared from the relatively non-volatile esters if there is any danger of drift on to susceptible crops. Volatile impurities in herbicides can also be a danger. The cresols that occur as impurities in MCPA and 2,4-D can cause taint in tomatoes as the result of vapour drift.

'*Blow off*'. This occurs primarily with DNOC and dinoseb and is very difficult to avoid. The safest course is that outlined under (4) above. If this is impossible and a susceptible crop is adjacent, an unsprayed strip 20 to 30 yards wide should be left.

With machines that do not possess a 'suck-back' device on the nozzles, damage can sometimes occur through drip from the nozzles while the machine is travelling over susceptible crops on its way between the filling station and the field being sprayed. Where the intervening crop is grassland, danger arises mainly from the herbicides that are poisonous to stock. The only recommendation that can be made is to route the machine to avoid as much damage as possible.

Crops particularly susceptible to MCPA and 2,4-D are tomatoes, beet, brassicas and other crucifers, lettuce, tree fruits, and many flowers.

SECTION (iv) DECONTAMINATION OF SPRAYING MACHINES

It is not recommended that the same sprayer equipment be used for both weed and insect control. This is particularly important when changing from a chemical such as 2,4-D to an insecticide, and most particularly when the oil-based 2,4-D preparations have been used, which in practice are extremely difficult to clean out. Damage to susceptible crops has sometimes been attributed to spray drift when the real cause has been the failure to make sure that the spraying machine was clean before it was used for spraying a susceptible crop with some other chemical.

If, however, for reasons of economy it is not possible to keep one machine for herbicides and another for insecticides the following decontamination recommendations are suggested:

(1) At the end of each day's work the sprayer should be emptied, filled with water and sprayed out on an area of waste ground where there is no danger from residues of poisonous substances. The machine should then be refilled and left overnight. This will prevent the chemical drying and caking inside and eventually flaking off to block the nozzles. If spraying of the same chemical is to continue on the following day, the water left overnight in the tank may be used to prepare the required concentration of herbicides.

(2) With dinitro compounds simply wash with water until the washings are colourless. The addition of a synthetic detergent will often speed up the process.

(3) When the growth regulating herbicides have been used one of the following routines should be carried out:

(a) Wash through thoroughly by filling with a solution of synthetic detergent. The inside of the tank, its ceiling and lid should be scrubbed, and the solution circulated through the pump and back into the tank. After this treatment two further washings with water are required and if possible the machine (and particularly rubber hose lines) should stand overnight completely full of water containing detergent.

(b) Thoroughly flush the equipment with plenty of water. Then, fill the tank with water and add two pounds of washing soda or soda ash per 100 gallons of water. The soda ash is more effective, but is somewhat corrosive to equipment. Soda ash is approximately a 50 : 50 mixture of lye and washing soda. Wash the inside of the tank thoroughly with this solution, running some through the pump and making sure that the solution goes through all the system. All lines must be thoroughly washed out. Leave this mixture in the tank for 8 to 12 hours. Wash out the tank, pump, hose and nozzles again with the soda ash mixture, then run fresh water through the pumps, all hoses and nozzles. After that, rinse out thoroughly and completely with additional fresh water.

(c) Another method calls for use of activated charcoal. It is faster but more expensive. For example, 2,4-D-amine can usually be removed by rinsing the sprayer for about two minutes with a 1 per cent solution of activated charcoal. Always follow this with a thorough rinse in clean water.

(d) Decontamination of machines following the use of the ester formulations of growth regulator weed killers is more difficult, but the following procedure has given satisfactory results. Put tractor vaporizing oil into the tank to a depth of 6 inches and then circulate through the pump. Use either a mop or a scrubbing brush to wash down the sides of the tank, and also its ceiling, and then spray through the pipe lines. The procedure thereafter is the same as is described above for cleaning the tank after using either the sodium or amine salts of weed killers, i.e. use a detergent or similar preparation and plenty of water. It is most important to clean the tank immediately after using ester formulations. As the method advocated will also remove grease it is advisable to re-grease the pump after treatment.

(e) For hand spray equipment such as a 3 gallon garden sprayer, where the cost factor is not so important, household ammonia is handy to use. Thoroughly rinse the equipment out with fresh water after spraying with 2,4-D. Fill the spray equipment with the ammonia solution, using one half cup of ammonia to 3 gallons of water. Let the equipment soak for 18 to 24 hours. Always spray some of this mixture through the pump, hose and nozzles, at the beginning and end of the soaking period.

(f) As a safety check, when the time permits, it is possible to be fairly sure that all of the 2,4-D is out of the sprayer if the tank is filled with clean water and a few seedlings of very sensitive plants are then sprayed. Beans or tomatoes are good examples. If the plants are not affected within a day or two, the equipment is probably safe for further use. It is more difficult to clean herbicides from old hoses than from most other parts of the sprayers.

Where a detergent has been used the final wash should always be with plain water in order to remove any detergent which might reduce the selectivity of the next herbicide to be used.

Machines with wooden tanks or other parts made of absorbent material should not be used for spraying insecticides or fungicides in addition to herbicides.

Chemicals other than wetting agents or mineral oils are not recommended. Some, e.g. permanganate, may remove the smell of the weed killers without affecting the active principle, thus giving a misleading impression of cleanliness. Many of the 2,4-D and MCPA preparations now on the market have been specially prepared to reduce the volatile impurities that were previously responsible for their smell and for causing the tainting in tomatoes etc.; the absence of smell cannot now be taken as an indication of cleanliness.

SECTION (v) THE MIXING OF HERBICIDES WITH EACH OTHER AND WITH INSECTICIDES OR NUTRIENTS

The mixing of herbicides to produce a combination of the weed killing effects of each constituent to control a varied weed population, or the use of herbicides in combination with insecticides or nutrient sprays offers many attractions. However, the practice of combining sprays should be approached with caution and only put into effect after considering all the relevant factors and possible risks of crop damage. Where combined applications are intended, manufacturers of the products concerned should always be consulted and their advice followed.

Advantages

The saving of time.
Reduced application costs.
Less mechanical damage, from one instead of two applications.
Weed control may be improved in some cases.
A wider range of weeds may be controlled.

Disadvantages

Correct timing for both constituents of a combined spray is often difficult and may be impossible.

The action of one consituent may impair or prevent the absorption of others, thus nullifying their effect.

Selectivity of herbicides may be reduced.

Physical properties of the diluted spray may be impaired by chemical reaction such as the formation of insoluble salts.

High volume application of the mixture may be necessary whereas the constituents may sometimes be applied separately at lower volumes.

MIXING

Successful mixing of two crop protection chemicals depends upon:

(1) chemical and physical compatibility. The two products must not interact chemically so that their phytotoxic properties are altered, and the mixture must form a sprayable fluid. Care should be taken that an oil, emulsifier, wetting agent etc. present in one product does not affect the selectivity of the other.

(2) the mode of action of each constituent being compatible. For example if MCPA is mixed with a contact herbicide such as DNOC, the rapid kill of foliage by the DNOC would prevent translocation of the slower-acting MCPA.

(3) the time of application being suitable for each chemical.

When combined sprays are used the following rules should always be observed:

(1) Never mix two preparations in concentrated form.

(2) Mineral deficiency and nutrient sprays and insecticides should be diluted with water in the spray tank before adding growth regulator herbicides.

(3) Mixed sprays should always be applied immediately after mixing and never left standing in the tank for long periods.

Some mixtures that may be thought particularly desirable are discussed in some detail below, whilst Table 18 gives a general indication of which mixtures are possible within a wider range of chemicals.

The information in this section of the Handbook is intended only as a general guide to the combination of herbicides with other sprays applied to farm crops. Where combined applications are intended, manufacturers of the products concerned should always be consulted and their advice followed.

THE COMPATIBILITY OF HERBICIDES

Where two herbicides are compatible in the respects outlined above there may be great advantage in mixing them. A better kill of weeds or a wider range of species may be controlled than where either herbicide is used alone. Examples of mixtures of herbicides with similar action are MCPB and MCPA, MCPA and 2,3,6-TBA, and chlorpropham and fenuron. There may also be advantages of mixing some herbicides with different modes of action. A foliar absorbed herbicide such as 2,4-D, used to kill deep-rooted perennial weeds, may be combined with a residual root-acting herbicide such as one of the substituted ureas or triazines which will kill more shallow-rooted weeds and also prevent re-establishment of weeds from seed. (See Chapter VI.)

COMPATIBILITY OF HERBICIDES AND INSECTICIDES

Conflicting principles govern the application of foliage insecticides and herbicides. With insecticide sprays the objective is to obtain maximum leaf coverage and adherence, whereas with herbicides, spray run-off from the crop may play an important part in selective action.

Higher spray pressures, to produce relatively small droplets, are required for insecticide than for herbicide sprays, so that when combined sprays are used a compromise is desirable.

Most insecticides used for spraying agricultural field crops are formulated as emulsions or dispersible liquids. These preparations contain oils or organic solvents, emulsifiers, and wetting agents, which may facilitate penetration of the herbicide when used in a combined spray and reduce selectivity, although weed control may be improved.

The following combinations of herbicides and insecticides may be used with reasonable safety and efficiency providing timing of both constituents of the mixture is correct for their intended purpose:

(1) Growth regulators (MCPA and 2,4-D) with insecticide emulsion sprays on cereals for combined control of weeds and leatherjackets or frit fly. Insecticide concentrates should not exceed about 5 per cent. Ester formulations of MCPA or 2,4-D are less suitable than metallic and amine salts for mixing with insecticide sprays. The addition of insecticide emulsions is liable to increase penetration of the herbicide into the plant tissues. Therefore, the combined spray may result in reduced selectivity of the herbicide.

(2) Petroleum oil herbicides with some insecticide emulsion sprays for combined control of weeds and carrot fly. Petroleum oil herbicides are not compatible with all solvents used for insecticide emulsions.

The following combinations of herbicides and insecticides are **not recommended** owing to risk of phytotoxicity:

(1) dinoseb and insecticide emulsions on peas or other legumes.

(2) DNOC and insecticide emulsions on cereals, except with winter wheat with heavy flag where heavy scorch is acceptable.

COMPATIBILITY OF HERBICIDES AND NUTRIENT SPRAYS

Mineral deficiency and nutrient sprays are most effective when applied in high volume, and one of the objections to mixing these with herbicides is that insoluble salts are sometimes formed.

Satisfactory combined sprays are:

(1) Manganese sulphate with dinoseb, for combined control of marsh spot and weeds in peas. If peas are scorched by dinoseb, absorption

of the manganese sulphate may be impaired to the detriment of marsh spot control.

(2) Manganese sulphate, copper sulphate and copper oxychloride with DNOC, applied to cereals.

(3) Urea, nitrate of soda or sulphate of ammonia with MCPA or 2,4-D (sodium, potassium or amine salts). High volume application in this case will be essential in order to dissolve the fertilizer, except with very low rates of fertilizer application.

(4) Copper sulphate and copper oxychloride with some MCPA and 2,4-D products. Some products are not suitable for this combined spray.

(5) Complete liquid fertilizers with some MCPA and 2,4-D products. These combined sprays may not be suitable owing to varying composition of the complete liquid fertilizers and differences in herbicide formulations.

A combined spray of manganese sulphate and MCPA or 2,4-D (sodium, potassium or amine salts) is not generally recommended owing to the likelihood of heavy precipitation in the spray tank, but medium to high volume applications have been used successfully with some formulations. The concentration should not exceed 1 lb of manganese sulphate in 5 gallons of water.

TABLE 18. THE COMPATIBILITY OF HERBICIDES, INSECTICIDES AND NUTRIENTS

Notes; This table must be used in conjunction with the notes on compatibility on pages 227 to 229, and with data given elsewhere in this book on the susceptibility of the crop. It must be ascertained that both constituents are safe to use for the purpose intended.

1 Chemicals can be mixed, but owing to variations between different products, manufacturers should be approached first.

2 Chemicals not compatible.

* Increased scorch will result.

† With ester formulations only or with pure dinitro compounds.

	MCPA	MCPB	2,4-D	2,4-DB	2,4-DES	2,4,5-T	2,3,6-TBA	Mecoprop	Dinoseb-amine	Dinoseb-ammonium	DNOC	Pentachlorophenol	Petroleum oils	Dalapon	Amino triazole	Fenuron	Neburon	Diuron	Monuron	Simazine	Chlorpropham	Propham	Borates	Chlorates
MCPB	1																							
2,4-D	1	1																						
2,4-DB	1	1	1																					
2,4-DES	1	1	1	1																				
2,4,5-T	1	1	1	1	1																			
2,3,6-TBA	1	1	1	1	1	1																		
Mecoprop	1	1	1	1	1	1	1																	
Dinoseb-amine	1*	1*	1*	1*	1*	1*	1*	1*																
Dinoseb-ammonium	1*	1*	1*	1*	1*	1*	1*	1*	1															
DNOC	1*	1*	1*	1*	1*	1*	1*	1*	1	1														
Pentachlorophenol	1	1	1	1	1	1	1	1	1	1	1													
Petroleum oils	1†	1†	1†	1†	1†	1†	1†	1†	1†	1†	1†	1												
Dalapon	1	1	1	1	1	1	1	1	1	1	1	1	2											
Amino triazole	1	1	1	1	1	1	1	1	1	1	1	1	2	1										
Fenuron	1	1	1	1	1	1	1	1	1	1	1	1	1	1	1									
Neburon	1	1	1	1	1	1	1	1	1	1	1	1	2	1	1	1								
Diuron	1	1	1	1	1	1	1	1	1	1	1	1	2	1	1	1	1							
Monuron	1	1	1	1	1	1	1	1	1	1	1	1	2	1	1	1	1	1						
Simazine	1	1	1	1	1	1	1	1	1	1	1	1	2	1	1	1	1	1	1					
Chlorpropham	1	1	1	1	1	1	1	1	1	1	1	1	1	1	1	1	1	1	1	1				
Propham	1	1	1	1	1	1	1	1	1	1	1	1	1	1	1	1	1	1	1	1	1			
Borates	1	1	1	1	1	1	1	1	1	1	1	1	2	1	1	1	1	1	1	1	1	1		
Chlorates	1	1	1	1	1	1	1	1	1	1	1	1	2	1	1	1	1	1	1	1	1	1	1	
Endothal	1	1	1	1	1	1	1	1	1	1	1	1	**2**	1	1	1	1	1	1	1	1	1	1	1
Urea	1	1	1	1	1	1	1	1	1	1	1	1	2	1	1	1	1	1	1	1	1	1	1	1
Copper	1	1	1	1	1	1	1	1	1	1	1	1	1	1	1	1	1	1	1	1	1	1	1	1
Manganese	1	1	1	1	1	1	1	1	1	1	1	1	2	1	1	1	1	1	1	1	1	1	1	1
DDT emulsion	1	1	1	1	1	1	1	1	1*	1*	1*	1	1	1	1	1	1	1	1	1	1	1	1	1
BHC emulsion	1	1	1	1	1	1	1	1	1*	1*	1*	1	1	1	1	1	1	1	1	1	1	1	1	1
[illegible]	1	1	1	1	1	1	1	1	1*	1*	1*	1	1	1	1	1	1	1	1	1	1	1	1	1

CHAPTER VIII

SAFEGUARDS FOR THE USER AND THE PUBLIC IN RELATION TO HERBICIDES

Among the wide range of chemicals being used or developed as herbicides it would be surprising if some were not toxic to animals. To safeguard wild life, the user of the herbicide and the consumer of the treated crop against the ensuing risks, there are in existence the Notification Scheme for Pesticides and the Agriculture (Poisonous Substances) Act and these are described in the first part of this Chapter. The civil liability of the user of herbicides is discussed in Section (ii) and this is followed in Section (iii) by an account of the extent to which insurance can be obtained to cover the various risks. Finally, there is a description of the Agricultural Chemicals Approval Scheme which is intended to ensure that the purchaser of a herbicide receives an efficient product with appropriate instructions for use.

SECTION (i) NOTIFICATION SCHEME FOR PESTICIDES AND THE AGRICULTURE (POISONOUS SUBSTANCES) ACT

THE NOTIFICATION SCHEME

The Notification Scheme for pesticides is a voluntary arrangement between Industry and the Government whereby no new pesticide product — a term which includes herbicides — is put on the market unless it is safe or, at least under the conditions of use agreed by the government, is unlikely to offer a hazard to users, consumers or treated crops and wild life. To observe the Scheme, a manufacturer, importer or distributor must first consider whether his new product, be it a new active ingredient or a new use or formulation of a current material, offers any hazards when used in the manner described on the label. If he decides that it offers no hazards then he may use his discretion (as allowed under the Scheme) and not notify. If in any doubt, he should notify under the Scheme. Having done so, the onus is upon him to provide all the evidence necessary to support adequately his claims regarding the safe use of his product.

Notification is made to the Ministry of Agriculture, Fisheries and Food, which administers the Scheme on behalf of a number of government departments: the Ministry of Agriculture, Fisheries and Food; the Ministry of Health and their Scottish equivalents and the Board of Trade, in collaboration with the Department of Scientific and Industrial Research (which includes the Laboratory of the Government Chemist); the Agricultural and Medical Research Councils and the Nature Conservancy. The departments look for advice in this matter to the inter-departmental Advisory Committee on Poisonous Substances Used in Agriculture and Food Storage. This was set up in 1954 and its principal function is to keep under continuous survey all risks arising from the use of pesticides in food production and storage and to recommend how such products should be used. It is presided over by an independent chairman and consists of administrative and technical representatives from the departments already mentioned, together with independent members drawn from outside government circles. Industry is not represented.

This Committee looks, in turn, for scientific assistance to a Scientific Subcommittee, also set up in 1954, and consisting of scientists from official sources, selected for their expert knowledge in the field of pesticides. Again, the trade is not represented.

A notification involving a herbicide is made to the Director of the Plant Pathology Laboratory, Ministry of Agriculture, Fisheries and Food. If the Director considers that the proposal might be dealt with without reference to the Scientific Subcommittee and the Advisory Committee, he will pass it through his Chief Chemist to an official toxicologist. If they confirm his opinion, the notification will be sent to the appropriate division of the Ministry of Agriculture to receive a 'Quick Clearance'. If, on the other hand, it appears to the Director that the notification must go through the committee procedure, or if it fails to secure clearance under the 'quick' procedure, it will be submitted to the Scientific Subcommittee, with the notifier's consent.

When a proposal is dealt with under the committee procedure, the data provided by the notifier and any other information that may be available, are presented to the Subcommittee and the notifier invited to be present when it is considered. The Subcommittee make recommendations to the Advisory Committee which, in turn, advises Departments. If Departments recommend precautions in the use of the chemical these will not be made public until the notifier has accepted them and has confirmed that his proposal is no longer confidential. The notifier will be advised of the proposed official recommendations in the same way as with a 'Quick Clearance'. The official recommendations are published as a loose-leaf dossier entitled 'Chemical Compounds used in Agriculture and Food Storage in Great Britain — User and Consumer Safety — Advice of Government Departments'. The advice is usually given in three parts: operator safety, consumer safety and wild life safety. On operator safety, Departments may consider that the product is either too toxic to use or that its use must be regulated by law (see below). On the other hand, they may consider that the product is insufficiently dangerous to justify regulating but that certain voluntary precautions should be taken; or that no special precautions need be taken other than common sense ones when handling any concentrated chemical.

The recommendations on consumer safety aim at ensuring that the treated crop at harvest contains no harmful residues. The use of the pesticide may be restricted to certain named edible crops, and advice is given about maximum rates and frequency of application, last date of application and a minimum interval between last application and harvesting. At present, in the U.K. there is no direct legislation for consumer protection, such as residue tolerances, with the sole exception of arsenic — for which the establishment of a tolerance has a historical background not connected with its use in agriculture. The consumer is also protected by the Food and Drugs Act and the Preservatives Regulations.

The recommendations for the protection of livestock, wild life and the public take the form of advice such as 'for the protection of animals do not allow to graze within x days of spraying'; 'to protect bees do not spray when orchards are in blossom'; 'to protect fish do not empty washings into ponds or water ways' and 'for the safety of children as well as animals, keep containers tightly closed in a safe place, and wash out used containers before disposing of them safely'.

The dossier is widely distributed in this country and copies are obtainable free of charge from the Ministry of Agriculture, Fisheries and Food. Widespread distribution enables consistent advice to be given whether it is on the label of the pesticide or in a trade journal, or given verbally from an official agricultural adviser or from a manufacturer's agent.

At the time this chapter went to press, few if any of the new herbicides listed in Chapter XIII had been placed on the market in the United Kingdom and they had not been cleared by Departments for commercial use. No doubt some have been or will be used in large-scale trials which may involve crops for consumption in which case the Notification Scheme becomes involved, for one of its aims, as already described, is to ensure that treated crops are safe to the consumer. Therefore, if, at any stage in the development of a pesticide and before marketing, a trial is carried out which involves a crop intended for consumption, the person carrying out that trial, whether he is the manufacturer or research worker must consider whether to notify the trial or not. If he decides to notify, the normal procedure is followed.

With a voluntary arrangement such as the Notification Scheme, emphasis is placed on the advantages of informal consultation at an early stage between those who are planning trials prior to marketing and those officials who will be responsible for steering a notification, once received, through the necessary procedure. With herbicides or any product to be used in agriculture, enquiries should be addressed in the first place to the Director of the Ministry of Agriculture's Plant Pathology Laboratory, Hatching Green, Harpenden, Herts. The Industry has co-operated closely in the operation of the Notification Scheme since its inception in 1957. Nevertheless, a safeguard still exists if a manufacturer should market a product whose use may be suspected of offering a hazard. When a chemical appears on the open market Departments can call upon the manufacturer to provide evidence in support of his claims that its use is safe. From then onwards the matter is treated as a notification. Although new products take up most of the Committee's time, pesticides already on the market are examined or reviewed as time permits. New or revised recommendations may be issued as the result of such studies.

AGRICULTURE (POISONOUS SUBSTANCES) ACT

The only legislation at present dealing with the safe use of pesticides in England, Scotland and Wales is the Agriculture (Poisonous Substances) Act, 1952. Users in Northern Ireland, the Channel Islands and the Isle of Man must consult the relevant regulations applying to those countries.

The object of this Act is indicated by its long title, 'An Act to provide for the protection of employees against the risks of poisoning by certain substances used in agriculture', and it is to be noted therefore that the provisions of the Act do not extend to the self-employed man or to members of the public, but only to the employees of contractors and farmers. The Act does not itself lay down the precautions to be observed when poisonous substances are used, since obviously these will vary from time to time as conditions change and scientific knowledge grows; it authorizes the Minister of Agriculture, Fisheries and Food and the Secretary of State for Scotland to make regulations, which may be amended or revoked at any time. Before making regulations the two Ministers are required to consult with the representative organizations of the industries concerned, although they are not legally bound by the advice which they are given. The Act provides for the appointment of inspectors who are charged with the duty of enforcing the Act and the regulations, and confers on them rights of entry on to land and other miscellaneous powers, such as the right to require the production of documents and to take statements. An inspector is also empowered to take samples of substances to which the Act applies, and it contains provision for such samples to be analysed by an approved analyst, whose certificate in any legal proceedings as to the result of any analysis is admissible in evidence without the need of calling the analyst in person as a witness.

The Regulations which are at present in force (which have replaced all earlier Regulations) are the Agriculture (Poisonous Substances) Regulations,

1956 to 1960 (Statutory Instruments: 1956 No. 445; 1957 No. 605; 1958 No. 566; 1960 No. 793). They extend only to the substances which are described in the Second Schedule to those Regulations, namely, among weed killers, to dinoseb, DNOC, endothal and potassium and sodium arsenites. The Regulations specify twelve separate operations (of which spraying a ground-crop is perhaps the most typical and the most important), and, according to where the substance used falls within the Second Schedule, lays down the protective clothing which a worker is required to wear when carrying them out. The five chemicals mentioned above are all included in Part II of the Second Schedule and Table 19 sets out in summarized form the requirements of the Regulations in relation to the wearing of protective clothing when handling and using dinoseb, DNOC, endothal and alkali arsenites. In

TABLE 19. PROTECTIVE CLOTHING REQUIRED FOR PARTICULAR OPERATIONS IN THE HANDLING AND USE OF DINOSEB, DNOC AND ENDOTHAL

Jobs for which protective clothing must be worn	Clothing, etc., to be worn
1. Opening a container, or diluting, mixing or transferring from one container to another.	Rubber gloves, rubber boots, face shield and either (a) an overall and rubber apron or (b) a mackintosh.
2. Washing or cleansing spraying apparatus.	Rubber boots, face-shield and either (a) an overall and rubber apron or (b) a mackintosh.
3. Spraying any groundcrop, except from aircraft or in a greenhouse.	Overall, hood, rubber gloves, rubber boots and either a face-shield or a dust-mask.
4. Spraying bushes, climbing plants (other than hops) or trees.	Rubber coat, rubber gloves, rubber boots, sou'wester and face-shield.
5. Soil application (other than in a greenhouse) by (a) unaccompanied driver or apparatus, (b) driver of tractor-*mounted* apparatus accompanied by on-foot operators,* or (c) any operator on foot.	Overall, rubber gloves and rubber boots.
6. Soil application in a greenhouse.	Overall, rubber gloves, rubber boots and rubber apron.

* A driver, so accompanied, of tractor-drawn apparatus is exempt from the regulations so long as he is driving and not performing any of the scheduled operations listed above.

addition, the Regulations prescribe that workers who handle potato plants which have been sprayed with arsenites within the previous ten days must wear overall, rubber gloves, rubber boots, and dust-mask. The Regulations impose an obligation not only on the employer to ensure that the worker wears the required protective clothing, but on the worker himself also. Therefore not only the employer but the worker, too, may be charged with infringing the Regulations. Moreover, Section II of the Act of 1952 makes it a specific offence for a worker wilfully to interfere with or misuse any appliance, clothing, equipment, facilities or other thing provided in pursuance of the Regulations, or wilfully and without reasonable cause to do anything likely to cause risk of poisoning to himself or others.

Other matters which are dealt with in the Regulations include the number of hours during which workers may be engaged on the specified operations; the age at which they may be employed; working in greenhouses; the provision and maintenance of protective clothing; the provision of washing facilities for workers; the notification of sickness; the training and supervision of workers; and the keeping of a register containing certain prescribed particulars.

In order to provide for special circumstances, inspectors are empowered to grant certificates of exemption if they are satisfied that any of the Regulations could reasonably be dispensed with if alternative conditions were observed, or if, by reason of exceptional circumstances or the small extent of the operations carried out, any of the provisions of the Regulations are unnecessary for the protection of the worker. For example, such certificates have been granted under this provision where spraying is carried our from an air-conditioned cab or when the worker is engaged on experimental work.

A person guilty of an offence against the Act or the Regulations is liable to a fine not exceeding fifty pounds and, in respect of an offence continued after conviction, to an additional fine not exceeding ten pounds for each day on which the contravention is continued.

A leaflet entitled 'The Safe Use of Poisonous Chemicals on the Farm' (APS/1), copies of which may be obtained free of charge from the Ministry of Agriculture, Fisheries and Food, Publications Room, Ruskin Avenue, Kew, Surrey, explains the requirements of the Regulations in non-legal language and gives some general advice on the safe use of pesticides.

When a chemical is prescribed under the Agricultural (Poisonous Substances) Regulations it is considered for inclusion in the Poisons law. Dinoseb, DNOC and endothal — and also mercuric chloride — are included in Part II of the Poisons List Order, 1952, which means they may be sold only by a retail chemist or by 'a listed seller of poisons', that is, someone such as an ironmonger or corn merchant who is registered with the local authority for the purpose. The Poisons Rules lay down the conditions under which listed poisons are labelled, packed, transported and stored in the shop. They also specify the conditions under which the chemicals may be purchased. For example, any of the five herbicides mentioned above may be purchased only by either producing a 'signed order' in a prescribed form or by attending the shop to sign the poisons book.

SECTION (ii) CIVIL LIABILITY OF USERS OF HERBICIDES

In dealing with civil liability it is important to appreciate that the law requires of persons who deal with things which are dangerous in themselves — such as dangerous chemicals — a very high standard of care indeed, so that in many cases it is unnecessary for the person injured to prove that the other party has been guilty of negligence. Although it is not possible to deal exhaustively with every type of case which could arise, the following are examples of relationships which might give rise to claims for damages.

EMPLOYER AND EMPLOYEE

Quite irrespective of the obligations laid down in the Agriculture (Poisonous Substances) Regulations, an employer owes to his workmen a duty to ensure that a safe system of work is adopted, and if the employer fails in this duty, he is liable for damages if a worker sustains injury in consequence. What constitutes a safe system of work is in every case a question of fact depending on the circumstances. Moreover, a worker who suffers damage through failure of the employer to comply with the Regulations, such as, e.g., to provide the proper protective clothing in connection with the use of poisonous substances specified in the Regulations, need not prove negligence on the part of his employer at all, but is entitled to bring an action for breach of statutory duty. It may be that in some cases the employer will have a defence to either of the above types of claim that the worker was himself guilty of contributory negligence, but if the alleged contributory negligence consists of failure to take steps which it was the employer's duty under the Regulations to ensure that the worker should take, such a defence is likely to fail.

DUTY TO NEIGHBOURS

If an occupier of land uses chemicals to spray his crops, and the chemicals escape and damage his neighbour's crops or livestock, in general it is true to say that he is absolutely liable and no question of negligence arises. The only defence which the occupier might have would be that the damage had occurred through the intervention of a third party or was due to an Act of God, but in practice neither of these defences is likely to be of much avail. If the spraying is undertaken by a contractor, the occupier will still be liable, but in such a case he will be able to recover indemnity from the contractor if he can show that the damage occurred through the contractor's negligence.

An occupier of land is under a duty to fence in his cattle, but he is under no obligation to fence out his neighbour's cattle. Consequently, in general, no legal redress exists if the cause of poisoning was that the cattle were trespassing on land which was being sprayed; but the position might be different if a fence was known to be weak, and the chemical used was known to be poisonous to cattle, and the occupier failed to issue a warning.

DUTY TO THE PUBLIC

Both an occupier of land and a contractor owe a duty to members of the public, e.g. persons lawfully passing along the highway (including any recognized footpath which crosses land which is being sprayed), to ensure that they are not injured by chemicals which are used. This responsibility also extends to persons visiting the land for the purpose of trade or business, and probably also to purely social visitors. There is, however, no duty or care owed to a mere trespasser, who therefore has no ground for complaint if he is injured while trespassing on land on which spraying operations are being carried out. An exception to this role, however, may arise in the case of young children, of whom the law does not expect the same standard of behaviour as of adults. If the operations being carried out are such as to constitute an 'irresistible lure' to children, e.g., spraying operations carried out by a helicopter, then it is the duty of the person responsible for carrying out the operation to see that effective measures are taken to exclude children; otherwise, if they are injured, the occupier or contractor is likely to be held liable.

CONTRACTOR'S DUTY TO OCCUPIER

In the absence of any special stipulation in the spraying contract, the contractor owes to the occupier of land for whom he has engaged to carry our spraying operations a duty to exercise proper care, and if through negligence the employer's livestock or crops are injured, the contractor will be held liable. It is, however, important to realize that there is nothing to prevent a contractor from limiting his liability to the occupier by making it a term of contract that his liability extends only to certain acts or omissions or is not to exceed a certain figure, or even excluding liability altogether so that he is not held responsible for any claims, however, caused. This, however, would not absolve the contractor from claims of negligence brought by the occupier's employees.

This statement of the law is by no means exhaustive, nor does it attempt to set out more than the basic principles which are involved, but as will be seen from even this brief summary, a heavy responsibility rests on both occupiers and contractors who make use of weed killers, more especially those which are poisonous, to ensure that every possible care is taken. It is, of course, normally possible for such persons to protect themselves against the possibility of civil claims by insurance. This, no doubt, is a prudent course and one which will be adopted in many cases.

SECTION (iii) INSURANCE IN RELATION TO THE USE OF HERBICIDES

Insurance cover can be obtained by occupiers of land, growers, contractors, merchants and manufacturers which will cover their legal liabilities resulting from the use of chemicals in agriculture arising out of injury or damage to crops, including the property of third parties, livestock and water pollution.

It can be generally stated that insurers would not be prepared to cover a grower who treats or sprays his own crops against damage thereto.

The grower may, however, insure his liability for damage caused to the crops, property and livestock belonging to a third party or neighbour where such damage or injury arises from drift. This type of insurance is becoming more widely accepted.

Some growers, in addition to doing their own spraying, also spray for other farmers, invariably without any specific form of contract, and thereby run considerable risk of not only having to pay for damage to the crops which they spray, but also for damage to the property of third parties.

Growers should therefore see that any insurance that they effect adequately indemnifies them in respect of all their operations.

Contractors are in a different position from that of growers, since they hold themselves out as specialists, and it is customary for contractors to undertake spraying for growers only on the terms and conditions of a printed form of contract the conditions of which the grower undertakes to accept.

There are various forms of contract in existence, but that most commonly used is the standard form which has been agreed between the National Farmers' Union and the National Association of Agricultural Contractors. Its conditions clearly set out the liabilities and the obligations of the contractor and impose certain duties on the grower.

It is a condition of a contractor's insurance that the contract shall be handed to the grower before spraying commences so that the grower may be aware of the terms and conditions under which the work is being carried out.

The contractor's policy gives indemnity in respect of the contractor's legal liability under the contract, and also indemnifies the contractor in respect of drift damage. It should, however, be understood that a policy of insurance excludes certain specific risks, for example, where contractors engage purely in experimental work with new chemicals which are not in commercial use.

Also no cover can be obtained which guarantees crop yields or guarantees the efficacy of the chemical used as to the control of weeds or pests.

It is a further condition of the contractor's insurance policy that he shall comply with the makers' instructions and recommendations as to the use of the chemical.

It should be stated that this type of insurance is of a hazardous class and it is therefore the type of insurance that every grower and contractor should seek to obtain.

The incidents which give rise to claims against growers and contractors are very varied: for example, where the machinery or equipment is not properly cleansed by employees, where hoses or attachments may become impregnated with growth-regulating herbicides, where wrong chemicals may be accidentally used, where losses occur through sudden changes in temperature or wind direction, where water or ground may become contaminated by carelessness of employees in either filling or emptying spraying apparatus.

These are some of the instances which give rise to claims against growers and contractors, and such incidents will occur even though the grower and contractor may take every possible step to see that the employees act carefully and with intelligence.

Apart from this, both growers and contractors frequently find themselves involved in claims concerning which there is considerable doubt as to whether they have a legal liability, and thus they may find themselves mulcted in very considerable costs in defending doubtful or unwarranted claims. Insurance policies protect the grower and contractor in such cases, which are not infrequent.

Another type of risk that contractors now run is that in connection with industrial spraying and spraying for local authorities.

In these cases the form of contract is essentially of a different type, and particularly in the case of public or local authorities the contractor is called upon to indemnify completely the principal against all claims however arising, and even going so far as to require the contractor to indemnify the principal against his negligence or that of his servants or agents.

This type of activity on the part of the contractors is increasing considerably, and it is essential that contractors should see that they are fully indemnified by their insurers under the contracts or indemnities which they have to give to their principals.

There is a growing tendency amongst merchants to engage the services of qualified persons to give advice to growers as to the treatment of their crops. As a result they therefore not only sell the chemicals but render themselves liable for wrong advice given.

Most merchants have adopted the attitude that they are only sellers of chemicals, and therefore pass any responsibilities on to the manufacturers or the contractors, but this is not always the case, and therefore merchants require proper insurance cover.

Manufacturers have a high degree of responsibility in respect of the chemicals which they market for agricultural use, and they are able to protect fully their liabilities under the Sale of Goods Act and in respect of negligence.

Many varied instances have occurred involving manufacturers in liabilities for considerable sums. For example, cases have arisen where wrong chemicals have been supplied, where there has been wrong labelling, and where the instructions as to use have not been clearly stated, and in respect of manufacturers it is the practice for them to engage a large technical advice staff who give direct advice to contractors and growers which may again involve liabilities where damage to crops arises.

Insurance cover should be looked upon as an essential part of the activities of manufacturers, merchants, contractors and growers, and it is recommended that they should carefully examine their existing insurances to see if they are adequate for their purposes, and should approach their brokers or insurance companies for advice.

SECTION (iv) AGRICULTURAL CHEMICALS APPROVAL SCHEME (INSECTICIDES, FUNGICIDES, HERBICIDES)

The purpose of this Scheme is to enable users to select and advisers to recommend efficient and appropriate proprietary brands of agricultural chemicals and to discourage the use of unsatisfactory products.

Included in the Scheme, which extends to Great Britain, Northern Ireland, the Channel Islands and the Isle of Man, are chemicals used for the control of plant pests and diseases, for weed destruction and growth-regulation, and for miscellaneous crop protection purposes. Rodenticides and chemicals used for purposes other than the protection of growing crops, e.g. for protection of stored products, veterinary or domestic uses, are not included.

Participation is voluntary and is open to manufacturers and their agents and also to the authorized agents of overseas manufacturers. The Scheme is operated on behalf of the Agricultural Departments of the United Kingdom by the Agricultural Chemicals Approval Organization at the Plant Pathology Laboratory, Harpenden, and a member of the Organization specializing in herbicides is attached to the A.R.C. Weed Research Organization, Begbroke Hill, Kidlington, Oxford. Full support to the principles of the Scheme is given by the Association of British Manufacturers of Agricultural Chemicals, the National Association of Corn and Agricultural Merchants and the National

Unions and Associations of farmers and growers in the United Kingdom.*
Under this Scheme, it is intended that products containing new chemicals
will be given official approval at the time of marketing.

Approval is granted to products by the Organization for specific uses under
United Kingdom* conditions when the recommendations made on the labels
are supported by satisfactory evidence from the manufacturers' field trials,

FIG. 5. The official mark of the Agricultural Chemicals Approval Scheme.

supplemented in appropriate cases by the results of work carried out by the
Advisory Services and Research Stations.

A Certificate of Approval, which is subject to annual renewal, is granted
to each product approved. The labels of approved products carry the iden-
tification mark shown in Fig. 5.

No product may receive approval under this Scheme until its safety in use
has been considered under another voluntary scheme — the Notification

* For the purposes of this Scheme the United Kingdom includes England, Scotland,
Wales, Northern Ireland, the Channel Islands, and the Isle of Man.

Scheme — and recommendations for its safe use has been published by the appropriate authorities.

A list of approved products is published on 1st February each year. Copies of the current list may be obtained free of charge from the Ministry of Agriculture, Fisheries and Food (Publications), Ruskin Avenue, Kew, Surrey, or from any of the Ministry's Regional and Divisional Offices. Copies can also be obtained from the main offices of the Agricultural Departments in Scotland, Northern Ireland, the Channel Islands and the Isle of Man.

Products approved too late for inclusion in the current List are announced in the journals *Agriculture* and *Scottish Agriculture*, before the next List appears.

Correspondence concerning the Scheme should be addressed to the Secretary, Agricultural Chemicals Approval Organization, Plant Pathology Laboratory, Hatching Green, Harpenden, Herts. Tel. Harpenden 5241.

CHAPTER IX

THE LAW CONCERNING WEED SEEDS AND INJURIOUS WEEDS

WEED SEEDS IN CROP SEED

The problem of controlling the distribution of weed seeds in crop seed was considered by the Committee on Transactions in Seeds, set up in 1954. The problem is difficult as it involves the seed producer, the seed merchant and the farmer.* The farmer naturally wants his crop seed to be free, if possible, from the seeds of weeds which are likely to reduce the economic value of his crop or contaminate the land on which it is grown. The seed merchant, on the other hand, cannot provide a cleaner sample than his seed cleaning plant can produce. Despite the ingenuity of modern cleaning machines some weed seeds cannot be removed by ordinary cleaning methods; others can be cleaned out but, beyond a certain point, only with a disproportionate loss of the crop seed which increases the price. The problem of 'dirty seed' is best dealt with at source by encouraging seed growers to harvest their seed as free as possible from weed seeds. Many of the weeds can not be controlled or eradicated in the seed crop by modern husbandry methods and herbicides. Legislation on weed seeds is designed to protect the farmer from unwittingly introducing weeds on his land in the crop seed he purchases; it therefore supplements the efforts made by seed producers and seed merchants to produce and sell clean seed.

THE LAW ON WEED SEEDS

Both the numbers of injurious weed seeds, and the percentage by weight of all weed seeds, in samples of crop seeds are dealt with in the Seed Regulations 1961, made under the Seeds Act 1920, amended by the Seeds Act 1925 and Section 12 of the Agriculture (Miscellaneous Provisions) Act 1954. Both the Act and the Regulations apply to farmer-to-farmer sales of crop seed equally with merchant-to-farmer sales.

The Seeds Act 1920 lays down that anyone selling crop seed of the kinds specified in the Regulations must, within seven days of sale or delivery, give to the buyer certain particulars about it including the analytical purity, the

* Report of the Committee on Transactions in Seeds. H.M.S.O., 1957.

germination, and the variety. These particulars must also be displayed on or near seed which is exposed for sale. The Act requires that tests to furnish the necessary particulars must be carried out either at an official seed testing station or at private stations licensed by the Ministry of Agriculture, Fisheries and Food; garden seeds, however, may also be tested in any other sufficient manner. There are certain exceptions to the provisions of the Act; these are seeds sold to a purchaser who intends to clean them before resale, or who gives a written undertaking that the seeds will be tested before resale, and seeds which are exported or are sold for purposes other than sowing.

The Seed Regulations 1961 define injurious weed seeds as seeds of:

Agropyron repens (couch-grass)
Alopecurus myosuroides (blackgrass)
Avena fatua and *Avena ludoviciana* (wild oat)
Cuscuta spp. (dodder)
Rumex spp. (docks and sorrels).

The Regulations require that the number of seeds of any of these injurious weeds must be ascertained in an official test on a sample of 8 oz of cereals and declared to the buyer. As from 1 August 1962 the number of seeds of any of the injurious weeds must be ascertained in the purity test on herbage and field seeds and declared to the buyer when more than one is present. The Regulations also require that the percentage by weight of all weed seeds, including any injurious weed seeds, must be ascertained in the purity test on

TABLE 20.   NUMBERS OF INJURIOUS WEED SEEDS SOWN PER ACRE WHEN ONE IN 8 OZ IS DECLARED FOR CEREALS, OR TWO IN A PURITY TEST ARE DECLARED FOR HERBAGE SEED

Weed	Crop seed	Weight examined	Assumed sowing rate (per acre)	Approximate number of weed seeds sown per acre
Avena fatua and *A. ludoviciana* (wild oat)	Cereals	8 oz	1·5 cwt	336
Rumex spp. (docks and sorrels)	Cereals	8 oz	1·5 cwt	336
	Herbage mixtures	5 g	16 lb	2880
Cuscuta spp. (dodder)	Red clover	5 g	10 lb	1800
	White clover	2 g	4 lb	1800
Alopecurus myosuroides (blackgrass) *Agropyron repens* (couch-grass)	Cocksfoot	2 g	8 lb	3600

17

TABLE 21. NUMBERS OF SEEDS OF WEEDS COMMONLY FOUND IN CEREAL SEED WHICH WOULD BE SOWN PER SQUARE YARD IF PRESENT AT THE RATE OF 3 PER CENT BY WEIGHT

(Assumed sowing rate: 1·5 cwt per acre)

Weed	Mean weight of 1000 seeds (g)	Approximate number of weed seeds sown per square yard
Galium aparine (cleavers)	13·1	30–40
Raphanus raphanistrum (wild radish)	7·9	60
Polygonum convolvulus (black bindweed)	7·0	70
Polygonum persicaria (redshank)	2·1	230
Polygonum aviculare (knotgrass)	1·7	280
Atriplex patula (common orache)	1·5	320

TABLE 22. NUMBERS OF SEEDS OF WEEDS COMMONLY FOUND IN MIXTURES OF HERBAGE SEED WHICH WOULD BE SOWN PER SQUARE YARD IF PRESENT AT THE RATE OF 3 PER CENT BY WEIGHT

(Assumed sowing rate 16 lb per acre)

Weed	Mean weight of 1000 seeds (g)	Approximate number of weed seeds sown per square yard
Poterium sanguisorba (salad burnet)	8·9	5
Bromus mollis (soft brome)	3·6	10
Geranium dissectum (cut-leaved cranesbill)	2·5	20
Ranunculus repens (creeping buttercup)	2·4	20
Sheradia arvensis (field madder)	1·6	30
Geranium molle (dove's foot cranesbill)	1·5	30
Plantago lanceolata (ribwort)	1·5	30
Lapsana communis (nipplewort)	1·5	30
Silene alba (white campion)	0·9	50
Vulpia myuros (rat's-tail fescue)	0·6	70
Prunella vulgaris (self-heal)	0·6	70
Chenopodium album (fat hen)	0·6	70
Stellaria media (chickweed)	0·5	90
Tripleurospermum maritimum spp. *inodorum* (scentless mayweed)	0·4	110
Holcus lanatus (Yorkshire fog)	0·3	150
Myosotis arvensis (forget-me-not)	0·3	150
Sonchus asper (spiny sowthistle)	0·3	150
Poa annua (annual meadowgrass)	0·2	230
Plantago major (greater plantain)	0·2	230
Cerastium holosteoides (mouse-ear chickweed)	0·1	450

cereals, herbage and field seeds and declared to the buyer when this exceeds 0·5 per cent.

Table 20 indicates the numbers of injurious weed seeds which will be sown per acre if the crop seed is contaminated at the level where a declaration must be made under the Regulations.

The Regulations do not at present implement the provision of the Act that it is not lawful to sell, or expose for sale, or knowingly to sow any seed which contains more than a prescribed percentage by weight of injurious weed seeds. The Committee on Transactions in Seeds recommended that the sowing of seed containing more than 3 per cent by weight of weed seeds, including the injurious weed seeds, should be prohibited. This is still under consideration but the numbers of seeds of different weed species, which would be sown per square yard when crop seed is contaminated by them at a level of 3 per cent by weight, are shown in Tables 21 and 22.

THE LAW ON INJURIOUS WEEDS

Legislation on injurious weeds dates from the Corn Production Acts of 1917 and 1920 and further provisions were introduced under a number of subsequent Acts. In July 1959 the previous enactments were repealed and all the provisions consolidated in the Weeds Act, 1959.

The injurous weeds to which the Weed Act applies are:

Cirsium vulgare (spear thistle)
Cirsium arvense (creeping thistle)
Rumex crispus (curled dock)
Rumex obtusifolius (broad-leaved dock)
Senecio jacobaea (ragwort)

and additional weeds may be prescribed by regulations.

The Minister has power under the Act to serve notice on an occupier of land requiring him, within the time specified in the notice, to take such action as may be necessary to prevent the injurious weeds from spreading. An occupier who unreasonably fails to comply with the requirements of such a notice is liable, on summary conviction, to a fine not exceeding £75, or for a second or subsequent offence, not exceeding £150; the Minister may also enter on the land and take the necessary action to prevent the weeds from spreading, recovering the cost of doing so from the occupier.

Since 1939, there have been changes in the delegation of the Minister's powers. At present the councils of county boroughs exercise the delegated powers on non-agricultural land within their areas, the Minister's divisional executive officers the powers on non-agricultural land outside the county boroughs, and the county agricultural executive committees on agricultural land within their areas.

CHAPTER X

WEEDS AND WEED SEEDS IN RELATION TO CROP SEED CERTIFICATION SCHEMES

INTRODUCTION

The main purpose of seed certification schemes is to ensure that the seed is correctly named for variety, and of a high standard of genetic purity. It is generally accepted also that the seed shall be of a high standard in other respects, and relative freedom from undesirable weed seeds is an important consideration.

Schemes for the production of high quality seed consist of two stages. Seed crops are inspected in the field, and if there is no further supervision after harvest, the produce is called 'field approved' seed. Where steps are taken to ensure the authenticity of the harvested and cleaned seed from approved fields the produce is called 'certified seed'.

Modern seed cleaning machinery in the hands of an efficient operator is capable of cleaning most dirty samples of seed to a satisfactory standard. Some weed seeds, however, are similar in size, shape and weight to the crop seeds in which they occur. To remove these is difficult and sometimes impossible. In any event, seed cleaning is a wasteful operation, since good seed is inevitably lost during the removal of impurities.

For these reasons, schemes for quality seed production lay stress on the importance of having the seed crop itself relatively free from objectionable weeds, and field approval depends not only on trueness to variety, but also on freedom from weeds. In certain cases, crops may only be entered for inspection if sown on fields which have been approved for the purpose.

Certified seed is always expected to meet high standards of purity on laboratory test. Purity standards, in so far as they cover weed seeds, are an attempt to attain a higher standard than that required by law.

All schemes in the United Kingdom are voluntary, but are well supported. In England and Wales, for instance, 20 to 25 per cent of the requirements of cereal seed is available from field approved crops, and 15 to 20 per cent of the herbage seed is 'British Certified', supplied in bags bearing a certificaton trade mark label authorized by the Board of Trade.

The following paragraphs set out the main points from the schemes in the United Kingdom applicable to weed plants in the field and weed seeds in the cleaned sample. These may be subject to revision in the light of experience. There are, of course, standards for other features, which are not listed here.

SECTION (i) SCHEMES IN ENGLAND AND WALES ADMINISTERED BY THE NATIONAL INSTITUTE OF AGRICULTURAL BOTANY

CEREALS (WHEAT, OATS AND BARLEY)

Field Approval Standards

For field approval not more than the following number of plants per acre in any cereal crop will be tolerated:

	Not more than
Allium vineale (wild onion)	3 per acre
Avena fatua and *A. ludoviciana* (wild oats)	3 ,, ,,
Scandix pecten-veneris (shepherd's needle)	3 ,, ,,
Raphanus raphanistrum (wild radish)	3 ,, ,,
Vicia spp. (wild tares or vetches)	20 ,, ,,
Galium aparine (cleavers)	50 ,, ,,

Under certain circumstances, approval may be granted even though the crop does contain more than the permitted number of one or more of the weeds listed above. In such instances the approval is deferred and is contingent upon the satisfactory cleaning of the produce and the observance of certain other conditions. For instance, except in special cases, deferment can be applied only in respect of:

Wild oats and shepherd's needle in wheat and barley.

Wild tare or vetches and cleavers in wheat, barley and oats.

The criteria for approval of the seed of the deferred crop are that two 7 lb samples of seed shall be completely free from any seeds listed in the Field Approval Standards. If a single seed of any of these weeds does occur in either of these two samples then approval will be given only if three further 7 lb samples are completely free.

Comprehensive Certification

In the Comprehensive Certification Scheme a 7 lb sample of seed is examined and a certificate refused if any weed seeds are found. Recleaning is permitted but a further 7 lb sample must be completely free from weed seeds before a certificate is issued.

GRASSES AND CLOVERS

Field Approval Standards

The following standards are applied to growing crops of all varieties in the field.

In each crop the weed plants scheduled for that crop and likely to be seed-bearing at time of harvest shall be given points according to the scale shown below. The maximum tolerance in any crop of normal seed expectation shall be *two points per square yard on average*.

Any crop containing dodder shall be rejected.

		Points per plant
(1) Ryegrasses, Meadow Fescue and Tall Fescue		
Carduus spp. and/or *Cirsium* spp.	(thistles)	1
Rumex spp.	(docks and sorrels)	1
Alopecurus myosuroides	(blackgrass)	2
Bromus spp.	(bromes)	2
(2) Cocksfoot and Red Fescue		
Carduus spp. and/or *Cirsium* spp.	(thistles)	1
Rumex spp.	(docks and sorrels)	1
Bromus mollis	(soft brome)	1
Alopecurus myosuroides	(blackgrass)	2
Holcus lanatus	(Yorkshire fog)	2
(3) Timothy		
Carduus spp. and/or *Cirsium* spp.	(thistles)	1
Rumex spp.	(docks and sorrels)	1
Silene alba	(white campion)	1
Plantago major	(greater plantain)	2
Crepis capillaris	(smooth hawk's beard)	2
Urtica spp.	(nettles)	2
Tripleurospermum maritimum ssp. *inodorum*	(scentless mayweed)	4
Sisymbrium officinale	(hedge mustard)	4
(4) Red Clover, Lucerne and Sainfoin		
Carduus spp. and/or *Cirsium* spp.	(thistles)	1
Rumex spp.	(docks and sorrels)	1
(5) White Clover		
Carduus spp. and/or *Cirsium* spp.	(thistles)	1
Rumex spp.	(docks and sorrels)	1
Silene alba	(white campion)	1
Geranium pusillum	(small-flowered cranes-bill)	2
Geranium molle	(dove's foot cranesbill)	2
Prunella vulgaris	(self-heal)	2

COMPREHENSIVE CERTIFICATION

The following standards apply to herbage seed lots entered for comprehensive certification:

(1) Total weed seed content shall not be more than 0·5 per cent by weight.

(2) In an official purity test there shall be no dodder.

(3) Seed shall only be certified if no declaration of injurious weed seed numbers is required under Schedule 2 of the Seeds Regulations, 1961 (see Chapter IX).

SECTION (ii) SCHEME FOR CEREALS ADMINISTERED BY THE WELSH SEED GROWERS' FEDERATION LTD

Fields intended for seed production must be inspected and approved prior to sowing, and must be known not to grow wild oats, wild vetches, wild onion and wild radish.

When the growing crop is inspected the following standards are applied:

	Maximum number of plants tolerated in 10 sample counts, each of 24 square yards	
	Stock seed	Certified seed
Avena fatua and *A. ludoviciana* (wild oats)	nil	nil
Allium vineale (wild onion)	} nil	nil
Bromus secalinus (rye-brome)		
Vicia spp. (tares)		
Raphanus raphanistrum (wild radish)	} nil	10
Scandix pecten-veneris (shepherd's needle)		
Cirsium spp. (thistles)	} 10	20
Rumex spp. (docks)		

After harvesting and cleaning, a 5 lb sample of the seed is examined and must satisfy the following standards:

	Maximum number of grains tolerated in 5 lb sample	
	Stock seed	Certified seed
Avena fatua, A. ludoviciana, Allium vineale, Bromus secalinus, Alopecurus myosuroides	} nil	nil
Vicia spp., *Raphanus raphanistrum, Rumex* spp., *Cirsium* spp., *Galium aparine*	} nil	1
Sinapis arvensis	nil	2
	nil	1

SECTION (iii) SCHEME FOR SEED OATS AND SEED BARLEY ADMINISTERED BY THE DEPARTMENT OF AGRICULTURE FOR SCOTLAND

SCOTTISH CERTIFIED GROWING CROPS — OATS AND BARLEY

INITIAL SEED SAMPLES

A 2 lb sample of the seed to be used for sowing is examined by the Department. It must not contain any seeds of *Avena fatua* and *A. ludoviciana* (wild oat) or *Raphanus raphanistrum* (wild radish); oat samples must not contain *Avena strigosa* (bristle-pointed oats). Not more than 2 seeds of the following group of weeds shall be found in oats and barley samples:

> *Galeopsis tetrahit* (hemp nettle)
> *Galium aparine* (cleavers)
> *Polygonum convolvulus* (black bindweed)
> *Sinapis arvensis* (charlock)
> *Vicia* spp. (wild vetches).

GROWING CROP STANDARDS

When the growing crops are inspected the following standards must be satisfied:

	Oat crops not more than	Barley crops not more than
Avena fatua and *A. ludoviciana* (wild oats)	nil	3 plants per acre
Avena strigosa (bristle oat)	2 plants in 100,000	—
Raphanus raphanistrum (wild radish)	100 plants per acre	100 plants per acre
Galium aparine (cleavers) *Sinapis arvensis* (charlock) *Vicia* spp. (tares) *Galeopsis tetrahit* (hemp nettle) *Polygonum convolvulus* (black bindweed)	500 plants per acre	500 plants per acre

SCOTTISH CERTIFIED STOCK SEED

Before a Stock Seed certificate is issued a 2 lb sample, drawn after cleaning of the harvested produce, must show 99 per cent purity and be free of any seeds of the weeds listed in the standards for field inspection.

SCOTTISH FIELD APPROVED CROPS

When the growing crop is inspected it must not contain more than 3 plants per acre of *Avena fatua* and *A. ludoviciana*, or more than 100 plants per acre of *Raphanus raphanistrum*, or more than 500 plants per acre of the above group of weeds, *Galium aparine*, etc. Oat crops must not contain more than 4 plants in 100,000 of *Avena strigosa*.

SECTION (iv) SCHEMES ADMINISTERED BY THE MINISTRY OF AGRICULTURE, NORTHERN IRELAND

Comprehensive schemes are in operation for the production of certified seed of oats, barley, perennial ryegrass and Italian ryegrass.

CEREALS

All fields are inspected prior to sowing and to be eligible for production of a crop for certification they must have a suitable cropping history and be free of evidence of presence of *Raphanus raphanistrum* (wild radish), *Avena fatua* and *A. ludoviciana* (wild oats), *A. strigosa* (bristle oat) and *Vicia* spp. (tares).

Growing crops are inspected, and counts on sample areas are made to determine the proportions of weeds and other impurities present. All crops containing troublesome weeds such as *Raphanus raphanistrum* are eliminated from the scheme at this stage.

While no rigid standards are set for cleaned seed, lots must have a high level of analytical purity and be virtually free of all weed impurities to be eligible for certification.

Official certificate labels are attached to all sacks under official seals. These labels state *inter alia*, the analytical purity and germination of the seed.

RYEGRASSES

As in the case of cereals, fields are inspected prior to approval for sowing to ensure that they have suitable cropping histories and are free of serious weed contamination.

Growing crops are inspected on three or four occasions prior to harvest. During the final inspection at the end of June or early July, sample area counts are taken.

All crops accepted as eligible for certification at this stage must not contain, on average, more than one plant of the following weeds in 5 square yards, *Alopecurus myosuroides* (blackgrass), *Bromus* spp. (soft brome), *Vulpia myuros* (rat's-tail fescue) and *Agropyron repens* (couch grass).

In a test carried out at the Official Seed Testing Station for Northern Ireland on an officially drawn, representative sample, the impurities must not exceed the following amounts:

	Maximum percentage by weight
Total content of weed seeds	0·3
Total weed seeds, *plus* other crop seeds	0·8
Total weed seeds, *plus* other crop seeds *plus* inert matter	1·5

FINAL CERTIFICATION

Each sealed sack of cleaned, certified seed bears an official label stating the purity and germination of the seed lot.

CHAPTER XI

WEEDS IN SEED CROPS

HERBAGE (GRASS AND LEGUMES) SEED

In seed crops weeds present a two-fold problem. As in all crops, they can hinder establishment, even to the extent of causing crop failure; they waste plant foods, reduce crop yields by competition and make harvest difficult. In addition, the presence of weed seeds can cause expense and loss of crop seed in cleaning; after cleaning sufficient numbers may still remain to reduce the value of the seed lot. In perennial crops, such as most herbage seed crops, the weeds which are important at seed harvest are frequently different from those which are important in the sowing year. Fast-growing smothering weeds, such as *Stellaria media* (chickweed) and *Polygonum* spp. may be controlled or crowded out by crop growth. Often, however, they give place to perennial weeds, especially grass weeds, whose seeds ripen with the crop seed and resemble it sufficiently in size, weight or shape to make cleaning difficult.

Herbage seed crops, especially those to be grown in wide drills or at low plant populations — as is often advisable for the best seed yields — should be sown on clean land, preferably after a crop in which weeds have been effectively destroyed. Even if this is not possible, it is worthwhile to give special attention to headlands and small areas of such weeds as *Agropyron repens* (couch grass) or *Alopecurus myosuroides* (blackgrass) in preparation for the seed crop. The responsibility for clean land and a weed-free seed crop must rest ultimately with the grower, who knows his land and its probable weeds, and can visit the crop regularly to check which weeds are present. He must decide on the method and timing of control measures.

The five weeds designated as injurious in the Seeds Regulations, 1961, (see Chapter IX) are important in herbage seed as in all agricultural seed. Other weeds of special importance in herbage seed are scheduled in the Field Inspection Scheme for herbage seed crops administered by the N.I.A.B. (see Chapter X) because of the special difficulty of cleaning the seeds out of crop seed. These two groups of weeds, and some others which may also present difficulty at cleaning, are shown in Table 23 under the crop in which they need special attention. A few species normally considered as crop plants are also included in Table 23 as they are treated as weeds in certain cases. The weeds fall in two categories, those which can be controlled by selective herbicides with varying degrees of effectiveness (e.g. broad-leaved weeds) and

TABLE 23. WEEDS OF IMPORTANCE IN HERBAGE SEED CROPS

I Injurious weed scheduled in Seeds Regulations, 1961.
S Species scheduled in N.I.A.B. field inspection standards.
D Other species likely to cause difficulty or losses in cleaning.

Weed	Annual (A), Biennial (B) or Perennial (P)	Rye-grasses	Meadow and tall fescues	Cocks-foot	Red fescue	Timothy	Red clover and lucerne	White clover	Sainfoin
Agropyron repens (couch grass)	P	I	I	I	I	I	I	I	I
Agrostis spp. (bent grass)	P					D			
Alopecurus myosuroides (blackgrass)	A	IS	IS	IS	IS	I	I	I	I
Avena fatua, A. ludoviciana (wild oats)	A	I	I	I	I	I	I	I	I
Bromus mollis (soft brome)	A, B	S	S	S	S				
Bromus spp. (sterile and other brome)	A, B, P	S	S	S	S	S	S	S	S
Carduus spp. (thistles)	B, P	S				D		D	
Cerastium holosteoides (mouse-ear chickweed)	A, P	D (in Italian)						D	
Chenopodium album (fat hen)	A								
Chrysanthemum segetum (corn marigold)	A	S							
Cirsium spp. (thistles)	B, P	S	S	S	S	S	S	S	S
Crepis capillaris (smooth hawk's beard)	A	IS	IS	IS	IS	S	IS	IS	IS
Cuscuta spp. (dodder)	A			D		IS			
Galium aparine (cleavers)	A								
Geranium dissectum (cut-leaved cranesbill)	A						D		
Geranium molle (dove's foot cranesbill)	A						D	S	
Geranium pusillum (small-flowered cranesbill)	A							S	
Holcus lanatus (Yorkshire fog)	P			S	S	D			

TABLE 23 (continued)

Weed	Annual (A), Biennial (B) or Perennial (P)	Rye-grasses	Meadow and tall fescues	Cocks-foot	Red fescue	Timothy	Red clover and lucerne	White clover	Sainfoin
Lapsana communis (nipplewort)	A				S				
Lolium spp. (ryegrasses)	A, B, P		S	D					
Medicago lupulina (trefoil)	A, P						D	D	
Myosotis arvensis (forget-me-not)	A					D		D	
Papaver rhoeas (corn poppy)	A					D			
Plantago lanceolata (ribgrass)	P								
Plantago major (greater plantain)	P	D							
Poa spp. (meadow grasses)	A, P		D	D	D	S	D	D	
Poterium spp. (burnets)	P					D			D
Prunella vulgaris (self-heal)	P				D	D		S	
Rumex spp. (docks and sorrels)	P	IS	IS	IS	IS	IS	IS	IS	IS
Sherardia arvensis (field madder)	A							D	
Silene alba (white campion)	A, B, P			D		S	D	S	
Sisymbrium officinale (hedge mustard)	A					S			
Sonchus spp. (sowthistles)	A, P		D						
Stellaria media (chickweed)	A					D		D	D
Trifolium dubium (suckling clover)	A							S	
Tripleurospermum maritimum ssp. *inodorum* (scentless mayweed)	A					S			
Urtica spp. (nettles)	A, P					S			
Vulpia spp. (rat's-tail fescues)	A				D				

those for which there is at present no selective herbicidal treatment (e.g. grass weeds in grass seed crops and such broad-leaved species as trefoil and suckling clover in clover seed crops). Information on the control of weeds in the first category and of some weeds in the second category, is given in Chapter V. In addition, inter-row cultivations, rogueing when numbers are not too great and ploughing, rotary cultivating or spraying round headlands are general control measures which may be applied in growing seed crops. Badly infested areas of the crop may have to be discarded from seed production.

The control measures which should be considered at particular stages in the life of a seed crop may be summarized as follows:

(a) Various pre-sowing and pre-emergence treatments are possible at sowing (see paragraphs 34, 36 and 38 in Chapter II).

(b) Shallow inter-row cultivations should be started as early as possible in a direct-sown wide-drilled crop. (A marker such as mustard or lettuce, sown at a few ounces per acre with the crop seed, may help by showing the rows early.)

(c) Spraying may be needed fairly soon after sowing in narrow-drilled direct-sown crops, where cultivations are not possible. The herbicide tolerances of grass and clover seedlings are shown in Chapter II. If spraying is necessary in undersown crops, the grass or clover seedlings should have reached the stages described in Chapter II. When undersown crops are cleared of the cover crop, those in wide drills should be cultivated and those in narrow drills may need herbicide treatments.

(d) Topping-over when the crop is established will help to control some broad-leaved weeds, but several cuts will be needed if *Avena fatua* (wild oats) or *Alopecurus myosuroides* (blackgrass) are to be prevented from seeding.

(e) For crops sown in the spring hand weeding of grass weeds in summer and autumn may be practicable if numbers are small, and this should be done, and the plants removed, before they set seed.

(f) Headlands should be ploughed, cultivated or sprayed as often as necessary to prevent encroachment of weeds such as *Anisantha sterilis* (barren brome).

(g) *Alopecurus myosuroides* (blackgrass) seedlings require special attention; no herbicide treatments against them can at present be recommended, although the autumn and winter of the sowing year is the period in which the most promising treatments have been made. In the absence of recommendations for herbicide treatments, inter-row cultivation remains the only effective control measure, and should if possible be repeated several times for maximum germination and seedling destruction.

(h) Inter-row work may be continued in late winter or early spring, but
after the crop has begun growth in the spring it may be damaged by
cultivations. They should therefore be as early as possible and, if
several are needed, progressively more shallow.

(i) The last opportunity to eliminate the weeds described in Table 23 will
occur in the spring and early summer. Herbicide treatments or hand
weeding should if possible be completed before the crop is officially
inspected under the Field Inspection Scheme.

The timing of herbicide treatments for grasses is important. Grass seed
crops can be sprayed in the spring before harvest with M C P A, 2,4-D, M C P B,
2,4-D B, mecoprop or M C P A/2,3,6-T B A mixture at the doses given in Chapter II.
Some of these herbicides may cause deformities in seed heads, or reduce seed
yields, if applied too early (when the head is being formed) or after the head
has emerged. Spraying should normally be carried out during the 4 to 5
weeks before heads begin to emerge from their sheaths, and Table 24 shows
the recommended safe period for each of the Aberystwyth grass varieties in a
normal season at Cambridge. These dates vary according to season, and should
also be adjusted for other parts of the country. Safe periods for other varieties
can be calculated if the normal time of ear emergence is known. In some cases
loss of yield has occurred from spraying too early or too late, but it may be
necessary to risk some damage in order to control certain weeds on which the

**TABLE 24.   SAFE PERIODS FOR USING GROWTH REGULATORS
ON ABERYSTWYTH GRASS VARIETIES IN SPRING BEFORE
SEED HARVEST**

(Based on the normal time of ear emergence at Cambridge)

Variety	Approximate extent of recommended safe period (Cambridge)	Normal start of ear emergence (Cambridge)
S.59 red fescue S.170 tall fescue	} April	4th week April to 1st week May
S.24 perennial ryegrass S.37 cocksfoot	} April	1st week May
S.26 cocksfoot S.215 meadow fescue	} 2nd week April to 1st week May	2nd week May
S.143 cocksfoot	mid-April to mid-May	2nd to 3rd week May
S.53 meadow fescue S.22 Italian ryegrass	} late April to mid-May	3rd week May
S.101 perennial ryegrass	late April to mid-May	3rd to 4th week May
S.23 perennial ryegrass	end April to end May	4th week May
S.50 timothy	end April to end May	4th week May to 1st week June
S.51 timothy	mid-May to early June	2nd week June
S.48 timothy	mid-May to mid-June	3rd week June

approval of the crop may depend. For example *Rumex* spp. (docks) and *Cirsium* spp. (thistles) may not be ready for spraying in early-heading grasses and *Tripleurospermum* sp. (mayweed) may be too advanced for spraying in timothy at the safe periods. Spraying in a very dry period is liable to cause some crop damage by scorching.

Although established clovers for mowing or grazing can be treated with M C P B or 2,4-D B, no recommendations can be made for spraying red clover for seed, nor for spraying white clover after shutting up for seed. The only recommended treatment for white clover is to examine it for important weeds early in the year, and if necessary spray with M C P B at 32 oz per acre by mid-May at the latest, to allow at least three weeks of grazing, or a silage cut, before shutting up for seed.

CEREAL SEED

Attention has been focused on the presence of weed seeds in cereal seeds by the Seeds Regulations, 1961, which requires declaration of the purity, the name and number of the five prescribed injurious weed seeds in an 8 oz sample, and the percentage by weight of all weed seeds present when this exceeds 0·5 per cent. In addition special attention has to be given to the presence of certain scheduled weeds in the seed crop when this is grown for Field Approval or Certification.

Some indication of the relative occurrence of the injurious weed seeds, the seeds of weeds scheduled under special schemes, and the common seed contaminants of cereal seed can be obtained from the records of samples analysed at the Official Seed Testing Station. The results of a survey of the reports for the 1960–61 seasons are shown in Table 25; where the frequencies of the weed seeds in the four main cereals are expressed as a percentage of the samples tested which contained at least one seed in 4 oz.

INJURIOUS WEED SEEDS

Seeds of *Agropyron repens* (couch grass) occurred at a frequency of 2 to 3 per cent in all four cereals, whereas seeds of *Alopecurus myosuroides* (blackgrass), reached this frequency only in oats, being present in 1 to 2 per cent of the wheat and barley samples, and absent in rye. These two weeds are particularly troublesome in cereals grown on heavy land in the south and east. There is at present no herbicide that may be used on cereal crops for the control of couch grass. Barban gives satisfactory control of blackgrass in winter cereals when applied at 5 oz. active ingredient (see paragraph 24 in Chapter II). Details of the control of these species by cultivation methods are given in Chapter V.

Seeds of *Avena fatua* and *A. ludoviciana* (wild oats) are a fairly frequent contaminant of cereal samples, ranging from 2 per cent in rye to 7 per cent in arley (see Table 25). Until recently careful cultivation was the only method f control but barban can now be used to check these weeds (see paragraph 3 in Chapter II).

Seeds of docks, principally *Rumex crispus* (curled dock), were confined ainly to rye and oats with a frequency of 3 per cent in each. Details of the ossible control measures are given in Chapter V.

SCHEDULED WEEDS

With the exception of *Avena fatua* and *Avena ludoviciana* (wild oats) mentioned above, and *Gallium aparine* (cleavers) the seeds of weeds scheduled in ield Approval and Certification schemes do not occur frequently in cereals. leavers are an important exception with a frequency ranging from 5 per cent rye to 13 per cent in barley (see Table 25). This weed can be controlled by arious herbicides suitable for use in cereal crops (see Chapter II, section (i) ereals).

The occurrence of wild oats and cleavers in numbers exceeding the prescribed standards in the seed crop are one of the most common causes of jection under the Field Approval Scheme. The occurrence of *Allium vineale* wild onion), *Vicia* spp. (tares) and *Raphanus raphanistrum* (wild radish), gether account for a much smaller proportion of rejected crops. These three eeds can all be controlled by herbicides (see Chapter V).

COMMON WEED SEED CONTAMINANTS

Polygonum convolvulus (black bindweed) was the most frequent contaminant all four cereals, being particularly common in barley with a frequency of 4 per cent. Seeds of *P. aviculare* (knotgrass), *P. persicaria* (redshank), and *lapathifolium* (pale persicaria) also occurred in the same samples.

Polygonum spp., *Atriplex patula* (common orache) and *Chenopodium album* at hen) can all be controlled by treatment with appropriate selective herbicides (see Chapter II, section (i) (Cereals).

FODDER, ROOT AND VEGETABLE SEED

he problem of weeds in the production of root and vegetable seeds is generally onsidered to be less serious than for cereal or herbage seed because of the ore intensive methods used. Many vegetable seed crops are transplanted om a seed bed, and hand harvested, but fodder and root crops such as kale, pe, turnips, mustard and beet can be drilled and may become badly infested ith weeds or plants of closely related crops, the seeds of which are difficult remove during cleaning. No injurious weed seeds are prescribed for root d vegetable seeds, but attention should be given to certain common weed eds which may be present in sufficient quantity to exceed the declarable inimum percentage for purity under the Seeds Regulations, 1961. Some

18

TABLE 25. WEEDS OF IMPORTANCE IN CEREAL SEED CROPS

Weed	Annual (A) Biennial (B) Perennial (P) or Bulb (Bb)	Injurious weed seeds (I)	Weeds scheduled in Certification or Field Approval Schemes (S)			Percentage frequency of samples containing at least one weed seed in 4 oz crop seed			
			N.I.A.B.	Scotland	Wales	Wheat	Barley	Oats	Rye
Agropyron repens (couch grass)	P	I				2	2	3	4
Agrostemma githago (corn cockle)	A					—	—	—	2
Allium vineale (wild onion)	Bb	I			S	T	—	T	—
Alopecurus myosuroides (blackgrass)	A					2	2	3	2
Atriplex patula (common orache)	A					3	3	3	2
Avena fatua, A. ludoviciana (wild oats)	A	I	S		S	4	7	4	2
A. strigosa (bristle oat)	A			S		T	T	T	—
Bromus mollis (soft brome)	A, B			S		T	T	T	T
Bromus secalinus (rye-brome)	A				S	1	—	T	—
Chenopodium album (fat hen)	A					T	2	3	3
Cirsium spp. (thistles)	B, P			S	S	T	T	T	T
Daucus carrota (wild carrot)	B			S	S	T	T	T	—
Galeopsis tetrahit (common hempnettle)	A		S			10	13	2	T
Galium aparine (cleavers)	A				S	T	T	7	5
Geranium dissectum (cut-leaved cranesbill)	A					T	T	T	2
Holcus lanatus (Yorkshire fog)	P					T	T	T	—
Polygonum aviculare (knot grass)	A					2	3	3	2
Polygonum convolvulus (black bindweed)	A			S		19	24	10	12

TABLE 25 (continued)

Weed	Annual (A) Biennial (B) Perennial (P) or Bulb (Bb)	Injurious weed seeds (I)	Weeds schedules in Certification or Field Approval Schemes (S)			(Percentage frequency of samples containing at least one weed seed in 4 oz crop seed)			
			N.I.A.B.	Scotland	Wales	Wheat	Barley	Oats	Rye
Polygonum lapathifolium (pale persicaria)	A					1	2	2	T
Polygonum persicaria (redshank)	A					2	3	6	T
Raphanus raphanistrum (wild radish)	A	I	S	S	S	T	1	T	2
Rumex spp. (docks and sorrels)	P					T	1	3	3
Scandix pecten-veneris (shepherd's needle)	A		S		S	T	T	T	—
Silene alba (white campion)	A, B, P			S		T	T	T	2
Sinapis arvensis (charlock)	A					T	2	2	T
Spergula arvensis (corn spurrey)	A			S		—	T	1	2
Stellaria media (chickweed)	A					T	1	T	1
Tripleurospermum maritimum ssp. *inodorum* (scentless mayweed)	A					T	T	T	4
Vicia spp. (tares)	A, P		S	S	S	T	T	1	3

T   (Trace) weed seeds occurring at a frequency of less than 1 per cent.
—   Seeds of the particular species were not recorded.

TABLE 26. WEEDS OF IMPORTANCE IN ROOT AND VEGETABLE SEEDS (1960–61)

(Percentage frequency of samples containing at least one weed seed in purity test)

Weeds	Annual (A) Biennial (B) or Perennial (P)	Turnip	Swede	Rape	Kale	Mustard	Cabbage	Brussels Sprouts	Cauliflower	Broccoli	Mangel	Sugar Beet	Fodder Beet	Onion	Leek	Carrot	Lettuce	Celery
Aethusa cynapium (fool's parsley)	A		T	T	T	T		1				T				2		
Amaranthus retroflexus (pig weed)	A			T		T										1	14	
Anagallis arvensis (scarlet pimpernel)	A						T				T	T		T		4	6	4
Atriplex patula (common orache)	A	1	1	1	T	5					1	T			4	7		1
Avena fatua (wild oats)	A				T	4						2						
Brassica juncea (brown mustard)	A	1	T	3		2	T	T										
Brassica nigra (black mustard)	A	4	2	3	1	2	T	T										
Chenopodium album (fat hen)	A		5	4	1	18	3	8	3	2	26	1		4		39	25	15
Cirsium spp. (thistles)	B, P	T	T	T		1		12	1			T			4	5	1	
Galium aparine (cleavers)	A	12	27	18	5	23	5		1	2		31	14					
Geranium dissectum (cut-leaved cranesbill)	A	2	4	5	4		2	4		T				T		24	2	1
Picris echioides (bristly ox-tongue)	A, B											T	T					
Poa annua (annual meadow grass)	A, P				T								T					
Polygonum aviculare (knotgrass)	A		3	3		4	T	4				T		4	7	10	4	4
Polygonum convolvulus (black bindweed)	A		2	5		31	2	9	2	3	47	48	41	8	4	T		
Polygonum lapathifolium (pale persicaria)	A		2	2		6	T	T				T		1		4		2
Polygonum persicaria (redshank)	A		T			2	T	1			T	T		1		6		2

TABLE 26 *(continued)*

Weeds	Annual (A) Biennial (B) or Perennial (P)	Turnip	Swede	Rape	Kale	Mustard	Cabbage	Brussels Sprouts	Cauliflower	Broccoli	Mangel	Sugar Beet	Fodder Beet	Onion	Leek	Carrot	Lettuce	Celery
Raphanus raphanistrum (wild radish)	A	3	—	—	—	T	—	—	—	—	T	2	3	—	—	—	—	—
Rumex spp. (docks and sorrels)	P	3	5	2	18	1	7	10	3	10	T	1	2	T	4	3	—	—
Senecio vulgaris (groundsel)	A	—	—	—	T	—	—	1	—	—	T	—	—	—	—	T	—	15
Sherardia arvensis (field madder)	A	3	5	2	2	2	2	T	—	2	—	—	—	—	2	2	—	—
Silene alba (white campion)	A, B, P	4	3	11	9	2	2	7	6	10	T	2	—	T	2	—	—	—
Sinapis arvensis (charlock)	A	—	—	—	7	34	6	6	—	—	T	—	—	T	4	—	—	—
Solanum nigrum (black nightshade)	A	—	—	—	—	—	—	6	6	11	T	2	—	—	—	10	—	—
Sonchus asper, S. coleraceus (annual sowthistles)	A	T	—	1	T	T	T	T	—	—	—	2	T	—	—	4	5	—
Stellaria media (chickweed)	A	17	4	2	—	T	1	9	1	2	—	—	T	—	—	3	5	2
Tripleurospermum maritimum ssp. *inodorum* (scentless mayweed)	A	—	—	1	1	—	—	2	—	—	—	T	—	—	—	3	—	1
Veronica spp. (speedwells)	A	2	1	T	—	—	—	—	1	2	T	T	T	T	—	1	1	2
Vicia spp. (tares)	A	—	1	T	—	T	T	6	—	2	—	1	—	—	—	—	—	—

T (Trace) weed seeds occurring at a frequency of less than 1 per cent.
— Seeds of the species were not recorded.

indication of the relative frequency of these weeds in samples analysed by the Official Seed Testing Station in 1960–61 is given in Table 26, expressed as a percentage of samples containing at least one weed seed in the purity test.

Polygonum convolvulus (black bindweed) was the most frequent weed species in samples of sugar beet (48 per cent), fodder beet (41 per cent), mangel (47 per cent) and onion (8 per cent), and was important in mustard (31 per cent). Seeds of this species can remain dormant in the soil for a number of years and may lead to subsequent infestation. Seeds of other *Polygonum* spp. (knotgrass and persicaria) were much less frequent except in carrot and leek seed. *Polygonum* spp. can now often be controlled by appropriate selective herbicides. *Sinapis arvensis* (charlock), *Raphanus raphanistrum* (wild radish), *Brassica nigra* (black mustard) and *B. juncea* (brown mustard) are serious weeds in the production of brassica seed crops owing to their similarity of growth habit and seed size. *Sinapis arvensis* was the most frequent weed seed found in the closely related cultivated mustard (34 per cent) and in broccoli (11 per cent) and was important in rape (11 per cent). Contaminated seed is difficult and expensive to clean and the presence of *Sinapis arvensis* in crop seed may prevent export to countries where it is a prohibited weed. Details of chemical methods for control of brassica weeds are given in Chapters II and III.

Seed of *Galium aparine* (cleavers) occurred mainly in samples of swede (27 per cent), rape (18 per cent), brussels sprouts (12 per cent), mangel (26 per cent), sugar beet (31 per cent) and mustard (23 per cent). The control of weeds in sugar beet and brussels sprouts is dealt with in Chapter II and of cleavers generally, in Chapter V.

Seeds of *Rumex* spp. (docks and sorrels) were found in all the crops in Table 26 except lettuce and celery. They are the most frequent contaminant of kale (18 per cent), cabbage (7 per cent) and brussels sprouts (10 per cent). In vegetable crops grown for market, *Rumex* spp. can be controlled by frequent cultivations but they can be serious in field crops such as kale, and in seed production. Herbicides that may be used on these crops are not very effective against established *Rumex* spp.

Seeds of *Chenopodium album* (fat hen) were particularly frequent in samples of carrot (39 per cent), lettuce (25 per cent) and celery (15 per cent). This weed can be controlled in carrots at the seedling stage by the use of contact pre-emergence sprays and certain mineral oils (see Chapter III). Although *Chenopodium album* is not of particular importance as a contaminant of beet seed, the plants may be difficult to control by chemical methods in these crops owing to close taxonomic relationship (see Chapters II and III).

Stellaria media (chickweed) is a very common weed in vegetable crops grown for market, but is not an important contaminant of the seeds except in turnip (17 per cent) and brussels sprouts (9 per cent). Details of the chemical control of *Stellaria media* is given in Chapters III and V.

CHAPTER XII

GRANTS PAYABLE TOWARDS THE COST OF WEED DESTRUCTION

AGRICULTURE

1. The eradication of bracken on pastoral land in England and Wales, Scotland and Northern Ireland may be aided by grants at the rate of 50 per cent towards the cost of cutting by hand or of cutting or crushing by private contractor. In addition, 50 per cent grants towards the cost of purchasing machinery of an approved type are payable in England and Wales.

2. The mechanical removal of bracken, whins, gorse, bushes, scrub, stumps, roots or other similar obstructions to cultivation, the cutting and spraying of rushes, the burning of heather or grass and the making of muir-burn may be included as parts of an approved scheme of improvement to hill and upland farms where livestock rearing is or will be practised under the Hill Farming and Livestock Rearing Acts. Grants are payable at the rate of 50 per cent.

3. In England, Scotland and Wales the clearance of scrub and the destruction of breeding places and cover for rabbits may be carried out with the aid of 50 per cent grants under the Pests Act, 1954; grants of up to 75 per cent are payable in certain circumstances. No such grants are available in Northern Ireland.

Full details may be obtained in the case of England and Wales from the Divisional Executive Offices of the Ministry of Agriculture, Fisheries and Food; in the case of Scotland from the Department of Agriculture for Scotland, St Andrew's House, Edinburgh, 1, or the Agricultural Executive Committee Offices; and in the case of Northern Ireland from the Ministry of Agriculture for Northern Ireland, Stormont, Belfast.

4. The following grants are payable to crofters in the Highlands and Islands of Scotland, details from the Crofters' Commission, 9 Ardross Terrace, Inverness:

(a) reclamation of rough or hill land — grants of up to 85 per cent of the gross cost of the approved operations less subsidies, subject to a maximum of £35 per acre;

(b) improvements of heath land and rough grazings by surface treatment. First year operations: grants of up to 85 per cent of the gross cost subject to a maximum of £11 per acre. Second year operations: these works will rank for grants of up to a maximum of £3 per acre if fertilizers to the value of £4 (net cost) per acre are applied.

(c) Bracken cutting — grants of 50 per cent of the approved cost on the basis of cutting twice a year for three years;

(d) removal of whins, gorse, bushes, scrub, stumps, boulders and similar obstructions to cultivations — grants of 50 per cent.

FORESTRY

Scrub clearance grants may be claimed in respect of the following:

(a) dedicated woodlands;

(b) approved woodlands;

(c) small woods or planting areas eligible for the small woods planting grant.

The grant is payable for the clearance of unproductive scrub, the clearing of which is estimated to cost more than £17 per acre, from which the owner undertakes to restock with trees.

The rates are:

(i) For areas estimated to cost more than £17 net per acre to clear, but less than £27 net: £8 10s. per acre.

(ii) For areas estimated to cost £27 net per acre or more to clear: £13 10s. per acre.

In order to ascertain whether any particular piece of land qualifies for a scrub clearance grant, owners should consult their local Conservator of Forests. The grant is available for schemes begun from 1958 onwards. It is payable in two instalments, the first of 75 per cent on completion of the clearance and planting, and the balance five years later, provided the area has been satisfactorily maintained. A minimum area of one acre, in one block, must be cleared in each year. The grant cannot be claimed for land concerning which another grant has been, or may be, paid for clearance of scrub under a rabbit clearing scheme. Neither can it be paid for clearing areas which have become scrub since 1948.

N.B. The Scrub Clearance Grant ends on 1st October 1963 and applications for the grant will be considered only for schemes to be completed by 30 September 1963.

CHAPTER XIII

NEW HERBICIDES

This chapter contains notes on a number of new herbicides now being developed. The notes provide a brief summary of knowledge regarding each chemical, and preliminary information on weed problems for which it appears promising, **but they are not in any sense recommendations.** In many instances these new herbicides have been discovered in the U.S.A. and the initial experiments conducted in North America. Caution is required, therefore, in extending the results to British conditions. Compounds in the very early stages of development are not included. Mention does not necessarily imply that the herbicide concerned is commercially available in Great Britain.

Full evaluation of the possible adverse effects on human health has not been completed for many of these herbicides and due caution should be used when handling and applying them. They should not be used on crops for food, under conditions where residues might remain at harvest, until their safety has been proved. These herbicides are subject to the provisions of the scheme for the Notification of Pesticides, co-ordinated by the Ministry of Agriculture, Fisheries and Food. A full account of this scheme appears in Chapter VIII.

The formulae and properties of these compounds are included in Table 28 (pages 286–317). The numbered position of each compound in this table is given in brackets at the end of the relevant heading in this chapter together with the common name approved by the British Standards Institution. Where there is no such approved common name but there is a name or abbreviation in use in this country the latter is given. Where only a trade name is in use in Britain at the present time it is given in inverted commas. Other abbreviations in use are given in Table 28.

Many diverse chemicals are mentioned in this chapter but wherever possible, herbicides which are related chemically, or in their biological effect, have been grouped together.

2-(2,4,5-Trichlorophenoxy)propionic Acid (fenoprop) (20)

This synthetic growth regulator was developed in the U.S.A. and found promising as a foliage spray for the control of woody plants. On some species, notably *Quercus* spp., it has been more effective than 2,4,5-T at similar doses. On the other hand it does not appear to be particularly efficient as a basal spray or stump treatment. It has also been used successfully for the control of emergent aquatic weeds and for submerged aquatic weeds in still water. Fenoprop has been applied in both water-soluble amine and emulsifiable ester formulations, and as a granular formulation for aquatic weeds.

More recently it has been tried out in Britain as a constituent of mixtures with other phenoxy herbicides to give a broader spectrum of post-emergence weed control in cereals. Fenoprop can control a similar range of broad-leaved weeds to mecoprop. It also kills germinating weed species and has a longer period of persistence in the soil than 2,4,5-T.

N-1-NAPHTHYLPHTHALAMIC ACID (naptalam) (83)

This compound has been used in North America to control weeds before emergence. Some effects are similar to those of synthetic growth regulators. Doses used range from 2 to 8 lb per acre and these are effective for three to eight weeks, but this is dependent to some extent on the soil type and its moisture content. It is generally applied as the sodium salt and the most widely adopted uses are for selective weed control in the cucurbitaceous crops such as melon and cucumber, in soyabean and groundnut, and as a granular formulation only for late application to potato.

3-AMINO-2,5-DICHLOROBENZOIC ACID ('Amiben') (27)

At doses of 2 to 4 lb per acre this herbicide, which has been developed in the U.S.A., shows promise for the selective pre-emergence control of many annual weeds, both grasses and dicots, in soyabeans and carrots and possibly in a variety of other vegetable crops, including French beans and potatoes. It also shows some post-emergence selectivity in soyabeans, though weed control is not so effective as from pre-emergence application. Water-soluble amine and ammonium salts and granular formulations have been used. 'Amiben' may be persistent in the soil for a few weeks. Plants treated post-emergence show epinastic and other effects typical of auxin type growth regulators. In most respects this compound is thought to be superior to 3-nitro-2,5-dichlorobenzoic acid ('Dinoben') (28) though strawberries are much more tolerant of this latter herbicide than of 'Amiben'.

2,3,6-TRICHLOROPHENYLACETIC ACID (fenac) (24)

This herbicide, which has been developed in the United States, produces some auxin type growth regulator effects and has a considerable effect on germinating weeds. 3 lb per acre has given good residual pre-emergence weed control in sugar cane and 2 lb per acre has been suggested for maize, which seems to recover after showing an initial response. American interest in its use on the latter crop is considerable because at rather higher doses preplanting it seems to control *Striga*. High doses, up to 16 lb per acre, are being used successfully for the control of *Convolvulus arvensis*, *Agropyron repens* and other perennial weeds, generally on fallow land, in North America. Fenac may have possibilities for soil sterilization, as it is persistent and resistant to leaching in the soil.

S-ETHYL NN-DIPROPYLTHIOLCARBAMATE (EPTC) (36)

This American herbicide is of the residual pre-emergence type which controls annual grasses and some broad-leaved weeds. It must be applied to a good seed-bed free of clods and be incorporated into the soil immediately after application. French beans and potatoes are among the crops reported to be tolerant of this herbicide. Doses are generally in the range 3 to 6 lb per acre and both granular and emulsifiable concentrate formulations are used. It has only a short period of persistence in the soil.

A number of other closely related thiolcarbamates are in the course of development and are thought to have improved selectivity. One of these — S-propyl N-butyl-N-ethylthiolcarbamate ('Tillam') (37) — has greater selectivity in sugar beet, though rather higher doses are needed than of EPTC, and it has the disadvantage from the British point of view that it is effective only on annual grass weeds and a very few dicot species. However, *Chenopodium album* is reported to be susceptible to EPTC and 'Tillam'.

2-CHLOROALLYL-NN-DIETHYLDITHIOCARBAMATE (CDEC) (35)

This compound has been used pre-emergence in North America in a variety of vegetable crops for the control of weeds, particularly annual grasses. Doses used range from 3 to 12 lb per acre and there is only a limited period of persistence in the soil.

SODIUM N-METHYLDITHIOCARBAMATE (metham-sodium) (40)

This compound undergoes decomposition in the presence of moisture in soil to form volatile end-products which are toxic to fungi, bacteria, nematodes, insects and weeds. Thus it acts as a soil fumigant. Doses range from 100 to 500 lb per acre and application is generally limited to areas such as seed-beds prior to sowing or planting. A variety of methods of application are suggested, but elaborate soil covering is not necessary as SMDC can be sealed in by further application of water. The soil needs to be moist and in good tilth and this fumigant is more effective in light soils than in heavy clay or organic soils. Under favourable conditions deep rooted perennial weeds as well as germinating weed seeds are killed. Crop damage may result from greenhouse use if the soil temperature is too low or the crop planted too soon after treatment. It may be necessary to wait several weeks before sowing or planting.

3,4,5,6-Tetrahydro-3,5-Dimethyl-2-Thio-2H-1,3,5-Thiadiazine (dazomet) (41)

This is another soil fumigant type of chemical developed in America, and like the preceding compound, the soil does not need to be covered after ap plication. Dose rates are of the order of 300 lb per acre and decomposition t(volatile toxic compounds occurs in warm moist soil. It is advocated that the fumigant should be cultivated into the soil and the area irrigated subsequently A variety of annual and perennial weeds, as well as other organisms, are con trolled; crops can be sown or planted three weeks after treatment.

NN-Diallylchloroacetamide (CDAA) (42)

This herbicide has been available in the U.S.A. for a considerable time, pri marily for the control of annual grasses as they germinate. A more recen development has been its use in a mixture with trichlorobenzyl chloride which enables it to control a much broader spectrum of weeds, including many annual dicotyledonous species at the time of germination. The main use is fo application, as an emulsion or in granules, to the soil surface at the time o ⌐owing maize; doses of about 3 lb per acre of CDAA plus 6 lb per acre of tri chlorobenzyl chloride are used. Onions may also be resistant to CDAA alon(when treated at the 3-leaf stage. Some rain after application is necessary fo best results, but excessive leaching can occur on sandy soil.

N-(3-Chloro-4-Methylphenyl)-2-Methylpentanamide ('Solan') (44)
N-(3,4-Dichlorophenyl)methacrylamide ('Dicryl') (45)

These herbicides, developed in the U.S.A., are absorbed through the foliage and are active when applied to a wide range of young annual weeds, including both grasses and broad-leaved species. Applied as emulsions at doses o around 4 lb per acre they cause cessation of growth, a gradual leaf necrosi and eventual death of susceptible species. These herbicides show only a limitec residual pre-emergence activity. Umbelliferous crops show considerable re sistance and 'Solan' may be of considerable interest for use in carrots. Cottor shows a useful resistance to 'Dicryl'. These herbicides may also have possi bilities as directed sprays or for dormant season application on other crops

N-(3,4-Dichlorophenyl)propionamide ('Stam F-34') (43)

This herbicide, discovered in the U.S.A., also enters through the leaves and controls many seedling monocotyledonous and dicotyledonous weeds, par ticularly grasses, at doses of 2 to 4 lb per acre as a foliage spray. It has little activity on weeds prior to emergence. It is in use for weed control in rice, and there is promising selectivity in potato.

NN-Dimethyldiphenylacetamide (diphenamid) (46)

This American herbicide controls annual grass weeds and a few dicotyledonous weeds prior to emergence at doses of 4 to 6 lb per acre. One of the more promising uses suggested is for newly planted and established strawberries.

Triazines (60–70)

A considerable number of substituted triazines, related to simazine, have been developed in Switzerland and their herbicidal properties investigated in Europe, North America and elsewhere. Their uses and properties vary according to their water solubility. With increasing solubility foliar uptake becomes more important and downward movement in soil more likely. Those whose development is likely to be pursued are shown in Table 27 together with

TABLE 27. THE STRUCTURE AND SOLUBILITY OF TRIAZINE HERBICIDES

The solubilities in water are given in parts per million below the common name or manufacturer's designation.

4	6	Cl chloro- triazines	OCH$_3$ methoxy- triazines	SCH$_3$ methylmercapto- triazines
NH.C$_2$H$_5$	NH.C$_2$H$_5$	simazine 5	simeton 300	simetryne 450
NH.C$_2$H$_5$	NH.iC$_3$H$_7$	atrazine 70	atraton 1800	ametryne 185
NH.iC$_3$H$_7$	NH.iC$_3$H$_7$	propazine 9	prometon 750	prometryne 48
NH.CH$_3$	NH.iC$_3$H$_7$			'G34360' 580
NH.C$_2$H$_5$	N(C$_2$H$_5$)$_2$	trietazine 20		

their solubilities in water and indicating their chemical relationship to each other.

There are some similarities and some differences between these herbicides in their selectivity. Thus maize is resistant to all the chloro-triazines listed and atrazine in particular is useful as an alternative to simazine in this crop under dry soil conditions. On the other hand there are some specific tolerances which may be useful, even though their weed control activity is lower than that of simazine or atrazine. Thus propazine shows greater selectivity in umbelliferous crops, particularly in carrots, while trietazine has been used successfully for the control of germinating weeds in potatoes.

The methoxy-triazines are more toxic to maize, and in general show little selectivity. However, they can enter the plant through the foliage and may be useful as general weedkillers. The same is true of atrazine which is highly active and may be an alternative to simazine as a non-selective herbicide. It should be noted that bushes and trees resistant to simazine may be damaged by atrazine.

The methylmercapto-triazines are of interest because of some selective properties in both pre-emergence and post-emergence situations. As an example, carrots have a useful degree of resistance to prometryne, and it may be possible to use some members of this group for weed control in potatoes.

All these triazine herbicides are generally used as wettable powders, but some can also be formulated as emulsifiable concentrates. They all may persist in the soil for many months and this aspect requires investigation and consideration when they are to be used on agricultural or horticultural land.

N'-(4-Chlorophenyl)-*NN*-Dimethyluronium Trichloroacetate ('monuron TCA') (56)
NN-Dimethyl-*N*'-Phenyluronium Trichloroacetate ('fenuron TCA') (55)

These combinations of monuron or fenuron with TCA as one compound are used in the U.S.A. primarily for total weed control on uncropped areas. Boht are prepared as granular formulations or as liquid concentrates. The fenuron compound is used at doses of 18 to 30 lb per acre, while rather higher doses of the monuron compound were originally suggested. Rainfall is relied on to take the material into the soil with subsequent uptake by root systems. Their effect is therefore reduced or delayed under dry conditions. A variety of annual, perennial and woody weeds are all reported to be controlled.

N'-(3,4-Dichlorophenyl)-*N*-Methoxy-*N*-Methylurea (linuron) (53)

This herbicide is closely related to diuron but is rather more water soluble and can enter plants through both foliage and roots to give pre- and post-emergence control of annual weeds. In the U.S.A. it is being introduced for pre-emergence use in maize at 0·75 to 3 lb per acre and in soyabean at 0·5 to 2 lb per acre, the higher rates being required in soil high in organic matter. 1·5 to 3 lb per acre can be used as a directed post-emergence spray in maize. In Britain possible use pre- and post-emergence in carrots and other umbelliferous crops, and pre-emergence in potato is under investigation. Linuron is thought to disappear from the soil in 3 to 4 months.

N'-(4-CHLOROPHENYL)-*N*-METHOXY-*N*-METHYLUREA ('Aresin') (52)

This is a similar herbicide to the previous one but no useful post-emergence selectivity has been found. It is suggested for pre-emergence use in dwarf bean and potato, and is thought to be more effective than linuron for the control of annual grasses.

N'-4-(4-CHLOROPHENOXY)PHENYL-*NN*-DIMETHYLUREA (chlorophenocarb) (54)

This Swiss soil-acting herbicide is reported to control a variety of germinating dicotyledonous weeds when applied at 2 to 5 lb per acre. Performance varies with soil type. Suggested uses are in strawberries, top and bush fruit and a variety of vegetables. It is thought to persist in the soil for a few weeks.

5-BROMO-3-ISOPROPYL-6-METHYLURACIL (isocil) (57)

This is a new American non-selective herbicide for total weed control applied as a wettable powder at 3 to 6 lb per acre for annual weeds and 4 to 20 lb per acre for perennials. It is slow acting, being dependent on uptake by roots, and is intended primarily for use on railways and industrial sites. It is reported to be effective on grasses and on the more adsorptive substrates.

5-AMINO-4-CHLORO-2-PHENYL-3-PYRIDAZONE (PCA) (58)

This German herbicide has a promising selectivity in sugar and fodder beet, both pre- and post-emergence. At doses of 1 to 3 lb per acre a variety of weeds are controlled, including species such as *Chenopodium album* (fat hen) and *Stellaria media* (chickweed). Germinating weeds are killed by uptake of herbicide from the soil. The optimum time for control is when the weeds are at the cotyledon stage; subsequently there is a rapid increase in resistance. This herbicide persists in the soil for a few weeks.

2,6-DINITRO-*NN*-DIPROPYL-4-TRIFLUOROMETHYLANILINE (trifluralin) (81)

This American herbicide is effective on a number of graminaceous and dicotyledonous weeds prior to emergence at doses of 1 to 6 lb per acre. The lower doses are effective only if incorporated into the soil. It is suggested for use in turf, woody ornamentals, established flowers and a range of vegetable crops.

DIMETHYL 2,3,5,6-TETRACHLOROTEREPHTHALATE ('Dacthal') (87)

This American pre-emergence herbicide is used for the control of annual grasses and a few dicot species, such as *Chenopodium album* (fat hen) and *Stellaria media* (chickweed) in strawberries and a number of vegetable crops. Doses of 8 lb per acre or more are needed and results may vary according to soil type and moisture conditions.

2,6-DICHLOROBENZONITRILE (dichlobenil) (78)

The herbicidal properties of this compound were discovered in both Britain and Holland. It is a very potent herbicide for the control of germinating weed seeds when applied at 1 to 4 lb per acre and incorporated into the soil, but has little selectivity. It may however have possibilities in transplanted or perennial crops or for total vegetation control. Providing it does not volatilize through being left on the soil surface this herbicide persists in the soil, the duration being markedly dependent on environmental conditions.

O-(2,4-DICHLOROPHENYL) *O'*-METHYL *N*-ISOPROPYL PHOSPHOROAMIDOTHIOATE ('Zytron') (80)

This herbicide has been tried out in emulsion, wettable powder and granular formulations at doses of 11 to 44 lb per acre for the control of *Digitaria* spp. both before and after emergence in American lawns. While not controlling a wide range of weeds it is effective on a number of other species, both dicotyledonous and graminaceous.

2-(2,4,5-TRICHLOROPHENOXY)ETHYL 2,2-DICHLOROPROPIONATE (erbon) (84)

This compound is being used in the U.S.A. for the non-selective control of vegetation at doses of 55 to 160 lb per acre. It can be absorbed through the leaves and translocated but the major effects result from root uptake. A wide range of monocotyledonous and dicotyledonous species are susceptible. Adequate rainfall is required for its action and it is persistent in the soil, killing germinating seedlings for a considerable period.

DI(METHOXYTHIOCARBONYL)DISULPHIDE (dimexan) (85)

This is primarily a contact herbicide used prior to crop emergence at doses of about 8 lb per acre. It may be applied to any crop that is drilled, not broadcast, unless drilled very shallowly. Dimexan is volatile and does not persist in soil. It is thought to penetrate in the vapour phase into the surface layer of soil immediately after application, killing some shallow germinating weeds which have not yet emerged.

DI(ETHOXYTHIOCARBONYL)DISULPHIDE ('Herbisan') (86)

This American herbicide behaves very similarly to dimexan. It is a contact pre-emergence weed killer and is suggested particularly for use in onions.

Prometryne (Gesagard by Fisons).
Apply 5-10 days after drilling. Post emergence use has the disadvantage that strut grass & mayweed are resistant to well grown.

Ametryne (Gesapax by Fisons)
Apply as a contact herbicide to the braird of weeds else before 10% of the potatoes have emerged. Ametryne has a stronger residual action.

GLOSSARY OF TECHNICAL TERMS

Acid equivalent, the amount of active ingredient expressed in terms of the parent acid. See Chapter VII, Section (ii).

Activated, see *formulation.*

Acute oral LD_{50}, in toxicological studies the dose required to kill 50 per cent of the test animals when given as a single dose by mouth. This means that the dose is expressed as the weight of chemical per unit weight of animal.

Application

  Band, where the herbicide is applied to bands and not to the entire area.

  Directed, where the herbicide is directed towards the ground or weeds to minimize contact with the crop.

  Overall, where the spray is applied uniformly over the whole area, as opposed to *band* application.

  Overhead, where the spray is applied over the crop, as opposed to application *directed* specifically to weeds.

  Post-emergence, application of a herbicide after the crop has emerged from the soil.

  Pre-emergence, application of a herbicide made after sowing but before the crop emerges from the soil, or prior to shoot emergence of an established perennial crop.

    Contact pre-emergence, — where a contact herbicide is applied to a weedy seed-bed before the crop emerges.

    Residual pre-emergence, — where a herbicide is applied to the soil before the crop emerges.

  Pre-planting, application of a herbicide made before planting the crop.

  Pre-sowing, application of a herbicide made before sowing the crop.

  Spot, application directed to patches of weed. This treatment is useful where the distribution of the weed is not sufficiently uniform or extensive to justify 'overall' treatment.

Auxin, a generic name for compounds characterized by their capacity to induce elongation in cells of shoots. Auxins may, and generally do, affect processes other than elongation, but elongation is considered critical.

Basal bark treatment, a treatment for killing trees and bushes in which a herbicide is applied (by sprayer or paint brush) to a band of bark encircling the basal 1 to 2 feet of the stem. (See page 137.)

Blow-off, the removal by high winds of a herbicide, such as DNOC, as solid particles, either from the foliage of treated plants or mixed with soil.

B.O.V., brown oil of vitriol. A commercial grade of sulphuric acid containing about 77 per cent by volume of sulphuric acid.

Contact herbicide, see *herbicide*.

Contact pre-emergence application, see *application*.

Defoliant, a chemical which, when applied to a plant, causes leaf fall.

Desiccant, a chemical which, when applied to a plant, causes the aerial parts to dry out. Generally used to facilitate harvesting.

Dose, the amount of active material applied per unit area. *Dosage, rate* and *dosage rate* are synonymous but dose is the preferred term.

Emulsifiable concentrate, see formulation.

Emulsifier, a surface-active agent which reduces interfacial tension and which can be used to facilitate formation of an emulsion of one liquid in another.

Emulsion, a mixture in which very small droplets of one liquid are suspended in another liquid, e.g. oil in water. When the emulsion consists of droplets of water in oil, the emulsion is known as an 'invert' emulsion.

Epinasty, the more rapid growth or elongation of the upper side of an organ, e.g. of a leaf, resulting in downward curling, but often incorrectly used in a more general sense to mean any curling or twisting of leaf blades, petioles, stems, etc. caused by uneven growth.

Formulation, the way in which the basic weed-killing chemicals are prepared for practical use.

    Activated, a formulation containing an activating agent which increases the effect of the herbicide.

    Emulsifiable concentrate, a concentrated solution of a herbicide and an emulsifier in a solvent, which will form an emulsion spontaneously when added to water with agitation.

    Granular, a type of formulation for dry application, in which a herbicide is adsorbed on, mixed with, or impregnated into a generally inert carrier in such a way that the final product consists of small granular particles.

    Wettable powder, a type of formulation in which a herbicide is adsorbed generally on an inert carrier, together with an added surface-acting agent, and finely ground so that it will form a suspension when agitated with water.

Frill-girdle, a series of overlapping cuts into the bark of a tree stem to form a girdle to which a herbicide is applied (see page 138).

Granular, see *formulation*.

Growth regulator, synthetic, see *plant growth regulator*.

Herbicide, a chemical which can kill or inhibit the growth of certain plants.

    Foliage treatment, where a herbicide is used so as to affect weeds through the leaves.

Soil treatment, where a herbicide is applied to the soil and where it persists in the soil and affects weeds through the roots.

Contact herbicide, a herbicide which only affects that part of the plant with which it comes into external contact; as opposed to a translocated herbicide.

Translocated herbicide, a herbicide which after penetration is capable of movement within the plant.

Residual soil treatment, a term sometimes used for soil treatment where the herbicide remains active in the soil for months (see page 9).

Soil sterilant treatment, where a herbicide is applied to the soil to prevent the growth of all vegetation for a considerable period. Weed seeds may or may not be affected according to the chemical and technique used. When applied to herbicide treatment the term 'soil sterilant' does not imply sterilization in the microbiological sense.

Total weed control, where a herbicide is used to kill all vegetation on un-cropped land in situations where selectivity is not required.

High volume spray, see *volume.*

Hormones, regulators produced by the plant, which in low concentrations regulate plant physiological processes. Hormones usually move within the plant from a site of production to a site of action.

Hypocotyl, that part of the stem of seedlings below the cotyledons.

Injurious weed seeds, see *weed seeds.*

Invert emulsion, see *emulsion.*

Leaf

   Trifoliate leaf, a leaf composed of three leaflets. In the seedling develop-ment of certain legumes, e.g. clovers and lucerne, the first true leaf is simple (unifoliate) and not trifoliate. The second and subsequent leaves are all trifoliate. The first trifoliate leaf in these crops is therefore the second true leaf (see Fig. 4).

   True leaf, a term used in defining the stage of growth of seedlings. Refers to all leaves other than the seed leaves or cotyledons.

Low volume spray, see *volume rate.*

Medium volume spray, see *volume rate.*

Necrosis, the death of plant tissue. Generally used in connection with local-ized death.

Non-selective treatment, see *herbicide, total weed control.*

Phytotoxic, toxic to at least some plants.

Plant growth regulator, synthetic, a synthetic organic compound, other than a nutrient, which in small amounts promotes, inhibits or otherwise modifies, growth.

Post-emergence, see *application.*

Pre-emergence, see *application.*

Pre-planting, see *application*.

Pre-sowing, see *application*.

Residual pre-emergence, see *application*.

Rhizome, a horizontal underground stem, of which the apex and the axillary buds are capable of producing aerial shoots.

Ring-barking, a method of killing trees by removing a ring of bark down to and including the cambium.

Scheduled weeds, see *weeds, scheduled*.

Selective herbicide, see *herbicide*.

Soil-sterilant herbicide, see *herbicide*.

Spot-treatment, see *application*.

Stale seed-bed, a seed bed which is prepared and left untouched to encourage weed germination and into which the crop is sown with a minimum of soil disturbance, before or after the weeds are killed with a herbicide. This enables pre-sowing and pre-emergence herbicides to be used with maximum efficiency.

Stolon, an above-ground creeping stem or runner capable of forming rootlets and shoots at the nodes and ultimately of forming new individuals.

Surface-active agents, also known as 'surfactants', substances, which when added to a liquid, affect the physical properties of the liquid surface. This enables them to be used for increasing the wetting properties of sprays and also for the formulation of emulsifiable liquids.

Synergism, the combined effect of two or more herbicides mixed together leading to a greater phytotoxic effect that would be predicted from the behaviour of each compound when applied singly.

Synthetic plant growth regulator, see *plant growth regulator*.

Translocated herbicide, see *herbicide*.

Trifoliate leaf stage, see *leaf*.

Volume rate, amount of liquid applied per unit area. The following definitions refer only to herbicide use.

    High volume spray, spray application of more than 60 gallons per acre. In this handbook the term implies a maximum rate of about 100 gallons per acre.

    Medium volume spray, spray application within the range of 20 to 60 gallons of liquid per acre.

    Low volume spray, spray application within the range of 5 to 20 gallons of liquid per acre.

    Very low volume spray, spray application within the range of 1 to 5 gallons of liquid per acre.

Weedkiller, see *herbicide*.

Weeds, scheduled, injurious weeds listed in the Weed Act, 1959 (see Chapter IX).

Weed seeds, injurious, weed seeds subject to statutory regulations, The Seeds Act, 1920, with the amendments of the 1925 Act and of Section 12 of the Agriculture (Miscellaneous Provisions) Act, 1954, provide the foundation for the Regulations in injurious weed seeds (see Chapter IX).

Wettable powder, see *formulation.*

Wetting agent, a surface-active agent which, when added to a liquid, increases its wetting properties.

APPENDIX II

LIST OF COMMON NAMES AND ABBREVIATIONS FOR HERBICIDES

An asterisk (*) signifies common names approved by B.S.I.
A double dagger (‡) signifies approval by the Weed Society of America.

acrolein‡	acrylaldehyde
ametryne*‡	4-ethylamino-6-isopropylamino-2-methylthio-1,3,5-triazine
amiben‡	3-amino-2,5-dichlorobenzoic acid
amitrole‡	3-amino-1,2,4-triazole
amitrole T‡	3-amino-1,2,4-triazole+ammonium thiocyanate
AMS	ammonium sulphamate
atraton*	4-ethylamino-6-isopropylamino-2-methoxy-1,3,5-triazine
atratone‡	see atraton
atrazine*‡	2-chloro-4-ethylamino-6-isopropylamino-1,3,5-triazine
barban*‡	4-chlorobut-2-ynyl-N-(3-chlorophenyl) carbamate
BiPC	butinol-N-(3-chlorophenyl) carbamate
CDAA	NN-diallylchloroacetamide
CDAA+TCBC	NN-diallylchloroacetamide+trichlorobenzylchloride
CDEA	2-chloro-NN-diethylacetamide
CDEC	2-chloroallyl-NN-diethyldithiocarbamate
chlorophenocarb	N'-4-(4-chlorophenoxy)phenyl-NN-dimethylurea
chlorpropham*	isopropyl-N-(3-chlorophenyl) carbamate
CIPC	see chlorpropham
CMPP	see mecoprop
CMU	see monuron
4-CPA*	4-chlorophenoxyacetic acid
4-CPB	4-(4-chlorophenoxy)butyric acid

2,4-D*‡	2,4-dichlorophenoxyacetic acid
dalapon*‡	2,2-dichloropropionic acid
dazomet*	3,4,5,6-tetrahydro-3,5-dimethyl-2-thio-2H-1,3,5-thiadiazine
2,4-DB*	4-(2,4-dichlorophenoxy)butyric acid
2,6-DBN	see dichlobenil
DCMA	N-(3,4-dichlorophenyl) methacrylamide
DCPA-dimethyl	dimethyl 2,3,5,6-tetrachloroterephthalate
2,4-DES*	2-(2,4-dichlorophenoxy)ethyl hydrogen sulphate
di-allate*	S-2,3-dichloroallyl NN-di-isopropylthiolcarbamate
dichlobenil*‡	2,6-dichlorobenzonitrile
dichlone*‡	2,3-dichloro-1,4-naphthoquinone
dichlorprop*	2-(2,4-dichlorophenoxy)propionic acid
dichloral urea	NN'-di-(2,2,2-trichloro-1-hydroxyethyl)urea
dimexan*	di(methoxythiocarbonyl)disulphide
dinoseb*	2-(1-methylpropyl)-4,6-dinitrophenol
diphenamid‡	NN-dimethyldiphenylacetamide
diquat*‡	1,1'-ethylene-2,2' bipyridylium-2A
diuron*‡	N'-(3,4-dichlorophenyl)-NN-dimethylurea
DMPA	O-(2,4-dichlorophenyl)s O'-methyl N-isopropyl phosphoro-amidothioate
DMTT	see dazomet
DNBP	see dinoseb
DNC	see DNOC
DNOC*	2-methyl-4,6-dinitrophenol
2,4-DP	see dichlorprop
DPA	N-(3,4-dichlorophenyl)propionamide
endothal*‡	7-oxabicyclo[2,2,1] heptane-2,4-dicarboxylic acid
EPTC	S-ethyl NN-dipropylthiolcarbamate
erbon‡	2-(2,4,5-trichlorophenoxy)ethyl 2,2-dichloropropionate
EXD	di(ethoxythiocarbonyl)disulphide
fenac‡	2,3,6-trichlorophenylacetic acid
fenoprop*	2-(2,4,5-trichlorophenoxy)propionic acid
fenuron*‡	NN-dimethyl-N'-phenylurea

ipazine*‡	2-chloro-4-diethylamino-6-isopropylamino-1,3,5-triazine
IPC	see propham
isocil*‡	5-bromo-3-isopropyl-6-methyluracil
linuron*‡	N'-(3,4-dichlorophenyl)-N-methoxy-N-methylurea
maleic hydrazide	1,2,3,6-tetrahydro-3,6-dioxopyridazine
MCPA*‡	4-chloro-2-methylphenoxyacetic acid
MCPB*	4-(4-chloro-2-methylphenoxy)butyric acid
MCPP	see mecoprop
mecoprop*	2-(4-chloro-2-methylphenoxy)propionic acid
metham*	N-methyldithiocarbamic acid
MH	see maleic hydrazide
monuron*‡	N'-(4-chlorophenyl)-NN-dimethylurea
naptalam*	N-1-naphthylphthalamic acid
neburon*‡	N'-butyl-N-(3,4-dichlorophenyl)-N'-methylurea
NPA	see naptalam
OMU	cyclooctyldimethylurea
paraquat*‡	1,1'-dimethyl-4,4'-bipyridylium-2A
PCA	5-amino-4-chloro-2-phenyl-3-pyridazone
PCP	pentachlorophenol
PDU	see fenuron
PEBC	S-propyl N-butyl-N-ethylthiolcarbamate
prometon*	4,6-bisisopropylamino-2-methoxy-1,3,5-triazine
prometone‡	see prometon
prometryne*‡	4,6-bisisopropylamino-2-methylthio-1,3,5-triazine
propazine*‡	2-chloro-4,6-bisisopropylamino-1,3,5-triazine
propham*	isopropyl N-phenylcarbamate
SES	see 2,4-DES
sesone‡	see 2,4-DES
silvex‡	see fenoprop
simazine*‡	2-chloro-4,6-bisethylamino-1,3,5-triazine
simeton*	4,6-bisethylamino-2-methoxy-1,3,5-triazine
simetone‡	see simeton
simetryne*‡	4,6-bisethylamino-2-methylthio-1,3,5-triazine

SMA	sodium monochloroacetate
SMDC	see metham
2,4,5-T*‡	2,4,5-trichlorophenoxyacetic acid
2,4,5-TB	4-(2,4,5-trichlorophenoxy)butyric acid
2,3,6-TBA	2,3,6-trichlorobenzoic acid
TCA	trichloroacetic acid
TCBC	trichlorobenzyl chloride
2,4,5-TP	see fenoprop
tri-allate*	S-2,3,3-trichloroallyl NN-di-isopropylthiolcarbamate
trietazine*‡	2-chloro-4-diethylamino-6-ethylamino-1,3,5-triazine
trifluralin‡	2,6-dinitro-NN-dipropyl-4-trifluoromethylaniline

APPENDIX III

PROPERTIES OF HERBICIDES

The information in Table 28 has been collected from a variety of published sources supplemented by data supplied by manufacturers of the chemicals concerned. A dash (−) indicates that no information has been obtained.

Inorganic chemicals are listed first, in simple alphabetical order. These are followed by the organic chemicals which are further sub-divided into the following groups: phenoxyacetic acids, phenoxypropionic acids, phenoxybutyric acids, phenylacetic and benzoic acids, halogenated aliphatic acids, carbamates, amides, ureas, diazines, triazines, phenols, quarternary ammonium compounds and miscellaneous. These groups are arranged in the order listed. The correct chemical name according to present rules of chemical nomenclature is given in heavy type. This is not always the same as the chemical name that is in current use, and the most generally used name is always given first. Other forms of the chemical name which have been used frequently are also listed.

Common or abbreviated names in current use are given in the next column, unless they are used solely as trade names. In certain instances the only shortened name in use in Britain at the time of going to press is a trade designation, which is then given in inverted commas. Names or abbreviations recommended by the British Standards Institution are indicated by an asterisk (*). Those marked by a circle (°) are draft recommendations by the International Organization for Standardization which have not yet been adopted by the British Standards Institution, at the time of going to press. Those names approved by the Weed Society of America are indicated by a double dagger (‡), while temporary designations by the Weed Society of America are marked by a dagger (†).

Where more than one form of a compound (e.g. various salts or esters) is in use, only the parent compound is included and the data given relate to the parent compound. In certain of these instances information on solubility of selected derivatives is given in addition. Where only one specific derivative is in use then this derivative and its properties are listed.

Solubilities are given in the form in which they were obtained originally, as it is not possible to convert from a w/w to a w/v basis without knowledge of the density of the solution.

The last column for the acute oral LD_{50} for rats gives an indication of

286

mammalian toxicity. This figure should not be used alone for an unqualified comparison between the hazards of one material and those of another. The acute oral toxicity is a measure of only one aspect of toxicity. Compounds differ markedly in their ease of entry through the skin so that chemicals which are similar in their oral toxicities may have widely different dermal toxicities Again, risks of chronic toxicity cannot be forecast from this figure and no guide is given as to possible carcinogenic or dermatitic properties. In addition it should be remembered that solvents and surface-active agents used in formulating some herbicides may have toxic properties of their own, and that formulation may increase the hazards from an already toxic compound, for instance by facilitating absorption through the skin.

In some instances more than one figure is available for the acute oral LD_{50} for rats. It is not surprising that some variation should be found in a biological estimation of this type and all such figures are entered to show the range obtained. As a standard for comparison, common aspirin which may be called 'slightly toxic' has an acute oral LD_{50} for rats of about 1200 mg/kg. In a few instances the existence of another toxic hazard not indicated by the acute toxicity is briefly indicated in this column. **Lack of any such additional comment should on no account be interpreted as indicating that no additional hazards are likely.**

TABLE 28. PROPERTIES OF HERBICIDES

No.	Compound	Common or abbreviated names	Formula	Molecular weight
INORGANIC CHEMICALS				
1.	ammonium sulphamate	A M S†	$(NH_4)O\cdot SO_2\cdot NH_2$	114·1
2.	calcium cyanamide	cyanamide	$CaCN_2$	80·1
3.	cupric sulphate penta-hydrate	copper sulphate	$CuSO_4\cdot 5H_2O$	249·7
4.	ferrous sulphate hepta-hydrate	iron sulphate	$FeSO_4\cdot 7H_2O$	278·1
5.	mercuric chloride	corrosive sublimate	$HgCl_2$	271·5
6.	mercurous chloride	calomel	$HgCl$	236·1
7.	potassium cyanate	—	$KCNO$	81·1
8.	potassium permanganate	—	$KMnO_4$	158·0
9.	sodium tetraborate deca-hydrate	borax	$Na_2B_4O_7\cdot 10H_2O$	381·4
10.	sodium chlorate	—	$NaClO_3$	106·5
11.	sodium nitrate	nitrate of soda	$NaNO_3$	85·0
12.	sulphuric acid	—	H_2SO_4	98·1

Melting point or physical state	Solubility	Types of formulation	Acute oral LD_{50} for rats (mg/kg)
130°C	water: 200 g/100 ml at 20°C soluble in alcohol and ketones	aqueous solution, dry solid	3900
solid	—	granular solid	1400 (rabbits)
150°C	water: 31·6 g/100 ml at 0°C methanol: 15·6 g/100 ml at 18°C	aqueous solution, dry salt	300
64°C	water: 15 g/100 ml at 0°C	aqueous solution	—
276°C	water: 6·9 g/100 ml at 20°C ethanol: 33 g/100 ml at 25°C	dry solid, solution	1–5
302°C	water: 0·2 mg/100 ml at 25°C	dry dressing	210
315°C	water: 63 g/100 ml at 10°C	aqueous solution	841 (mice)
solid	water: 6·4 g/100 ml at 20°C soluble in methanol and acetone	aqueous solution	—
75°C	water: 5·1 g/100 ml at 20°C insoluble in alcohol	aqueous solution, dry salt	—
248–250°C	water: 79 g/100 ml at 0°C	aqueous solution, dry salt	1200
307°C	water: 73 g/100 ml at 0°C	aqueous solution	—
liquid	miscible with water	undiluted acid, aqueous solution	—

289

TABLE 28 (*continued*)

No.	Compound	Common or abbreviated names	Formula	Molecular weight

PHENOXYACETIC ACIDS

13.	**4-chlorophenoxyacetic acid** p-chlorophenoxyacetic acid	4-CPA*†	$O \cdot CH_2 \cdot COOH$	186·6
14.	**4-chloro-2-methylphen-oxyacetic acid** 2-methyl-4-chlorophen-oxyacetic acid	MCPA*†	$O \cdot CH_2 \cdot COOH$ CH_3	200·6
15.	**2,4-dichlorophenoxyacetic acid**	2,4-D*‡	$O \cdot CH_2 \cdot COOH$ Cl	221·05
16.	**2,4,5-trichlorophen-oxyacetic acid**	2,4,5-T*†	$O \cdot CH_2 \cdot COOH$ Cl	255·5
17.	**sodium 2-(2,4-dichlorophen-oxy)ethyl sulphate**	2,4-DES-Na* sesone‡ disul°	$O \cdot CH_2 \cdot CH_2 \cdot O \cdot SO_2 \cdot ONa$ Cl	309·1

PHENOXYPROPIONIC ACIDS

| 18. | **2-(4-chloro-2-methyl-phenoxy)propionic acid** α-(4-chloro-2-methyl-phenoxy(propionic acid 2-(2-methyl-4-chloro-phenoxy)propionic acid | mecoprop* 2-(MCPP)† CMPP | CH_3 $O \cdot CH \cdot CO \cdot OH$ CH_3 | 214·7 |

Melting point or physical state	Solubility	Types of formulation	Acute oral LD$_{50}$ for rats (mg/kg)
157–158°C	water: 381 p.p.m. at 25°C	emulsifiable oil solution of esters	850
118–120°C	water: 0·055 g/100 ml at 20°C sodium salt: 27 per cent in water, 34 per cent in methanol, 0·1 per cent in benzene	aqueous solution of metal and amine salts, emulsifiable oil solution of esters, metal salts as dusts	700
138–142°C	water: 0·05 g/100 ml at 20°C triethanolamine salt: 440 g/100 ml in water at 32°C	aqueous solution of amine salts, emulsifiable oil solution of esters	375
154–157°C	water: 280 p.p.m. at 25°C	emulsifiable oil solution of esters alone or in mixture with 2,4-D esters	300 375 500
170°C	water: 25 per cent at room temperature	water-soluble powder	730 1400
93–94°C	water: 0·062 g/100 ml at 20°C sodium salt: >25 g/100 ml in water at 0°C diethanolamine salt: 58 g/100 ml in water at 20°C	aqueous solution of metal and amine salts	650 (mice)

TABLE 28 (*continued*)

No.	Compound	Common or abbreviated names	Formula	Molecular weight
19.	**2-(2,4-dichlorophenoxy)-propionic acid** α-(2,4-dichlorophenoxy)-propionic acid	dichlorprop* 2-(2,4-D P)† 2,4-D P	CH_3 $O \cdot CH \cdot COOH$ Cl Cl	235·1
20.	**2-(2,4,5-trichlorophenoxy)-propionic acid** α-(2,4,5-trichlorophenoxy)-propionic acid	fenoprop* silvex‡ 2,4,5-T P	CH_3 $O \cdot CH \cdot COOH$ Cl Cl Cl	269·5

PHENOXYBUTYRIC ACIDS

No.	Compound	Common or abbreviated names	Formula	Molecular weight
21.	**4-(4-chloro-2-methylphen-oxy)butyric acid** γ-(4-chloro-2-methylphen-oxy)butyric acid 4-(2-methyl-4-chlorophen-oxy)butyric acid	MCPB* 4-(MCPB)†	$O \cdot CH_2 \cdot CH_2 \cdot CH_2 \cdot COOH$ CH_3 Cl	228·7
22.	**4-(2,4-dichlorophenoxy)-butyric acid** γ-(2,4-dichlorophenoxy)-butyric acid	2,4-DB* 4-(2,4-DB)†	$O \cdot CH_2 \cdot CH_2 \cdot CH_2 \cdot COOH$ Cl Cl	249·1
23.	**4-(2,4,5-trichlorophenoxy)-butyric acid** γ-(2,4,5-trichlorophenoxy)-butyric acid	2,4,5-TB 4-(2,4,5-T B)†	$O \cdot CH_2 \cdot CH_2 \cdot CH_2 \cdot COOH$ Cl Cl Cl	283·6

Melting point or physical state	Solubility	Types of formulation	Acute oral LD_{50} for rats (mg/kg)
117·5–118·1°C	water: 0·035 g/100 ml at 20°C potassium salt: 90 g acid equivalent/100 ml at 20°C	aqueous solution of metal and amine salts	800
179–181°C	water: 0·014 g/100 ml at 25°C	aqueous solution of salts, emulsifiable oil solution of esters, granular formulation	650
100°C	water: 44 p.p.m. alcohol: 15 per cent acetone: >20 per cent	aqueous solution of metal salts	700 (as sodium salt on mice)
117–119°C	water: 53 p.p.m. at room temperature acetone: 10 per cent	aqueous solution of metal salts	—
114–115°C	insoluble in water acetone: >10 per cent sodium salt: >20 per cent in water at 25°C	aqueous solution of metal salts	—

TABLE 28 (*continued*)

No.	Compound	Common or abbreviated names	Formula	Molecular weight

PHENYLACETIC AND BENZOIC ACIDS

No.	Compound	Common or abbreviated names	Formula	Molecular weight
24.	2,3,6-trichlorophenylacetic acid	fenac‡		239·5
25.	2,3,6-trichlorobenzoic acid	2,3,6-TBA†		225·5
26.	2-methoxy-3,6-dichloro-benzoic acid	'Banvel D' dicamba‡		221·1
27.	3-amino-2,5-dichloroben-zoic acid	amiben‡		206·0
28.	2,5-dichloro-3-nitrobenzoic acid	'Dinoben'		236·0

HALOGENATED ALIPHATIC ACIDS

No.	Compound	Common or abbreviated names	Formula	Molecular weight
29.	sodium monochloroacetate	SMA	$CH_2Cl \cdot COONa$	116·5
30.	trichloroacetic acid	TCA†	$CCl_3 \cdot COOH$	163·4

Melting point or physical state	Solubility	Types of formulation	Acute oral LD$_{50}$ for rats (mg/kg)
—	water: 200 p.p.m. at 28°C	water soluble salts, emulsifiable formulation of esters, wettable powder, granular formulation	1780
125°C	water: 7700 p.p.m. at 22°C soluble in alcohol and acetone	aqueous solution of salts, oil solution of acid	705 1500
114–116°C	water: very slightly soluble sodium salt: 38 g a.e./100 ml in water dimethylamine salt: >72 g. a.e./100 ml in water	aqueous solution of salts, alone or in mixture with MCPA	1040 1100
200–201°C	water: 0·07 g/100 g ethanol: 17·3 g/100 g	aqueous solution of amine salts, granular formulation	5620
220–221°C	water: very slightly soluble ethanol: moderately soluble	aqueous solution of amine salts, granular formulation	3500
solid	water: 85 g/100 ml at 20°C	dry water-soluble salt	76 650
57°C	water: 120 g/100 ml at 25°C soluble in alcohol	water-soluble sodium and ammonium salts	3320 5000

TABLE 28 (*continued*)

No.	Compound	Common or abbreviated names	Formula	Molecular weight
31.	**sodium 2,2-dichloro-propionate** sodium αα-dichloropropionate	dalapon-Na*‡	$CH_3 \cdot CCl_2 \cdot COONa$	165·0

CARBAMATES

No.	Compound	Common or abbreviated names	Formula	Molecular weight
32.	**isopropyl *N*-phenylcarbamate**	propham* IPC†		179·2
33.	**isopropyl *N*-(3-chlorophenyl)carbamate**	chlorpropham* CIPC†		213·7
34.	4-chloro-2-butynyl *N*-(3-chlorophenyl)carbamate **4-chlorobut-2-ynyl *N*-(3-chlorophenyl) carbamate**	barban*‡		258·1
35.	**2-chloroallyl *NN*-diethyl-dithiocarbamate**	CDEC†		223·8
36.	***S*-ethyl *NN*-dipropylthiol-carbamate** ethyl di-*n*-propylthiol-carbamate	EPTC†		189·3
37.	***S*-propyl *N*-butyl-*N*-ethylthiolcarbamate** *n*-propyl ethyl-*n*-butyl-thiolcarbamate	PEBC† 'Tillam'		203·4

Melting point or physical state	Solubility	Types of formulation	Acute oral LD$_{50}$ for rats (mg/kg)
93–197°C	water: 90 g/100 ml at 25°C	water-soluble powder	6590–8120
°C	water: variously cited at 100 and 250 p.p.m.	emulsifiable liquid concentrate, wettable powder, mixture with endothal in emulsifiable concentrate	1000
5–41°C	water: variously cited at 80 and 108 p.p.m.	emulsifiable liquid concentrate alone or in mixture with fenuron or diuron, wettable powder, granular formulation	3800 5000
-	aromatic hydrocarbons: 10 per cent more soluble in ketones	emulsifiable liquid concentrate	600 dermal toxicity slight but liable to cause skin irritation
liquid	water: about 0·01 per cent at 25°C	emulsifiable liquid concentrate	850
liquid	water: 375 p.p.m. at 20°C miscible with methanol, acetone, benzene, xylene	emulsifiable liquid concentrate, granular formulation	1630
liquid	water: 92 p.p.m. at 21°C miscible with methanol, acetone, benzene, xylene	emulsifiable liquid concentrate, granular formulation	1120

TABLE 28 (*continued*)

No.	Compound	Common or abbreviated names	Formula	Molecular weight
38.	*S*-2,3-dichlorallyl *NN*-di-isopropylthiolcarbamate	di-allate* DATC†	CH_3, CH_3, CH_3, CH_3 CH, CH $N \cdot C \cdot S \cdot CH_2 \cdot C \, Cl = CHCl$ with $\overset{O}{\overset{\|}{C}}$	270·2
39.	*S*-2,3,3-trichlorallyl *NN*-di-isopropylthiolcarbamate	tri-allate*	CH_3, CH_3, CH_3, CH_3 CH, CH $N \cdot C \cdot S \cdot CH_2 \cdot C \, Cl = C \, Cl_2$ with $\overset{O}{\overset{\|}{C}}$	304·7
40.	sodium *N*-methyldithio-carbamate	metham-Na* SMDC†	$CH_3 \cdot NH \cdot \overset{S}{\overset{\|}{C}} \cdot S \cdot Na$	129·2
41.	3,5-dimethyltetrahydro-1,3,5,2*H*-thiadiazine-2-thione **3,4,5,6-tetrahydro-3,5-dimethyl-2-thio-2*H*-1,3,5-thiadiazine** tetrahydro-3,5-dimethyl-2*H*-1,3,5-thiadiazine-2-thione	dazomet* DMTT†	$S = C$ ring with $S-CH_2$, $N-CH_3$, $N-CH_2$, CH_3	162·3

Note: Chemically, compound 41 should be grouped with compounds 57–59, but is included here because it is thought to become active by degradation to compounds similar to compound 40.

Melting point or physical state	Solubility	Types of formulation	Acute oral LD$_{50}$ for rats (mg/kg)
liquid	water: 40 p.p.m. at 25°C miscible with alcohol, acetone, xylene, benzene and kerosene	emulsifiable liquid concentrate	393
liquid	insoluble in water miscible with alcohol, acetone, benzene	emulsifiable liquid concentrate	1340–1810
solid	water: 72·2 g/100 ml at 20°C moderately soluble in alcohol, sparingly soluble in other organic solvents	concentrated solution	820
9·5°C	water: 0·12 per cent at 30°C acetone: 19·4 per cent at 30°C	wettable powder, granular	500

TABLE 28 (*continued*)

No.	Compound	Common or abbreviated names	Formula	Molecular weight

AMIDES

No.	Compound	Common or abbreviated names	Formula	Molecular weight
42.	*NN*-**diallylchloroacetamide** 2-chloro-*NN*-diallylacetamide	CDAA†		173·6
43.	3,4-dichloropropionanilide *N*-**(3,4-dichlorophenyl)propionamide**	DPA† 'Stam F-34'		218·1
44.	*N*-**(3-chloro-4-methylphenyl)-2-methylpentanamide**	solan‡		239·8
45.	*N*-**(3,4-dichlorophenyl)-methacrylamide**	dicryl‡		230·1
46.	*NN*-**dimethyldiphenylacetamide**	diphenamid‡		239·3

Melting point or physical state	Solubility	Types of formulation	Acute oral LD_{50} for rats (mg/kg)
liquid	water: 1·97 per cent at 25°C	emulsifiable liquid concentrate, alone or with trichlorobenzyl chloride, granular formulation	700 only slight toxicity from application to rabbit skin but serious skin and eye irritant
91–92°C	water: 225 p.p.m. at room temperature ethanol: 54 per cent at 25°C isophorone: 60 per cent at 25°C	emulsifiable liquid concentrate	1384
85–86°C	insoluble in water xylene: 20–30 per cent at room temperature isophorone: 55 per cent at room temperature	emulsifiable liquid concentrate	>10000
127–128°C	insoluble in water xylene: <5 per cent acetone: 20 per cent pyridine: 33 per cent	emulsifiable liquid concentrate	3160
134·5–135·5°C	water: 0·024 g/100 ml at 25°C acetone: 19·0 g/100 ml at 25°C dimethylformamide: 16·0 g/100 ml at 25°C xylene: 5·0 g/100 ml at 25°C	wettable powder, granular formulation	1050

TABLE 28 (*continued*)

No.	Compound	Common or abbreviated names	Formula	Molecular weight
			UREAS	
47.	*NN'*-**di-(2,2,2-trichloro-1-hydroxyethyl)urea**	DCU† dichloral urea	$CCl_3 \cdot CH \cdot NH \cdot C \cdot NH \cdot CH \cdot CCl_3$ with OH, O, OH groups	354·9
48.	*NN*-**dimethyl-*N'*-phenylurea** 3-phenyl-1,1-dimethylurea	fenuron*‡		164·2
49.	*N'*-**(4-chlorophenyl)-*NN*-dimethylurea** 3-(*p*-chlorophenyl)-1,1-dimethylurea	monuron*‡		198·7
50.	*N'*-**(3,4-dichlorophenyl)-*NN*-dimethylurea** 3-(3,4-dichlorophenyl)-1,1-dimethylurea	diuron*‡		233·1
51.	*N*-**butyl-*N'*-(3,4-dichloro-phenyl)-*N*-methylurea** 1-*n*-butyl-3-(3,4-dichloro-phenyl)-1-methylurea	neburon*‡		275·2
52.	*N'*-**(4-chlorophenyl)-*N*-methoxy-*N*-methylurea**	'Aresin'		214·7

Melting point or physical state	Solubility	Types of formulation	Acute oral LD$_{50}$ for rats (mg/kg)
191°C (decomposes on melting)	low solubility in water only moderate solubility in most organic solvents, more soluble in cyclic ketones such as isophorone	wettable powder	>31600
136°C	water: 2900 p.p.m. at 24°C	wettable powder, also in mixtures with chlorpropham or 2,4-DES	7500
167–174°C	water: 230 p.p.m. at 25°C	wettable powder	3700
150–155°C	water: 42 p.p.m. at 25°C	wettable powder	3600
102–103°C	water: 4·8 p.p.m. at 24°C	wettable powder	>11000
solid	water: 580 p.p.m. readily soluble in alcohol, acetone, benzene	wettable powder	2250

TABLE 28 (*continued*)

No.	Compound	Common or abbreviated names	Formula	Molecular weight
53.	N'-(3,4-dichlorophenyl)-N-methoxy-N-methylurea	linuron*‡ harnitane		249·1
54.	N'-4-(4-chlorophenoxy)-phenyl-NN-dimethylurea	chlorophenocarb		290·8
55.	NN-dimethyl-N'-phenyl-uronium trichloroacetate 3-phenyl-1,1-dimethyl-urea trichloroacetate	fenuron-TCA†		327·6
56.	N'-(4-chlorophenyl)-NN-dimethyluronium trichloro-acetate 3-(p-chlorophenyl)-1,1-dimethylurea trichloracetate	monuron-TCA†		362·1

DIAZINES

No.	Compound	Common or abbreviated names	Formula	Molecular weight
57.	5-bromo-3-isopropyl-6-methyluracil	isocil*‡		247·1

Melting point or physical state	Solubility	Types of formulation	Acute oral LD$_{50}$ for rats (mg/kg)
3–94°C	water: 75 p.p.m. at 25°C soluble in alcohol, acetone, benzene, xylene, toluene	wettable powder	1500 3500
51–152°C	water: 0·00037 g/100 ml at 20°C	wettable powder	>1000
-	—	liquid concentrate and granular formulations	—
-	—	granular formulation	3700
8–159°C	water: 2150 p.p.m. at 25°C soluble in ethanol, acetone, and with strong bases in aqueous solution slightly soluble in herbicidal oils	wettable powder	3400

TABLE 28 (*continued*)

No.	Compound	Common or abbreviated names	Formula	Molecular weight
58.	1-phenyl-4-amino-5-chloro-pyridazone-6 **5-amino-4-chloro-2-phenyl-3-pyridazone**	PCA		221·7
59.	maleic hydrazide **1,2,3,6-tetrahydro-3,6-dioxopyridazine** 1,2-dihydropyridazine-3,6-dione	MH†		112·1

TRIAZINES

No.	Compound	Common or abbreviated names	Formula	Molecular weight
60.	**2-chloro-4,6-bisethylamino-1,3,5-triazine**	simazine*‡		201·7
61.	**2-chloro-4-ethylamino-6-isopropylamino-1,3,5-triazine**	atrazine*‡		215·7
62.	**2-chloro-4,6-bisisopropyl-amino-1,3,5-triazine**	propazine*‡		229·7

306

Melting point or physical state	Solubility	Types of formulation	Acute oral LD_{50} for rats (mg/kg)
02°C	water: 0·03 per cent at 20°C methanol: 3·54 per cent at 20°C	wettable powder, emulsifiable liquid concentrate	3600
96–298°C	water: 0·6 g/100 g at 25°C alcohol: 0·1 g/100 g at 25°C acetone: 0·1 g/100 g at 25°C dimethyl formamide: 2·4 g/100 g at 25°C	aqueous solution of salts	4000 5800
24–225°C	water: 5 p.p.m. at 20–22°C methanol: 400 p.p.m. petroleum ether: 2 p.p.m.	wettable powder	>5000
73–175°C	water: 70 p.p.m. at 20–22°C chloroform: 5·2 per cent	wettable powder	2000–3000 3080
12–214°C	water: 8·6 p.p.m. at 20–22°C	wettable powder	>5000

TABLE 28 (*continued*)

No.	Compound	Common or abbreviated names	Formula	Molecular weight
63.	**2-chloro-4-diethylamino-6-ethylamino-1,3,5-triazine**	trietazine*‡		229·7
64.	**4,6-bisethylamino-2-methoxy-1,3,5-triazine**	simeton* simetone‡		197·2
65.	**4-ethylamino-6-isopropyl-amino-2-methoxy-1,3,5-triazine**	atraton* atratone‡		211·3
66.	**4,6-bisisopropylamino-2-methoxy-1,3,5-triazine**	prometon* prometone‡		225·3
67.	**2-methylmercapto-4,6-bis-ethylamino-s-triazine 4,6-bisethylamino-2-methylthio-1,3,5-triazine**	simetryne*‡		213·3

Melting point or physical state	Solubility	Types of formulation	Acute oral LD$_{50}$ for rats (mg/kg)
–	water: 20 p.p.m. at 20–22°C	wettable powder	3750
–	water: 3200 p.p.m. at 20–22°C	wettable powder	535
94–96°C	water: 1800 p.p.m. at 20–22°C readily soluble in organic solvents	wettable powder	2400 1465
91–92°C	water: 750 p.p.m. at 20–22°C benzene: >25 per cent methanol, acetone: >50 per cent	wettable powder	2980
–	water: 450 p.p.m. at 20–22°C	wettable powder	–

TABLE 28 (*continued*)

No.	Compound	Common or abbreviated names	Formula	Molecular weight
68.	2-methylmercapto-4-ethyl-amino-6-isopropylamino-*s*-triazine **4-ethylamino-6-isopropyl-amino-2-methylthio-1,3,5-triazine**	ametryne*‡		227·3
69.	2-methylmercapto-4,6-bis-isopropylamino-*s*-triazine **4,6-bisisopropylamino-2-methylthio-1,3,5-triazine**	prometryne*‡		241·4
70.	2-methylmercapto-4-iso-propylamino-6-methyl-amino-*s*-triazine **4-isopropylamino-6-methyl-amino-2-methylthio-1,3,5-triazine**	'G-34360' desmetryne		213·3

PHENOLS

No.	Compound	Common or abbreviated names	Formula	Molecular weight
71.	3,5-dinitro-*o*-cresol **2-methyl-4,6-dinitrophenol** 2,4-dinitro-6-methylphenol	DNOC* DNC†		198·1
72.	2,4-dinitro-6-*s*-butylphenol **2-(1-methylpropyl)-4,6-dinitrophenol**	dinoseb* DNBP†		240·2

Melting point or physical state	Solubility	Types of formulation	Acute oral LD$_{50}$ for rats (mg/kg)
—	water: 185 p.p.m.	wettable powder	—
118–120°C	water: 48 p.p.m. at 20°C	wettable powder	3750
—	water: 580 p.p.m.	wettable powder	—
86°C	water: 130 p.p.m. alcohol: 3·5 per cent	aqueous solution of salts, aqueous suspensions, oil solutions emulsifiable or otherwise	7–10 40
38–42°C	water: 0·1 g/100 ml at room temperature	aqueous solution of salts, aqueous suspensions, oil solutions emulsifiable or otherwise	40 50

TABLE 28 (*continued*)

No.	Compound	Common or abbreviated names	Formula	Molecular weight
73.	**pentachlorophenol**	PCP†		266·4

QUATERNARY AMMONIUM COMPOUNDS

No.	Compound	Common or abbreviated names	Formula	Molecular weight
74.	**1,1′-ethylene-2,2′-dipyridylium dibromide** **9,10-dihydro-8a,10a-diazoniaphenanthrene dibromide**	diquat-dibromide*‡		344·1 (cation 184·2)
75.	**1,1′-dimethyl-4,4′-bipyridylium dimethylsulphate**	paraquat-di-(methyl sulphate)*‡		408·5 (cation 186·3)

MISCELLANEOUS

No.	Compound	Common or abbreviated names	Formula	Molecular weight
76.	**acrylaldehyde**	acrolein‡	$CH_2 = CH \cdot \overset{O}{\overset{\|}{C}}H$	56·1
77.	**3-amino-1,2,4-triazole**	amitrole°‡ ATA		84·1
78.	**2,6-dichlorobenzonitrile**	dichlobenil*‡ 2,6-DBN		172·0

Melting point or physical state	Solubility	Types of formulation	Acute oral LD_{50} for rats (mg/kg)
190–191°C	water: 20–25 p.p.m. at 20°C sodium salt: 33 per cent in water	emulsifiable oil solutions, aqueous solution of sodium salt	78 210
>320°C	water: 70 g/100 ml at 20°C	aqueous solution	400–440
—	very soluble in water	aqueous solution, also as aqueous solution of the dichloride	157
—	water: 20·8 per cent at 20°C	liquid for injection under water	42 potent irritant and lachrymator
153–154°C	water: 28 g/100 g at 23°C	aqueous solution, with or without ammonium thiocyanate as activator	1100
141–144°C	water: 10–20 p.p.m. at 25°C alcohol: 5 per cent at 15°C acetone: 8 per cent at 15°C medium solubility in xylene and high aromatic petroleum fractions	wettable powder, granular formulation	>1500 2710

TABLE 28 (*continued*)

No.	Compound	Common or abbreviated names	Formula	Molecular weight
79.	**2,3-dichloro-1,4-naphthaquinone**	dichlone*‡		227·1
80.	***O*-(2,4-dichlorophenyl)** *O′*-**methyl** *N*-**isopropyl phosphoroamidothioate**	DMPA† 'Zytron'		314·2
81.	2,6-dinitro-*N,N*-di-*n*-propyl-*α,α,α*-trifluoro-*p*-toluidine **2,6-dinitro-*NN*-dipropyl-4-trifluoromethylaniline**	trifluralin‡		335·3
82.	disodium 3,6-endoxohexahydrophthalate **disodium 7-oxabicyclo-[2,2,1]heptane-2,3-dicarboxylate**	endothal-Na*‡		230·1
83.	*N*-1-**naphthylphthalamic acid**	naptalam* NPA†		291·3
84.	**2-(2,4,5-trichlorophenoxy)-ethyl 2,2-dichloropropionate** 2-(2,4,5-trichlorophenoxy)-ethyl *αα*-dichloropropionate	erbon°‡		366·5

314

Melting point or physical state	Solubility	Types of formulation	Acute oral LD$_{50}$ for rats (mg/kg)
—	—	wettable powder	1300 concentrated chemical can be skin irritant
—	—	emulsifiable liquid concentrate, wettable powder, granular formulation	>1000 (dogs and cats)
46–47°C	water: 0·0024 g/100 ml at 27°C acetone: 40 g/100 ml at 27°C xylene: 58 g/100 ml at 27°C	emulsifiable liquid concentrate, granular formulation	>10000
263–266°C	water: about 21 per cent	aqueous solution	35 38 80
175–185°C	water: 0·2 per cent slightly soluble in ethanol, acetone and benzene	aqueous solution of sodium salt, granular formulation	>8200
—	—	emulsifiable concentrate	—

TABLE 28 (*continued*)

No.	Compound	Common or abbreviated names	Formula	Molecular weight
85.	dimethylxanthic disulphide **di(methoxythiocarbonyl)-disulphide**	dimexan	$CH_3 \cdot O \cdot \overset{\overset{S}{\|}}{C} \cdot S \cdot S \cdot \overset{\overset{S}{\|}}{C} \cdot O \cdot CH_3$	214·4
86.	ethyl xanthogen disulphide **di(ethoxythiocarbonyl)di-sulphide** diethylxanthic disulphide	EXD† 'Herbisan'	$CH_3 CH_2 \cdot O \cdot \overset{\overset{S}{\|}}{C} \cdot S \cdot S \cdot \overset{\overset{S}{\|}}{C} \cdot O \cdot CH_2 \cdot CH_3$	242·4
87.	dimethyl ester of tetra-chloroterephthalic acid **dimethyl 2,3,5,6-tetra-chloroterephthalate**	DCPA-dimethyl† 'Dacthal'		332·0

Melting point or physical state	Solubility	Types of formulation	Acute oral LD_{50} for rats (mg/kg)
22·5–23	—	emulsifiable concentrate	240
27–29°C	—	emulsifiable concentrate	603
156°C	water: $<0·5$ p.p.m. acetone: 10 per cent at 25°C benzene: 25 per cent at 25°C xylene: 14 per cent at 25°C	wettable powder, granular formulation	>3000

APPENDIX IV

THE COST OF HERBICIDES

The comparison of prices shown in Table 29 is based on the cost per lb of acid equivalent or active ingredient in 1962. This cost varies quite widely depending upon formulation. The comparisons are therefore only approximate. In the table, MCPA, the most widely used selective herbicide, is taken as the unit cost and the cost of other herbicides are compared with it. The approximate comparative cost coupled with the dose required (the range of doses most used in agriculture, horticulture and forestry are shown) will give an indication of the relative cost of chemical treatments.

The total cost of treatment will depend additionally, of course, upon such costs as are incurred in applying the herbicide, incorporating it into the soil where this is necessary and so on.

TABLE 29.   A COMPARISON OF THE AVERAGE COST PER POUND ACID EQUIVALENT OR ACTIVE INGREDIENT AND RANGE OF SELECTIVE DOSES OF HERBICIDES (APPROXIMATE)

	Approximate comparative cost MCPA: 1	Range of doses used selectively (lb per acre)
MCPA-salt	1	0·25–2·0
trichloroacetic acid-salt	0·5	15·0–20·0
DNOC	0·5	4·0–8·0
2,4-D-amine	1	0·25–2·0
mecoprop-salt	1	1·5–2·5
dichlorprop-salt	1	1·5–2·5
dalapon-salt	1·25	8·0–12·0
pentachlorphenol	1·5	3·0–4·0
2,4-D-ester	2	0·25–1·0
MCPB-salt	2	1·0–2·0
2,4-DB-salt	2	1·0–2·0
propham	2	3·0–4·0
chlorpropham	2·5	1·0–2·0
dinoseb	3	1·0–2·0
MCPA + 2,3,4-TBA (total a.e.)	2·5	1·0
amino triazole (activated)	3·5	4·0
maleic hydrazide	3·5	4·0–6·0
di-allate	4·5	1·0–1·5
MCPA + 3,6-chloro-2-methoxybenzoic acid (total a.e.)	4·5	1·25
propham plus endothal (total a.i.)	5	3·5–7·0
simazine	10	0·5–2·0
atrazine	10	0·5–2·0
2,4,5-TB-salt	10	1·0–2·0
barban	20	0·3–0·6

Weight

1 ounce (oz)		= 28·3 grammes (g)
1 pound (lb)	= 16·0 oz	= 454 grammes
1 hundredweight (cwt)	= 112 lb	= 50·8 kilogrammes (Kg)

Conversion factors

ounces to grammes	× 28·3
pounds to grammes	× 454
pounds to kilogrammes	× 0·454
hundredweights to kilogrammes	× 50·8

Volume

1 pint		= 0·568 litres (l)
1 gallon (gal)	= 8 pints	= 4·55 litres
1 fluid ounce	= 1·73 cubic inches or 0·05 pints	= 28·4 mililitres

Conversion factors

pints to litres	× 0·568
gallons to litres	× 4·55
gallons to millilitres (ml)	×4545

Length

1 inch (in.)		= 2·54 centimetres (cm)
1 foot (ft)	= 12 in.	= 30·5 centimetres
1 yard (yd)	= 3 ft	= 0·914 metres (m)
1 mile	= 1760 yd	= 1·61 kilometres (Km)

Conversion factors

inches to centimetres	× 2·54
feet to metres	× 0·305
yards to metres	× 0·914
miles to kilometres	× 1·61

Area

1 square inch		= 6·45 sq. cm
1 square yard		= 0·836 sq. metres
1 acre	= 4840 square yards	= 0·405 hectares

Conversion factors

square feet to square metres	× 0·093
square yards to square metres	× 0·836
acres to hectares	× 0·405

Other conversions

1 lb per acre	=	1·12 kilograms per hectare *or* 1120 grams per hectare
1 gallon per acre	=	11·2 litres per hectare
1 cwt per acre	=	1·25 quintals per hectare
1 kilogram per hectare	=	0·9 lb per acre *or* 14·2 oz per acre
1 litre per hectare	=	0·09 gallons per acre *or* 0·7 pints per acre
1 quintal per hectare	=	0·8 cwt per acre

320

ISH AND METRIC MENSURATION (Approximate)

100 grammes			=	3·53 ounces
1 kilogramme	=	100g	=	2·20 pounds
1 quintal	=	100Kg	=	220 pounds

grammes to ounces	×	0·0353
grammes to pounds	×	0·00220
kilogrammes to pounds	×	2·20
kilogrammes to hundredweights	×	0·020

100 millilitres (ml)			=	0·176 pints
1 litre	=	1000 ml	=	1·76 pints
1000 litres	=	1 kilolitre	=	220 gallons
1 cubic centimetre (cc)	=	1·0 ml	=	0·00176 pints

litres to pints	×	1·76
litres to gallons	×	0·220
millilitres to gallons	×	0·00022

1 millimetre (mm)			=	0·0394 inches
1 centimetre	=	10 mm	=	0·394 inches
1 metre	=	100 cm	=	39·4 inches or 3·28 feet
1 kilometre	=	1000 m	=	1094 yards or 0·621 miles

centimetres to inches	×	0·394
metres to feet	×	3·28
metres to yards	×	1·09
kilometres to miles	×	0·621

1 square metre	=	10·8 square feet or 1·20 square yards
1 hectare	=	2·47 acres

square metres to square feet	×	10·8
square metres to square yards	×	1·20
hectares to acres	×	2·47

321

INDEX TO THE RECOMMENDATIONS FOR THE USE OF HERBICIDES ON CROPS.

This index is to help the reader to see at a glance which herbicides may be considered for any particular crop, which type of weed will be controlled and the method of using the herbicide. Herbicides that are recommended tentatively are inserted in square brackets. It is stressed that the citation of a herbicide in the index for any paticular crop does not mean that the herbicide is necessarily safe or effective under all conditions, but rather that it should be considered as a candidate when the choice of treatment is made with the help of detailed comment in the paragraphs to which reference is made.

pre-em = pre-emergence
post-em = post-emergence
dicot = dicotyledonous weeds, i.e. broad-leaved weeds.

Crop	Candidate herbicides	Application: pre- or post-weed emergence	Stage of crop	Type of weed controlled	Paragraph reference
Anemones	I Contact pre-em sprays (see paragraphs 151–158)	post	pre-em	seedling grasses and/ or dicots	276
Apples	II PCP	post	pre-em	seedling dicots	277
	I Simazine	pre	established	seedling grasses or dicots	229, 233
	II MCPA, 2,4-D	post	established	annual and perennial dicots	230
	III Dalapon	post	established	annual and perennial grasses	231
	IV Amino triazole (activated)	post	established	annual and perennial dicots and grasses	232
	V [Diuron]	pre	established	annual grasses and dicots	234
	VI [Diuron + amino triazole (activated)]	pre	established	annual and perennial grasses and dicots	235

INDEX TO THE RECOMMENDATIONS FOR THE USE OF HERBICIDES ON CROPS—*continued*

Crop	Candidate herbicides	Application: pre- or post-weed emergence	Stage of crop	Type of weed controlled	Paragraph reference
Blackcurrants	I Simazine, chlorpropham	pre	established	seedling grasses and dicots	236, 237
	II Dalapon	post	established	annual and perennial grasses	238
	III 2,4,5-TB, MCPB	post	established	perennial dicots	239
	IV Paraquat, diquat	post	established	grasses, annual dicots, creeping buttercup	240, 241
	V [Diuron]	pre	established	seedling grasses or dicots	242
Brussels sprouts (direct sown)	I Contact pre-em sprays (see paragraphs 151–158)	post	pre-em	seedling grasses and/ or dicots	178
	II Sodium monochlorocaetate	post	post-em	seedling dicots	178
Brussels sprouts (trans-planted)	I Sodium monochloroacetate	post	post-planting	seedling dicots	180
Bulbs (daffodils and tulips)	I Contact pre-em sprays (see paragraphs 151–158)	post	pre-em	seedling grasses and/ or dicots	281
	II PCP	post	immediately pre-em	seedling dicots	282
	III Chlorpropham	pre	post-em	seedling grasses and] dicots	284
	IV Chlorpropham, chlorproph-am + fenuron, chlorproph-am + diuron	pre	pre-em	seedling grasses and dicots	283, 285, 286
Cabbage (direct-sown)	I Contact pre-em sprays (see paragraphs 151–158)	post	pre-em	seedling grasses and/ or dicots	181
	II Sodium monochloroacetate	post	post-em	seedling dicots	182

22

INDEX TO THE RECOMMENDATIONS FOR THE USE OF HERBICIDES ON CROPS—*continued*

Crop	Candidate herbicides	Application: pre- or post-weed emergence	Stage of crop	Type of weed controlled	Paragraph reference
Clovers	I MCPA, 2,4-D	post	post-em	annual and perennial dicots	91
	II MCPB, 2,4-DB, MCPA + MCPB, 2,4-D + 2,4-DB	post	post-em	annual and perennial dicots	92
	III Dinoseb	post	post-em	seedling dicots	94
Clovers	I Dinoseb, diquat, DNOC, sulphuric acid, PCP, sodium monochloroacetate	pre-harvest desiccation			131–136
Clover (white for seed)	I MCPB	post	post-em	annual and perennial dicots	112
	II Dinoseb, diquat, DNOC, sulphuric acid, PCP, sodium monochloroacetate	pre-harvest desiccation			131–136
Dahlias	I Cresylic acids	post	established	seedling grasses and dicots	290
Flax	I MCPA	post	post-em	annual and perennial dicots	53
	II DNOC	post	post-em	seedling dicots	54
	Contact pre-em sprays (see paragraphs 151–158)	post	pre-em	seedling grasses and dicots	280
Flowers (annual and biennial)	I Formalin, chloropicrin, vaporizing oils	pre	pre-sowing	annual grasses and dicots	331
Forest nurseries (a) Seedbeds	II Diquat	post	pre-sowing	annual dicots	333

INDEX TO THE RECOMMENDATIONS FOR THE USE OF HERBICIDES ON CROPS—*continued*

Crop	Candidate herbicides	Application: pre- or post-weed emergence	Stage of crop	Type of weed controlled	Paragraph reference
Grasses (for seed)	I [MCPA, 2,4-D, mecoprop, dichlorprop, MCPA + 2,3,6-TBA]	post	post-em	annual and perennial dicots	110
Grasses (seedling)	I [MCPA, 2,4-D, MCPB, 2, 4-DB, mecoprop, MCPA + 2,3,6-TBA]	post	post-em	annual and perennial dicots	90
	II Dinoseb	post	post-em	seedling dicots	90
Grassland (leys in first year)	I MCPA, 2, 4-D, MCPB, 2, 4-DB	post	post-em	annual and perennial dicots	87 et seq.
Grassland (established)	I MCPA, 2,4-D, MCPB, 2,4-DB	post	post-em	annual and perennial dicots	103 et seq.
Kale	I Sulphyric acid, sodium mono-chloroacetate	post	post-em	seedling dicots	55, 56
	II PCP, diquat, paraquat, sulphuric acid, cresylic acid	post	pre-sowing	seedling grasses and/or dicots	57
	III [G,34360]	post	post-em	seedling dicots	58
	IV [Sodium or potassium cyanate]	post	post-em	seedling dicots	59
	V Gas liquor	post	post-em	seedling dicots	60
Lawns and sports turf	I MCPA, 2,4-D, mecoprop	post	—	annual or perennial dicots	308 et seq.
	II Lawn sand	post	—	Sagina procumbens, other dicots and mosses	322, 326
	III Calomel, mercuric chloride, potassium permanganate	post	—	mosses	323, 328

INDEX TO THE RECOMMENDATIONS FOR THE USE OF HERBICIDES ON CROPS—*continued*

Crop	Candidate herbicides	Application: pre- or post-weed emergence	Stage of crop	Type of weed controlled	Paragraph reference
Pea-field, dry and vining	I Dinoseb	post	post-em	seedling dicots	72, 73
	II MCPB	post	post-em	annual and perennial dicots	74
	III TCA, propham	pre	pre-sowing	wild-oats	75, 76
	IV Chlorpropham + fenuron, chlorpropham + diuron	pre	pre-em	annual grasses and dicots	77
	V [Barban]	post	post-em	wild oats	78
	VI [Dinoseb]	post	pre-em	seedling dicots	79
Peas (for picking green)	I Contact pre-em sprays (see paragraphs 151–158)	pre	pre-em	seedling grasses and/ or dicots	214
	II Dinoseb	post	post-em	seedling dicots	215
	III MCPB	post	post-em	annual and perennial dicots	216
	IV Chlorpropham + fenuron, chlorpropham + diuron	pre	pre-em	seedling dicots	217
	V Dinoseb	post	pre-em	seedling dicots	218
Pears	I Simazine	pre	established	annual grasses and dicots	229, 233
	II MCPA, 2,4-D	post	established	annual and perennial dicots	230
	III Dalapon	post	established	annual and perennial grasses	231
	IV Amino triazole (activated)	post	established	annual and perennial dicots and grasses	232
	V [Diuron]	pre	established	annual grasses and dicots	234
	VI [Diuron + amino triazole (activated)]	post	established	annual and perennial grasses and dicots	235

INDEX TO THE RECOMMENDATIONS FOR THE USE OF HERBICIDES ON CROPS—*continued*

Crop	Candidate herbicides	Application: pre- or post-weed emergence	Stage of crop	Type of weed controlled	Paragraph reference
Shrubs	I 2,4-DES	pre	established	annual dicots	302
Strawberries	I Dinoseb	post	dormant season	annual dicots	267
	II 2,4-DES	pre	fruiting beds	annual dicots	268
	III [Simazine, chlorpropham]	pre	late-season	seedling grasses and dicots	269
	IV [Paraquat, diquat]	post	inter-row directed	runners, grasses and annual dicots	271
Sward destruction	I [2,4-D, MCPA, dalapon, amino triazole, paraquat]				85
Sweet corn	I Simazine, atrazine	pre	pre-em	seedling grasses and dicots	222
Willow (a) Stoolbeds	I Simazine	pre	post-em	annual grasses and dicots	343
(b) Cutting beds and transplant lines	II Dalapon	post	post-em	perennial grasses	343
	I Vaporizing oil, PCP	post	post-em	annual grasses and dicots	342

INDEX

1. Weed species are indexed under botanical names (*Flora of the British Isles*, 2nd ed., Clapham, Tutin and Warburg) and under the common name used in the text. Common names of two or more words are, in general, indexed under the last word, e.g. White campion is indexed under Campion, white.
2. Crops and ornamental species (excepting tree species) are indexed under common name only. Tree species are indexed under common and botanical names.
3. Page numbers printed in heavy type indicate the principal references for that subject.

Buttercups (*Ranunculus* spp.) grassland 63, 69, 70, non-selective control 197

Buttercups, water (*Ranunculus* spp.) 203, 204

Buttercup, Bermuda (*Oxalis pes-caprae*) 179–80

Buttercup, bulbous (*Ranunculus bulbosus*) 77, 123, 158

Buttercup, corn (*Ranunculus arvensis*) 40, 52, 158, 166

Buttercup, creeping (*Ranunculus repens*) 77, 158, 246, blackcurrants 105, forestry seedbeds 128, gooseberries 106, non-selective control 194, raspberries 107–8, shrubs 115, turf 123

Buttercup, hairy (*Ranunculus sardous*) 158

Buttercup, meadow (*Ranunculus acris*) 77, 157

N - butyl - *N'* - (3,4 -dichlorophenyl) *N* - methylurea, see Neburon

1 - *n* - butyl - 3 - (3,4 - dichlorophenyl (-1-methylurea, see Neburon

Buxus sempervirens 141

Cabbage, weeds in seed crops 261, 264–6

Calcium cyanamide 5, asparagus 88, properties 288–9

Calcium hypochlorite 206

Calculations, acid equivalents 217–20, application rates 217–20, dilutions 217–20, spray volumes 216–7

Calendula 111

Calibration, sprayers 214–7

Callitriche spp. 204

Calluna vulgaris 71, 142, 192, grants for destruction 267

Calomel, see Mercurous chloride

Calystegia sepium 19, 148, 177, blackcurrants 105, non-selective control 193

Campion, bladder (*Silene vulgaris*) 160

Campion, night-flowering (*Silene noctiflorum*) 159

Campion, red (*Silene dioica*) 159

Campion, white (*Silene album*) 18, 52, 159, **181**

Cane fruits, see Soft fruits

Capsella bursa-pastoris 38, 52, 148, 163, 165

Cardamine hirsuta 148

Cardaria draba 148, **176–7**, 192, 197

Carduus spp. 250, 256

Carduus nutans 148

Carex spp. 148, 202

Carpinus betulus 142

Carrots 27, **93–4**, Amiben 270, dalapon 170, linuron 274, propazine 274, Solan 272, weeds in seed crops 261, 264–6

Carrot, wild (*Daucus carota*) 151

Cats, ear (*Hypochoeris radicata*) 122, 153, 197

Cauliflower, weeds in seed crops 261, 264–6

CDAA **272**, properties 300–1

CDAA + trichlorobenzyl chloride 272

Cedar, western red (*Thuja plizata*) 125, 127, 128

CDEC 271, properties 296–7

Celandine, lesser (*Ranunculus ficaria*) 123

Celery **94**, weeds in seed crops 261, 264–6

Centaurea cyanus 111, 148

Centaurea nigra 148, non-selective control 197, turf 122

Centaurea scabiosa 148

Centrifugal pumps 212

Cerastium arvense 148

Cerastium glomeratum 149

Cerastium holosteodes 38, 149, 246, in seed crops 256, turf 122

Ceratophyllum spp. 203

Cereals 15, 29–50, barban 20, 32, cereal pea mixtures 47, di-allate 22, dichlorprop 17, 32, dinoseb 32, DNOC 26, 32, DNOC insecticide mixtures 228, docks 181, dredge corn 47, 2,4-D 15–16, 29, 32, 2,4-DB 17, 32, 2,4-D + MCPA 17, 2,4-D + 2,4-DB 17, 2,4-DB + MCPA 17, 32, fenoprop 270, growth stages 30–31, herbicide volumes 33, MCPA 15–16, 29, 32, MCPA + 3,6-dichloro-2-methoxy benzoic acid 32, MCPA + MCPB 17, 32, MCPA + 2,3,6-TBA 17–18, 32, MCPB 17, 32, mecoprop 17, 32, recommendations 34, 35, 36, seed certification 249, 253, seed purity 245, spraying procedures 220, sulphuric acid 14, 32, 33–34, 2,3,6-TBA 18, TCA 168, undersown 16, 29, 32, **48–50**, 65, 258, weeds in seed crops **260–3**, wild oats 175–6

Cereal mixtures 47, cereal pea mixtures 47

23

WEEDKILLER
WEEDKILLER
WEEDKILLER
WEEDKILLER
WEEDKILLER
WEEDKILLER

Growth of a Weedkiller..

It happens hundreds of times a year in Boots research laboratories. A small phial of chemical is mixed with solvent and sprayed onto a tray of weeds and plants. Once in a while that chemical shows promise as a weedkiller. The discovery made, development begins. What is the right strength? How much should it be diluted? Likely answers are found in the laboratories before work begins in the field. Eventually the problem is solved—in local conditions. The new chemical must still be tried out in different parts of the country. Does it work as well in heavy land? Does rainfall affect it? Can it be safely applied? If there are still no snags, a number of farmers will be invited to try it as part of their normal operations. And, when all is well, the new weedkiller can be launched—three, four or even five years after the first sign that it might be useful. In this way, Boots have made many notable advances in hormone weedkilling. The first commercial 2,4D formulation in Great Britain. The first reliable MCPA at reduced rates of application. The first control for cleavers and chickweed, CMPP. The discovery that 2,4DP controls Redshank. And other potential winners are going through the same thorough, cautious process of development at this moment.

THE FARMER'S CHEMISTS

One year's seeds . . .

seven years' weeds

So the saying goes. Nowadays weeds are effectively controlled by the use of 20 MULE TEAM herbicides. Destroying existing vegetation and preventing new growth for long periods, these non-selective herbicides can be safely and easily applied without risk of fire, toxicity to animals or damage to installations. Formulated to suit the needs of industry, public utilities, local authorities and river boards, the 20 MULE TEAM range includes herbicides based on monuron, chlorates, borates, 2, 4-D and dalapon.

Industrial weed spraying carried out by contract—with guaranteed results

BORAX CONSOLIDATED LIMITED

BORAX HOUSE, CARLISLE PLACE, LONDON SW1

20 MULE TEAM *Registered Trade Mark*

BX194B

For Highway and Industrial Weed Control

Treatment of expansion joints
at London Airport

Fisons Pest Control

is second to none

There is no organisation in the world better equipped to deal with weed, pest and disease problems than Fisons Pest Control.

This is a strong claim to make, but it can be made deliberately in the light of past achievement and present development.

All Fisons Pest Control products are based upon exhaustive research and intensive testing. And, through its subsidiary Fisons Farmwork, the company is kept constantly in touch with the practical side of weed and pest control.

But this is only a part of the story. Efficient distribution .. the capacity to get products from the laboratory and on to the market as quickly as possible .. a long experience of farming problems .. All this—and much more—is behind the organisation which makes Fisons Pest Control second to none.

FISONS PEST CONTROL

...you will find the right selective weedkiller in the May & Baker range

2,4-D ester
General weedkiller in wheat, barley and grassland.

2,4-DB
Kills general weeds in seedling lucerne.

2,4-DB/MCPA
Kills redshank and general weeds in undersown and straight cereals, and direct reseeds.

2,4-DP/MCPA
New wide spectrum weedkiller for complex weed problems in straight cereals.

2,4-D/2,4,5-T
Kills scrub, nettles and other herbaceous weeds.

CMPP
Controls cleavers, chickweed and general weeds in cereals.

MCPA
General weedkiller in cereals and grassland.

MCPB
For safe weed control in peas.

MCPB/MCPA
For use in undersown cereals and direct-sown leys.

TCA
Controls wild oat and couch grass.

The range of M&B brand crop protection chemicals also contains:

A quick-acting systemic insecticide containing phosphamidon.

Two fungicides for complete protection against potato blight, one containing ziram and copper, the other containing maneb.

These products are all commercially available under M&B brand names.

HA1983

MAY & BAKER LTD Dagenham · Essex · Tel: DOMinion 3060 Ext. 344

selective weedkillers

Plant Protection's lead in selective
weed killing started when they
introduced MCPA—
the first hormone weedkiller.
That lead has been maintained and
Plant Protection can now offer a
comprehensive range of selective
weedkillers which will answer
most of the farmer's weed problems.

PLANT PROTECTION LTD.
A subsidiary company of
Imperial Chemical Industries Limited

MEMO TO BUYER:

Stanton and Staveley, Limited, are long established Suppliers of Sodium Chlorate for weed killing, and Sulphuric Acid for crop Spraying.

They maintain an excellent delivery Service, and the quality of their products is first class.

Send them out next enquiry, please.

J.B.

Chemical Sales Office:

STANTON AND STAVELEY, LIMITED
NEAR CHESTERFIELD
Telephone: Chesterfield 7214

also at LONDON GLASGOW BIRMINGHAM MANCHESTER LEEDS CARDIFF BRISTOL EXETER BELFAST

By Appointment
Agricultural Spraying
Contractors

To
H.M. Queen
Elizabeth II

LONGMATES
(E. C. Longmate, Ltd.)
SPRAYING SPECIALISTS

The introduction of new materials continues. We have been Manufacturers of Crop Spraying Chemicals and Agricultural and Horticultural Spraying Contractors since 1920 and our Advisory Service is fully abreast of developments.

HEAD OFFICE
TERRINGTON ST. JOHN, Near WISBECH, CAMBRIDGESHIRE
Telephone: Terrington St. John 301 (three lines)

Ready Summer 1963

Crop Production in a Weed-Free Environment
The Second Symposium of the British Weed Control Council

CONTENTS

The Problem of Weed Seeds in the Soil: H. A. ROBERTS

The Effects of Cultivation in the Absence of Weeds

1 Physical
    (a) Oxygenation: J. C. HAWKINS
    (b) Water Acceptance: E. J. WINTER
    (c) Fertilizer Availability: G. W. COOKE
    (d) Root Penetration: A. TROUGHTON
    (e) Compaction: J. PRINGLE AND F. HUNTER
    (f) Erosion: A. J. LOW

2 Biological: W. T. WILLIAMS

Crop spacing and Management under Weed-Free Conditions: J. K. A. BLEASDALE

Crop Situations where Cultivations for Weed Control may be Eliminated by Use of Herbicides
    (a) Agriculture: J. G. ELLIOTT AND P. J. BOYLE
    (b) Horticulture: D. W. ROBINSON
    (c) Forestry: G. D. HOLMES

August 1963   100 pages   Illustrated   About 25s.

BLACKWELL SCIENTIFIC PUBLICATIONS · OXFORD